1990

University of St. Francis
GEN 801.95 B646

W9-AED-633
3 0301 00000000 2

# SUBJECTIVE CRITICISM

David Bleich

# SUBJECTIVE CRITICISM

*The Johns Hopkins University Press*
*Baltimore and London*

LIBRARY
College of St. Francis
JOLIET, ILLINOIS

Copyright © 1978 by The Johns Hopkins University Press

All rights reserved.

Manufactured in the United States of America

The Johns Hopkins University Press, Baltimore, Maryland 21218
The Johns Hopkins Press Ltd., London

Originally published, 1978
Johns Hopkins Paperbacks edition, 1981

**Library of Congress Cataloging in Publication Data**

Bleich, David.
   Subjective criticism.

   Includes index.
   1. Philology—Study and teaching. 2. English
philology—Study and teaching. 3. Criticism. I. Title.
P51.B55        410'.7        77–12968

      ISBN 0–8018–2032–4 (hardcover)
      ISBN 0–8018–2093–6 (paperback)

LIBRARY
College of St. Francis
JOLIET, ILLINOIS

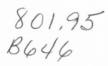

801.95
B646

# CONTENTS

137.535

# SUBJECTIVE CRITICISM

*Introduction*

# LANGUAGE, LITERACY, AND CRITICISM

Most of us who have grown up and gone to school in the United States have a fairly good idea of what the subject English is. We remember it in terms of what we did in the classroom—grammar, spelling, punctuation, reading and discussion of literature, essay writing, and related activities. For many of us, even those with scientific or mathematical inclinations, it was a relatively easy subject, sometimes fun, sometimes irksome, but rarely insurmountably difficult or impenetrable. Moreover, by the time we studied English in high school or college, we had been exposed to a series of preparatory activities in elementary school, so that throughout our school careers, some form of the subject always took up a considerable part of our time.

If, in college, we took an English course beyond composition and introduction to literature, English turned into Criticism, a somewhat narrower subject, but one that occupies the offerings of English departments in most universities. This subject is also not arcane and is relatively accessible to people with a variety of interests: it is simply the organized discussion of literature. Advanced students of English learn and practice Criticism. At least on the surface, Criticism, like the other practices associated with English, seems to be a sensible enterprise that interests and enlightens its students.

Throughout the range of its activities, then, English is conceived as a rather benign subject, making few taxing demands, and dealing with issues about which most people think in a state of relaxation (as opposed to politics or sex, which more easily arouse strong feelings). When I was an undergraduate in a large, scientifically oriented university, English and the other humanities were often viewed as indulgences or slack spots in a stern curriculum of quantitative rigor. Viewing the subject from its professional side, we come upon the fact of its great size. No university discipline, either in colleges of education or of arts and sciences, has a greater population of practitioners. If we include foreign language and comparative literature departments and their counterparts in education, we discover that the language and literature discipline is the most widespread in all phases of pedagogy and scholarship. We may therefore ask why such an apparently undemanding subject occupies the professional energies of so many people. To say that people do what is easiest cannot be the answer, since then even more would be engaged in this work. I think, rather, that the answer must concern issues of educational demand as well as psychological factors of personal taste and intellectual aspiration. To put the matter in more familiar terms, it must be that language and literature are in some way very important not only to the many who teach it, but to the majority of citizens, since otherwise funds would not be forthcoming to support so vast a professional enterprise. The mystery of this situation arises because from a topical standpoint the subject matter seems neither urgent nor pragmatically indispensable.

I think some light is shed on this problem by observing the analogy between the language and literature profession and the current function of institutional religion. In every city and town across this country there is at least one building affiliated with an organized religion; in most cities there are many more than one building. These buildings house congregations that contribute money for the maintenance of the building and what it stands for. Probably a majority of American citizens have some sort of religious affiliation in either membership or sponsorship or both. This majority, however, are not religiously observant in any important way. While many attend services, few go regularly, and even fewer actually perform in their daily lives anything that resembles religious ritual. Yet how many in this majority would deny that they believe in God? The verbal acknowledgement of this belief is given independently of which activities in daily life represent an enactment of the belief.

In a similar way, people "believe" in English. Every city and town has one or more buildings for the purpose of teaching this and other subjects. Public monies from taxes support the enterprise. Few people doubt that it should be taught. In the majority of adult lives, however, the material usually taught in English has almost no discernible role. True, most know how to read and write, but how different is such a skill from a perfunctory public declaration of faith in God? Unless there are observable consequences to literacy, it is as inert as the declaration of faith. Nevertheless, both literacy and the need to declare one's faith often seem more necessary in our civilization than many things that are pragmatically more urgent.

A general historical perspective is helpful in this regard. The first verse of the Gospel According to St. John says: "In the beginning was the Word, and the Word was with God, and the Word was God." From the earliest stages of civilization, people perceived a connection between language and faith. More than this, they felt an utter identity between certain words and the source of those words, God. Even though the passage above first says that the Word preceded God, it finally declares that the Word and God are one and the same: both are to be believed, and it is in both at the same time that one has faith. Consider the ordinary sentence, "I believe you." This actually means, "I believe what you say—your words," but in common parlance we do not make the distinction between the person and what he says. While this is not always the case, it is almost always the case *to begin with* in an interpersonal exchange. It takes a considerable length of conversation for us to decide to dissociate a person's words from our overall sense of the person. The idea that relates language and God, therefore, is the idea of belief, which helps to explain the fact of seemingly universal concern without an accompanying sense of universal urgency. The belief in God and the belief in words must represent something so fundamental in human psychology that institutions for the preservation of these beliefs proliferate; for many the mere existence of such institutions satisfies the implications of the belief, and no further demands for actualization need be made.

If we accept a certain degree of truth-value in the passage from John, language is psychologically prior to God; religious activity developed later than language, but it necessarily became attached to language consciousness. From what we know of the earliest civilizations, literacy was a privilege of the rich; only in the last century or so has this circumstance changed. For most of the past, those who had "the word" also had the power. Because of this concentration of literacy, literature, history, science, and religion were all manifested through what we call mythology. That is, knowledge was identified with literacy. In the Christian era, literacy continued to be concentrated among members of a wealthy oligarchy, the church, but a new story was introduced, that of a single God, and his wife and son. For the masses of dependent poor, this story had considerable interest, since they too were born in mangers and they too anticipated a merciless, ignominious death. The story was the most important "word" one could believe; those who told the story were the most important people one could believe. The advantage of believing the story was that it promised the day would come when the poor would live like the rich. In order to hasten this day, one had to believe the word, and pay money to those who spoke it. Thus literacy was associated with the pleasures and privileges of being alive; yet in an everyday sense, it was inaccessible to most people. Until very recently the belief in the power of literacy remained a functional substitute for actual literacy. This view helps us to understand the present-day similarity between attitudes toward English and attitudes toward religion; both seem intimately bound up with our existence and fate, yet all we can do—or need do, perhaps—is *believe* in their existence and their importance.

Consider one further element that helps to ratify my analogy. For many centuries now, the "word" has been publicly accessible mainly through the book. We know the word of God because it is written in the Bible. One can see and write words as well as hear them. Similarly, in English, we first learn to read from a book (and a teacher), and later we read literature (stories about people), just like the ones in the Bible. A book transforms words that are originally made only of air into something unmistakably tangible—black and white pages that each person can handle for himself. Since a book requires a reader, however, and since few in the past were literate, specially appointed people made it their full-time business to read the book and to tell others what it said. These readers' lives were sustained by the illiterate public. Anyone with access to the book had an especially important place in society. Such people had a special power that did not seem to have to do with being rich—that is, the power to say what the words meant. Since everyone knows that words have to have meanings, the tasks of telling what something says and of telling what it means are, to an illiterate person, one and the same. In an illiterate society, the regulation of verbal meanings lay in the hands of those who could read; the regulation of meaning is thus bound up with the exercise of power. It was just as Carroll's Humpty Dumpty said: meanings are utterly subjective, and what counts is who is master.

Today, we receive the Bible and other literature from our ancestors along with a whole array of "readings" by privileged and prominent readers. We may now readily recognize such readings as the work of "critics," whose interpretive task continues with purposes not unlike those of the past. A critic's normal job is to tell others what books say and mean, and to discuss the sayings and the meanings with other readers. Critics are usually paid out of public funds under the agreement that most people want to know what books say and mean and that, for one reason or another, this majority cannot perform the critical function for itself. Thus, critics, like the clerics of the past, command a large measure of public and pedagogical faith in their words.

The social institutions connected with reading and literacy are not in essence radically different from those which obtained in the past, when few were literate. Although the handling and teaching of language is now controlled by lawyers as much as by English teachers, both of these groups exercise publicly delegated authority. More importantly, the fundamental fact of our automatic, simultaneous belief in words and their speakers has not changed. The use of language, even by all of us who are now literate, depends on the *belief* in meanings. I stress that the handling of language and literature depends not on certain knowledge of meanings, but belief in them. These beliefs have no other source than the accumulated social uses of language. We believe in the meanings given words by certain authoritative people or groups of people (authors). We likewise believe in the meanings of poems and laws as they are interpreted by critics and justices. The meanings of individual words, and of aggregates of words, depend altogether on those who read the words and tell the meanings to others. It is not possible to separate the meaning of words and of literature from the way language and literature are handled by speakers and readers.

Matters that concern belief are difficult to discuss. We do not usually associate acts of belief with a search for reliable knowledge. Because language development is so intimately connected with the growth of automatic belief systems in us, the teaching of language and literature often boils down to simple supervision of natural growth processes. Yet for just this reason, institutions that foster and facilitate such growth are considered important. The relaxed character of the subject English is testimony not so much to its operational simplicity as to most people's intuitive sense of the closeness of the subject to common experiences of growing and living. Usually, we do not question a person about his religious beliefs; we accept that these beliefs help to tell him who he is and where he stands. A belief derives its strength and its adaptive function exactly because it is independent of decisive proof. A person's language, grounded as it is in a whole series of unquestioned beliefs, is a similar foundation of self-knowledge and self-esteem. Perhaps more importantly, it is a means to observe one's own growth and to integrate it with the growth of others.

Literary pedagogy has enacted this viewpoint by proceeding on the axiom that "literature is a reflection of people, and in it we can see human problems and concerns that we are going through ourselves." Unfortunately, the benign and homiletic character of this axiom is narcotic. Its extraordinary generality, rooted as it is in centuries of habitual religious thinking, directs our attention away from the physical details of our actual reading experience or speaking experience, and toward the need to develop behaviors compliant with received moral authority. It is always "man" that a work of literature reflects, or a fictitious figure that it describes. The fact that this work, when read, becomes a reflection of a particular reader is left out of consideration. Those discussing a work usually pretend that they did not experience it in a direct emotional way. By rendering a reading experience as representative of a general human principle, they omit the subjective immediacy of this experience to them, the readers. This strategic omission makes the traditional subject of English seem benign, as opposed to what more quantitative disciplines seem to be: rigorous, problematical, taxing to mental concentration. In the study of language and literature, the demand for personal self-exploration that we might naturally expect is systematically excluded from public attention. Even in the teaching of language alone, words all have "objective" meanings, and learning to speak or write is a mechanical matter of developing skills. And in the university, the writing of paragraphs is taught as a function of some proposed intrinsic form that all good paragraphs should have. It is not so much that teachers are unaware that writing represents thoughts and feelings, but that the vast majority of teachers are unable to say what the connection is between having thoughts and feelings and writing them down. The personal and emotional connection we have to language and literature is just not consciously explored in our educational system, and it works only as a silent justification for the wide professional enterprise of English.

This silence is traceable to two factors: the decline of religious authority over subjective matters and the lack of any widely accepted context for validating subjective experience. As a result, the standards for literary and linguistic knowledge have been developed in imitation of the well-established quantitative sciences. New Criticism has formulated "objective" explications of literature, and Generative Grammarians have formulated distinct logical rules to explain linguistic functioning. By and large, however, the objective standard of knowledge when applied to the language-dependent disciplines has actually lost a good deal of its authority. Students electing these disciplines because of their promise of subjective and social involvement are increasingly disappointed by the acrobatic maneuvers of their teachers to present literary and linguistic knowledge "objectively."

Such disaffection is not limited to students. Recently, language-oriented disciplines have become less orthodox than they were earlier in this century. In publications addressed to the professions and in classroom practice, ideas and techniques from various branches of the humanities and social sciences have been amalgamated in the search for more satisfying forms of thought. Many important inquiries are under way to reduce the distance between actual reading experiences and conceptualizations put forth as literary and linguistic knowledge.

In this study, I will discuss those inquiries which I think are especially useful in developing forms of thought that have major consequences for our daily subjective experience and for our organized efforts at maximizing the value of pedagogical practices. Underlying my discussion is my argument for the recognition of the subjective paradigm, which I think is considerably more compelling and pragmatically consequential than the currently prevailing objective paradigm. I will try to show that under the new paradigm, our present conception of language may be productively altered; such alteration implies new conceptions of the act of interpretation, the act of reading, and the pedagogy of language and literature.

In Chapters Six through Ten, I will place special emphasis on the significance of actual classroom experiences I have had using subjective forms of thought. I will discuss four specific contexts for the organized pursuit of literary and linguistic knowledge, and I will try to show how existing curricular practices may be changed and enlarged to make the subject of "English" more directly and satisfyingly answerable to our subjective experiences of language and literature.

Too often in current practice, academic thought is segregated from the classroom cultivation of literacy and language awareness. My view is that subjective thinking can end such segregation and can make important new knowledge, and the means for acquiring such knowledge, available on a much larger scale than heretofore considered possible.

# Chapter One

# THE SUBJECTIVE PARADIGM

The concept of a thought paradigm as I am using it was introduced by T. S. Kuhn in his important treatise *The Structure of Scientific Revolutions* (1962). According to Kuhn, a paradigm is a model that describes the cognitive state of mind of those systematically observing something in human experience. The model is usually constituted of "Law, Theory, application, and instrumentation together," and from it springs "particular coherent traditions of scientific research. These are the traditions which the historian describes under such rubrics as 'Ptolemaic astronomy' (or 'Copernican'), 'Aristotelian dynamics' (or 'Newtonian'), 'corpuscular optics' (or 'wave optics'), and so on. A paradigm is recognized in two basic ways. First it is "sufficiently unprecedented to attract an enduring group of adherents away from competing modes of scientific activity"; second, and simultaneously, it is "sufficiently open-ended to leave all sorts of problems for the redefined group of practitioners to resolve."[1] A paradigm's existence is therefore defined by the behavior of the group of its adherents. Thus, Kuhn writes, "a paradigm is what the members of a scientific community share, *and*, conversely, a scientific community consists of men who share a paradigm."[2] In a literal sense a paradigm governs scientific activity only and directly by the consent of the governed. It is a shared mental structure, a set of beliefs about the nature of reality subscribed to by a group of thinkers large enough to exercise leadership for those similarly wishing to observe and understand human experience.

A paradigm is perhaps even more than this; it is, in Kuhn's term, a

1. T. S. Kuhn, *The Structure of Scientific Revolutions* (Chicago, 1962), p. 10.
2. Ibid., p. 176 (from Postscript, 1969).

"world-view." For example: after the Copernican revolution, "Western astronomers first saw change in the previously immutable heavens"; however, "the Chinese, whose cosmological beliefs did not preclude celestial change, had recorded the appearance of many new stars at a much earlier date." This means, Kuhn argues, that "after Copernicus, astronomers lived in a different world. In any case, their research responded as though that were the case."[3] Perhaps a more familiar and dramatic example is the change in the conception of space as a result of Einstein's general theory of relativity. Newtonian space was conceived as a giant jungle gym, an unchanging grid defined at each point by imaginary straight lines. The theory of relativity said that space was Riemannian, that is, curved under the influence of the gravitational fields produced by heavenly bodies; the shortest distance between any two points is defined by the combined gravitational fields of bodies in the area; hence the distance that anything had to traverse from here to there was no longer straight but curved according to the calculations of Riemannian geometry. This is a "different universe" from that imagined by Newton.

Kuhn's work shows that all perception takes place through a paradigm. The paradigmatic perception of reality at any moment in history *is* the reality at that time. The implication of this thought is that for all practical purposes, reality is invented and not observed or discovered by human beings. Kuhn claims that the "philosophical paradigm initiated by Descartes and developed at the same time as Newtonian dynamics" is no longer adequate to modern experience. "Today," he argues, "research in parts of philosophy, psychology, linguistics, and even art history, all converge to suggest that the traditional paradigm is somehow askew."[4] Kuhn's idea that paradigms govern science has led to the suspicion in many and the conviction in some that the notion of objectivity is itself *only* a paradigm, and that consensually validated perception is a more useful way of understanding what is real at this time.

Kuhn does not announce an alternative to the objective paradigm. He says that "none of these crisis-producing subjects has yet produced a viable alternative to the traditional epistemological paradigm."[5] Yet parts of his own work do suggest what I think is just such an alternative. Toward the very end of his treatise, Kuhn observes that he has discussed science for all of those pages without ever mentioning the word "truth." He explains this fact by maintaining that "we have to relinquish the notion, explicit or implicit, that changes of paradigm carry scientists and those who learn from them closer and closer to the

3. Ibid., p. 116.
4. Ibid., p. 121.
5. Ibid.

truth."[6] A change in paradigm is *not progress toward* anything but *development from* something. Under the influence of religious thought, evolution was taken for granted to be proceeding ever closer to perfection. The perfection of human knowledge is absolute truth. Kuhn's work shows that we may eliminate the ideas of progressive evolution and absolute truth because the history of science suggests that new paradigms are devised *only to meet the epistemological needs of the present* or of any age that creates such a paradigm. This argument implies the paradigm under which Kuhn is working—a Darwinian paradigm, which holds that paradigm formation is a human form of organismic adaptation and that its purpose is to better insure human survival as a species at any historical moment. The notion of objective truth is unnecessary for this purpose, as it the conception of human development as a march toward perfection.

The recent thinking of the late, well-known biologist C. H. Waddington coincides with Kuhn's formulations about the nature of progress. Waddington first points out that "to biologists who look at their materials with unprejudiced eyes, the notion of improvement— which implies value—is . . . inescapable." But he then says that the origin of the *idea* of improvement must be a part of the process of biological observation: "In order to recognize that something worthy of being called 'improvement' has occurred while a rabbit's egg is developing into an adult rabbit, we do not need to apply any *a priori* notion of what an animal ought to be like, or any yardstick external to the developing system itself. And adult rabbit is just more of a rabbit than a rabbit's egg is. The system defines its own criterion, and it is by this inherent criterion that it is judged to have improved."[7] Waddington thus shows that "improvement," or progress, is an abstraction of our observation of natural growth; and it makes no more sense to infer the perfection of mankind from the present state than it does to infer the adult rabbit from our observation of the rabbit egg, since it is only after we have seen the adult rabbit that we judge this adult to be an improvement. Kuhn's thought paradigm is analogous to this one of organismic development, which is grounded in the idea of "development from" as opposed to "growth toward."

While Waddington, like Kuhn, is not yet willing to claim definitive status for a new paradigm, he does believe that "changes of world-view that have been occurring in the last fifty years are amongst the most far-reaching in the whole history of human thought."[8] Using M. C. Goodall's terminology, Waddington describes how a "Third Science," following the "Second Science" of the last 300 years, and the "First

---

6. Ibid., p. 170.
7. C. H. Waddington, *Behind Appearance* (Cambridge, Mass., 1970), p. 107.
8. Ibid., p. 1.

Science" of pre-Renaissance thought, is now bringing about fundamental changes in our common conception of what reality is. The key feature of Third Science is the involvement of the scientist:

> The scientist himself, or man in general in his activity as an observer, comes to be incorporated into science in a way which is completely outside the Second Science paradigm. And finally he also becomes involved in science not only as a maker of it but as a subject for its study, not only as an individual with a psychology, but as a member of a set of societies which are themselves examples of organization. Third Science, which is still nascent and has not yet arrived at a definitive inclusive paradigm of its own, will certainly have the human and social sciences as very important factors in its make-up.[9]

In going a small step farther than Kuhn by including the human and social sciences in his sense of the newly forming paradigm, and in relating these sciences to the increasing involvement of the scientist in the process of observation, Waddington suggests the full dimensionality of subjectivity in the emerging conceptions of knowledge.

If, therefore, we accept the notion that civilization has proceeded according to a series of successive paradigm formations aimed at maximizing phylogenetic adaptability, we are led to consider seriously the objective paradigm as now being maladaptive. The subjective paradigm, instead, views knowledge as created by the scientific community in the name of all mankind for the purpose of insuring the survival of our species.

Consider now the nature and purposes of the objective paradigm. The reason Kuhn attributes its origin to Descartes is that the latter first articulated the modern mind-matter duality which is the basis of the paradigm. This belief holds that there are two levels of existence—matter, the level of things, and mind, the level of experience. Thus, if we connected the nerve endings in my finger to your brain, and then slammed the door on my finger, you would feel the pain. Likewise, there are primary qualities of things, like size and shape, which are a function of matter, and secondary qualities, like color and smell, which are a function of mind. Pain and color are subjective and take place only in the mind; nerve endings and size are objective and exist in objective reality. This duality is not just a description of cognition but a philosophical correlative of what is probably a much more influential thought, the religious dichotomy of body and soul. The adaptive advantage of the cognitive dualism is that it leaves room in thought for the coexistence of religious cosmologies and secular ones. It is an intellectual compromise which works hand in hand with the European Protestant compromise between Church doctrine and Church power.

9. Ibid, pp. 2-3.

Taken together, the two compromises work something like this: if we confine soul and mind issues, including emotional and sexual life, to the private life of mankind and to the authority of personal conscience, we may deal "objectively" and technologically with everything else, including society and government; in fact, we will now create governments in the name of "freedom," and they will protect and hide the sexual, emotional, and intellectual lives of mankind with the ideas of "privacy" and "individual liberty," while concentrating all public efforts on creating ever more goods and services and reducing the social power of religious institutions. In this light the dualism of mind and matter was, for the seventeenth century, a creative solution to a problem that concerned not just philosophers, but, really, all constituents of society at that time.

The manifestations of this paradigm are legion. I suppose the most familiar one is Newtonian mechanics, terrestrial and celestial. Newton said that heavenly and earthly bodies move according to three mathematical laws of motion and the law of universal gravitation. With the ingenious mathematical invention, calculus, not only was the motion of all macrocosmic matter explained, but future motions, especially of celestial bodies, were predictable. The equation of predictability with the certainty of mathematical logic boosted objective science in the eighteenth century into the status of absolute truth. This truth, in turn, demonstrated the certainty of divine control of the universe. The efficacy of the subject-object duality was thus a cause for celebration. Imagine the tremendous comfort the eighteenth-century man derived in learning of the lawfulness of the heavens and the obvious corollary that such remarkable order can only have come from the infinite bounty and wisdom of the Lord. Clearly, the Great Order was there since Creation, and God's Gift of Reason has shown man His greater glory. How can this wonderful God not save our souls as part of the plan?

The paradigm of objective truth defined by the mind-matter duality obtains in influential contexts today, most notably in behaviorist psychology. Probably the foremost philosophical defender of objective knowledge is Karl Popper, who writes: "Although I do not think that we can ever describe, by our universal laws, an *ultimate* essence of the world, I do not doubt that we may seek to probe deeper and deeper into the structure of our world or, as we might say, into the properties of the world that are more and more essential, or of greater and greater depth."[10] Unmistakably, Popper describes scientific progress as moving ever closer to scientific truth. Using Kuhn's insight, we may identify this logic with the supervention of religious wishes on

10. Karl R. Popper, *Objective Knowledge* (Oxford, 1972), p. 196.

evolution. The essay Stephen Dedalus wrote contained the "heresy" that the soul in relation to the Creator was "without a possibility of ever approaching nearer." When this heresy was called to his attention (by, of all people, his English teacher), he corrected it with the phrase "without a possibility of ever reaching."[11] This is precisely Popper's attitude with regard to the world's "ultimate essence": without the possibility of ever reaching. I think that the origin of this attitude is in the religious dogma of human helplessness and inner corruption. The notion of objective truth has the same epistemological status as God: it is an invented frame of reference aimed at maintaining prevailing social practices. There is reason to suspect that Popper understands the subjectivity of scientific work but that he needs to deny this understanding. in discussing "depth," he says: "I believe this word 'deeper' defies any attempt at exhaustive logical analysis, but that it is nevertheless a guide to our intuitions. . . . the 'depth' of a scientific theory seems to be most closely related to its simplicity and so to the wealth of its content." A theory needs a "rich content" and a "certain coherence and compactness." To him compactness is "intuitively fairly clear," but "so difficult to analyze. . . . I do not think that we can do much more than refer here to an intuitive idea, not that we need to do much more."[12] Popper is at last driven to metaphors of richness and depth and to an open acknowledgement of the intuitive basis of these standards for evaluating scientific theories. He has arrived at a point where formulaic knowledge is no longer explicable on a logical basis, which suggests to me his implicit perception of the subjective nature of knowledge.

From historical and psychological perspectives, Popper's difficulties are understandable. He is faced with the inadequacies of a thought paradigm, not a more local scientific paradigm. This thought paradigm is at least 300 years old, and perhaps even older. The habit of viewing the world objectively is not an arbitrary or mutational development in human culture. It is connected with, though not caused by, a developmental event common to every human being, namely, the acquisition of the ability to objectify experience which appears in the infant at about eighteen months of age. In the next chapter, I will discuss how this ability is decisively connected with syntactical language and with the symbol-making capacity in general. While these psychological connections, in coordination with historical considerations, help explain the tenacity of the objective paradigm, they also give us grounds to understand exactly the sense in which "objective reality" is a construction of, and hence a subordinate

11. James Joyce, *A Portrait of the Artist as a Young Man* (1916; rpt. New York, 1956), p. 79.
12. Popper, *Objective Knowledge*, p. 197.

function of, our subjective perspective. In the past fifty or sixty years, we have been finding it increasingly necessary to consciously remove the capacity for objectification from the status of a paradigm—an assumed and almost unconscious presupposition—and reconceive it in the light of the subjective paradigm.

In an essay published in March 1975, Gunther Stent discussed the problems raised originally by Niels Bohr about his own work:

At the turn of this century, physics had progressed to a stage at which problems could be studied which involve either tiny subatomic or immense cosmic events on scales of time, space, and mass billions of times smaller or larger than our direct experience. Now, according to Bohr, "there arose difficulties of orienting ourselves in a domain of experience far from that to the description of which our means of expression are adapted." For it turned out that the description of phenomena in this domain in ordinary, everyday language leads to contradictions or mutually incompatible pictures of reality. In order to resolve these contradictions, time and space had to be denatured into generalized concepts whose meaning no longer matched that provided by intuition. Eventually it appeared also that the intuitive notion of causality is not a useful one for giving account of events at the atomic and subatomic level. All of these developments were the consequence of the discovery that the rational use of intuitive linguistic concepts to communicate experience actually embodies hitherto unnoticed presuppositions. And it is these presuppositions which lead to contradictions when the attempt is made to communicate events outside the experimental domain.[13]

The "hitherto unnoticed presuppositions" Stent mentions may be understood directly as the objective paradigm, which does conceptualize the intuitive notions of space, time, and causality, and whose intuitive nature is demonstrated by the multilingual use of the concepts. In physics, however, methods of observation and experimentation have gone beyond the capability of language, beyond the scope of developmental intuition; and those using these methods have, in effect, tried to develop a new language. The attempt has exposed the local basis of everyday language and thought, and is one of the main grounds on which Kuhn's new view of science is based.

There are three particular formulations in modern physics that forced the reevaluation of our epistemological presuppositions: Einstein's relativity, Bohr's complementarity, and Heisenberg's uncertainty. Einstein's relativity, which is based on the universal invariance of the speed of light, forced us to believe that hitherto invariant parameters of space, time, and mass must now be conceived of as variable, depending on the frame of reference from which we are observing them. According to this way of thinking, minutes can last

13. Gunther Stent, "Limits to the Scientific Understanding of Man," *Science*, 21 March 1975, p. 1055.

hours and still be minutes, and yards can stretch into miles while still remaining yards. These last two clauses of mine show how relativity has altered everyday linguistic semantics. Bohr's complementarity was devised in order to account for the apparent paradox that light observed in one context behaves like a wave and observed in another context behaves like a stream of particles. The idea of complementarity eliminated the expectation, derived from the objective paradigm, that light, which seems experientially one essential thing, must also be ontologically one essential thing. (Like Popper, Bohr renounces the quest for essences, but unlike Popper, Bohr makes no pretense that his way of thinking about light gets any deeper or closer to the ultimate truth.) Finally, Heisenberg's uncertainty principle holds that all the parameters of subatomic particles—location, velocity, and mass—cannot be specified at once, as one can do with Newtonian particles. If one of the parameters is specified, the other can be described only statistically. The reason is that the process of observation interferes with what is being observed in such a way that the object of observation appears changed by the act of observation. Here again we see the strain on everyday semantics: our sense of the idea "object" is just that it remains unchanged by our perception of it: an object is something that our perception renders permanent.

Heisenberg himself drew the conclusion of subjectivity from his work:

The objective reality of the elementary particles has been strangely dispersed, not into the fog of some new ill-defined or still unexplained conception of reality, but into the transparent clarity of a mathematics that no longer describes the behaviour of the elementary particles but only our knowledge of this behaviour. . . . If, starting from the condition of modern science, we try to find out where the bases have started to shift, we get the impression that it would not be too crude an oversimplification to say that *for the first time in the course of history modern man on this earth now confronts himself alone, and that he no longer has partners or opponents.* . . . Even in science, *the object of research is no longer nature itself, but man's investigation of nature.*

In the same discussion, Heisenberg quotes Eddington:

We have found that where science has progressed the farthest, the mind has but regained from nature that which mind has put into nature. We have found a strange foot print on the shores of the unknown. We have devised profound theories, one after another, to account for its origin. At last, we have succeeded in reconstructing the creature that made the footprint. And lo! It is our own.[14]

Heisenberg, Eddington, and others whom I will discuss shortly have added up a series of recent developments in science and have come to

14. Werner Heisenberg, *The Physicist's Conception of Nature* (London, 1958), pp. 17, 24.

an unexpected conclusion: the limits of the capacity for objectification have been reached, and any new knowledge—and even knowledge established in the past if viewed in widest generality—is a function of the means of observation and perception.

The formulations of Einstein, Bohr, and Heisenberg, therefore, all make sense as a manifestation of the subjective paradigm, because in each case the role of the observer is paramount. An observer is a subject, and his means of perception define the essence of the object and even its existence to begin with. An object is circumscribed and delimited by a subject's motives, his curiosities, and above all, his language. Under the subjective paradigm, new truth is created by a new use of language and a new structure of thought. The establishment of new knowledge is the activity of the intellecting mind adapting itself to ontogenetic and phylogenetic developmental demands. Knowledge is made by people and not found.

This view of knowledge is so alien to traditional ways of thinking that it challenges the rationality of those who try to define the context of modern science without changing its epistemological presuppositions. Herbert J. Muller takes pains to show how science is like poetry, how it is like theology, how "scientific laws are not chips off the old block, Reality,"[15] how a comprehensive scientific law does not "reduce by one the number of absolute truths to be discovered."[16] Muller continues:

Science is first of all the creation of scientists, who are also men with temperaments, special interests, predispositions. (Bertrand Russell has noted, for example, the divergent developments in animal psychology under Thorndike and Koehler: "Animals studied by Ameicans rush about frantically, with an incredible display of hustle and pep, and at last achieve the desired result by chance. Animals studied by Germans sit still and think, and at last evolve the solution out of their inner consciousness.") More significantly, science is the creation of a definite type of mentality, which has been interested in certain kinds of phenomena but notoriously indifferent to others, averse to seeming "wild data." Most significantly, it is the creation of a culture, a society with special interests. . . . There is an obvious correspondence between the long reign of classical mechanics and the needs of industry. Today . . . science . . . is the more profoundly a fashion of the times.[17]

It would seem that Muller's statement has all the ingredients of the subjective paradigm, but we soon learn that this is not the case at all:

The physicist "invents" theories, "creates" causes, but he does not invent and create at random, he cannot play fast and loose with nature. His "laws" are convenient descriptions of an actual lawfulness; that night follows day and all apples fall down are not arbitrary assumptions. His whole scheme is not a

15. Herbert J. Muller, *Science and Criticism* (1943; rpt. New York, 1956), p. 65.
16. Ibid, p. 66 (quoted from William H. George, with no reference given).
17. Ibid.

literal copy of reality, but neither is it mere fiction or artifact. . . . In the language of common sense, our knowledge is approximate, but it is approximate to *something*, it is a knowledge of appearance, but these are appearances of something. . . . modern physics . . . has been a solid gain, a genuine *advance* in knowledge. One should be able to reject Newton's absolutes without rejecting all objective knowledge and becoming a scientific atheist.[18]

Muller's formulations are hardly distinguishable from Popper's, and his religious metaphor documents the religious dimension of the objective paradigm: Let us not be dogmatic, but God exists nevertheless. Muller believes in the autonomy of what is "out there" and believes that one can "advance" toward it. But I wonder in reading these statements how scientists, societies, and cultures can "first of all" create science if it is the object after all upon which science is modeled. Muller's two passages represent another example of the contradictions the objective paradigm has produced in our thinking. The subjective paradigm aims *to remove contradictions from thought,* regardless of what we decide is objective. The objective paradigm requires that reality exist without contradiction. We see now that this requirement cannot be met.

Alfred North Whitehead was aware of the philosophic magnitude of modern science's epistemological challenge and considered the subjective paradigm as a possible solution. He believed that traditional ideas have to be "refashioned" and wished to settle "whether this refashioning of ideas is to be carried out on an objectivist basis or on a subjectivist basis." He rejected the subjective basis on three grounds. First, the direct "interrogation of our perceptive experience" makes it appear that we are *within* a world of colours, sounds, and other sense objects, related in space and time to enduring objects such as stones, trees, and human bodies." Second, "historical knowledge tells us" of a past before mankind existed and of a universe in which there is "something happening" now. Third, the human "instinct for action" "seems to issue in an instinct for self-transcendence" in the same way as "sense-perception seems to give knowledge of what lies beyond individuality." Finally, he observed that "with the exception of those who are content with themselves as forming the entire universe, solitary amid nothing, everyone wants to struggle back to some sort of objectivist position. I do not understand how a common world of thought can be established in the absence of a common world of sense."[19]

18. Ibid., pp. 88-89.
19. Alfred North Whitehead, *Science and the Modern World* (1925; rpt. New York, 1967), pp. 88-90.

Under the subjective paradigm, the common world of thought is established on just such a basis as the common world of sense. The latter world is subjective, determined by extended negotiation among perceivers. The three reasons Whitehead gave for rejecting subjectivity beg the question altogether. The need for the subjective paradigm arose just because what appears to be overwhelmingly apparent can no longer be believed to underlie a whole array of scientific experiences, three of which I discussed above. These experiences have called into question both the authority of historical knowledge and our inferences of ongoing events in the universe. The increasing complication of our means of perceiving the celestial universe has shown that we need to change *our notion* of "something happening" to a position that gives authority to our means of perception. Finally, the so-called instinct for action which "seems" to give knowledge does just that: it *seems* to give knowledge. But whether this knowledge is beyond the community of mankind's agreement is in no way determinable. The idea of self-transcendence makes sense only in theological terms. If we divest the idea of God from it, it can refer only to interpersonal and social activity. The "instinct for action" leads neither to some quasi-mystical association with things, as Whitehead's concept of "organism" would have us believe, nor to a fully mystical connection with God, whom Whitehead would likewise have us keep in the picture. Except insofar as individuals deal with other individuals and groups deal with other groups, self-transcendence is imaginary, and can apply referentially only to the soul's leaving the body—at death or at any other time.

The work of Popper and Muller fulfills, in large part, Whitehead's wish to have others join him in his struggle back to an objectivist position; others do share his trepidation about tampering with objectivity. But since Whitehead wrote in 1925, others who were trained in the physical sciences and many who came from the biological, social, and psychological disciplines have been considerably less fearful of developing new modes of thought more accomodating of the kinds of knowledge needed in our time.

Edmund Husserl was almost an exact contemporary of Whitehead's and, like him, was an accomplished and creative mathematician. Also, like Whitehead, his work in mathematics led him to philosophical reconsiderations of the nature of science; this, in turn, led him to formulate the concept of "transcendental subjectivity," which does seem similar to "self-transcendence." In Husserl's work, however, I am able to separate his forceful understanding of the nature of subjectivity from his impulse to transcendentalism  because the latter contains no theological dimension and is thus not motivated by the "struggle" back to objectivity. In contrast, Whitehead's concept of organism needs the theological dimension just because it is an objectivist theory. The philosophy of these two men are responses to the same problem; Husserl believed that it had to be solved on the subjective basis that Whitehead rejected.

Husserl's most important contribution in this regard is his last and unfinished treatise, *The Crisis of European Sciences*, first published in 1938. He names his problem as "the enigma of subjectivity" and the "enigma of psychological subject matter and method."[20] The problem arises from two angles. First, "if we cease being immersed in our scientific thinking, we become aware that we scientists are, after all, human beings and as such are among the components of the life-world which always exists for us, ever pregiven; and thus all of science is pulled, along with us, into the—merely "subjective-relative"—life-world."[21] Restated interrogatively, the question is, if scientists are bound by the life-world (the world of subjective experience), doesn't this reduce science to mere subjective relativism? The other side of the question, Husserl says, is "But can the world, and human existence in it, truthfully have a meaning if the sciences recognize as true only what is objectively established?" Thus, the very fact that one *can* be both objective and subjective is the heart of the problem: "The paradoxical interrelationships of the 'objectively true world' and the 'life-world' make enigmatic the manner of being of both."[22]

While Husserl does not claim to solve the problem finally, his way of understanding science anew insists on its communal basis, just as Kuhn's way of understanding science does: "The whole edifice of doctrine in the objective sciences are structures attained through certain activities of scientists bound together in their collaborative work. . . . attained through a continued building-up of activities the later of which always presuppose the results of the earlier." The internal dialectic of the scientific community creates the "edifice" of science. He further claims that perception itself is communally grounded: "The thing itself is actually that which no one experiences as really seen, since it is always in motion, always, and for everyone, a unity for consciousness of the openly endless multiplicity of changing experiences and experienced things, one's own and those of others. The cosubjects of this experience themselves make up, for me and for one another, an openly endless horizon of human beings who are capable of meeting and then entering into actual contact with me and with one another." Perception is validated by the interpersonal contact of the "cosubjects" of an experience. The multiplicity of such

20. Edmund Husserl, *The Crisis of European Sciences and Transcendental Phenomenology*, tr. David Carr (Evanston, Ill., 1970), p. 5.
21. Ibid., p. 131.
22. Ibid., pp. 67, 131.

cosubjects invalidates absolute objectivity, and instead grounds what is taken for objectivity on communal authority. Knowledge is created by the human community: "Thus in general the world exists not only for isolated men but for the community of men; and this is due to the fact that even what is straightforwardly perceptual is communalized."[23] In spite of whatever frustrations Husserl had in formulating what he thought was a complete philosophical position, his starting point was his consistent conviction of the subjective and communal basis of all human knowledge, both quantitative and hermeneutic.

The development of physicist P. W. Bridgman's thinking follows a path somewhat analogous to that of Husserl's thought. Starting from a position seemingly geared exclusively for research in the positivistic tradition, Bridgman ultimately makes use of his original mode of thought to conceive of knowledge as a function of subjectivity, even as far as grounding knowledge in communal action and decision.

One of Bridgman's major contributions to science is his concept of the operational definition, or operationalism. This principle holds that the definition of a natural object is created by the operations used to measure it. In agreement with the principle of complementarity, light "is" a wave when wave measurements apply, and it "is" a particle when particle measurements apply. Perhaps more familiarly, the operational definition of a table is the aggregate of human behaviors which use it as a table: if a camp trunk is used regularly as a dining site, it is then a dinner table. It is only through such operations that we can say we "know" what anything "is." Bridgman reports that in his early work he tended to separate the object-plus-defining-operations from the mental techniques of understanding objects, but he eventually came to the position that "it is not profitable to separate the one problem (understanding the world) from the other (understanding the process of understanding) the way I did."[24]

On the basis of Bridgman's observations, Floyd Matson argues that "it might be said that Bridgman, having extracted meaning and relevance from the human subject through an ingenious feat of surgery, spent the balance of his career trying to put them back."[25] This characterization portrays his development as an about-face from the desire to eliminate subjectivity from our thinking to a reverse desire to make it an inclusive principle of mental functioning. I think, however, that we can more profitably view the change as a *natural consequence of his original formulations of operationalism*. Bridgman writes: "Any new insights which I may have been acquiring over the years cannot be dissociated from my constant practise of 'operational

23. Ibid., pp. 131, 164, 163.
24. P. W. Bridgman, *The Way Things Are* (Cambridge, Mass., 1959), p. 2.
25. Floyd W. Matson, *The Broken Image* (1964; rpt. New York, 1966), p. 238.

analysis,' which continually reveals itself as a fruitful line of attack."[26] Operationalism was originally a subjectively grounded form of thought, and Bridgman's simple following of the consequences of his own thought ultimately made clear its subjective nature. Unlike his friend and colleague B. F. Skinner, Bridgman understood that if behaviors are used to define realities, the perception of behavior is likewise a behavior that defines the "thing perceived."

When Bridgman tried to record and communicate his developing thoughts, he began to believe that operationalism describes how knowledge has to be treated in the hermeneutic disciplines. The underlying principle is that "operations are performed by individuals."[27] This applies to verbal operations as well as to mathematical:

A spoken or written word was spoken or written by someone, and part of that recognition of the word as activity is a recognition of who it was that said it or wrote it. When I make a statement, even as cold and impersonal a statement as a proposition of Euclid, it is I that am making the statement, and the fact that it is I that am making the statement is part of the picture of the activity. . . . Attention to the activity aspect of all our communication inevitably forces mention of the maker of the communication.[28]

If this is the case with any form of intellection, Bridgman reasons, the obvious consequence is that "we never get away from ourselves." This is a situation of unprecedented generality, a problem "associated with, but incomparably more complicated than, the problem of the role of the observer to which quantum theory has devoted so much attention."[29]

The "conceptual revolution" in physics, therefore, is "not really a revolution in new realms of high velocities or the very small, but is properly a conceptual revolution on the macroscopic level of everyday life. . . . It is still *we* who have the new concepts, and the material which goes into the formation of the concepts still comes to *us* through the same old sense."[30] The generality of this way of thinking leads Bridgman to understand social interaction in a way which, as I will discuss in connection with Roger Poole, demands personal responsibility for one's perceptions and behavior: "I now understand my fellows in terms of myself rather than myself in terms of my fellows. My fellow, I believe, understands me and his fellows in the same way. Society is a group of individuals, each thinking of others in this way. I believe that the first person approach receives its most important application, and the failure to adopt the approach has its most serious consequences, in

26. Bridgman, *The Way Things Are*, p. 2.
27. Ibid.
28. Ibid., p. 4.
29. Ibid., p. 6.
30. Ibid., p. 8.

a social setting."[31] Bridgman here claims that whatever else is the case, one's own perceptual and intellectual initiative is the operational path toward social adaptation. Unless this endogenous form of a person's social activity is recognized, social regulation and organization is severely inhibited. The later development of Bridgman's thinking is thus less a rebellion against objectivity than a rigorous pursuit of the intellectual consequenes of following objectivity as far as it can go. Operationalism was a response to the needs of the objective paradigm, but when fully followed through and understood, it is a statement of the subjective paradigm.

Michael Polanyi's elaborate treatise *Personal Knowledge* (1958), while an admirable attempt to deal with subjectivity in an extended philosophical context, is disappointingly influenced by the same religious thought paradigms that generated the belief in objectivity. In certain fundamental points, his work is nevertheless consistent with the present concept of subjectivity. He observes, for example, that "objectivism requires a specifiably functioning mindless knower. To accept the indeterminacy of knowledge requires, on the contrary, that we accredit a person entitled to shape his knowing according to his own judgment, unspecifiably." Because of the self-denying feature of objective observation, the buildup of modern science has created the fiction of autonomous facts. He likens this development to the effect of the medieval church: "Now it has turned out the modern scientism fetters thought as cruelly as ever churches had done. It offers no scope for our most vital beliefs, and it forces us to disguise them in farcically inadequate terms."[32] Unfortunately, Polanyi's search for personal knowledge is linked to a nostalgia for the very medievalism he finds so stifling. He reaffirms Augustine's principle that "all knowledge is a gift of grace," and he distinguishes belief from subjectivity. In seeking to "restore to us once more the power for the deliberate holding of unproven beliefs," Polanyi's conception of personal knowledge is antisocial. It remains in the retrograde religious context of individual moral responsibility alone, as if beliefs were not socially formulated. Like Whitehead, he speaks of man's capacity for self-transcendence and seeks to restore our knowledge of Good and Evil but now in the "blinding light of our new analytical powers."[33] Being a personalist rather than a subjectivist, he does not manifest Husserl's urgent awareness of the connection between personal knowledge and the human community. We may observe, nevertheless, that he is importantly affected by at least a rudimentary imperative to understand knowledge as ground in the subjective initiative of people rather than in the objective transcendence of things.

---

31. Ibid., p. 251.
32. Michael Polanyi, *Personal Knowledge* (1958; rpt. New York, 1964), pp. 264, 265.
33. Ibid., p. 268.

In the past forty years there have been serious efforts to understand the social origins of knowledge. These efforts have come from the Frankfurt group of neo-Marxists, who, in spite of sometimes embarrassing intrusions of received dogma, mount persuasive arguments for the socially subjective character of knowledge. I will mention two of these efforts.

At the end of the 1920s, Karl Mannheim, in his essay "The Sociology of Knowledge," outlines what is essentially the form of the subjective paradigm without its content. The content as presently understood makes no distinction between knowledge gained in the quantitative sciences and that gained through hermeneutics. Mannheim still makes this distinction and tries to make room for the social origins of knowledge by denying that the natural sciences are necessarily relative to their culture of origin:

The natural sciences have been selected as the ideal to which all knowledge should aspire. It is only because natural science, especially in its quantifiable phases, is largely detachable from the historical-social perspective of the investigator that the ideal of true knowledge was so construed that all attempts to attain a type of knowledge aiming at the comprehension of quality are considered as methods of inferior value. For quality contains elements more or less intertwined with the *Weltanschauung* of the knowing subject.[34]

Kuhn's view of the exact sciences, which sees them as culture-determined after all, says that both forms of knowledge are qualitatively determined and that there can no longer be "ideals of true knowledge." With regard to particular researches in the social sciences, Mannheim writes: "The approach to a problem, the level on which the problem happens to be formulated, the stage of abstraction and the stage of concreteness that one hopes to attain, are all and in the same way bound up with the social existence." As a general principle, knowledge is not dependent on a preexistent theory of knowledge: "New forms of knowledge, in the last analysis, grow out of the conditions of collective life and do not depend for their emergence upon the prior demonstration by a theory of knowledge that they are possible; they do not therefore need to be first legitimized by an epistemology."[35] Because knowledge freely emerges from collective life, its nature cannot be either specified or limited in advance. This concept of knowledge coincides with Kuhn's concept of revolutionary science.

We should bear in mind that by the phrase "conditions of collective life" Mannheim is referring to the economic and class structures of the society in which science is developed. These factors add considerable

34. Karl Mannheim, *Ideology and Utopia*, tr. Louis Wirth and Edward Shils (1929; rpt. New York, 1963), pp. 290-91.
35. Ibid., pp. 278, 289.

137,535

specificity to the ideas of community discussed by Husserl and Kuhn, and they thus add to our understanding of the dimensions of the subjective paradigm.

Jürgen Habermas's major study *Knowledge and Human Interests* (1968) increases the sophistication of Mannheim's formulations by describing how social existence represents a definable syndrome of motives, particularly those of self-preservation and of pleasure. Because knowledge is produced by such motives, knowledge and human interest form a unified basis of civilization. In the past, science depended on the separation of knowledge from interest:

Because science must secure the objectivity of its statements against the pressure and seduction of particular interests, it deludes itself about the fundamental interests to which it owes not only its impetus but the *conditions of possible objectivity* themselves. . . . If knowledge could ever outwit its innate human interest, it would be by comprehending that the mediation of subject and object that philosophical consciousness attributes exclusively to *its own* synthesis is produced originally by interests.[36]

Kuhn's work gives us grounds for believing this argument: subjective and communal needs themselves produced the separation of subject and object. From the time of Descartes on, religious interests have fostered the separation, and these same interests limited the thought of Whitehead, Popper, Muller, and Polanyi. The growth of human interests other than religious has brought recognition to the subjective paradigm.

Habermas's thought paradigm is not Darwinian. It is animated, rather, by the Marxian idea of evolution toward a utopian society. Habermas believes that human language "raises us out of nature" and guides "mankind's evolution toward autonomy and responsibility." He argues that knowledge is "an instrument (that) transcends mere self-preservation" and that, similarly, the "enticing natural force" libido "urges toward utopian fulfillment."[37] The Marxian nature of the concept of interest thus separates two biologically grounded features of the human being from phylogenetic development and posits the interest-motivated but independently driven development toward the social ideals of autonomy and responsibility. According to the Darwinian paradigm, such a motivational element as an evolution-toward-an-ideal is not viable. In this sense, overgeneralized Marxist thought embarrasses an otherwise far-reaching view of the function of knowledge.

A recent study by Roger Poole, *Towards Deep Subjectivity* (1972), is able to show just how ethical considerations represent an important

36. Jürgen Habermas, *Knowledge and Human Interests*, tr. Jeremy J. Shapiro (1965, 1968; rpt. Boston, 1972), pp. 311-12.

37. Ibid., pp. 314, 315, 313, 312.

aspect of the subjective paradigm without deriving them from either religious or Marxist traditions. Though not explicitly labeled as such, Poole's concept of ethics is Darwinian, and is consistent with Husserl's and Bridgman's formulations regarding the basis of social interaction. On this ground Poole can argue that interpersonal exchanges of knowledge and interpersonal allocations of responsibility function in exactly the same way. Knowledge and responsibility are both governed by the subjective paradigm on levels ranging from two people to the community of nations.

Poole achieves this synthesis of ideas with a new idea of his own, ethical space, the primary unit of which is the human body: "The body is the locus of all ethical experience, and all experience is, because spatial, ethical. There can be no act which does not take place in ethical space. There can be no 'flaccid' act, no act devoid of all significance, no unconditioned act."[38] Ethical space is meant to be in part metaphoric but in part real. It is metaphoric in the sense that every human act, even private ones, has some consequence for some other human beings; such acts must touch on other people's personal "space." It is real, however, in the sense that every human body—and every nation—does need a certain measure of real space in order to live, as well as a certain stake in the inventory of environmental resources. In this context, metaphorical space and actual space are identical. We may thereby understand how getting along with one another and conquering disease are two activities with the same purpose—enhancing the conditions of being alive. The idea of ethical space is especially compelling because its function is conceived exactly as the function of celestial space in general relativity, namely, that the number and needs of human bodies "curve" the space according to themselves. If space is improperly allocated, either through hoarding of wealth, ecological contamination, or the use of nuclear weapons, the human race will become maladaptive, and life will end. Poole claims that the need for subjectivity is dictated by the imminence of all of these threats to human life. The new form of thought can help produce the large-scale perceptions needed to understand the *interconnectedness* of the threats and increase the sense of urgency in reducing them. This argument suggests the Darwinian basis of the ethical and political reach of the subjective paradigm: it is a matter of survival of the human species.

Poole discusses how governments may use context-free objective facts at once to prevaricate and to disclaim responsibility. A typical example would be the public announcement that cites statistics pertaining either to military operations or economic conditions. Because statistics always seem context-free, they function like a

38. Roger Poole, *Towards Deep Subjectivity* (New York, 1972), p. 27.

Rorschach blot. The public decides, on an individual basis, what truth such announcements have. Ordinarily, the citizen imagines that he has a relationship with his government and that the announcement is true to the relationship. The presumed objectivity of the facts, however, gives the government the option of denying its connection with those facts: "We don't know which of our soldiers killed the civilian women and children; the fact is: this many are dead." In this way the government can lie to the public about its public responsibility, because regardless of which soldiers did the killing, the government is responsible. Therefore, the facts cannot be objective; they are a function of the government's relationship to the public.

Floyd Matson describes a similar situation offered by Joseph Tussman, in which the supposed need for objectivity negates responsibility. A judge is trying to make a decision. In order to render an "objective" decision, Matson explains, the judge will "take account of the statistical trends" as well as of the "role-expectations that significant interest-groups have of him." The judge would also consider proddings of conscience as "only a disease of the inner ear," simply because conscience is not an objective factor. Thus, Matson concludes, "If he is not to be laughed out of court, the judge must look upon himself and his role objectively, from the outside; and in so doing he becomes, in the fullest sense of the word, irresponsible. He has refused to judge."[39] Much as what follows from Poole's discussion, the meaning of responsibility is to look on neither the facts of a case nor on oneself objectively. Facts can acquire meaning only as a function of someone's subjectivity. The action of such facts—or the operations, as Bridgman calls such action—is also necessarily subjective. Responsibility does not exist, therefore, without subjectivity.

This brings us to the nub of Poole's argument: "Subjectivity itself thus turns out to be, not only an intentionality, a meaning-conferring ability, but a relationship. It is (I think) impossible to have an objective relationship with anything at all: at the very least it would be intentional and thus subjective, even if it were relatively passionless, like my relation to the pillar-box. It does not move me to strong feelings about it, but I have decided all the same that it is red."[40] The unspoken proposition in this statement is that the instrument of subjectivity and of intersubjectivity is language, since that is what we use to announce intention and to confer meaning. To decide that something is or is not red, true, or free is simultaneously a subjective act and a linguistic act. Every linguistic act has cognitive, expressive, interpersonal, and ethical dimensions that render such acts subjective. Rather than raising human beings out of nature, language is part of the human means of

39. Matson, *The Broken Image*, pp. 233-34.
40. Poole, *Towards Deep Subjectivity*, pp. 95-96.

adaptation in nature. When this part is cancelled by violence or other destructive and nonsymbolic behavior, we lose our only natural means of survival. Unlike the animals, we depend on language and thought—on self-awareness—and not on the accidents of vegetation and prey, to protect, preserve, and prolong our lives.

The efforts of Piaget to understand the nature of intelligence, which he identifies with language and thought, have produced the belief that it is best conceived as an organ of the body: "Cognitive functions are an extension of organic regulations and constitute a differentiated organ for regulating exchanges with the external world."[41] Like an organ, it is, on the one hand, an independent system, and on the other hand, it is a contributing element to the individual's biological and social homeostasis. In *The Origins of Intelligence in Children* (1952), Piaget argues that intelligence is grounded in two universal circumstances—the development of sensorimotor intelligence, which most animals also have, and a dialectic relationship between mother and child, which no animals have. These two conditions foster natural growth to where human activity is controlled by consciousness and its agent, language, in a way that permits indefinite periods of time to elapse between the first impulse and the sensorimotor fulfillment of its demand. This capacity for conscious control is what Piaget calls representational intelligence. He characterizes it as an internalization, or mentalization, of the sensorimotor behaviors that were established in the earlier stages of bodily growth. In the next chapter, I will discuss his reasoning and his findings in greater detail; now, I am calling attention to the aspect of subjectivity in his concept of intelligence.

Piaget seems willing to extend this understanding of intelligence to its social function. He suggests, in particular, that there is a "continuity" between the function of intelligence in the individual and the function of the individual in the social group:

The social group . . . plays the same role that the "population" does in genetics and consequently in instinct. In this sense, society is the supreme unit, and the individual can only achieve his inventions and intellectual constructions insofar as he is the seat of collective interactions that are naturally dependent, in level and value, on society as a whole. The great man who at anytime seems to be launching some new line of thought is simply the point of intersection of synthesis of ideas which have been elaborated by a continuous process of cooperation, and, even if he is opposed to current opinions, he represents a response to underlying needs which arise outside himself. This is why social environment is able to do so effectively for the intelligence what genetic recombinations of the population did for evolutionary variation of the transindividual cycle of the instincts.[42]

41. Jean Piaget, *Biology and Knowledge*, tr. Beatrix Walsh (1967; rpt. Chicago, 1971), p. 369.
42. Ibid., p. 368.

Others have conceived of the great man as Piaget does, but metaphorically, Piaget means his description literally and as a manifestation of the Darwinian paradigm. Large-scale intellectual construction is achieved, he suggests, by methods identical to those used by infants in small-scale constructions. This points up the subjective meaning of the term *environment*, which is "that which a person objectifies as part of the natural process of intellection." Objectification proceeds from normal biological functions, which are the bases of psychological functions, which, in turn, are the bases of social functions. This reasoning gives considerable support to the claim that meaning is constructed and conferred on objects and not extracted from them; the construction of meaning is motivated by organismic adaptation.

Before Piaget began his now successful efforts to illuminate processes of intellection, psychoanalysis had come upon the clinical necessity to understand certain intellectual processes in subjective terms. Like Bridgman's operational analysis, psychoanalysis reached subjectivity by exhausting the capacities of the objective paradigm with which it started. That is, Freud first assumed that his hermeneutic method did uncover original causes of dreams and neurosis. Gradually, however, he realized that most of the clinical interpretations he adduced could not be conceived in objective terms. I will discuss in some detail psychoanalytic hermeneutics in Chapter Three, which deals with interpretation in general; here I will record two items, a practice Freud came upon early and a principle he articulated late in his career.

While he was working with his first patients who complained of hysterical symptoms, Freud started to conclude that he had to view patients' fantasies of sexual contact with their parents with the same authority as remembered facts of such contact. He thus began treating memories and fantasies identically in the attempt to relieve the symptoms of hysteria. The epistemological import of the success of this practice we see now: the patient's own subjectivity actually controls what is or is not a fact. The patient's psychological homeostasis defines the degree of fact and fantasy. In the ordinary neurotic patient this control is subject to regulation by his interpersonal relationships. In the psychotic patient, who cannot be treated analytically, the regulation of fact and fantasy is beyond control by a relationship situation; to put it another way, his language cannot be used as a means of psychological and social self-regulation, as it is in neurotic patients and in the everyday lives of people in general. Therefore, in an important sense, psychological interpretation worked best when conceived as independent of actual facts and as a subjectively motivated construction by both patient and therapist *after* either fact or fantasy, aimed at present-time psychosocial adaptation: interpretation did not function as the recovery of original factual causes of feelings and behaviors.

Late in his career, increasingly impatient with the attempts to discredit psychoanalysis with the argument that it is not scientific, Freud formulated the epistemological principles which he thought applied simultaneously to his science as well as to any organized pursuit of knowledge. These principles constitute one of the earliest attempts to change our conception of knowledge in the direction of subjectivity:

> In the first place, our organization—that is, our mental apparatus—has been developed precisely in the attempt to explore the external world, and it must therefore have realized in its structure some degree of expediency; in the second place, it is itself a constituent part of the world which we set out to investigate, and it readily admits of such an investigation; thirdly, the task of science is fully covered if we limit it to showing how the world must appear to us in consequence of the particular character of our organization; fourthly, the ultimate findings of science, precisely because of the way in which they are acquired, are determined not only by our organization but by the things which have affected that organization; finally, the problem of the nature of the world without regard to our percipient mental apparatus is an empty abstraction, devoid of practical interest.[43]

Although, with the exception of this statement, these principles functioned for Freud mainly as axiomatic presuppositions, it is not surprising to find that one or more of them describe the work of each of those I cited earlier as having contributed significantly to the understanding of subjectivity. For example, the first, third, and fourth statements apply to Piaget's work on adaptation; Husserl arrived at the second and fifth statements through phenomenology, as did Heisenberg and Bridgman through physics. Poole's work follows and expands upon Husserl's; Mannheim's and Habermas's thought relate to the third statement. When Freud made these statements, the quantitative sciences were in the midst of change in the direction Freud outlined.

It might seem that subjective thinking would be least applicable in matters of visual perception, as compared with perception through the other senses or with the perception of linguistic meaning. Over the past few decades, however, psychologists and art critics have shown that the subjectivity of visual perception is at least equal to that of semantic perception, especially in cases where the act of seeing is considered of central importance. For example, if a married couple passes a rose on a walk and both observe "rose red" and then forget about it, there is agreement: they saw the same "objective" color. But if the same couple is looking at various styles of rose red carpeting for their prospective home, their perceptions of the color will be heavily influenced by what each had in mind in general for their home. The carpeting will be "seen" in the preimagined context; there would be no point in explaining to each party what the "actual" color is. The "operational" use of the color red in this case defines it.

In *Art and Illusion* (1956), E. H. Gombrich tried to articulate this problem in terms more general than had been used by gestalt, behavioral, or psychoanalytic psychology. In the many studies of perceptual variability, he finds the "news of a radical reorientation of all traditional ideas about the human mind."[44] The important new belief is that perception takes place as a gradual differentiation of originally perceived wholes rather than as a buildup of originally perceived parts. This means that the mind creates its own perceptual paradigms from prior experience, and these paradigms are then invoked, automatically, in subsequent perception. The preexisting paradigm, like an optical lens, interprets the visual experience. Gombrich uses a common perceptual experiment—the rabbit-duck drawing—to demonstrate this thought. If you think "rabbit" while viewing it, it looks like a rabbit; if you think "duck," it looks like a duck. Gombrich draws two conclusions that are of interest in the present context. First, "to see the shape apart from its interpretation . . . is not really possible." Thus, the shape has no objective existence except if we *decide* that it is "just" a shape. But this latter option proves the point: only we can decide on what the shape is, or on whether it is only a shape. The second conclusion is that "we cannot experience alternative readings at the same time." As a result, "though we may be intellectually aware of the fact that any given experience *must* be an illusion, we cannot, strictly speaking, watch ourselves having an illusion."[45] Even though we know we can shift paradigms, we still may experience only one at a time. Therefore, our subjective circumstance determines both which paradigm we will use and what initiative we will take to change paradigms. There is thus no way to establish an independent object that all viewers must perceive identically.

Toward the end of his treatise, Gombrich reaches a conclusion related to the one just above: "There is no 'objective' sense in which a human being can look 'the size of an ant' simply because an ant crawling on our pillow will look gigantic in comparison with a man in the distance. In Professor E. G. Boring's words, 'Phenomenal size, like physical size, is relative and has no meaning except as a relation

44. E. H. Gombrich, *Art and Illusion* (1956; Princeton, 1960), p. 27.
45. Ibid., pp. 5-6.

between objects.' "[46] This conclusion means that the notion of size is completely subjective, regardless of whether we think of size as a percept or as an attribute of an object. Gombrich's statement that a human being cannot even "look" the size of an ant articulates the principle that any judgment of size involves a mental calculation that compares the percept to previous perceptions. Since, perceptually, an object never has a constant size, it can never look the size of something else. I have already discussed how relativity forces us to vary our conception of physical size.

My survey of intellectual developments in various fields is intended to suggest that for the past few decades, knowledge in the physical sciences and in the social and psychological sciences has been hermeneutically derived. To make a distinction between the interpretive and quantitative sciences for the purpose of assigning more or less authority to one of them is no longer possible. The subjective paradigm suggests that knowledge in general comes through synthesized interpretations.

There has never been any doubt that literary criticism was a major constituent of the humanistic disciplines we have traditionally understood as hermeneutic. Yet at the very time when Mannheim, Freud, and the physical scientists were looking to subjective forms of thought to better authorize knowledge, criticism turned in the opposite direction, emphasizing the "scientific" attitude, featuring the objective autonomy of a work of art. Having no language to rationalize and organize older forms of topical impressionistic criticism, "new" critics tried to hypostasize a literary text as a document with an internally coherent objective meaning. At the same time the traditional practices of literary judgment and evaluation were retained, so that criticism began to resemble the biblical hermeneutics of centuries back. For example, T. S. Eliot felt justified in claiming that *Hamlet* is an "artistic failure" because there is no "objective correlative" for the emotion the play aroused in him.[47] Had he held his own subjectivity in higher esteem, however, he might have delivered a similar judgment with less presumption, greater candor, and greater authority. He thus would have reported that he could not understand how or why he is responding to the play because he does not perceive the occasion of his response in the play. What he did present was a value judgment in the form and syntax of fact. Partially as a result of Eliot's leadership, such statements became common critical practice. In this practice, two aspects of the objective paradigm are combined—the religious assumption that ministers have special access to the absolute truth and

46. Ibid., p. 301.
47. T. S. Eliot, *The Sacred Wood* (New York, 1928), p. 98.

the scientistic assumption that an object of art is independent of human perception. This is not surprising, though, in the light of the long-standing association of religious interests and the objective paradigm.

Two major modern critics have tried to bring new language and thought into literary hermeneutics, though ultimately, objective thinking prevailed in their work. In 1925, I. A. Richards tried to remove the mysticism from aesthetic thought. He argued that aesthetic emotion is no different from any other emotion and that, therefore, it is ordinary human feeling occurring under the influence of aesthetic perception. He further argued that it is the job of critics to present value judgments and that such judgments derive from the subjective economy of appetites and drives. He maintained that psychology is indispensable if we are to understand the human interest in literature, and he tried to outline what such a psychology might look like. Finally, he dismissed the mind-body problem altogether because it arises from our failure to make a distinction "as to when we are making a statement and when merely inciting an attitude."[48] That is, if we understand the motive of our own pronouncements, the question of what is objective and what subjective would not arise. This much of Richards' argument is in accord with the subjective paradigm.

As a rule, however, this thinking is not applied in his own critical practice. Although he says he feels awkward about it, he also proffers his belief that he as a critic is an "expert in matters of taste" and that a critic "ought then to be ready with reasons of a clear and convincing kind as to why his preferences are worth attention."[49] In *Principles of Literary Criticism,* which articulates the theory I outlined above, Richards presents highly subjective judgments of good and bad poetry, supported by equally subjective reasons. Yet, rather than using his psychological considerations to explain his personal judgments, he uses only his assumption of his expertise in taste to authorize the judgments. Richards did not develop his proposed psychology much further, and he did not publicly change his opinion about the critic's expertise. In fact, in *Practical Criticism,* which is a pioneering attempt to examine in detail how actual readers read, Richards again relies on his own authority simply to judge correct and incorrect readings. Therefore, the subjective factors that Richards acknowledged in his theory as being part of the reading process were omitted from systematic, conscious consideration in his practice of criticism.

The work of Northrop Frye has played a comparably prominent role in critical thinking of recent decades. His emphasis on the search for and definition of archetypal themes has widened the critical tradition he received. Yet for him the ideal of knowledge is still the quantitative

48. I. A. Richards, *Principles of Literary Criticism* (1925; rpt. New York, n.d.), p. 84.
49. Ibid., pp. 36, 37.

sciences. He believes that criticism should imitate physics: criticism, the subject, studies literature, the object, just as physics studies nature. Even though he shows how the frontier sciences in this century are social and behavioral, he still hopes that the "science" of words will one day be as reliable as mathematics. The classification system he devised for literature is neither more nor less certain than a persuasive interpretation. In the future, in different cultural circumstances, other criteria for classification may be adduced, or the act of literary classification may not be considered knowledge at all.

Frye believes that a certain area of literary response is inaccessible in an ultimate sense; this is the *nous*, the knowledge of literature, as opposed to the *dianoia*, knowledge about literature. Frye pursues the latter, objective knowledge. The *nous* is experiential and yields only subjective value judgments. This knowledge cannot be sought by a subject of study. This could be a defensible position for Frye if his own sense of his relationship to knowledge were less personal. Frye explains why one seeks knowledge in the first place: "The knowledge of most worth, for a genuine student, is that body of knowledge to which he has already made an unconscious commitment. I speak of an unconscious commitment because for a genuine student, knowledge, like marriage, is too important a matter to be left entirely to conscious choice."[50] The question "What knowledge is most worth having," he suggests, should be rephrased as "With what body of knowledge do you wish to identify yourself?" Thus, he subjectifies the "worth" and keeps the knowledge objective. But if the knowledge most valuable to us arrives through unconscious commitment, and if we commit ourselves by processes similar to those experienced in getting married, and if knowledge is something *we identify ourselves with,* in what sense can it be objective? In what sense is it independent of communal or personal function? I do not think it is a coincidence that Frye is an ordained minister. More than Richards, I think, he is committed to the objectivity of knowledge, which he characterizes as an undiscovered person with whom one can both identify and marry. But ultimately it is not a real person, and like the memory of one's parents, this person is a part of oneself. Knowledge cannot be either a parent, a spouse, or a god, though we may think of it that way at times; rather, it is the subjective construction of our minds, which are, after all, more accessible to us than anything else.

The subjective grounding of both feelings and knowledge was seriously explored in modern literature long before the scientists and philosophers started taking it into account. In *The Modern Psychological Novel,* Leon Edel shows how a whole series of authors, in many Western countries at about the same time (the turn of this century), began, as he

50. Northrop Frye, *The Stubborn Structure* (London, 1970), p. 3.

puts it, to "turn inward." He says that while these authors, each like those of previous times, portrayed subjective experience, each presented it in forms and languages that were far different from anything that came before. Hamlet's "To be or not to be speech," for example, "gives us no feeling of his surroundings or the sensory experiences . . . at the time of utterance."[51] Modern subjectivity, he suggests, is the scene not just of different thoughts, but of different kinds of thoughts, all occurring in peremptory succession to one another. In portraying the near simultaneity of the sensory, the trivial, the past, and the logic of the present, the subjective novelists were aiming at more than verisimilitude; they expressed the recognition that *every element of subjective experience is potentially meaningful.* Before Freud started consciously using this principle in his technique of free association, experimental writers like Dujardin presented in fiction trivial subjective experiences which had meaning to the reporting character and which invited the reader to share this meaning. As this literary style came into the hands of the great novelists of the twentieth century—Joyce, Woolf, Faulkner, for example—it became a widespread expression of the discovery of subjectivity as a fundamental and pervasive fact of modern experience.

The subjective novel also helped bring to the fore the fact of subjectivity in the reading experience. In discussing James's "The Turn of the Screw," Edel says that "the reader's mind is forced to hold to two levels of awareness: *the story as told,* and *the story to be deduced.* This is the calculated risk Henry James took in writing for audiences not prepared to read him so actively."[52] Active reading of this tale involves a situation of subjective choice for the reader. If you believe the narrator, then the ghosts are "real." The governess is then thought of as having given an "objective" account of the events at Bly. If you do not always believe the narrator, then you consider part of the story "real" and part "imaginary," especially the ghosts. When the reader is aware of this choice of viewpoints, the language of the story becomes multivalued, not simply in its metaphorical function, as in most other literature, but in its *referential* function.

Active reading involves other kinds of subjective initiatives as well. Reading *The Sound and the Fury* can require a great degree of ratiocination; *Ulysses* requires background information; and the poetry of Eliot and Pound demands a high level of erudition. Most modern subjective literature seems to require some sort of supplementary effort on the part of the reader in order for the reading experience to become meaningful.

51. Leon Edel, *The Modern Psychological Novel* (New York, 1955), p. 56.
52. Ibid., p. 50.

Most fundamentally, subjective literature calls attention to the complex subjective actions of languge. If we are not conscious of language use, we are not aware of how decisively it defines our realities. Joyce's later work portrays different realities by using different languages and different styles of the same language. In fact, reality is identified with linguistic reality. Linguistic manipulation calls into question the homogeneity of consciousness. If we start believing that the meanings of words are synthesized and arbitrary, we are made aware of the great extent to which we place trust in things that we know of only through linguistic action. The stability of consciousness depends on the stability of our language. The subjective novelists made deliberate use of the psychological fundamentality of language, its absolute governance of our daily sanity, and its uniqueness as a means toward both intellectual enlightenment and the management of our emotional lives.

The subjective paradigm is a development of modern culture on the largest scale. Its presence may be noted in every phase of cultural activity. In creating new awareness of the determining role played by language in these activities, it also suggests new ways to understand the human ontogenesis of language and symbolic thought, as well as the capabilities and limits of our natural tendency to objectify experience.

# Chapter Two

# THE MOTIVATIONAL CHARACTER
# OF LANGUAGE
# AND SYMBOL FORMATION

Under the objective paradigm knowledge is pursued on the scientist's assumption that what he is observing is now and will continue to be independent of him and his act of observation. The object of knowledge is thought of as having no connection with the knowing subject. The explanation of that object (or process) is thought of as belonging to that object; the explanation is that which we know about the object, and it is conceived to be as independent of the subject as the object is. Therefore, knowledge about an object is as objective as the object itself.

In this way, the objective paradigm established the criteria of explanatory adequacy. The different ways of identifying these criteria include universality (the explanation has to obtain in every case of the object), repeatability (every time the object or process is deliberately repeated, the explanation works) and predictability (the behavior of the object or process may be predicted by our prior knowledge of the explanation). These standards of explanation are all met when the object of explanation is representable through some variety of mathematical formalism or symbolic logic. The representation constitutes the explanation. Because this kind of explanation has prevailed for the last few centuries, Hume's uncontradicted argument against a necessary connection between cause and effect has not been assimilated into our conception of knowledge. Mathematical explanation demonstrates just such a necessary connection among parts of objects of explanation. Because the explanation is identified with its object, necessary connections seem to be true of the object. It is a contradiction in our thought that both Hume's argument and mathematical explanation are considered true.

The subjective paradigm removes this contradiction by reconceiving what constitutes explanatory adequacy. In particular, it considers mathematical representation a subcategory of a more general explanatory act, *resymbolization*. Symbolization occurs in the perception and identification of experiences; resymbolization, when the first acts of perception and identification produce in us a need, desire, or demand for explanation. This conception of explanation is consistent with Kuhn's description of scientific evolution; with acts of historical, philosophical, and literary explanation; and with artistic and religious activity. Resymbolization is governed by subjective factors only. A community of thinkers is both the original synthesizer and the final authority for the resymbolization and its ranges of applicability and value. An adequate explanation may or may not meet the criteria of predictability or repeatability. But if the community finds the explanation satisfactory for its own needs, this alone is enough to render it adequate. It is a moot question whether superstitions disappear because they have been discovered to be "erroneous" beliefs, or because the beliefs have come into conflict with more urgent adaptive demands in the community. There are many urban buildings today which do not have thirteenth floors. For some purposes the concept of the thirteenth floor obtains; for others, there is only the twelfth and fourteenth. The subjective paradigm came about because mathematical explanation was considered adequate for ever fewer purposes.

The decreasing adequacy of formal logical explanation was accompanied by an increasing awareness of the role of language in the production of knowledge. This awareness is an acknowledgement that knowledge is far more subjective than previously conceived. In any case, the result has been that language is now an object of organized inquiry on an unprecedented scale. It has also proved particularly unyielding to formal logical explanation. The problem has been that the study of language enacts our condition of subjectivity. Because we think in language, it is not possible to think about language as an object. Being so decisively tied to mental functioning in general, the conception of language as a formal system does not accord with its use. Many have recognized this and have introduced semantic considerations in order to increase the accord. Yet both the generative semanticists and the speech-act theorists retain a formal system of logical rules as their basic framework of explanation. The subjective paradigm does not disallow the use of formal rules as part of an explanation; it does propose, however, that a satisfactory explanation of language behavior will entail the use of concepts more commensurate with the subjective experience of language, and particularly with our common feeling of dominion over the language we use.

These considerations translate the problem of the nature of language into the problem of how to understand our own mental development. From his own viewpoint, Chomsky has already defined the problem in these terms. To understand our language is to understand our minds. He is in agreement with Piaget that language or intelligence, or both, are to be conceived as organs of the body. He is in dispute with Piaget over whether the latter's formulation of the developmental stages of intelligence constitutes an explanation of language and thought. Chomsky's reasoning is that because language has been largely describable as a system of formal syntactic rules, we are justified in seeking the source of those rules in a mathematically describable structure present in human genes. Such a system of genetically based rules would constitute an adequate explanation of the stages of cognitive development, including the means of transition between stages, from birth through the development of adult language. Chomsky claims that Piaget's formulations give only a description of the shift from stage to stage, and not an explanation. Presumably, if the genetic information that stage 6 follows stage 5 could be isolated, this would constitute an explanation, since the full program of development would be mathematically available by inspection of the genes in advance.[1]

Let us assume that what Chomsky's thinking implies can be done, namely, that we can extract from genes mathematical information that formulates how infantile development schemata grow stagewise into linguistic competence. Rather than explaining the nature of language, this information explains the origin of linguistic rules. The problem arises if we consider that the purpose of seeking the new genetic knowledge was to allay the serious doubt that a formal system of rules explained language. This doubt had to do with the dependency between language and mental functioning in general. Unless we claim that the genetic knowledge will also explain mental functioning through a system of rules, we are left with a version of the original transformational rules whose explanatory power is only slightly improved. Seeking a logical or mathematical explanation of language

1. The views that I am attributing to Noam Chomsky in this discussion are my sense of remarks he made at an informal discussion at the University of British Columbia in February 1976. On that occasion, the issue had been what constituted an adequate explanation of the infant's movement through stages in the development of his intelligence. Chomsky reported that he had just returned from discussions with Piaget on how to explain the infant's shift of stages; Chomsky, somewhat hyperbolically, but somewhat seriously as well, characterized Piaget's way of explaining the shift as "a miracle." Piaget believes that description of the assimilation and accommodation behaviors constitutes an acceptable explanation, but Chomsky's reasoning implied (to me) that he thought a genetic explanation would be far superior. He held physics up as, in his word, the "best" science, which suggested to me that the sort of mathematical explanation it uses is the kind Chomsky seeks to "explain" the stagewise development of intelligence and language.

or mind or both assumes that, ultimately, both are objective entities. But the difficulties arising in pursuit of such an explanation suggest that explanation will be more forthcoming if we limit the degree to which both are objectified and then reformulate the original question, What is language? in the direction proposed by Heisenberg about knowledge in general: What is the nature of our investigation of, or understanding of, language?

The problem is analogous to trying to explain an automobile race. Many kinds of knowledge have to enter into the explanation. Much of it can easily be called objective knowledge: the workings of a souped-up internal combustion engine, the length of the track, the degree of incline on the curves, and so on. Other items might be classified as objective or subjective: the rules of the race are specifiable "objectively," but they were invented by those who race for the purpose of insuring the best possible race. Finally, there is purely subjective knowledge having to do with the motives and action of the drivers—in their history as drivers and in their performance on that particular occasion. Given all of these possible forms of knowledge, the question is, How are we to combine them into an explanation? In order to answer this question, it is necessary to know the circumstances under which an explanation of the race was requested. Why are we explaining this race, to whom, and what is meant by an explanation in this instance? Depending on the answers to these questions, we can combine the material appropriately to create an explanation. Its correctness, however, will be determined solely by the person who asked for the explanation, in negotiation with the explainer. What a person *wants to know* determines explanatory adequacy. This is exactly the case in the investigation of language.

Under the objective paradigm, the first question automatically is, What is it? Under the subjective paradigm, the first question is, What do I want to know? I think it is obvious that this latter question actually precedes the former; the former question *assumes* that I want to know what language *is*, and that the more formally and precisely I can specify "language," the better the explanation. The latter question uses as its criterion of adequacy the satisfaction of the community of askers and of the community of co-askers. In principle, this criterion will allow a superstitious or otherwise irrational answer to prevail; yet if that is what the human community chooses, it can't be helped.

The concept of resymbolization is especially useful in dealing with this new epistemological circumstance in which we find ourselves. It is capable of encompassing, in a single framework of thought, both the traditional types of mathematically represented knowledge as well as the newer sorts of subjective knowledge that are increasingly determining the course of organized civilized activity. The concept rests on a way of understanding language that can accommodate both its description in terms of formal rules as well as our subjective experience of it as an instrument of free human initiative. In this way, it deals with the difficulty of our conception of language as being simultaneously an object of knowledge and a medium of knowledge.

Modern attention to symbolic activity began about fifty years ago with Ernst Cassirer's *Philosophy of Symbolic Forms*, which proposed that all knowledge (quantitative and hermeneutic) and all art may be conceived as different varieties of symbolic forms. Human beings are always performing a basic mental function—the formation of symbols. All cultural artifacts are ascribable to symbol formation; the synthesizing of symbols is a primary mental act from which quantitative, verbal, and sensory acts derive. Cassirer believed that this activity was phylogenetic in scope and origin, and his work presents arguments and evidence to support his claim.[2]

Susanne Langer pursues Cassirer's thought in the study of art and

2. Readers familiar with Cassirer's work will perceive its considerable influence on the present study. For example, the idea of the common origin of language and religion discussed in my Introduction is explored by Cassirer in *The Philosophy of Symbolic Forms* and in *Essay on Man* as the reciprocal phylogenetic development of language and myth. A more specific seminal thought is the following passage: "For theoretical science, the enduring and necessary elements in experience are 'objective'—but which contents are said to be enduring and necessary depends on the general methodological standard applied to the experience and on the level of cognition at that time, that is, on the totality of its empirically and theoretically assured insights. Seen in this context, the way in which we apply the conceptual opposition of subjective and objective in giving form to the world of experience, in constructing nature, appears to be not so much the *solution* to the problem of cognition, as its perfect *expression*" (*Philosophy of Symbolic Forms*, 1925, rpt. New Haven, 1965, I, 90-91). This thought underlies Kuhn's study discussed in Chapter One, and itself originates from Kant's influence on Cassirer. Of direct relevance in this chapter is the history of the philosophic perception of how symbol formation and subjectivity are related. Cassirer's understanding of the phylogenesis of language is consistent with the view of linguistic ontogenesis discussed later in this chapter. Following Darwin's view of emotion as attenuated action, Cassirer reasons that in human beings, "the sensory drive, instead of proceeding directly towards its object, instead of satisfying itself and losing itself in the object, encounters a kind of inhibition and reversal, in which a new *consciousness* of the same drive is born" (*Philosophy of Symbolic Forms*, I, 180). Consciousness is characterized as originating in an inhibitory function. In ontogenetic development, the temper tantrum is the culmination of the self-inhibitory "no" phase preceding and accompanying language acquisition and self-awareness. René Spitz in *No and Yes* (New York, 1957) and in *The First Year of Life* (New York, 1965), writing from an orthodox Freudian (and Darwinian) standpoint, places considerable stress on the uniquely human act of gestural negation as it begins in the first months of life. He sees the early "no" as the infant's first truly semantic act. Cassirer further links the act of objectification to the development of the inhibitory tendency: he says that the human infant's "clutching at the distance" "is one of the first steps by which the perceiving and desiring I removes a perceived and desired content from himself and so forms it into an 'object,' and 'objective' content" (p. 181). The object-concept, in this account, is a compensatory event, permitted by neurophysiological capacity and motivated by frustration. Thus, both self-consciousness and the capacity for objectification (the combination of which is the symbol-making capacity) originate from accumulated feelings of disjunction from one's own experience. This development is species specific for human beings.

aesthetic experience and introduced psychological considerations in this connection:

I believe there is a primary need in man, which other creatures probably do not have, and which actuates all his apparently unzoological aims, his wistful fancies, his consciousness of value, his utterly impractical enthusiasms, and his awareness of a "Beyond" filled with holiness. Despite the fact that this need gives rise to almost everything that we commonly assign to the "higher" life, it is not itself a "higher" form of some "lower" need; it is quite essential, imperious, and general, and may be called "high" only in the sense that it belongs exclusively (I think) to a very complex and perhaps recent genus. . . . This basic need, which certainly is obvious only in man, is the *need of symbolization*. . . .

The material furnished by the senses is constantly wrought into *symbols*, which are our elementary ideas. Some of these ideas can be combined and manipulated in the manner we call "reasoning." Others do not lend themselves to this use, but are naturally telescoped into dreams, or vapor off in conscious fantasy; and a vast number of them build the most typical and fundamental edifice of the human mind—religion.[3]

Langer brings in psychological concerns by characterizing symbol formation as a "basic need." Cassirer's work was oriented almost exclusively around issues of cognition and epistemology; Langer's thinking is oriented about issues of affectivity, and she proposes that all art forms have the generic function of expressing human feeling. The need for artistic symbolization results in the public expression in sensory and sometimes verbal terms of personal affective states.

An important result of Cassirer's and Langer's assumptions is their view of language as having a special status in the array of symbolic forms. Langer writes that "speech is, in fact, the readiest active termination of that basic process in the human brain which may be called the *symbolic transformation of experiences*.[4] Language, unlike other forms of symbolic expression, occupies approximately the same status in every human society. While all cultures paint, dance, and sing, they do not all do each to the same degree, and the number of persons who practice these arts varies from culture to culture. For language, this sort of variation does not obtain. All people speak, and all learn to speak at about the same infantile age. Speech grows and develops in each individual regardless of whether it becomes an art form, an instrument of science, or a medium of soothsaying. That is, the "readiest active termination" of the symbol-making capacity grows from its intimate connection with the natural biological developments of sight, hearing, and vocalization and their history of

3. Susanne K. Langer, *Philosophy in a New Key* (1942; rpt. New York, 1964), pp. 45, 46.
4. Ibid., p. 48.

intercoordination with the infant's bodily development. Thus, if a child is allowed to grow under normal ecological and social conditions, he will learn to speak. The level of linguistic complexity at which all members of a society may mutually interact is extremely high, and such interaction involves no unique talent or special allocation of psychological energy. Language is, in these senses, the basic and universal behavior that argues most strongly for exploring further what may be meant by a "need of symbolization."

To a large extent, the idea of a need is self-evident for Langer; the need of symbolization is analogous to the needs for food, air, or exercise. Her thinking of it in these terms is itself an important contribution to understanding it. In general, however, psychologists have reached no clear consensus of what a need is. When applied to symbolization and language, the idea is further complicated because the linguistic function seems so heavily dependent on intrapsychic factors. Furthermore, the general function of language seems so exactly opposite to other organismically grounded needs; that is, it is more often than not a *substitute* for sensorimotor behavior and a systematic *inhibition* of bodily action. Language permits a whole series of ordinary animal behaviors to come under the dominion of conscious control and initiative. In fact, *language is the means and agency of our characteristic human self-awareness.* Therefore, in order to discuss and understand it, our traditional thought structure of causality has to be enlarged.

In psychological discourse, a need is adduced as the cause of certain behaviors: the "cause" of eating is hunger, which is the need to eat. In thinking so automatically of a need as a cause, we also automatically think of the necessary connection between the need and the behavior. Yet we also know that especially in psychological matters there is no such necessary connection; sometimes the same need results in different behaviors. So instead of thinking either of a need or a cause of behavior, we may better use the idea of a motive. Consider the following example.

We would normally think that the swing of a bat causes the ball to fly to center field. Yet, that is not how the activity of batting is regularly conceived; rather, we think that it is the batter who causes the ball to move. But except perhaps in legal contracts, the idea of a cause is not ascribed to a person's initiative. Once we think of a batter waiting at home plate to hit the ball, the subsequent act of hitting it is most easily conceived as having been motivated; thus, *a motive is a subjectively regulated cause* and is the name for causes originating in human initiative. If we isolate the bat and the ball, there is sense in speaking of a cause, just for that context. But if we take the batter into account, remember that he once decided to become a professional athlete, note that he is looking over the pitcher, think that he is deciding on which pitch to hit, causality is an inadequate idea for understanding the action at home plate, and motivation is far more promising. In explaining baseball, the technology of batting is subordinate to the intentionality of the batters, which is what gives the game its human interest to begin with.

In some contexts, a cause or a need may be used to explain behavior just as easily as a motive. If a cause may be used, it is less disputable than a need; if a need is used, it is less disputable than a motive. In general, needs and causes are used to explain behaviors that are considerably less disputable than those we would explain with motives, which we apply in discussing the most important matters of interpersonal experience. In particular, motivation is necessary as an explanatory principle when we aim to understand deliberate behavior or other human action in which choice figures prominently. Most forms of psychological explanation try to conceptualize behavior by making acts of choice seem inevitable, as being causally determined by a principle because causal determination was the absolutely prevailing means of scientific explanation. At the same time, psychological explanation is without point if it does not encompass the ever-present subjective experience of conscious deliberation and self-awareness. Since all behavior is not ascribable to conscious planning, however, the explanatory principles have to be applicable to other conditions as well. Understood in various ways, motivation can fruitfully explain habitual behaviors, unconscious behaviors (behaviors of which we are not aware until someone else informs us about them), and deliberate behaviors. All of these behaviors are manifested in the ways we use language. In fact, language behaviors are keys to motivation as much as motivation is the key to language.

I think we have a particularly good view of how and why this is the case when we consider the onset of language and symbolic, representational thought in the infant. The subject has been studied for many decades and has long been considered the source of the knowledge we want about language behavior. In the last few years, it has been studied in the light of Chomsky's formulations about language; nevertheless, most researchers are not optimistic that the desired understanding will soon be forthcoming. David McNeill writes, for example, that "the immediate prospects of explaining the acquisition of language are bleak."[5] Lois Bloom's extensive experience observing infantile behavior led her to warn that "one cannot know the mind of a child with anything even approaching certainty or conviction."[6] Her most important conclusions bear out Piaget's

---

5. David McNeill, "The Development of Language," in *Carmichael's Manual of Child Psychology*, ed. P. H. Mussen (New York, 1970), I, p. 1063.
6. Lois Bloom, *One Word at a Time* (The Hague, 1975), p. 132.

formulations: "Grammatical function depends upon underlying cognitive function."[7] Few have gone even slightly beyond this in claiming new knowledge about the infant's acquisition of language. In no case has the question of motivation been introduced.

Let me review some of the well-established facts about the problem. It is generally accepted that when an infant is about eighteen months old, his speech undergoes a relatively discrete change from one-word utterances, usually naming, to two-or-more-word grammatical usages. Often, the change is rapid—from one week to the next. Piaget's work further shows that no matter what mode of activity is observed— language, object constancy, causality, conceptions of space and time, imitation, ludic activity—the use of symbolic or representational thought, which occurs at the transition between the sensorimotor stage and its own stage, also begins in the middle of the second year.[8] Specifically of interest here is the appearance of grammatical language together with representational thought.

Both Piaget and Sinclair de Zwart claim that language acquisition cannot be viewed separately from the general capacity for symbol formation.[9] The appearance of the latter is to be conceived as a new construction from schemata learned in the previous sensorimotor stages. The acquisition of new schemata is the result of interaction between mother and infant. Although Piaget does not specify in principle the nature of this interaction, he does consider it a causal

7. Ibid, p. 131. Bloom is skeptical about the idea of language competence. She writes that "the view that language development results from prior linguistic knowledge of the nature of sentences as proposed by McNeill, cannot be taken as hypothesis or theory until such prior linguistic knowledge is identified or otherwise described. There is an important distinction between the innate propensity or capacity to acquire language and the idea that such innate capacity takes the form of linguistic notions of either form or substance. There is simply no evidence that children have knowledge of linguistic structure before they use structure in their speech. . . . If one believes, with Piaget, that developmental change occurs as a function of the child's manipulating and interacting with his environment, then the idea that single-word utterances reflect prior linguistic knowledge of sentences becomes even less tenable" (pp. 130-31). Bloom's skepticism about linguistic competence derives from the limits she perceived in what one can know about the child's mind. While many inferences may be made, she holds to the view that only observations of the child's actual usages is an adequate authorization for knowledge about infantile language development. She therefore rejects, in principle, the view that mathematical formulations will constitute an explanation of language, since such formulations apply only to linguistic competence, which, in turn, is based on the objectification of language as independent of behavior.

8. Piaget's three main works which discuss this transition are *Play, Dreams, and Imitation in Childhood* (New York, 1952), *The Origins of Intelligence in Children* (New York, 1952), and *The Construction of Reality in the Child* (New York, 1954). Also see Eric Lenneberg's investigations of nontechnological societies, which have not "cast the slightest doubt on perfect chronological commensurability of language development throughout the world," in "The Capacity for Language Acquisition," in *The Structure of Language*, ed. J. J. Fodor and J. J. Katz (Englewood Cliffs, N. J., 1964).

9. Jean Piaget, "Piaget's Theory," in Mussen, *Carmichael's Manual of Child Psychology*, vol. I; H. S. de Zwart, "Developmental Psycholinguistics," in *Studies in Cognitive Development*, ed. D. Elkind and J. H. Flavell (New York, 1969).

factor in the development of intelligence. His explanatory framework is the concept of *construction*, which the infant will do only in dialectic interaction with the mother figure. As I suggested earlier, for Chomsky, interaction and construction do not qualify as explanations; rather, the discovery of a formal genetic pattern prefiguring this development would thus qualify.

The emphases of both Piaget and Chomsky have been on cognition as an independent mental capacity. Some efforts have been made to show that Chomsky's logical order of transformational rules is an accurate description of language performance development,[10] and therefore, that the cognitive structure of greatest interest is the linguistic one alone rather than a generalized structure that Piaget describes. Neither Piaget nor Chomsky, however, view affective development as being a determining feature of cognition.

Meanwhile, the psychoanalysts, who have been studying affective development, have been meeting difficulty in relating conceptualizations of affective life to the cognitive considerations of Piaget and Chomsky. W. G. Cobliner tries to apply psychoanalytic concepts such as the libidinal object and psychic energy dynamics as explanations of the behaviors Piaget detailed. He seeks to coordinate the growth of the libidinal object—either a person or a toy of special value to the child—with the growth of the permanent cognitive object—the capacity in the child for knowing that a hidden object continues to exist even though he cannot see it. He says that the "constancy of the libidinal object must be preceded by the formation of the corresponding permanent object."[11] But unless there is direct evidence to the contrary—which there is not—it is more likely, given Piaget's basic conception, that both sorts of objects appear coordinately with one another.

Peter Wolff proposes a consideration that would put Piaget in contradiction with psychoanalysis.[12] He says that if Piaget's observations regarding the late arrival (eighteen months) of "detachable" images are correct, then Freud's suggestion that the hungry infant hallucinates the breast cannot be true. Piaget's argument

10. Carol Chomsky, *The Acquisition of Syntax in Children of Five to Ten* (Cambridge, Mass., 1969).

11. W. G. Cobliner, "Appendix: The Geneva School of Genetic Psychology and Psychoanalysis: Parallels and Counterparts," in Spitz, *The First Year of Life*, p. 348; italics in original. Cobliner says, however, that this thought applies only to the mother: "The fact that in the mother's case the permanent object has already been achieved does not, by the same token, mean that the infant has, in general, reached the stage of the permanent object." It would be of interest to document in experience whether this is the case. In the infant, many behaviors that resemble those proceeding from concepts of permanent objects may simply be sensorimotor habits.

12. Peter H. Wolff, "Cognitive Considerations for a Psychoanalytic Theory of Language Acquisition," in *Motives and Thought*, ed. R. R. Holt (New York, 1967).

is that at the stage of representational thought, the infant is able to produce images *independently* of need—independently, that is, of sensorimotor stimulation. Freud's model presupposes that the internal stimulation of hunger is automatically linked with a mental copy of satisfaction experiences and that the hunger and the hallucination are part of a single schema. The inability of this schema to produce satisfaction results in frustration and a motor crying response. In contrast, Piaget's argument is that the independent representational image tends to function as a substitute satisfaction and thus helps to reduce frustration. Therefore, while there is no contradiction between the affective and cognitive developmental schedule, neither has there been demonstrated any decisive correspondence or interaction. Existing reports of infantile behavior—those which describe systematically actual behavior—suggest that before the onset of representational thought, it may not be useful to distinguish between the affective and the cognitive, since both modes are directly dependent on experience. The response of naming and of crying are both stimulated by some immediate sensorimotor experience. After the onset of representational thought, however, affect remains experience-dependent (even if the experience is the sudden memory or thought of something), while conceptual thought takes place independently of experience: it can be consciously initiated. This suggests that there may be a determining connection between affectivity and cognition in the transition into symbol-making, representational thought.

Because most of the relatively recent child-language studies assumed Chomsky's model,[13] there has been little interest in either the semantic or expressive aspects of the collected language samples. Typically, the

---

13. By "model," I mean epistemological model, which defines the options for research. These options include attempts to define "steady-state" cognitive structures in adults or "initial state" innate structures in infants. In *Reflections on Language* (New York, 1975), Chomsky distinguishes between "problems" in the study of language and "mysteries." The former are those research tasks which are, in principle at least, soluble using his model. The latter are those tasks for which "some fundamental insights are lacking" (p. 138). These include "how humans make use of these cognitive structures, how and why they make choices and behave as they do; although there is much that we can say as human beings with intuition and insight, there is little, I believe, that we can say as scientists. What I have called elsewhere 'the creative aspect of language use' remains as much a mystery to us as it was to the Cartesians who discussed it, in part, in the context of the problem of 'other minds.' Some would reject this evaluation of the state of our understanding" (pp. 138-139). I am one of those who reject the evaluation because the subjective paradigm proposes the insight that is lacking if the objective paradigm prevails. Within his epistemology, Chomsky is fully consistent; the difficulties of gaining knowledge from his work reflect on the inadequacy of his epistemological paradigm. What Chomsky considers mysteries, I consider problems of greater interest and importance than the ones he proposes. Specifically, the issue of will or choice or initiative is more likely to enlighten questions of language than the abstract definition of linguistic structures. This issue is further discussed toward the end of Chapter Four.

attempt has been to specify the structure of the language. Braine first introduced the "pivot-open" structure, which was subsequently explored by Brown and by McNeill, though more recently, Bloom found it inapplicable.[14] Admittedly, it is not easy to organize the semantic content of a child's language because the meanings are arbitrary and idiosyncratic much of the time. Yet, as Winnicott and Stevenson did in studying many children's "transitional objects" (a very young child's specially treasured item, like a blanket or a teddy bear), one may define behavioral regularities within the system of the child's own experiential vocabulary.[15]

Comparison of lists of children's vocabulary compiled by different observers reveals consequential semantic similarities, which imply cognitive-affective behavioral similarities among preverbal infants. Lois Bloom's list of word frequencies shows that prominent on each child's list are the child's name, *Mommy, away* or *all gone*, and the name of some object, like *'chine* (*machine*). Often the name of a younger sibling appears, or just the word *baby*. Piaget's samples from children already having acquired language show phrases like "mommy gone" and "duck swim in lake, gone away." In children of fifteen and eighteen months, Werner and Kaplan similarly report phrases like "biscuit gone" and "gone bird."[16] We also know from everyday domestic experience of infants of this age that they are especially interested in hiding games and other forms of playful appearances and disappearances, including that of their own arms, legs, and head when being dressed. It is not surprising that many language samples reflect this interest. More importantly, language behavior takes an active part in such interests. For example, the parent will name the missing item, the child will find it, and it will be named again, so that after a while the child has two different schemata to handle: the invariance of the name and the transience of the object. Two such schemata are coordinated when the child ultimately catches on to language.

Werner and Kaplan also report a somewhat oppositely directed

14. M. D. S. Braine, "The Ontogeny of English Phrase Structure: The First Phase," *Language*, 39 (1963), 1-13; Roger Brown, *Psycholinguistics* (New York, 1970); David McNeill, *The Acquisition of Language* (New York, 1970); Bloom, *One Word at a Time*. Throughout his study, Bloom argues that "pivot-grammar" is, in many contexts, only a "superficial description" of language behavior. Braine's concept may also be seen as having observed language behavior from the traditional objective framework.

15. D. W. Winnicott, "Transitional Objects and Transitional Phenomena," in *Collected Papers* (London, 1958), pp. 229-42; O. Stevenson, "The First Treasured Possession," in *The Psychoanalytic Study of the Child*, vol. IX (London, 1954). These essays are the original definitions of transitional phenomena on which Norman Holland bases his epistemological claims, discussed in Chapter Four.

16. Lois Bloom, *Language Development: Form and Function in Emerging Grammars* (Cambridge, Mass., 1970); Piaget, *Play, Dreams, and Imitation*; Heinz Werner and Bernard Kaplan, *Symbol Formation* (New York, 1963), p. 146.

behavior that accompanies infantile symbol-formation: the development of the infant's sharing experience with the mother figure.[17] The common act of referential pointing often starts with the mother's invitation, but soon eventuates in the child's using the same gesture for the same purpose with the mother. This is one of the beginnings of *cognitive stereoscopy*, or *dialectical perception*. That is, the act of objectification is grounded in the infant's experience of a mutuality of perception. It is as if the mother's perception validates the child's perception; the mother's response is obviously an affective as well as a cognitive act. From very early, the cognitive choice of an object of attention is also an occasion of the child's receiving attention. In any case, the child's isolation of an object from all other objects is almost always connected with an experience of social interaction. Likewise, the child sees that naming has to be done with two people present, even though he practices the names when alone. The child learns to name things *to* someone; he begins knowing that it is important to someone else that he name things. The child's early sense of cognitive stereoscopy lays the groundwork for notions of two-ness and separateness that are instrumental in the use of syntactical language.

The preverbal infant's special attentions to appearance and disappearance of objects and people and his development of sensorimotor naming schemata in coordination with the mother figure suggest a means of conceptualizing the onset of representational thought in terms of motivation. *The motive for the mental representation of absent objects and people is the frustration of their absence to the child.* The experience of sharing associated with the naming process gives the cognitive act of naming its emotional force. Because this force is specifically associated with sharing, it is particularly suited to help compensate for the opposite of sharing—the frustration of absence. When an infant learns to think and say *that* a person *is* "gone" or "away," the act of attaching "goneness" to the conjured and presumably desired object is an act of control or management by the child that substitutes a cognitive initiative for an affective frustration. In this way, the first acts of predication are motivated into existence.

It is now widely held that all human languages seem to be founded on the act of predication. That is, even the most complex acts of language may be viewed as necessary logical variants of predicative acts. Predication is not simply a linguistic structure; it is the elemental form of conceptual thought.

When the infant performs his first predicative acts, they are often, perhaps usually, not done with nouns and verbs. It has been observed, however, that early grammatical utterances represent the systematic

17. Werner and Kaplan, *Symbol Formation*, p. 43.

combination of two *classes of usages*, one of them almost always a noun or a name. We may call the naming class "topic" and the other "comment." In the presyntactic period, the naming activity is at first only a coordination of vocal schemata with perceptual or motor schemata. Although it often appears to be an act of identification, it is not an act of symbol formation until it is also an act of predication. In the later stages of one-word naming, this word could involve a silent predication or, as is sometimes the case, a topic involving a word and a comment involving a behavior. But unless the comment class has also become verbal, it is not possible to be sure that a predication has taken place. The verbalization of the comment completes the prototypical adult predication by rendering the topic independent of sensorimotor experience and establishing the autonomy of mental action. Essentially, the second verbal class, comment, marks the internal (subjective) appearance of a new mental category—an act of symbol formation consisting of two parts, each dependent on the other, confined strictly to words, and modeled on the child's negotiative behaviors with objects and people. The linkage of topic and comment creates a dependent relationship between two ideas that reduces the frustration of, and that substitutes for, each idea's dependency on real experience.

Piaget's name for this linkage is "internal reciprocal assimilation" of schemata. He describes the action as each schema's being "assimilated" to the other at the same time. The dependency is such that one cannot tell which schema is assimilating and which accommodating; thus, they are assimilated to one another. His phrase also suggests that a single new schema is formed by synthesis of the two previous ones. One of Piaget's observations which demonstrates how this synthesis works is that of a sixteen-month-old girl who wishes to open a matchbox to get a toy she knows is inside. After studying the situation and seeing that her finger cannot fit into the opening as it now is, she opens and closes her mouth several times, and then deliberately opens the matchbox to get the toy. The child here used her mouth to represent with her body (mind?) the small opening she saw in the matchbox. Obviously, she already had the schema of sticking her finger into an opening to get a toy. But she seemed to have no notion of the controllability of the box opening. She had long since used the schema of opening and closing her mouth, and she was accustomed, as every child of that age is, to putting her finger in her mouth. Therefore, the body was used to represent "subjectively" what was perceived as an external, or objective, situation. In the child's mind, a perception schema, with its frustration, was reciprocally assimilated with a previously established bodily schema, where the frustration was motivating the thought. At the same time, the child was able to view both the similarity and the difference between herself and the matchbox, thus suggesting the fact of what I previously called cognitive stereoscopy. The bodily representation of the matchbox had to involve the mental coordination of two different schemata, and this coordination is of a copulative and thus predicative nature: "the matchbox is my mouth," or "finger in mouth is finger in matchbox," or some similar and purely visual but nevertheless predicative act. Finally, the act of visual predication is motivated—by a frustration however small or inconsequential; yet it is a typical sort of frustration for a child of that age, and it is one of a very large class of behaviors in which the child can get objects out of hard-to-reach places, play with them, return them. These objects include the mothering figure. The motive itself is a familiar piece of experience; therefore, its force is not simply local but operates generally in the child's growth stage. The child is motivated to get back to and/or get to the desired object. The mental means to do this are thus motivated into the child's mind, and the motor action follows automatically. Once having fully acquired representational thought, the child may delay the motor action indefinitely as soon as the mental representation has taken place.

It is clear from Piaget's many data, as well as from ordinary experience of infants, that the child's body, and his consciousness of it, plays a very important role in both the motives for and means of symbol formation. In the presyntactic period, the child begins to use his mouth less frequently to examine new objects, and his attention is increasingly drawn to the excremental activity in the lower part of his body. There can be little doubt that the "objects" which the child sees coming from his body must fall into the same category as the many other objects that are becoming valuable to him. These objects are perhaps more important, however, because there is some question as to whether they are actually a part of this body. The infant is known to become very emotional about his feces, either in a positive way, when he is enthusiastic about having made such an interesting product, or in a negative way, when he might not want to part with this product. Already familiar schemata of frustration quickly become attached to the enforced habits of controlling the use of excremental matter. At the same time, the sense of frustration increases when growing muscular capabilities cannot reach their desired ends. Because of the convergence of these factors, the child in the middle of the second year begins to respond to the all too familiar experience of frustration with temper tantrums. This behavior is the undirected flaying about of both muscles and voice at full tilt: the bodily agencies previously under conscious discipline are now released, are on their own, so to speak. Because of these behaviors, in turn, because of the need to control excrement, and because of the practical domestic need to control many of the quickly growing muscular functions, self-inhibitory behaviors gain considerable importance for the child. Such behaviors have two directions—to desist from new behaviors and to retain with extra strength those he already has. In other words, the child can *do* "no," regardless of whether he can say it and mean it when he says it. Because of what he actually "knows" in a sensorimotor way, the child seems to have become stubborn and self-willed.

This overall emotional condition is the motive for the development of representational thought. Presented in somewhat different terms it is really the same motive I ascribed to Piaget's little girl, her motive being simply a small, detailed manifestation of this larger condition. There are many dimensions to the "condition" of infantile frustration in this developmental stage. Language use is part of each dimension, and it therefore forms the child's first means of unifying his disparate experiences, since each of these experiences may be referred to naming schemata and are so referred, for the most part. There are thus two large classes of experience: language, and everything else (but especially the child's own body and its products). In the acquisition of language, the child learns to subordinate the larger motions and potentialities of his body through a very narrow set of vocal behaviors. These vocal schemata and their source, mental representation, allow the child to subjectivize his interaction with whatever is around him. He may conjure up situations before they happen, and he may reconstitute them afterwards. He may hold onto ("retain") situations that are transient in experience, or he may ignore an unpleasant scene by thinking of something else. Through language, the child's sense of initiative is released, as is his awareness of himself. The motive for this development is an accumulation of circumstances, cognitive and affective, in which the child's sense of loss of both particular objects and people, and of a sense of well-being, can no longer be handled by any sensorimotor means, and the full resources of consciousness available to human beings have at last to be activated.

This description of the motive behind language acquisition is not strictly in accord with my earlier description of what a motive is. It is obvious that the child does not *decide* to acquire language. But let me delay consideration of this issue until after I have presented a particular case which I think will be helpful in understanding the kinds of motives I am looking into.

Helen Keller's acquisition of language when she was about 6 1/2 makes something clear about a child's mental development that is not so clear when we observe infants directly: that the capacity for syntactical language and for self-awareness are parts of the same act of growth. Without language, it is not possible to distinguish between awareness and self-awareness. Language makes us self-aware and persuades us of the self-awareness of others. In this sense our perception of experience is cognitively stereoscopic. Self-awareness in conjunction with the direct awareness of things produces the subjectivity of our thought processes and defines them as a necessarily *subjective dialectic*. In contrast, we have no way of interacting with animals except on the assumption of their mere awareness, which renders all such interaction mechanical or, in Langer's term, signific rather than symbolic. Without language, all speech is imperative of experience; language is a necessary accompaniment of experience. With language, speech is the deliberate control of, and subjective manipulation of, experience.[18] Helen Keller's account, unlike any other available, details the transition from a sensorimotor state of consciousness, without language, to a symbolic state in which language activated her awareness of herself.[19] In addition, we are helped considerably by Helen Keller's teacher's account, that of Anne Sullivan, which goes a long way toward defining her pupil's psychological perspective at the time.

A few days after Miss Sullivan took full control of Helen and her education, she reports the following:

I had a battle royal with Helen this morning. Although I try very hard not to force issues, I find it very difficult to avoid them.

Helen's table manners are appalling. She puts her hands in our plates and helps herself, and when the dishes are passed, she grabs them and takes out whatever she wants. This morning I would not let her put her hand in my plate. She persisted, and a contest of wills followed. Naturally the family was much disturbed, and left the room. I locked the dining-room door, and proceeded to eat my breakfast, though the food almost choked me. Helen was

18. Those experimenting with teaching chimpanzees sign language have sought to ascertain if language in the human sense is after all limited to humans. While many of the chimpanzees' achievements are impressive, however, there is still no reason to suppose that their use of language is any different from that of the prelinguistic infant, whose complex sensorimotor behaviors and vocalizations sometimes resemble conceptually motivated behavior. See Beatrice T. Gardner and R. Allen Gardner, "Teaching Sign Language to a Chimpanzee," *Science*, 165 (1969), 664-72, and David Premack, "Language in a Chimpanzee?" *Science*, 172 (1971), 808-22.

19. Three earlier discussions of Helen Keller's acquisition of language present viewpoint consistent with the one I am developing; they are in Langer, *Philosophy in a New Key*, Werner and Kaplan, *Symbol Formation*, and Hartvig Dahl, "Observations on a 'Natural Experiment': Helen Keller," *Journal of the American Psychoanalytic Association*, 13, No. 3, (1965), 533-50. Langer emphasizes the discrete and "miraculous" nature of the acquisition of the symbol-making capacity, and sees Keller's experience as evidence for the endemic status of symbol-making in humans. Werner and Kaplan emphasize the analogy between the pouring water and the pouring words, claiming that such experiential analogies are of fundamental importance in the infantile acquisition of language. Dahl understands Keller's achievement as evidence for the shift in infants from primary to secondary process thinking which occurs with language acquisition. None of these views, however, constitutes a motivational explanation, even though they are consistent with such an explanation.

lying on the floor, kicking and screaming and trying to pull my chair from under me. She kept this up for half an hour, then she got up to see what I was doing. I let her see that I was eating, but did not let her put her hand in the plate. She pinched me, and I slapped her every time she did it. Then she went all round the table to see who was there, and finding no one but me, she seemed bewildered. After a few minutes she came back to her place and began to eat her breakfast with her fingers. I gave her a spoon, which she threw on the floor. I forced her out of the chair and made her pick it up. Finally I succeeded in getting her back in her chair again, and held the spoon in her hand, compelling her to take up the food with it and put it in her mouth. In a few minutes she yielded and finished her breakfast peaceably. Then we had another tussle over folding her napkin. When she had finished, she threw it on the floor and ran toward the door. Finding it locked, she began to kick and scream all over again. It was another hour before I succeeded in getting her napkin folded. Then I let her out into the warm sunshine and went to my room and threw myself on the bed exhausted. I had a good cry and felt better. I suppose I shall have many such battles with the little woman before she learns the only two essential things I can teach her, obedience and love. [7 March 1887][20]

Miss Sullivan's treatment of Helen was not disciplinary. The immediate goal was only to establish in the girl's mind that new eating procedures were going to be used and that Helen, if she did not submit to them, would be forced to use them. Obviously, Helen's eating habits were the result of her parents' complete indulgence; having no way to communicate subtleties, they had allowed Helen to develop the sensorimotor habits that served her bodily necessities. Pitying Helen for her sorry fortune, the family bore the discomfort so that Helen might be at least partially compensated. She was allowed the luxuries of the prelinguistic sensorimotor life for the five years following the illness which, at nineteen months of age, took away her eyesight and hearing. Though growing physically, Helen was treated essentially as if she were still in her second year. It is clear, in retrospect, that her brain developed quite normally, but for all practical psychosocial purposes, she was a two-year-old child with a seven-year-old body. Miss Sullivan arrived with no particular method, but with a very ordinary plan: she would, at all costs, *treat* Helen like a normal girl of seven. It was this normal treatment that resulted in Helen's three temper tantrums.

The first occurred when she tried to put her hands in Miss Sullivan's plate and was forbidden; the second when she refused to eat her breakfast with a spoon; and the third, when she refused to fold her napkin after finishing. The tantrums came as a result of her unwillingness to perform a new behavior and her frustration at being

20. Anne Sullivan, in Helen Keller, *The Story of My Life*, (1902; rpt. New York, 1961), pp. 263-64.

forbidden the old ones. I do not think Helen considered her customary means of procuring food at the dinner table a privilege. More likely, she considered these means a familiar ritual which helped enhance her sense of stability. From her standpoint, Miss Sullivan's new rules were a fearful and irrational intrusion into a sensible way of life. She had no way of knowing why the new teacher had arrived, or whether it could be at all good for her. In any case, Miss Sullivan did present to Helen an experience she had not had previously: contact with one who gives constant attention and love but tries to change her behavior at the same time. Given that Helen was almost seven years old and of normal intelligence, it is not surprising that after two weeks she completely adjusted, emotionally, to Miss Sullivan's ways and demands. Thus, the temper tantrum phase, which normally lasts for months in the infant, was overcome in two weeks. To Miss Sullivan, this was a "miracle."

A miracle has happened! The light of understanding has shone upon my little pupil's mind, and behold, all things are changed!

The wild little creature of two weeks ago has been transformed into a gentle child. She is sitting by me as I write, her face serene and happy, crocheting a long red chain of Scotch wool. She learned the stitch this week, and is very proud of her achievement. When she succeeded in making a chain that would reach across the room, she patted herself on the arm and put the first work of her hands lovingly against her cheek. She lets me kiss her now, and when she is in a particularly gentle mood, she will sit in my lap for a minute or two; but she does not return my caresses. The great step—the step that counts—has been taken. The little savage has learned her first lesson in obedience, and finds the yoke easy. It now remains my pleasant task to direct and mould the beautiful intelligence that is beginning to stir in the child-soul. [20 March 1887][21]

Helen had begun living with Miss Sullivan only, since Miss Sullivan thought there would be no progress unless she had complete control of Helen. Miss Sullivan's simple procedure involved only that she would become Helen's "mother." The "miracle" is that Helen responded ordinarily and became completely dependent on her teacher-mother. In this spirit, she gives to her teacher "the first work of her hands," but she is only passively affectionate. Miss Sullivan, like many parents, interprets a high level of obedience as "understanding." At a sensorimotor level, it is understanding, in the sense of organized physical compliance with what is demanded, but conceptual initiative was still not possible. Miss Sullivan says that because of this new attitude she was able to teach Helen "eighteen nouns and three verbs." Helen describes the same facts from a somewhat different perspective:

I was not conscious of any change or process going on in my brain when my teacher began to instruct me. I merely felt keen delight in obtaining more

21. Ibid., p. 268.

easily what I wanted by means of the finger motions she taught me. I thought only of objects, and only objects I wanted. . . . It is true that my bodily sensations were extremely acute; but beyond a crude connection with physical wants they were not associated or directed. They had little relation to each other, to me, or to the experience of others.[22]

In view of Helen's report, Miss Sullivan was still justified in claiming the beginning of intelligent behavior, in the sense of Helen's initiatives now being directed by words: Helen wrote that she could fulfill her wants more easily now. On the other hand, Helen plainly notes the lack of relation of either words or sensations with each other and with people. Each sensation was unconnected with other experiences. There was no inner sense of the organization or control of these experiences; each seemed to just happen. "Understanding" in this situation could only mean acceptance of Miss Sullivan's supreme authority. But this was a necessary step to Helen's main achievement of two weeks later, as Miss Sullivan describes:

I must write you a line this morning because something very important has happened. Helen has taken the second great step in her education. She has learned that *everything has a name, and that the manual alphabet is the key to everything she wants to know.*

In a previous letter I think I wrote you that "mug" and "milk" had given Helen more trouble than all the rest. She confused the nouns with the verb "drink." She didn't know the word for "drink," but went through the pantomime of drinking whenever she spelled "mug" or "milk." This morning, while she was washing, she wanted to know the name for "water." When she wants to know the name of anything, she points to it and pats my hand. I spelled "w-a-t-e-r" and thought no more about it until after breakfast. Then it occurred to me that with the help of this new word I might succeed in straightening out the "mug-milk" difficulty. We went out to the pump-house, and I made Helen hold her mug under the spout while I pumped. As the cold water gushed forth, filling the mug, I spelled "w-a-t-e-r" in Helen's free hand. The word coming so close upon the sensation of cold water rushing over her hand seemed to startle her. She dropped the mug and stood as one transfixed. A new light came into her face. She spelled "water" several times. Then she dropped on the ground and asked for its name and pointed to the pump and the trellis, and suddenly turning round she asked for my name. I spelled "Teacher." Just then the nurse brought Helen's little sister into the pump-house, and Helen spelled "baby" and pointed to the nurse. All the way back to the house she was highly excited, and learned the name of every object she touched, so that in a few hours she had added thirty new words to her vocabulary. [5 April 1887][23]

22. Helen Keller, *The World I Live In* (New York, 1910), pp. 116-17.
23. Keller, *The Story of My Life*, pp. 273-74.

Helen's acquisition of the symbol-making capacity differed from that of infants in its onset as a sudden "aha!" experience. This was partly due to Helen's age, but there were other factors involved which I will discuss shortly. From Miss Sullivan's account, it might also seem that the activity of drinking played an important role in Helen's ultimate comprehension. But until this account is understood in conjunction with Helen's own description of those events, which tells the state of her relationship with Miss Sullivan at the time, we cannot fully account for the important change in Helen's mental capability and her awareness of that capability. Here, then, is Helen's version of the same events:

One day, while I was playing with my new doll, Miss Sullivan put my big rag doll into my lap also, spelled "d-o-l-l" and tried to make me understand that "d-o-l-l" applied to both. Earlier in the day we had had a tussle over the words "m-u-g" and "w-a-t-e-r." Miss Sullivan had tried to impress it upon me that "m-u-g" is *mug* and that "w-a-t-e-r" is *water*, but I persisted in confounding the two. In despair she had dropped the subject for the time, only to renew it at the first opportunity. I became impatient at her repeated attempts, and seizing the new doll, I dashed it upon the floor. I was keenly delighted when I felt the fragments of the broken doll at my feet. Neither sorrow nor regret followed my passionate outburts. I had not loved the doll . . . .

We walked down the path to the well-house, attracted by the fragrance of the honeysuckle with which it was covered. Some one was drawing water and my teacher placed my hand upon the spout. As the cool stream gushed over one hand she spelled into the other the word *water*, first slowly, then rapidly. I stood still, my whole attention fixed upon the motions of her fingers. Suddenly I felt a misty consciousness as of something forgotten—a thrill of returning thought; and somehow the mystery of language was revealed to me. . . .

. . .On entering the door I remembered the doll I had broken. I felt my way to the hearth and picked up the pieces. I tried vainly to put them together. Then my eyes filled with tears; for I realized what I had done. [24]

The main difference between the two accounts is that Helen includes the significant story of her dolls, which is part of an atmosphere of great frustration on the way to the climactic event. The new doll was one brought by Miss Sullivan to Helen; it had been made by the students at the Perkins School for the Blind, where Miss Sullivan had also been a student, especially for Helen. Helen had "known" this doll for as long as she had known her new teacher, and *doll* was the first finger-word she had learned. Helen had obviously thought that this word applied only to the new doll, while Miss Sullivan was trying to teach her that *doll* was a generic name, or a concept which included many different dolls; that is, she was trying to transform in Helen's mind the finger-word from a local signifier to a general symbol. Helen, however, could not understand what was going on and had, expectably, a temper tantrum. Her report also indicates that this tantrum came in the context of a previous frustration that day, when Helen could not be brought to distinguish, through the words, between the mug and the water in it. The moment of Helen's enlightenment, therefore, was preceded, that day, by two major experiences of frustration with the words and with her teacher.

Helen's dashing of the doll was a behavior similar to that of throwing the spoon and the napkin on the floor in the dining room episode previously described. But the doll was both a more personal item for her and a key point of connection between her and her teacher. Breaking it was a highly personal act and a message of sorts to Miss Sullivan. She was "delighted" at its destruction since she had not loved it anyway: it had begun to represent the enormous frustration involved in getting along with the person who had brought it. By breaking it, Helen separated herself from her teacher-mother and thereby tried to reaffirm and protect the old, familiar part of her self. This is the same function that tantrums serve in infants. The outburst seemed to clear the slate; then there was a new, refreshing, cool, fragrant experience in the well-house. She was thrilled by a "returning thought," and she "realized" what she had done in breaking the doll.

I had mentioned earlier that Helen became ill at nineteen months of age, at which time she did know the word for water, or some version of the word. When she speaks of a "returning thought" and the "misty consciousness as of something forgotten," it is almost certain that she is alluding to the memory of that word and its meaning. Until the time of her illness, she had experienced a normal mental development; if she was not already at the point of representational thought, she must have been very close to it. When she became ill, it was as if she remained in that sensorimotor stage for five years. There can be little doubt that had she not developed normally up to that point, the acquisition of the symbolic capacity and the ensuing intellectual development would hardly have been possible. Miss Keller was as much prepared to acquire language as any normal child of nineteen months. In cases of congenital deafness and blindness that I have seen, the children have not been able to develop a functional conceptual intelligence, even though they have been taught and supervised since infancy.[25] This fact

25. In the spring of 1971, the Perkins School in Watertown, Massachusetts, generously allowed me to peruse the medical records of enrolled students who were congenitally deaf and blind, and they further permitted me to observe some of these children in their normal classroom activity. Of all the students whose records I studied, six could be classified as having almost total congenital deafness and blindness. Only one of these students reached the functional proficiency of an eleven-year-old, and this, at the age of about twenty. The other five led essentially sensorimotor lives; even if one supposes that

suggests, though it does not prove, that interpersonal interaction is a more fundamental factor in language acquisition than the genetic program of mental development. Miss Keller's achievement as an adult is singular in terms of stamina and perseverence. The early linguistic accomplishment, however, grew largely from the good fortune of having a teacher who could reactivate a suspended normal mental development.

Psychologically, Miss Sullivan was more a mother than a teacher. After Helen's illness, her mother had normal maternal authority over her except for one key item: she could not speak to her daughter. This problem altered what might otherwise have been the normal exercise of authority. Miss Sullivan assumed normal authority and combined it with "normal" speech; that is, in every circumstance that a mother tells a child something, Miss Sullivan spelled out words into Helen's hands. Miss Sullivan knew from the trying experience of her own childhood that such "normal" treatment is what works best with sensorily handicapped children. By bringing the new "touch-words" to Helen and by assuming full authority over her behavior, Miss Sullivan re-created the necessary form of interpersonal relationship for the development of language and conceptual thought. In particular, the basic infantile dialectic of separation and return, observable in infants as appearance and disappearance schemata, was reinstated into Helen's experience in full emotional and cognitive dimension.

The frustrating feeling of separation kept returning to Helen in spite of her new, "obedient" behavior. The inability to catch on to the finger language was identical, to Helen, to a separation from her teacher and thus an affective as well as a cognitive confusion. The doll episode introduced a new semantic aspect to this situation—namely, the old and new dolls easily became emblematic of old and new *selves*. The old doll uses her hands to remove food from people's plates; the new uses hands to speak. The old doll doesn't have a finger name; the new doll is "d-o-l-l." In this way, a whole syndrome of sensorimotor meaning enlarged Helen's basic sense of relationship with Miss Sullivan.

This is the interpersonal situation into which the water experience at

---

there was conceptual intelligence in these children, there was no way to recognize it in their regular behaviors, which could be just as easily explained as Helen's before she acquired language. The well-known cases of deaf-blind children who have grown up to lead functional lives—with the suitable mechanical adjustments—are those of children who lost their sensory functions well after they had acquired language. If language competence were an independent and innate mechanism, both it and general self-awareness would not be so decisively influenced by sensory functionality. The early loss of this functionality halted the interactional behaviors which normally develop sensorimotor intelligence and then language; the result is that the only sort of intelligence *finally* developed is confined to the sensorimotor level, since it is governed only by whatever sensory contingencies appear in the child's experience.

the well-house entered. It is difficult to say that the close juxtaposition of the tantrum over the doll and the recognition of water was anything but fortuitous. I can more easily claim, however, that some such juxtaposition would have taken place sooner or later anyway. Or, better, Helen's growing motive to find a reliable way to get back to Miss Sullivan would eventually have seized upon a similar situation. In any case, in remembering the word *water*, Helen was actually returning to her original, pre-illness self. But she was doing this as a result of the need to cope with a *present* contingency. The recognition of the word was a reconstitution of self, in which the past and the present were unified as features of the same self. The path to this unification was that the old object water and the new object water were preceived for the first time stereoscopically—simultaneous views of the "same" thing, the abstraction of which resulted in the concept of water as denoted by the finger-word for it. But to have a concept is to have the symbol-forming capacity, language, which meant that all the finger-words were concepts—names—and this was the solution to the frustrating reappearance of those words in her experience with Miss Sullivan. Conceptual thought was thus motivated into existence in Helen's mind.

The idea that everything had a name means that physical experience is systematically coordinated with mental experience. The totality of experience is double, or dialectical. We do not think of a thing without a name or a name without a thing; that is the nature of human self-awareness. The name tells what something *is*; that is, the name *objectifies* the thing. The mere fact that things have names reifies our sense of the objectivity of things. Our sense of reality depends on our separation between the concept and the experience, a separation which appears to us as an identity of concept and experience. When Helen begins to ask the names for everything, she is actually asking to identify objects for and by herself, to repeat with other objects what she has just learned on the first object, her self. Only because the self has become both a subject and an object may an "object" be an experience and a concept. Helen was able to "realize" what she had done to her new doll because she was then able to translate the doll from an experience into a concept, which rendered the doll an "object." As a concept, it was reconstituted in her mind, but now that there was a difference between a concept and an experience, she saw that if only she had had the concept, her experience would have been under her management. Before, all experience had been peremptory. But the simultaneous apprehension of concept and experience creates the capability for mental initiative.

*The ability to form and use a symbol is the same as the capacity for predication.* The recognition of the word *water* is the appearance in Helen's mind of the thought "*Water* is a word." The motive for the subsequent initiative is the inward sense of the pragmatic efficacy of the first predication.

This is the same as saying that the pleasure in eating pizza once becomes a motive for a subsequent eating when the contingency arises. But more than this, the motive acts to create the new contingency. It *converts* a new experience situation into an occasion for a new predication, in Helen's case. Language is built up when previous predications are reciprocally assimilated to a present experience, rendering that experience into a new concept. The development of language may thus be conceived as motivated, from infancy into adult complexity.

In Helen's first language experiences, touching things was analogous to seeing, hearing, *and* touching things for the normal infant. The touch-words were analogous to the infant's vocalizations. What facilitates an infant's learning to speak is the natural sensory distinction between vocalization and perception; different organs are used for speaking as opposed to seeing and hearing. With sight and hearing absent, the same sense—touch—had to develop two modes of functioning previously developed by sight and hearing independently. Miss Sullivan successfully transferred the previous schemata of sensory functioning to the purely manual function. Within this function, the two classes of experience—language and everything else—were established. When the experience of water was related to the word *water*, the relationship of predication was established. In language, a copulative predication resembles a pure identity. It is really, however, a mentally legislated identity, as the mind is *declaring* the identity of the word and the thing. Subsequent adult predications are declared identities in exactly the same way; this is true of sentences ranging from "The sun is round" to "Freedom is best." Just as Helen's predication "*Water* is a word" is not comprehensible without our knowing its motive, adult sentences—and treatises and poems—are not comprehensible until we think of them as an individual's motivated act.

In Miss Sullivan's description of Helen's behavior after her acquisition of language, she reports a decided change in her emotional bearing: "Helen got up this morning like a radiant fairy. She has flitted from object to object, asking the name of everything and kissing me for very gladness. Last night when I got in bed, she stole into my arms of her own accord and kissed me for the first time, and I thought my heart would burst, so full was it of joy."[26] In the description of how Helen changed from a "savage" into a "gentle child," Miss Sullivan had reported that while Helen would let herself be caressed, she would not take the initiative for affection. Now, however, the capability for such initiative has come, and it is directly related to the initiatives for knowledge. This is really the fulfillment of Miss Sullivan's second aim:

26. In Keller, *The Story of My Life*, p. 274.

the first was obedience, the second, love. It is possible to conceive of the first aim as love also, since many animals "love" their keepers in just the same way—obedience and compliance. Human love, however, requires cognitive objectification, which renders things objects and people subjects. In a love relationship, the lover has to conceive the objects of his love as a *subject*, the same as himself and different at the same time. One cannot have a relationship with an object, since an object is a functional creation of our minds. Another subject is an object only if his relationship to me is not social in any way. But this situation is almost impossible, because even the person standing in line before me has a social relationship to me. The essence of an object lies in the unnegotiable permanence we all agree to accord it; but a subject, like myself, is defined by its principles of growth and by socially negotiated alteration. Knowledge of objects is shaped and motivated by intersubjective knowledge; love, as the ancient Hebrew word suggests, is likewise a function of such knowledge.

In retrospect, Helen Keller reports that subjective self-awareness was the source of her first and subsequent knowledge:

When I learned the meaning of "I" and "me" and found that I was something, I began to think. Then consciousness first existed for me. Thus it was not the sense of touch that brought me knowledge. It was the awakening of my soul that first rendered my senses their value, their cognizance of objects, names, qualities, and properties. Thought made me conscious of love, joy, and all the emotions. I was eager to know, then to understand, afterward to reflect on what I knew and understood, and blind impetus, which had before driven me hither and thither at the dictates of my sensations, vanished forever.
From reminiscences like these I conclude that it is the opening of the two faculties, freedom of will, or choice, and rationality, or the power of thinking from one thing to another, which makes it possible to come into being first as a child, afterward as a man.[27]

Miss Keller here draws the distinction I raised toward the beginning of this chapter, the distinction between consciousness and self-consciousness, between feeling guided by "impetus" and by "choice." This difference is a fact because it is a feeling, or an awareness; in the context of self-awareness, knowledge and feelings are identical, and the difference represents the subjective foundation of subsequent mental development, through language and thought in general.

I am now in a position to discuss the consideration that because Helen Keller and developing infants did not decide to acquire language, this development cannot be thought of as motivated. The example I gave to demonstrate motivation was that of an adult

27. Keller, *The World I Live In*, pp. 117, 116.

professional athlete behaving with full consciousness; the infant, on the other hand, is just acquiring this sort of consciousness, so how can his acquisition of it be described as motivated? In my earlier discussion, I did stipulate that motivation is normally used to explain behavior where acts of choice enter prominently, but this does not deny that motivation may also be used where we would not ordinarily ascribe a choice. I further formulated a motive as a subjectively regulated cause; this formulation also does not necessitate the inclusion of consciously initiated decision in a motivated behavior. But using motivation to explain infantile language acquisition does require further comment.

It is fairly common to regard goal-directed behavior of animals as motivated. For example, we easily think of a rat's learning to get through the maze in the quickest way as being motivated by the cheese at the end of the maze. At the same time, we do not think of the rat as having decided to get the cheese by running through the maze. And the standard behaviorist explanation of the rat's action as "conditioning" is conceptually inadequate to explain the complexity of the rat's slowly refining movements. Therefore, the concept of motivation is introduced to explain what can only be the rat's mental regulation of his motor behavior in the service of re-creating an organismically important condition—the eating of the cheese. Because we have isolated cheese-eating as the rat's goal, we also think of this goal as the rat's motive and, therefore, as the *regulatory principle of its behavior*. The whole sensorimotor apparatus is mobilized and directed by that motive.

Our familiar means of thinking of animal, infantile, and adult behavior in terms of motives is part of a much wider assumption of what constitutes an adequate explanation of living things. This is the assumption of adaptedness which originated with Darwin. It holds that all living things, especially animals, actively strive to preserve, protect, and prolong their lives and to enhance the life of the species. Each piece of local behavior is organized by a motive that is visibly a part of the adaptational teleology of living things. Infantile motivation is similar to animal motivation in its manifest goal-directedness. In the human infant, *the acquisition of language and representational thought transforms goal-directedness into the organ of consciousness*. This produces our capacity to view ourselves in terms of unconscious motives, in which we *assume* that all of our behavior is motivated; however, our knowledge of our behavior can become available only through language and thought. We are thus motivated to acquire self-awareness, which in turn gives us the capacity to regulate and to produce further, more complicated, more adaptive motives to govern growth.

Consciousness, which includes language, intelligence, thought, and affect, may be thought of as an organ motivated to define objects and cognizant of itself in terms of motives. In this way the concept of motivation keeps rational thought processes consistent with Heisenberg's formulation that the object of scientific research is now "man's investigation of nature" and with Freud's view that the mind "is itself a constituent part of the world which we set out to investigate." Objects come into existence by a subjective act of discrimination, and they gain authority and credibility through intersubjective ratification. Motives come into existence in just the same way, and they gain explanatory authority in the same way. The ideas of motivation, of consciousness as an organ, and of the subjective paradigm permit the study of language-dependent experiences to proceed by including local instances of formal logical explanation but by disallowing such explanation its absolute constraining authority. Once we admit that language is susceptible to objectification in only a limited way, a more general and satisfying explanation of language experience becomes available.

*The idea of resymbolization is both an explanation of language use and an explanation of explanation.* It explains the linguistic report of facts in terms of the motives of the reporter, and it explains the accepted explanation of acts in terms of the motives of those seeking the explanation. The many linguistic functions, in all disciplines and among all people, may be understood as originating in different motives which eventuate in the same mental act of resymbolization. But following the formulation of Cassirer and Langer, symbolic activity other than language may be conceived as similarly motivated. The symbolic formalism of the arts, the humanities, and the quantitative sciences can be most fruitfully understood in terms of the motives of those who create and use it, with special regard for individual and communal occasions of creation and response.

When scientific explanation follows from the acceptance of a paradigm, this paradigm is constituted by a communal motive; mathematical formalism is an instrument of this motive. Mathematical systems resymbolize those experiences which the original belief in the paradigm has deemed "presently adaptive to understand." Artistic expression and historical explanation likewise proceed from communal motives, represented by styles or schools, but the local formalism is color or words rather than mathematics. My linguistically articulated response to a work of art is just as much a symbolic explanation of experience as are Newton's laws of motion. The structure of motivation in each case is different, but both explanations are motivated resymbolizations.

The distinction between symbolization and resymbolization corresponds, respectively, to the use of language as simple denotation and as complex explanation. Symbolization involves ordinary acts of naming and predication of the elementary sort first learned by infants. Resymbolization refers to the mentation performed in conscious response to rudimentary symbolizations. When we become aware that a symbolic objectification system is unsatisfactory, we try to resymbolize or explain it. As Kuhn discusses, such explanation can actually change the object of attention from, say (to use his examples), a swinging stone into a pendulum or Euclidian space into Riemannian space. The motive for such important changes grows from personal and communal subjectivity. Resymbolization rewords (or reworks) established symbols in a direction more adaptive to present needs.

When the assumptions of objectivity are in effect, and when the resymbolization is mathematical, the latter is verbally presented in terms of causality. The explanatory statement resymbolizes the item in question by presenting it as the effect of a cause. Such statements are both predictive and retroactive. The involvement of past and future instances of the item in a single name has the same stereoscopic effect of insight that Helen Keller experienced. The presentation of an item in terms of its cause constitutes a new predication which is meant to be taken as an objective fact. The symbolic nature of both the item and its new predication does not seem pertinent. It becomes pertinent when statements of cause-and-effect facts become contradictory.

The use of motives as explanations localizes causes in persons or communities and is nonpredictive; it is only retrospective. The form of motivational explanation is similar to that of causal explanation, however, because the linguistic forms of both are predications. Regardless of their content, predications originate in subjective development and are the foundation of language. The subjective paradigm reduces the scope of the claims made by motivational explanation from that of those made by causal explanation. Rather than categorically affirming the existence of an item's cause, the motivational explanation *proposes* that an item *looks as if* it is motivated in thus and such a way. By consciously aiming for communal validation, the explainer is seeking relative truth value, as opposed to absolute truth. Ultimately, the only criterion of validation is the explanation's viability for the present, where viability refers to communal negotiation under existing standards of rationality. It is not determinable in these cases whether the explanation actually applies to the past event. Our source of satisfaction with the motivational explanation comes from our resynthesizing our memories of, and other symbolic representations of, the past. The success of the explanation derives from its meeting present demands rather than from the certain recovery of past truth. The explanation is thus neither predictive nor necessarily retroactive. It resymbolizes the item under inquiry, and the community that originally sought explanation validates the resymbolization. This sort of explanation is commonly known as *interpretation*.

# Chapter Three

# THE LOGIC OF INTERPRETATION

Although artistic performers are often said to render interpretations, the term on almost all other occasions refers to an act of linguistic explanation. It implies that something requires an explanation and that someone has made the requisition. The interpretation, though it may be formulated at various levels of complexity, will boil down to a predication of the form "this means that," and those engaged in synthesizing it will have produced what to them is a new piece of knowledge. The interpreting community, and each of its members, will have incrementally enhanced their understandings of their own experience and thereby, presumably, have improved their own adaptive capability. Even at the ordinary level of, say, hikers reading a map, interpretation has this adaptive, communal function; experience is resymbolized into a form in which consciousness may take more initiatives with it.

This formulation may be applied to even the oldest types of interpretation, such as astrology and prophecy. The interpreter's role was to enlighten others about experiences generally deemed obscure or mysterious. Any anomaly of human experience is susceptible to interpretive treatment. But also, the basic facts of life and death have always produced so great a sense of subjective anomaly that they have occupied the forefront of interpretive activity. Whatever its degree of success, interpretation has consistently been the first and fundamental means of coping with the unsettling disharmonies of experience. It is about as deeply rooted in phylogenetic behavior as speech, and it is a natural consequence of speech.

Interpretation has not always had the same level of authority as a path to knowledge. Just as today, a particular interpretation of the Bible will have a different sort of authority in the mind of the believer and the agnostic, interpretive authority has been determined by the communal beliefs and by the particular shape of belief in the interpreting individuals. In more contemporary times, while mathematical interpretation has held sway, verbal interpretation has had relatively less authority: science, it is intuited, is knowledge—interpretation is only opinion. But in one particular area—clinical psychology—the principle has been, starting with Freud, that interpretive knowledge is as scientifically authoritative as any other knowledge.

I have supported this principle by trying to show the senses in which quantitative knowledge ultimately rests on acts of interpretation and the interpretation, in turn, is dependent on the motivational character of language. Yet, unless I adduce a subjective logic of interpretation that resymbolizes the traditional notion of it in a more adaptive way, I will have no strong claim for any new interpretive authority. That is, unless we understand interpretation as a new systematic means of producing helpful knowledge, and unless there is a communal motive for believing in this means, there would be no point in setting any greater stock in interpretation now than we have in the past.

Freud's faith in the authority of interpretation came about mainly from his success in interpreting dreams. His interpretation of other forms of behavior was founded on his interpretation of dreams. Conceptually, his claim was simply that dreams are caused by wishes and that these wishes may be discovered by examining the dream in connection with the dreamer's free-associative thoughts given immediately after reporting the dream. The dream itself disguises the wish because, as a rule, it would disturb the sleep of the dreamer to experience the wish directly in the dream. In this way Freud explained dreams in terms of a series of adaptive motives—to release feelings and to preserve sleep. The appeal of this logic was that, for the first time, dream interpretation was not superstitious and was, on the contrary, visibly related to the overall functioning of the individual. A mysterious human experience was rendered, in principle, comprehensible.

In practice, the procedure for recovering dream-wishes leaves doubt as to whether wishes "objectively" cause dreams or whether it is therapeutically pragmatic to think that they do. I suspect that the latter is the case. No matter how many wishes one may announce on a given day, there is no way to predict whether those wishes will then appear in disguised form during a dream. This consideration makes it sensible to entertain the idea that dream interpretation has meaning only in retrospect. Only after the dream has taken place and after the associations have been collected can a decision be reached regarding the wish fulfilled by the dream. Dream interpretation from the outset, therefore, must have utilized the logic of the subjective paradigm.

Wittgenstein raised such doubts about the objective causation of dreams by wishes:

To say that dreams are wish fulfillments is very important chiefly because it points to the sort of interpretation that is wanted—the sort of thing that would be an interpretation of a dream. . . . And some dreams obviously are wish fulfillments; such as the sexual dreams of adults, for instance. But it seems muddled to say that *all* dreams are hallucinated wish fulfillments. . . . Partly because this doesn't seem to fit with dreams that spring from fear rather than from longing. Partly because the majority of dreams that Freud considers have to be regarded as *camouflaged* wish fulfillments; and in this case they simply don't fulfill the wish. *Ex hypothesi* the wish is not allowed to be fulfilled, and something else is hallucinated instead. If the wish is cheated in this way, then the dream can hardly be called the fulfillment of it. Also it becomes impossible to say whether it is the wish or the censor that is cheated. Apparently both are, and the result is that neither is satisfied. So that, the dream is not an hallucinated satisfaction of anything.[1]

Before engaging this argument I would like to note that it does not faithfully represent Freud's sense of how a dream is a fulfillment of a wish. Freud did confront the fact that a dream fulfills wishes even though the dream's manifest content does not seem like a wish fulfillment; Freud's logic is the inverse of Wittgenstein's, namely, that both wish and censor are partly appeased by the dream work. Wittgenstein's point, however, is productively understood in the light of his first sentence: postulating a wish behind the dream is a means of defining what type of interpretation is sought. He thereby implies that one need not claim that the wish actually causes the dream. In other parts of this discussion, Wittgenstein stresses that the wish theory of dream interpretation is a way of proceeding with a post facto synthesis of dream and free association by the dreamer into a piece of self-knowledge.

First, Wittgenstein poses the relatively simple problem of the dream symbol: "Consider the difficulty that if a symbol in a dream is not understood, it does not seem to be a symbol at all. So why call it one? But suppose I have a dream and accept a certain interpretation of it. *Then*—when I superimpose the interpretation on the dream—I can say, 'Oh yes, the table obviously corresponds to the woman, this to that,

1. Ludwig Wittgenstein, *Lectures and Conversations*, ed. Cyril Barrett (1938; compiled and published Berkeley, 1967), p. 47. The notes for the conversations on Freud were compiled by Rush Rhees. Although I am citing only a small part of Wittgenstein's work, many of his considerations of aesthetics, meaning, and language are concerned with the issues I have been discussing and derive from the assumption of our pervasive dependence on language. He observes, especially with regard to aesthetics and psychology, that explanation is far more a matter of persuasion than of proof. He argues, however, that the same is the case for mathematics and physics, where the acceptability depends on how much "charm" an explanation has for the mathematician (p. 28).

etc.' "[2] The assumption here is that a symbol has no intrinsic meaning but is given a meaning by the perceiver's subsequent use of the symbol. In the case of dreams, though, it is not simply the subsequent perception of the symbol which creates the meaning, but the act of assuming that the whole dream has meaning, part of which is the local meaning of the symbol. Before meaning is conferred on a symbol, there is considerable reflective intervention in the dream report, the response to the report, and in the conceptualization of the report. Functionally, the symbol does not even exist until the subjective initiative of interpretation creates a defining context for it. The act of perceiving a wish in a dream is just such an initiative, which permits the perception of special significances in individual dream symbols.

When a dream is interpreted we might say that it is fitted into a context in which it ceases to be puzzling. In a sense the dreamer re-dreams his dream in surroundings such that its aspect changes. . . . What is done in interpreting dreams is not all of one sort. There is a work of interpretation which, so to speak, still belongs to the dream itself. In considering what a dream is, it is important to consider what happens to it, the way its aspect changes when it is brought into relation with others things remembered, for instance. On first awaking a dream may impress one in various ways. One may be terrified and anxious; or when one has written the dream down one may have a certain sort of thrill, feel a very lively interest in it, feel intrigued by it. If one now remembers certain events in the previous day and connects what was dreamed with these, this already makes a difference, changes the aspect of the dream. If reflecting on the dream then leads one to remember certain things in early childhood, this will give it a different aspect still. And so on.[3]

While accepting Freud's technique of dream interpretation through free association, Wittgenstein presents it in a somewhat different light; Freud did think of his interpretive work as "of one sort" in that the intervening steps mattered much less than the wish that was finally reached. Wittgenstein views the associative process as a successive enlargment of the dream's context of observation. By slowing down the associative accumulation, he shows that it may be stopped at any point and a context of interpretation may be declared. The point of dream interpretation is to find a suitable context in which the dream "ceases to be puzzling." Freud dealt with the apparent multiplicity of applicable contexts by saying that the dream was overdetermined, that all of these contexts were actually contributions to the original dream, whose highly economical work condensed them neatly. In this way Freud was able to maintain that he was recovering the dream's precipitating causes. Figure 1 is a drawing that might help clarify the difference in outlook between Freud and Wittgenstein. Freud's view of dreaming

2. Ibid., p. 44.
3. Ibid., p. 46.

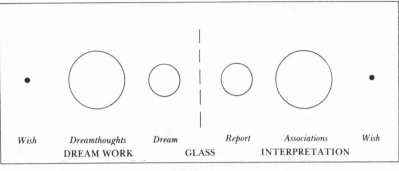

Wish        Dreamthoughts    Dream        Report      Associations      Wish
            DREAM WORK                   GLASS              INTERPRETATION

*Figure 1*

and dream interpretation uses the center line as a metaphorical two-way mirror, where the analytic identification of the wish is conceived as the naming of the dream's source. The interpretive process is thought to reveal and reflect something that has factually taken place. Interpretive work duplicates the dream work in consciousness. Even though one cannot get beyond the glass, the work of interpretation positively identifies what has happened, in the past, behind the glass. The therapeutic effect is attributed to this identification. Wittgenstein's sense of dream interpretation treats the glass as if it was a normal mirror, in that the image on the other side is totally virtual. Although the actual process of dream interpretation remains the same as Freud's, there is no additional stipulation that the product of the interpretation, the wish, be conceived as the actual precipitating cause of the dream. It may resemble such a recovery, but the plane of psychological reality is confined to the right side of the glass. The advantage of this view is that it simplifies our understanding of dream interpretation and suggests a new logic of interpretation in general. We are now concentrating attention on our conscious activity and proposing that the therapeutic effect is due to the activity of interpretation rather than to the interpretation's having recovered the cause of the dream.

The recent discovery that dreaming occurs in neurophysiological cycles supports the more subjective conception of dream interpretation. It is now known that dreams occur, as part of a cyclical sleep rhythm, about every ninety minutes; that each person has about four or five dreams a night; that sexual stimulation accompanies dreaming; that the deprivation of dream time produces severe psychological effects; and that prolonged deprivation (three or four days) results in psychotic symptoms. Although these facts are not understood now, the sheer physiological regularity of the process suggests that wish fulfillment is a less appropriate explanation than it was when only the semantic element of dreams was known. We would not say that digestion or elimination fulfills wishes even though we do wish to digest and eliminate.

Suppose, for example, that a person remembers two of his five dreams in one night, and after interpretation it is decided that each dream fulfills a wish. What then is the status of the unremembered dreams? In an interpretive context, the unremembered dream simply does not exist. In a physiological context, it may well exist, but to understand the polygraph lines that recorded the dream as wish fulfillments is not possible in principle. In the case of digestion, which is likewise a physiological process, we would conclude that the gastrointestinal breakdown of our dinner fulfilled a "wish" to assimilate nourishment into our bodies. But there is no need to define digestion as wish fulfillment—and thus as motivated activity—since its self-regulatory mechanism is already defined physiologically. Conscious initiative does not play a role in digestion or heartbeat or metabolism. As soon as a dream is remembered and reported, it becomes subject to language and consciousness, and, willy-nilly, interpretation. The physiological regularity of dream activity thus serves to better demarcate the organ-like function of consciousness; just as the lungs do one thing with blood and the kidneys do another, the physiological brain does one thing with dreams and consciousness does another. Consciousness works with dreams in terms of wishes or motives.

Freud spent considerable energy trying to justify the causal action of wishes in dreams through a complex series of drives and shifts of psychic "forces." Most of these speculations remain fruitless today, and they are conspicuously devoid of physiological documentation.[4] On

4. Many psychoanalysts allow that the dynamic and structural formulations of psychoanalysis have little bearing on practice and are therefore of interest mainly as intellectual curiosities. Few of these analysts, however, have presented formal arguments to this effect. Roy Schafer's recent study, *A New Language for Psychoanalysis* (New Haven, 1976), does make a very strong case against the traditional theoretical language of psychoanalysis, and especially against the problems it causes when seriously applied in practice. The solution he advances is to abandon the old language completely, which necessarily implies abandonment of ideas like the unconscious mind, the ego, the libido, and other thing-like mental agencies. He reconceives psychoanalysis as a body of thought that proposes only reasons for (not causes of) human behavior, and he observes that most therapy is conducted this way anyhow. Schafer forcefully claims that it makes a consequential difference to an individual if he thinks that "I acted unconsciously" as opposed to "My unconscious mind made me do it." The former emphasizes the responsibility of the subject in each of his actions; the latter implies that the behavior originating in the subject is not the subject's responsibility. By and large Schafer retains the traditional psychoanalytic concepts pertaining to mental life, but sees them only as means of referring to human actions. In this sense, he is proposing to change the language of psychoanalysis and characterize it mainly as a disciplined form of negotiation. As a result, his substantive proposals amount to a set of rules for how to go

the other hand, the interpretive *practices* that he began and the vocabulary of human motives that he formulated have become part of our language, our thinking, and our daily experience. Moreover, some of his most prominent and far-reaching discussions of dream interpretation show that he does not positively identify the cause of a dream but that, rather, *he conceptualizes it in terms of a motive more pertinent to the occasion of interpretation than to the occasion of the dream.* Consider first what is probably his most celebrated dream, that of 23-24 July 1895, more familiarly known as the dream of Irma's injection.

A large hall—numerous guests, whom we were receiving.—Among them was Irma. I at once took her on one side, as though to answer her letter and to reproach her for not having accepted my 'solution' yet. I said to her: 'If you still get pains, it's really only your fault.' She replied: 'If you only knew what pains I've got now in my throat and stomach and abdomen—it's choking me'— I was alarmed and looked at her. She looked pale and puffy. I thought to myself that after all I must be missing some organic trouble. I took her to the window and looked down her throat, and she showed signs of recalcitrance, like women with artificial dentures. I thought to myself that there was really no need for her to do that.—She then opened her mouth properly and on the right I found a big white patch; at another place I saw extensive whitish grey scabs upon some remarkable curly structures which were evidently modelled

---

about changing the traditional language. His implication is that once the abstract, metaphorical nouns of mental life are converted into "action" adverbs, we will have taken a significant step in telling more of the truth about ourselves to one another. This is probably the case, but it is definitely not a conceptual solution to the problem of objectification. The origin of the concept of the unconscious mind is undoubtedly Freud's observation that "people do things unconsciously." Because of the multiplicity of the observations, Freud simplified them by *constructing* an entity called "the unconscious mind." This noun became reified into a monolithic force as it was passed to succeeding generations who understood the construction as an objective reality and added to its features. Regardless of the value of the embellishments, to convert the "unconscious mind" and related substantive concepts *back* into adverbial formulations simply as a matter of usage can be only a partial solution to the problem of maladaptive objectifications. The question is not Shall we objectify certain things? but Which things shall we objectify? For example, shall we, at every instance, say of a third person, "He acted smartly," instead of "He is a smart fellow"? Of course, we will not; there are suitable occasions for each usage. The latter sentence may not be the "objective" truth each time it is used; but its truth value is much different from that of the former statement, and it may be much more appropriate. By a similar reasoning, the mere reduction of nominal usages and their conversion into adverbials does not speak to the demand of all language users for items to be objectified. Schafer implicitly proposes that the subject himself be objectified, and this I cannot dispute. But this alone does not amount to a new proposal, since we objectify ourselves as a matter of course. Within the purview of psychoanalytic interests, the issue is what, besides the subject, is to be objectified in a theory of human behavior, and what shall be the principles of objectification? Schafer proposes that less and less ought to be objectified. Yet, is not human experience considerably improverished if, say, I am restricted to saying "I spoke angrily" rather than "I had an angry feeling when I spoke"? To me each sentence has an independently important meaning. To eliminate certain linguistic usages cannot be a fruitful path to new knowledge. The work of Leon Levy, which made similar, but much less restrictive, proposals about fifteen years ago, is discussed subsequently in this chapter.

on the turbinal bones of the nose.—I at once called in Dr. M., and he repeated the examination and confirmed it. . . . Dr. M. looked quite different from usual; he was very pale, he walked with a limp and his chin was clean-shaven . . . . . . My friend Otto was now standing beside her as well, and my friend Leopold was percussing her through her bodice and saying: 'She has a dull area low down on the left.' He also indicated that a portion of the skin on the left shoulder was infiltrated. (I noticed this, just as he did, in spite of her dress.) . . . M. said, 'There's no doubt it's an infection, but no matter; dysentery will supervene and the toxin will be eliminated.' . . . We were directly aware, too, of the origin of her infection. Not long before, when she was feeling unwell, my friend Otto had given her an injection of a preparation of propyl, propyls . . . propionic acid . . . trimethylamin (and I saw before me the formula for this printed in heavy type). . . . Injections of that sort ought not to be made so thoughtlessly. . . . And probably the syringe had not been clean.[5]

Freud said that all of the thoughts in this dream could "be collected into a single group of ideas and labelled, as it were, 'concern about my own and other people's health—professional conscientiousness.' "[6] He derived this meaning, through many steps, from the topical correspondence between the events of the dream and an event of the previous day—Otto's informing Freud that Irma was better but not quite well yet. The motive for the dream was to fulfill the wish that he not be held responsible for Irma's failure to recuperate completely. Let us consider whether Freud's discussion shows that in fact the wish caused the dream, or if the role of motivation in dreaming and intepretation can be better understood otherwise.

In pursuing this issue, there is an immediate difficulty, namely, that there is no record of Freud's state of mind before the dream. In his preamble Freud reports on the events that preceded the dream and tells something of what his state of mind was—but this report was made considerably after the dream, and perhaps after Freud had decided that this dream had led him to the "secret of dreams" in general. We cannot tell the extent to which his remembered predream state corresponded to his actual predream state. There is just as much reason to suppose that what was remembered in the ambitious mood in which *The Interpretation of Dreams* was prepared was shaped by the motives for ratifying that mood, even under the assumption that Freud was as candid and accurate as possible. In this light the dream seems to be an occasion appropriated to construct an interpretation enhancing the postdream state of mind.

Freud reports that some years before the dream he had begun analyzing himself or, in more ordinary terms, had started a major

5. Sigmund Freud, *The Interpretation of Dreams*, tr. and ed. James Strachey (1900; rpt. New York, 1965), pp. 139-40; italics in original.
6. Ibid., p. 153.

effort to understand where he had been and where he was going. During his earlier experiences as a physician, he was concerned with his professional conscientiousness. Schur and Grinstein present biographical material about Freud's use of cocaine and the casualties which resulted from this use; concern with conscientiousness was associated with this difficult period in his life, and the concern did precede in Freud's mind the occurrence of the Irma dream.[7]

Yet the temporal precedence of this concern is not enough to justify Freud's claim that the dream's "content was the fulfillment of a wish and its (the dream's) motive was a wish." In his interpretation, Freud takes almost every single detail of the dream and shows how it connects with some facet of his experience. He brings in other instances where his patients actually did not fare so well, other instances of injections, of recalcitrant female patients, of the failure of his colleagues. Every associated detail makes sense as a contribution to the thesis that Freud "was not responsible for the persistence of Irma's pains, but that Otto was."[8] The associations, however, were first brought together only after the dream, piece by piece. The thesis of nonresponsibility may be obtained directly from the dream-report, the last part of which states that Otto had mistreated Irma with a syringe that "probably" had not been clean. The associations were not needed to maintain that Freud's meaning applied to the dream.

The compelling force of the meaning is that Freud believed it to be true of himself. Someone else, unless he were analyzing Freud, could not take the associations and conclude that the meaning of the dream was other than what Freud said it was; and even in analysis with this other person, Freud would still have had to believe the meaning for it to be "true." Before the process of interpretation begins, it is assumed that Freud's meaning will be "the" meaning. But this still does not show that Freud's meaning states the wish that caused the dream; rather, Freud's meaning is a sensible way of conceiving the materials that appear in the dream. Freud's discussion definitely shows that sentiments in dreams often correspond to sentiments in waking life, particularly those feelings experienced just before the dream. In this case, the preceding feelings could be called Freud's belief in his nonresponsibility, or his conviction of his colleagues' incompetence. The dream may be conceived as expressing different sorts of feelings which may or may not have amounted to a wish. Even though Freud had, the evening before the dream, written Irma's history for Dr. M, this does not show that Freud's wish for nonresponsibility then caused that particular dream on that night. It shows only that matters of the previous day's attention appear in nocturnal dreams.

7. Max Schur, *Freud: Living and Dying* (New York, 1972), p. 29; Alexander Grinstein, *On Sigmund Freud's Dreams* (Detroit, 1968).
   8. *Interpretation of Dreams*, p. 151.

If the interpretive procedure Freud used on dreams, and then on many other aspects of human behavior, cannot be said to recover the dream's motive, in what sense is the motivational explanation the cornerstone of this procedure? If the logic of dream interpretation is not after all an instance of the pragmatic utility of searching for motives, how else may one think of its contribution? These questions are answered by considering that the logic of dream interpretation pertains to interpretation rather than to dreams. *The motive articulated by the interpretation was the motive for the interpretation and not the dream.* The wish in question motivates the interpreter(s) to *name* that wish; the conception of the dream as a fulfilled wish is an adaptive resymbolization of the dream experience. This produces the illusion that the wish actually caused the dream.

It is never possible to know that a subsequently articulated wish is an objective entity which caused a particular dream. In regard to a dream, the wish first comes into existence only when it is conceptualized during interpretation. Once it is named, the dreamer uses it to test both his dream experience and the associated behaviors and memories to see if any or all of these experiences make more sense to him as being organized by the newly named motive. If they do make sense, the work of interpretation has had its desired effect—to increase the person's understanding of himself and his history. The source of this good effect is that the person has himself reconstructed his experience and has renamed or resymbolized it. In the therapy situation, this action is authorized by the therapist, and the dreamer's reconstruction creates the cognitive stereoscopy necessary for his early confidence; if therapy is successfully completed, the person has internalized the system of authorization as well as the habits of interpretation. Therapy thereby helps a person create for himself a much more conscious means of self-regulation.[9]

Interpretation does not discover the motives of dreams; rather, dreams are the motive for interpretation. Like other forms of behavior that bring a person to seek help, they create occasions for subjective disharmony. Sometimes these occasions are widespread in the person's

9. In Freud's early psychoanalytic practice, he was often frustrated when his patients did not accept his interpretations as given, and as a result Freud was not able to ameliorate their complaints. He consequently tried to enlarge psychoanalytic therapy in the direction of making the interpretive authority of the analyst credible to, and hence binding on, the patient. This effort led to the increase in interpretive authority of *both* analyst and patient. Freud conceived the patient as naturally "resisting" cure, and he reunderstood the patient's relationship with the analyst as a substitute version of the patient's relationship with a previous authority figure in his life (the "transference" neurosis). These ideas helped Freud persuade the patient of his own actions within the therapeutic situation and thus helped motivate the patient to construct new strategies of self-acceptance and self-transformation. Psychoanalytic practice became effective when it found the means to *teach* each individual to interpret his subjective and intersubjective experiences.

experience, and they thus require a long, extensive investigation and discussion. But in the common dream, as Freud's work showed, our past experiences are brought together in unfamiliar forms and attached to unfamiliar feelings; on the most benign occasion, we still would like to have a way to bring sense to these unfamiliarities. The mere isolation of the dream report and its analysis will not bring this sense. Only if, through association, we allow ourselves to choose dream elements and then seek their correspondence with other elements in our memory do we make the interpretive occasion susceptible to resymbolization. The dialectic between our memory of the dream elements and our memory in general makes interpretation possible. Because by conscious decision, our attention is on the dream, the interpretation appears to have isolated the dream's cause. In practice, however, the interpretation—motivated at least by the local desire to understand a small experience, but usually by a more urgent need to better handle large segments of experience—makes the dream experience appear to be a sensible part of what we now consciously know about ourselves.

The report of a dream is already an interpretation of it; succeeding reports of the same dream usually are different from one another. The actual experience of a dream is highly visual or otherwise sensory, and as yet, unreproducible. Since the only way to reproduce a dream experience is linguistically, the "translation" has to involve a resymbolization to or for another person, which renders the experience an occasion of intersubjective negotiation. As in the case of infantile symbolization, the interpersonal setting of dream interpretation also contributes a strong motive for resymbolization. Both therapist and dreamer seek an interpretation. Both also desire that each should be satisfied with the interpretation. The dreamer stipulates that the therapist has more authority, as if the latter were a parent and a teacher. The motive to validate this affective relationship combines with the motive to synthesize, for the dreamer, a new piece of self-knowledge. The importance of Freud's dream studies is less that he discovered what in essence dreams are than it is that they are pieces of experience uniquely suited for applying our natural conscious motives for interpretation in the service of subjective self-enhancement.

A dream may be interpreted and reinterpreted indefinitely; ever more wishes may be seen as having contributed to the dream. It is far less likely, however, that the dreamer is developing greater and greater insight into the past event than it is that he is developing newer sorts of self-awareness which bring the memory of the original experience into presently applicable perspectives. Without any claim that the following considerations do or did apply to Freud's mind, consider these formulations as the *motive for the interpretation*: in addition to Freud's announced motive as the wish for nonresponsibility for Irma's continuing illness and for the vindication of his professional conscientiousness, personal ambition and the wish for leadership are part of the motivational explanation.

The interpretation of the Irma dream was the keynote of Freud's major new book. The "one fresh piece of knowledge" that Freud attributed to the interpretation is one of the underlying principles of all his subsequent work, as well as a major principle of previous work in hysteria. Not long after the dream book was published, and about five years after the dream, Freud wrote to Fliess some of his thoughts on revisiting the house in which the dream occurred: "Do you suppose that some day a marble tablet will be placed on the house, inscribed with these words? 'In This House, on July 24th, 1895 the Secret of Dreams was Revealed to Dr. Sgm. Freud.' At the moment there seems little prospect of it."[10] Freud had confided, as much as fifteen years earlier, similarly ambitious thoughts to his fiancée. Before the dream book, he had had high hopes for his "botanical monograph" on cocaine, but the clinical use of this drug did not bring unequivocally good results. In *The Interpretation of Dreams*, in his interpretation of another of his dreams, the "dream of the botanical monograph," Freud compares his dream vision of the monograph "lying before me" to Fliess's sympathetic vision of Freud's dream book "lying before me."[11] Freud was considering the dream book to have accomplished for him what the botanical monograph had failed to do—establish a major new piece of knowledge. It is therefore just as likely that Freud's interpretation of the Irma dream was motivated by the wish to synthesize an important principle about dreams as it was to announce the cause of this dream and of dreams in general.

The particular wish for nonresponsibility is easily translated into a wish to distinguish himself from his colleagues, a wish that was present as much after the dream and before the interpretation—regardless of the dream—as it was there as a cause before the dream. In his interpretation, Freud identified "trimethylamin" as being sexually connected; the dream thus may be read that Otto gave Irma an injection of sexual material with a dirty syringe. Freud had also referred to Irma's widowhood as a possible cause of her disease. He mentions other widows, as well as his poor treatment of his pregnant wife. These facts are readily explained with Freud's principle of understanding dream wishes in sexual terms. Otto and the other colleagues are inadequate sexual rivals with "dirty syringes." Their poor sexual behavior toward Irma prolongs her illness. The dreamer

10. *Interpretation of Dreams*, p. 154.
11. Ibid., pp. 204-5.

must be the right doctor, far from being responsible for the illness. This is the doctor who, in dispute with Breuer (M in the dream), insisted on the sexual etiology of hysteria, the disease with which Irma is afflicted. Can this oedipal configuration—sexual wishes toward Irma and other widows alongside denigration of his wife and derision of the sexual authority of colleagues—be thought of as the particular motive for the dream, or is it a more generally present motive which the occasion of the dream helped Freud to articulate and then assign in retrospect as the cause of the dream? The content of this motive, whether given the oedipal slant or not, shows it to be more clearly connected with interpretation than with dreaming. Even Freud's use of the oedipal theme was the interpretive application of an explanatory paradigm—in retrospect—that was subsequently viewed as a cause. Like interpretations, oedipal configurations are ways of conceiving a piece of experience, motivated by the feeling that the experience needs explanation. Therefore, Freud's motive of nonresponsibility is a resymbolization of his previous symbolizations of the dream—the report and the associations, motivated by the aggregate of disharmonious feelings aroused by attention to the dream and its associative elaborations and by the overall orientation of personality both before and after the dream.

In retrospect, it seems clear that Freud's concern with conscientiousness was connected with his work's departure from established practices and forms of thought. Even after his work became widely recognized, there was always the charge, in some important quarters, that it was "unscientific." From this standpoint, many other dreams, both before and after the Irma dream, could just as well have been motivated by the wish for self-justification. But this wish is much more easily understood as a conscious motive activating conscious activity, rather than as an unconscious motive causing "unconscious" dreaming. This assumption, derived from the subjective paradigm, produces no change in therapeutic and related interpretive *practices*. It does, however, create authority to greatly enlarge the purview of these practices, to reduce concern with the cumbersome superstructure of the id and the ego and the imaginary circuitry of psychic energy, and to apply motivational explanation to new areas with much greater confidence. In Freud's often-discussed case history of the "Wolf Man," he takes a major step in this direction, namely, toward the indeterminacy of dream causation and the establishment of a new epistemological attitude based on this indeterminacy.

In this case, the interpretation of the patient's complaints was based largely on the interpretation of a single dream, one reported by the patient as having been dreamt on the eve of his fourth birthday. Here is the dream:

I dreamt that it was night and I was lying in my bed. (My bed stood with its foot towards the window; in front of the window there was a row of old walnut trees. I know it was winter when I had the dream, and night-time.) Suddenly the window opened of its own accord, and I was terrified to see that some white wolves were sitting on the big walnut tree in front of the window. There were six or seven of them. The wolves were quite white, and looked more like foxes or sheep-dogs, for they had big tails like foxes and they had their ears pricked like dogs when they are attending to something. In great terror, evidently of being eaten up by the wolves, I screamed.[12]

Introducing his discussion of the dream, Freud comments: "This interpretation was a task that dragged on over several years. The patient related the dream at a very early state of the analysis and very soon came to share my conviction that the causes of his infantile neurosis lay concealed behind it. In the course of the treatment we often came back to the dream, but it was only during the last months of the analysis that it became possible to understand it completely, and only then thanks to spontaneous work on the patient's part."[13] It is especially important that Freud did not consider this dream understood until the end of the analysis and that it took all the intervening associations, as well as "spontaneous work on the patient's part," to bring about this result. Furthermore, all of the facts brought to bear on the interpretation were given by the patient in retrospect of perhaps ten to fifteen years: he had come into treatment at age eighteen, and Freud is discussing his childhood. Therefore, understanding of the patient's complaints and understanding of the childhood dream amounted to the same act of interpretation, based on the patient's rendition of the facts and on the mutual reconceptualization of them.

The interpretation of the dream was that it symbolized the patient's infantile viewing of his parents in the act of coitus from behind, at five in the afternoon and his interruption of this act by passing a stool and waking up. The original viewing occurred when the patient was eighteen months of age, and the memory of this scene returned to motivate the wolf-dream; the opening of the window corresponds to the child's opening his eyes originally; the immobility of the wolves is an inverse correspondence to the violence scene of intercourse. The child's terror during the dream resulted from his natural attachment of his then-present oedipal disposition to the unconscious memory of the "primal scene." Of course, the complete interpretation is much more elaborate than this, as it accounts for each detail of the dream. Now, I would like to consider only the single problem that the patient

12. Sigmund Freud, *Three Case Histories*, ed. Philip Rieff (1918; rpt. New York, 1963), p. 213; italics in original.
13. Ibid., pp. 217-18.

did not actually remember that such a scene took place, that there was no other direct evidence that it happened, but that, nevertheless, patient and therapist considered it a correct interpretation of the dream.

Among the pieces of indirect evidence, collected through the entire analytic process, were the following: the patient could not enjoy intercourse except from the rear; he was stimulated at age 2 1/2 by a view of the maid on her hands and knees, and subsequently by other women in that position; he had developed a wolf-phobia, after the dream, that was directly connected with fear of his father; he suffered, for long periods of time, from irregularities of the bowel; he had, as a child, seen animals in intercourse from the rear; he had, in boyhood, gotten depressed at five in the afternoon during his bouts with malaria. Still other facts of a similar nature were remembered or complained about by the patient. The interpretation was developed by Freud's reconceiving all of these facts toward the end I indicated above.

If both Freud and his patient considered the "primal scene" interpretation of the dream correct as inferred, despite the patient's failure to remember the scene, the criteria of interpretive adequacy are the issue. "Correctness" must mean something different from "recovery of the prior event the memory of which caused the dream." In dealing with this problem Freud redefined "correctness" according to subjective criteria. He considered that the interpretation was only a retrospective fantasy on the part of the patient. There is a lengthy discussion about whether infants of that age can perceive such scenes and/or understand them and/or remember them. But even if it were possible for the infant to assimilate the primal scene and reproduce it in a dream, Freud reasons, there is no evidence that this particular infant did so. The question thus is, How can a retrospective fantasy be considered a correct interpretation? The principles Freud proposes to answer this question resemble the logic of resymbolization I discussed in the previous chapter.

The first principle is addressed to "the practical analyst," who, Freud assumes, doubts that a child could assimilate the primal scene. He observes: "It must be admitted that, if this interpretation of these scenes from infancy were the right one, the practice of analysis would not in the first instance be altered in any respect."[14] This statement claims priority for the interpretive procedure over the establishment of facts. If a patient's own resynthesis of his personal history proceeds as this patient's did, it does not depend absolutely on the truth of any one particular fact. Interpretive practice, rather than recovery of facts, produces therapeutic results. This leads to the second and more encompassing principle:

14. Ibid., p. 237.

If neurotics are endowed with the evil characteristic of diverting their interest from the present and of attaching it to these regressive substitutes, the products of their imagination, then there is nothing for it but to follow upon their tracks and bring these unconscious productions into consciousness; for, if we disregard their objective unimportance, they are of the utmost importance from our point of view, since they are the bearers and possessors of the interest which we want to set free so as to be able to direct it on to the problems of the present. The analysis would have to run precisely the same course as one which had a *naif* faith in the truth of the phantasies.[15]

This conclusion is much the same as that of the first principle, but it is given in a different context. In the first context, the truth of the (in this case) primal scene fantasy may be disregarded, and the analysis proceeds in the same way. In the second context, the truth of the fantasy is also not important, but its *truth value* is very important, and the analysis proceeds in the same way. The truth value of a fantasy is that it is the "bearer and possessor of the interest which we want to set free so as to be able to direct it on to the problems of the present." The fantasy is taken to represent something of the patient's *present mind*, which is the one whose complaints need attention. From the viewpoint of the subjective present, the fantasy represents the patient's view of his past, and it may symbolize, for example, his current attitude toward his parents. Although such fantasies are "objectively unimportant," they are "of the utmost importance from our point of view,"—that is, subjectively to the patient and intersubjectively to the therapeutic relationship. Therefore, the interpretation of this therapeutic relationship's central dream is not the recovery of the dream's original cause, but a presently determined conceptualization of the dream experience in the context of the patient's overall self-concept.

Perhaps as many as twenty-five years before this case was published, Freud had come upon this same principle of truth value, when repeatedly in cases of hysteria, patients reported memories of sexual contact with their parents, according to the oedipal paradigm for either sex. Freud finally began to believe that they could not all be true but, instead, were either partially true or wholly imaginary. In any event, he had even decided that the act of articulating the fantasy was of primary psychological importance, while its historical truth might or might not be a factor; analysis was based more on psychological importance than on historical truth. From its very beginning, analytic interpretive practice was marked by its almost exclusive reliance on consciously given reports of fact and feeling and the intersubjective negotiation of these reports. All of these considerations lead to the following conclusion: *The logic of interpretation is that its resymbolizing activity is motivated and organized by the conscious desires created by*

15. Ibid.

*disharmonious feelings and/or self-images; the goal of these desires is increasing
the individual's sense of psychological and social adaptability.*

Instead of searching for the necessary cause of a patient's complaint
or a person's particular dream, interpreter and dreamer try to
reconstruct their perception and experience of the interpretive
occasion and then find the context in which it "ceases to be puzzling."
Even though this conception of interpretation seems to violate certain
commonsense notions of it, it is the only way to understand its
functional efficacy without searching for proofs and objective causes
that cannot exist in a form and on a scale on which a viable community
of observers will agree. In the contemporary community of
psychological thought, this point of view has already been broached,
though it remains a minority opinion. Two particular formulations are
of interest: Leon Levy's *Psychological Interpretation* (1963) and Samuel
Novey's *The Second Look* (1967).

Levy begins with the idea that interpretation is the fundamental act
of psychotherapy. His definition of interpretation, however, may
describe almost any act of intellection: "Psychological interpretation,
viewed as behavior, is engaged in whenever a state exists that seems
refractory to other efforts at mitigation or understanding. In essence,
it consists of bringing an alternate frame of reference, or language
system, to bear upon a set of observations of behaviors, with the end in
view of making them more amenable to manipulation."[16] Of special
interest here is the thought that interpretation is the use of a new
language system to conceptualize in an enlightening way a commonly
agreed-upon experience. The definition presupposes that an
interpreter is called upon just because he speaks a different language.
A person seeking interpretation of his behavior, meanwhile, is seeking
an adequate language with which to think and speak of himself. Levy
proposes that interpretive understanding amounts to the translation of
disturbing experiences into a language that will better manage them.
This formulation is consistent with the explanation of infantile
language acquisition as a "translation" from sensorimotor language
into the more adaptive conceptual language. The new languages
acquired by infant and patient get their characteristic shapes,
respectively, from negotiation with parent and therapist. In each case
the change in systems of symbolization is dependent on the motives
defining the influencing relationships.

This logic applies to the question of the applicability of alternative
interpretations. Levy writes that "the making of one [interpretation]
does not imply that any other one is untrue; the choice is made simply
on the basis of consistency with the interpreter's orientation and

16. Leon Levy, *Psychological Interpretation* (New York, 1963), p. 7.

purposes at the moment." The orientation and purpose are functions of the interpreter's language system. A different system may also be applicable to the same interpretive occasion. The question of an interpretation's correspondence with an objective situation is not relevant, since the situation is defined to begin with intersubjectively by the community of, in this case, therapist and patient. Therefore, Levy observes, "the interpretation of an event is not a search for the true meaning of the event. Every event is subject to a vast range of interpretations. In psychological interpretation we apply the particular construction which we believe will best suit our purposes and which is consistent with the theoretical frame of reference we bring to the situation."[17] The abandonment of objectivity and of the search for provable causation naturally leads to the renunciation of the search for "true meanings." It is assumed in this viewpoint that truth is what all parties *feel* when an interpretation is accepted. Beyond the emotional durability of this feeling and its versatility in situations beyond that of the original interpretation, there is no meaning for truth.

The concept of "the unconscious mind" may now be understood in a new light. Rather than being an independent object, Levy describes it as an idea which facilitates theoretical discussion for some people. In practice it is not an observable "thing," in the same way that intelligence or imagination are not objects. Both of the latter nouns are really only adjectives which describe mental functioning. Levy argues that the "unconscious" is "brought in to provide a residence for" a motive of which a person was not hitherto aware. A person's view of his own behavior alongside an interpreter's descriptions of it in terms of unconscious motives simply "represents two differing constructions of the same situation, nothing more."[18] The system of interpretation that assumes a person's lack of awareness of certain things is something that this person is likely to accept, since he seeks interpretation when he believes he does not know—is unconscious of—why he is suffering or reporting a complaint. If the unconscious mind is not an object, it requires no act of faith of the form: "I believe that I have an unconscious mind, and it is doing all these things to me." To increase conscious dominion over experience is an aim different from localizing the cause of complaint in an item, which, by definition, one does not control.

Samuel Novey's treatise, like Levy's, is oriented around the determining nature of the subjective present in interpretive situations. He says that a person's life history as it appears in a therapeutic situation is already a product of the patient's interpretation of his own memory. The participants in theory "get the view of prior events to be

17. Ibid., pp. 9-10.
18. Ibid., p. 24.

looked at again—not prior events as they happened, but today's view of those events."[19] Interpretation is thus a resymbolization of the presentational form of the patient's life history. This epistemological status of "the past" implies that the interpretive basis of any historical discipline is far greater than we nominally assume, as Carl L. Becker describes:

When we really get down to hard facts, what the historian is always dealing with is an *affirmation*—an affirmation of the fact that something is true. There is thus a distinction of capital importance between the ephemeral event which disappears, and the affirmation about the event which persists. For all practical purposes it is this affirmation about the event that constitutes for us the historical fact. If so the historical fact is not the past event, but a symbol which enables us to re-create it imaginatively. Of a symbol it is hardly worthwhile to say that it is cold or hard. It is dangerous to say even that it is true or false. The safest thing to say about a symbol is that it is more or less appropriate.[20]

Becker's formulation suggests that our cultural or phylogenetic past, as we know it, is very much like our memory of a dream, in the sense that we subject it to an interpretive process and understand it in terms of a fitting symbol. While historical events must once have been facts, our relationship to such facts can only be symbolic and therefore not assessable by standards of objective truth. Viewed in objective terms, this necessary symbolic handling of the past is a definite limitation. From a subjective viewpoint, the past is resymbolized rather than recovered with an awareness of present interests.[21]

Novey gives an example of how such thinking works in everyday experience, in contrast to the broad historical perspective and Freud's dramatic primal scene discussion:

In adult life, a sister and brother compare their memories of a past event.

Sister's version: "When we were younger, you were Mother's favorite. You used to bring home chocolate eclairs and give them to her."

Brother's version: "No, that is not entirely correct. As I remember it, I would, in fact, give them to Mother, and she would say, 'Thank you, son. Your little brother *loves* chocolate eclairs.' "[22]

In each version, the presumed fact of the eclairs' disposition is subordinate to the perception of the significant relationships. Both siblings now remember their childhood relationship with their mother as being disturbed by another person; the sister sees this brother as the

19. Samuel Novey, *The Second Look* (Baltimore, 1968), p. ix.

20. Carl L. Becker, "What Are Historical Facts?" *Western Political Quarterly*, 8, No. 3 (1955), quoted by Novey, *Second Look*, p. 23.

21. A similar and more recent concept of historiography is given in the work of Hayden V. White, *Metahistory: The Historical Imagination in Nineteenth-Century Europe* (Baltimore, 1973).

22. Novey, *Second Look*, p. 33.

culprit; the brother sees the younger brother as the culprit. Factually, it is possible for both of the above versions to have been true: this brother may well have been favored over the sister, but the younger brother may have been favored over this brother. The point is that because a perspectival context is not used, the present brother sees his memory as a correction of the sister's memory, thereby calling attention indirectly to the additional influence of the present relationship on the historical perception. The resolution of this dispute would lie not in the determination of what actually happened to the eclairs, but in a new conceptualization of agreed-upon mutual memories, and more importantly, in a newly negotiated awareness of the present relationship between the siblings: "Emphasis is placed upon the fact that a consensus is arrived at with the patient and that certain commonly agreed-upon prior experiences which appeal to a sense of logic and order bear influence upon the present state of affairs. A coherent and continuous picture which makes good sense is sought."[23]

Novey's stress of subjective historical perspective is similar to Gombrich's priority of visual perspective and Poole's priority of ethical perspective. In each instance, facts are formulated by perspectives and not discovered independently. The experience of insight results from the construction of a perspective most satisfying to the present communal initiative. The effort to create a "coherent and continuous picture which makes good sense" grounds the search for any sort of knowledge in the logic of interpretation.

In understanding an act of interpretation as a resymbolization, I have presupposed that a symbolization is always the occasion of interpretation. This means that one does not interpret a table or a chair unless it is mentally removed from its functional context—the context in which no one questions its existence or purpose—and conceived as a symbolic object, an item of deliberate contemplation. In discussing the interpretation of dreams and other human behavior, it was not necessary to announce the distinction between a symbolic object and a real object, since those phenomena had to be linguistically presented as the prerequisite for their interpretation. Aesthetic objects, however, which form a class of experiences also axiomatically taken for granted as occasions of interpretation, do not seem to require symbolization to become available for interpretation. In everyday experience, aesthetic objects are usually pregiven, and the encounter with such objects seems to issue in interpretation immediately. That is, aesthetic objects seem to function as real objects, with the exception that they are directly susceptible to interpretation. The aesthetic object has many of the trappings of the real object, its tangibility, and its manifest reality to almost every test of perception. When an interpretation is presented in

23. Ibid., p. 34.

terms of these real features of the aesthetic object, the interpretation seems to be just an intelligent description of the object, much as a table may be described as a flat surface elevated from the ground by four legs. But as we are equally well aware, such descriptions of aesthetic objects do not finally pass for interpretations, which are judgments of meaning or other kinds of resymbolization. Ultimately, an aesthetic object is symbolic, and there is no recourse but to think of it that way.

The difference between a symbolic object and a real object is that the former's existence depends on an act of subjective initiative, and its subsequent level of reality varies according to the value assigned to it by communal motives. A real object, by definition, is not variable. Its reality lies precisely in the fact of the community's universal agreement about it. For a multitude of objects, there is no reason to dispute their objective reality. Insofar as they are not a subject of dispute, however, they are functionally nonexistent. According to the assumptions of the objective paradigm, this argument is an absurdity, since, *by assumption*, real objects are the absolute standard of reality; and the reality of any item or process is determined by the same sensorimotor tests which establish real objects. The subjective paradigm says that the level of primary reality is symbolic because that is how the organ of consciousness functions. Consciousness takes real objects for granted and directs its efforts either toward symbolic manipulation of real objects or toward symbolic manipulation of objects of its own creation—symbolic objects. In either case, reality is *defined* symbolically. Reality is *explained* by resymbolization, which is the conceptualization of symbolized objects and processes in terms of subjective motives.

A more general formulation is to say that reality is defined subjectively, which means "by subjects." Subjects—or, from now on, people—decide what shall be real objects and what symbolic objects. I therefore conceive human perception to be governed by three possible perceptual initiatives: to see each experience as a real object, a symbolic object, or a person. The subjective perspective is constant and creates the occasions for perspectival shifts. Unlike the perception of real objects and symbolic objects, the perception by people of other people is negotiated with those people—not always, of course, but in any consequential context. People are "real," by universal agreement, but often they are only symbols, as when we live only with memories of people, or images of them. Most of the important people in our lives are cosubjects of our experience, and we confer reality onto them and then continuously renegotiate this reality with them. These negotiations are the ultimate authority for which objects are real and which symbolic and which communities shall be formed. In this way the subjective paradigm defines cognition.

With these considerations in mind, we may apply the logic of interpretation to aesthetic objects. The prevailing conception of aesthetic experience holds that it is ultimately an act of communication between an artist or a performer and a perceiver or an audience. Some element of human experience originates in an artist and through symbolic expression is transmitted to his audience. This situation is assumed to obtain even when the artist is long since dead and when the artist is not aware of the constituents of his audience. The act of interpretation is considered an effort to reconstruct the artist's original experience and the associated communicative intention. It would seem that interpretation thus conceived follows the logic of motivational explanation. But this is not the case any more than Freud's interpretation of dreams recovered the actual cause of particular dreams. In order to make this point, I will consider Freud's application of his interpretive logic to an aesthetic object, the *Moses* of Michelangelo.

The structure of Freud's argument is that great works of art like the *Moses* have a powerful effect on him, and yet he is "unable to say what the work represents to him." Critical praise of the work hardly solves this problem. Therefore, "it can only be the artist's intention in so far as he has succeeded in expressing it in his work and conveying it to us, that grips us so powerfully." In order to discover this intention, "I must find out the meaning and content of what is represented in the work, I must in other words, be able to *interpret* it."[24] The occasion of interpretation is the work's effect on him; the purpose of interpretation is to explain this effect to himself; a satisfactory explanation will name the artist's intention. In this argument, the work of art corresponds to a dream; the artist's intention, to the wish motivating the dream. If the artist's original intention is recovered, both the meaning of the work and its effect are explained.

Freud ultimately reveals none of Michelangelo's intentions. Toward the end of his essay, he seems aware of this fact as he asks, "What if we have shared the fate of so many interpeters who have thought to see quite clearly things which the artist did not intend either consciously or unconsciously? I cannot tell."[25] He admits that he has brought forth no evidence that the artist's intention corresponds to his interpretation. If Freud did not achieve his stated purpose, how are we to conceive the satisfaction his elaborate interpretation seemed to have brought him? The answer is that the interpretation explains the effect on Freud *regardless of the artist's intention.* That is, the interpretation explains the interpreter's "intention"—his perception of and response to the work of art.

24. Sigmund Freud, "The *Moses* of Michelangelo" (1914), in *Character and Culture*, ed. Philip Rieff (New York, 1963), p. 81.
25. Ibid., p. 105.

Freud writes that he gets pleasure from works of art when he can "explain to [himself] what their effect is due to." He continues: "Whenever I cannot do this, I am almost incapable of obtaining any pleasure. Some rationalistic, or perhaps analytic, turn of mind in me rebels against being moved by a thing without knowing why I am thus affected and what it is that affects me."[26] Here is the general motive in Freud's personality for interpreting works of art—to release his own pleasure. The actual interpretation gives this motive a particular form.

After speaking briefly of *Hamlet*, Freud calls the *Moses* "another of these inscrutable and wonderful works of art." Commenting that "no piece of statuary has ever made a stronger impression on me than this," he says:

How often have I mounted the steep steps of the unlovely Corso Cavour to the lonely place where the deserted church stands, and have essayed to support the angry scorn of the hero's glance! Sometimes I have crept cautiously out of the half-gloom of the interior as though I myself belonged to the mob upon whom his eye is turned—the mob which can hold fast no conviction, which has neither faith nor patience and which rejoices when it has regained its illusory idols.[27]

After surveying a series of critical opinions which suggest that the statue represents Moses just before he is about to spring up and destroy the tablets after seeing the faithlessness of his people in the desert, Freud reports that this interpretation does not seem to work for him:

I can recollect my own disillusionment when during my first visits to the church, I used to sit down in front of the statue in the expectation that I should now see how it would start up on its raised floor, hurl the Tables of the Law to the ground and let fly his wrath. Nothing of the kind happened. Instead, the stone image became more and more transfixed, an almost oppressively solemn calm emanated from it, and I was obliged to realize that something was represented here that could stay without change; that this Moses would remain sitting like this in his wrath forever.[28]

In this second statement Freud says that a key feature of the statue is not that it is about to jump up, but that it seems to him eternally fixed in its wrath. This, presumably, is the *feeling* he gets about the figure of Moses. If it were the real Moses, he would not vent his wrath upon the "mob," among whom Freud had earlier imagined himself. He thus feels the anger communicated, but no threat from its results.

In the first statement, Freud describes his imaginary relationship with the hero, where the quality of the affect is brought out by the "unlovely" street in a "lonely" and "deserted" church; Freud "crept cautiously" through this "half-gloom" only to try to bear up under

26. Ibid., pp. 80-81.
27. Ibid., pp. 82-83.
28. Ibid., p. 90.

Moses's anger. But rather than identifying with his hero, he imagines himself one of the contemptible, idolatrous mob which has incurred the anger of its leader. Freud's pleasure and excitement are unabashed, as if he were himself heroic in his attempt to withstand "the angry scorn of the hero's glance."

The sources of pleasure for Freud are, first, looking into the eyes of the angry hero, and then, perceiving that after all the anger will be confined to the glance. He took the exciting risk of confronting the anger and yet avoided it at the same time, as it remains in the same restrained pose "forever." If these are the pleasures, what role does his identification with the vulgar mob play in them, and how does the act of interpretation release them?

Freud says that the statue represents "not the inception of a violent action but the remains of a movement that has already taken place." He pictures Moses as first sitting calmly holding the tablets of the law at his side, facing front. He then envisions the figure hearing the clamor of the mob around the golden calf; Moses turns his head left, moves his left foot back, ready to spring up. At the same time his right hand plunges into his beard in anger. As he does so, the tablets are held to his side only by his right forearm and elbow. They then slip forward because they are so precariously held. Feeling that they are about to fall, Moses quickly draws his right hand back, but his hand having been so deeply plunged into his beard, draws back, to the right side, the left side of the beard. This new movement, which brings him into the position shown by the statue, Freud explains, shows that Moses has overcome the temptation to vent his wrath on the people and will, instead, save the tablets: "He will now remain seated and still in his frozen wrath and in his pain mingled with contempt."[29] Freud does observe that this interpretation is not consistent with the account in Exodus, in which Moses breaks the tablets, but he dismisses the Biblical account as full of "incongruities and contradictions." He proposes instead that Michelangelo "has added something new and more than human to the figure of Moses; so that the giant frame with its tremendous physical power becomes only a concrete expression of the highest mental achievement that is possible in a man, that of struggling successfully against an inward passion for the sake of a cause to which he has devoted himself."[30]

In this interpretation of the figure, which Freud gratuitously attributes to Michelangelo, he expresses his admiration for the hero, which derives from Freud's imagined perception of the human emotion this figure represents. The statement releases the beholder's own deep heroic sentiment, which, alongside the other sources of

29. Ibid., p. 99.
30. Ibid., pp. 102, 103.

pleasure, accounts for Freud's great fascination with the sculpture. In the earlier descriptions of his affective response, Freud did not mention his identification with the *Moses*; but the act of interpretation in its singular capacity of motivational understanding brings the interpreter considerably closer to his "hero" and its creator.

In the second volume of his biography of Freud, Jones suggests that at the time this essay was written Freud was smarting from the "defection" of Jung, as well as of Adler and Stekel earlier. Freud had considerable wrath for the vulgar and fickle "mob" of professionals as well as for his erstwhile associates who ignored, ridiculed, or criticized his work. But he neither vented his anger nor gave up on his thinking; instead, he successfully struggled against this anger and persevered. When the "mob" became idolators, Freud kept his own hand on the "law" of science he developed and shrewdly translated what felt like betrayal into "resistance."

Almost thirty years before this essay was written, Freud wrote to his fiancée: "Now for a long time I have known that I am not a genius and cannot understand how I ever could have wanted to be one."[31] In these more ordinary days it seemed that life would actually be more ordinary for Freud in spite of his thoughts of personal greatness. During these days he had himself tried to withstand the "angry scorn" of skeptical superiors like Meynert and Brücke, but it turned out that the scorn was only in the glance and did not harm him.[32] Nevertheless, at the time, it took courage and maturity to endure the attitude of his supervisors and to confront the possibility that his life just might develop ordinarily.

Freud's response to the sculpture, as it is recorded in the essay, symbolizes first being a humble element in a leader's constituency, and then being the inwardly struggling leader himself. Freud's interpretation, particularly the scenario of movements leading up to the present form and the statement of what was "more than human" in the figure, resymbolizes the response. In this way, the series of three phases Freud proposes as the interpretation of the figure corresponds much more to the three phases of Freud's recorded response than to any known intention of the artist, which Freud admits he did not recover anyway. The first phase, in which the hero is serene in his accomplishment of having brought the law, resymbolizes Freud's sense of obsequious creeping into the presence of his hero and, if viewed motivationally, removes the even imaginary humiliation Freud

---

31. To Martha Bernays, 2 February 1886, in Ernst L. Freud, ed., *Letters of Sigmund Freud* (New York, 1960), p. 200.

32. Freud reports this in his discussion of the "*non vixit*" dream in *The Interpretation of Dreams*, p. 458. Freud writes how his supervisor, Brücke, greeted him one morning when Freud was late for work in the laboratory: "What overwhelmed me were the terrible blue eyes with which he looked at me and by which I was reduced to nothing."

attaches to his behavior. The second phase, in which Moses angrily clutches his beard at seeing the mob's betrayal, resymbolizes Freud's bearing up under the glance; viewed motivationally, Moses's anger is directed against himself and not at his humble subject. Finally, the present pose, in which the hero has subdued his anger and saved the law, corresponds exactly to Freud's sense of himself at the time of writing, where the motive for the resymbolization is simple identification. In the final interpretation, Freud names his pleasure in the "giant frame with its tremendous physical power" and, more importantly, his perception of and identification with "the highest mental achievement that is possible in a man," the successful struggle against one's own passion to preserve one's life's work, the "law" of his own and of human life.

In Freud's life, the act of interpretation brought him to his own "highest mental achievement." He became a leader by virtue of the fact that many others could accept and use the kind of interpretation he practiced. His fascination with, and interpretation of, the *Moses* is an expression of and an understanding of his own leadership. Within this frame of reference, neither he nor we need consider the artist's intention in order to assimilate Freud's interpretation of the work. Like the interpretation of dreams, the interpretation of an aesthetic object is motivated not by a wish to know the artist's intention—though this is an admissible enterprise in a different context—but by the desire to create knowledge on one's own behalf and on behalf of one's community from the subjective experience of the work of art.

From the standpoint of the intellectual traditions of our culture, it is much easier to accept the subjectivity of dream interpretation, or even of Freud's interpretation of works of art, than it is to conceive of organized attention to literature and authors in terms of the subjective paradigm. For reasons I will discuss in Chapter Nine, it is psychologically important for most readers to think of their reading experience as being governed in some way by the author. For other reasons, it is of genuine interest to learn how and why literary artists create their work, and I will explore this interest in the same context. Now, however, it is germane to inquire why the concept of literary communication from author to reader is not admissible to the logic of literary interpretation.

E. D. Hirsch, Jr., in *Validity in Interpretation* (1967), argues with great care and precision that determination of the author's meaning in a work of literature is not only admissible but is the only possible foundation for achieving valid interpretations. Given his assumptions, his argument cannot be improved. I am therefore inquiring into his argument with a view toward contesting the assumptions.

Early in his study Hirsch allows the human basis of verbal meaning: "A word sequence means nothing in particular until somebody either means something by it or understands something from it. There is no magic land of meanings outside human consciousness. Whenever meaning is connected to words, a person is making the connection, and the particular meanings he lends to them are never the only legitimate ones under the norms and conventions of his language."[33] He defines understanding as how a person constructs verbal meaning, while interpretation is the explanation of this meaning—to someone else, presumably. Thus, the interpretation of a given sentence involves, say, my explaining its meaning to you. In contrast to interpretation, there is another act, criticism, which is the explanation of a judgment. Just as understanding constructs meaning, judgment names—or actually, judges—significance, which is the relationship between meaning and anything else—for example, values or historical circumstances. The nub of Hirsch's treatise involves these two points: first, in order for the discipline of literary studies to make sense and avoid confusion, the distinction between meaning and significance has to be carefully maintained and followed; second, acts of interpretation can be validated by criteria which, in principle, all readers can accept. Thus, there are actually two branches in the literary discipline—the branch which proposes judgments of significance for public debate and the branch which defines the most valid interpretation of any given work or language sample.

Because the branch which judges significance follows the assumption of the subjective paradigm, I can subscribe to it without dispute. But the principle that it is possible to define a most valid interpretation (using Hirsch's sense of interpretation) is inapplicable to literary study. This principle stands on the assumption that the author's meaning is recoverable. The assumption is not useful because in the vast majority of literature the nominal meaning of the words is already well-known; in cases where the nominal meaning is not known, either it can be discovered with trivial sorts of intellection or it cannot be discovered, so that in either case the acts of understanding or of interpretation are trivial or impossible.

Hirsch gives major authority to the author's meaning because of his belief about language, cited above, that follows from subjective considerations, namely, that verbal meaning is always constructed by a human mind. Because it makes more sense to think that the meaning of a text was constructed by the author rather than the reader, we should therefore ground all interpretive processes on the determination of the author's meaning. The problems begin because any procedure for recovering the author's meaning is necessarily either personally or culturally subjective. Hirsch denies that his own procedure for recovering the meaning is subjective, but consider his argument: "A

33. E. D. Hirsch, Jr., *Validity in Interpretation* (New Haven, 1967), p. 4.

good many disciplines do not pretend to certainty, and the more sophisticated the methodology of the discipline, the less likely that its goal will be defined as certainty of knowledge. Since genuine certainty in interpretation is impossible, the aim of the discipline must be to reach a consensus, on the basis of what is known, that correct understanding has *probably* been achieved."[34] First, the most that Hirsch seeks is the probability of "correct understanding," rather than certainty. Hirsch outlines certain sensible techniques that we normally use to determine obscure textual meanings. Ultimately, both the correctness of understanding and the probability of correctness rest on the *consensus* within the discipline. If this is so, the motives of the community of students are more decisive in determining correctness than this community's objective perception of meaning. If Hirsch were willing to say that consensus determines correctness, it would also have to determine the objectivity of the meaning.

But this subjective argument is not Hirsch's. His view is, rather, that we share the meaning of most words with authors; this helps make the meaning objective and determinate. In addition, literary forms and conventions create meaning, and we can know how such forms work in most cases. Therefore, the author's verbal meaning is objectively determinable. But this objective meaning, based on certain sharing and certain knowledge of generic forms, is a trivial occasion for interpretation, since what we share is not in dispute to begin with and functions as any real object. In literary practice, the author's verbal meaning is rarely an interpretive occasion; it arises only when all that is universally certain has been exposed and interpretive choices become subjectively necessary. Hirsch is applying the standard of consensus only in the trivial case of determining the nominal verbal meanings. In the really difficult cases of verbal ambiguity, such as the meaning of the word "still" in Keats's line "Thou still unravished bride of quietness," there are neither the means nor the purpose to determine objectively the author's intended verbal meaning. The task of interpretation as explaining my understanding of the line to you remains subjective on the issue of greatest concern.

The pragmatic effect of Hirsch's grounding literary interpretation on the recovery of the author's meaning is to devalue the act of interpretation. Interpretation is not a decoding or an analytical process; it is a synthesis of new meaning based on the assumption that the old shared meanings of words and works are not in question, but that the *present perception* of these meanings have created the experiential circumstance for resymbolization. In this way, the logic of interpretation excludes consideration of whether and how the author

34. Ibid., p. 17.

is communicating anything to us and explains, instead, the motives and processes developed by the interpreter(s) on the interpretive occasion.

The occasion of special interest in this study is the act of reading where comprehension of nominal meanings is not an issue. There is further particular emphasis on reading literature—verbally formulated aesthetic objects. Although one implication of my claim that the logic of interpretation derives from the subjective paradigm is to demonstrate the need for a new means of conceiving processes of conscious intellection and symbol formation, the main aim of my discussions is to discover how to make use of our ubiquitous dependency on language. In view of language's determining role in almost all conscious activity, it has become increasingly necessary to greatly enlarge our awareness of this role. Technological means of human adaptation are decreasingly effective by themselves. The kind of knowledge made available by language awareness—personal, interpersonal, and communal knowledge—is at this time a more likely contributor to survival than the more traditional sorts of objective knowledge.

Literature is the locus for the organized cultivation of new language elements and habits. It has been traditionally conceived as play or amusement or art or nonsense, but these roles only contribute to its importance as a prime occasion for tangibly enlarging mental capacity and strength. Insofar as literature has been treated as a real object and criticism pursued as the local description of that object, the growth of language awareness is essentially inhibited; the decisive subjective action we all take with literature is subordinated, in educational practices and depressing cultural lethargy, to the dissemination of information and the moralistic, coercive demand to read carefully. To treat literature as a symbolic object is to shift our attention from acts of informational perception first to the perceptual initiatives we automatically take with a work, and then to the more deliberate conceptualizations we try to synthesize from these initiatives. I have identified these latter conceptualizations as resymbolizations—the familiar act of interpretation; I am now saying that interpretation as an explanatory procedure is motivated by the first perceptual initiatives toward a symbolic object, and I am identifying these initiatives as subjective *response*.

# Chapter Four

# EPISTEMOLOGICAL ASSUMPTIONS
# IN THE STUDY OF RESPONSE

When interpretation is conceived as motivated resymbolization, the idea of response, which otherwise has an inapplicably wide range of nominal meanings, becomes specifiable in experience. Generally, response is a peremptory perceptual act that translates a sensory experience into consciousness. The sensory experience has become part of the sense of self, and in this way, we have identified it. Identification always takes place automatically and may thus often be erroneous; a configuration of lights on a country road at night may be identified at first either as a stopped vehicle nearby or a town in the distance. The identification is a peremptory act; subsequently, its truth value may or may not be determined by different sorts of interpretation, depending on the motive created by the original identification.

Consider the responses, and their respective consequences, to two different real objects. I am at a dinner table with another person, who interrupts my conversation by saying, "Could you pass the salt, please." My visual identification of the salt is my response, and its consequence is the motor act of passing it. The latter act did not interpret or resymbolize my response but, rather, removed the idea of the salt from consciousness so that my conversation could continue. The response of identification was the most complex level of intellection I reached in that parenthetical behavior. But suppose I am in the country, and I identify in the distance Mt. Rainier, which, like the salt, is a real object and registers in consciousness in the same way. I may not take note of it and may direct my attention to something else, so that I remove the identification from consciousness just as I did with the salt. Since I am not so disposed, I think about the mountain, and this entails a series of deliberate reviews of the scene. My motive for having directed consciousness in this way is found in the fact that my original identification was *evaluative*; it was not simply "Mt. Rainier" that I saw, but it was "the magnificent Mt. Rainier." Because there was no situational motive to regulate my response in advance, my evaluation of the scene is automatically attached to my identification of it. This means that I have peremptorily converted the real mountain into a symbolic mountain, since it is now primarily a function of my self-awareness. In this instance, the response is an act of symbolization; if I then conceptualize the symbolization, I will have interpreted my perceptual experience of the mountain. I will not, however, have interpreted the mountain, whose status as a real object is no longer relevant to me. When there is no prior motivational constraint on my perceptual initiatives, response will be an act of evaluative symbolization, which is the only basis on which an interpretation may proceed.

This conception of response and its connection to interpretation becomes especially useful in the efforts to understand the mental handling of aesthetic experience. When we decide that an object is aesthetic, it means that we have cleared the motivational ground by the simple act of confronting the object. The universally agreed-upon boundaries of the aesthetic object represent a collective declaration that the perceptual symbolization of the object will be the ground for all further discussion of it and that, furthermore, this object is no longer "real"—that is, for example, Michelangelo's *Moses* is no longer a block of stone in the shape of a seated man, but is a symbolic representation of something. The object of attention is not the item itself but is the response of those who observe it. The assumption derived from the objective paradigm that all observers have the same perceptual response to a symbolic object creates the illusion that the object is real and that its meaning must reside in it. The assumption of the subjective paradigm is that collective similarity of response can be determined only by each individual's announcement of his response and subsequent communally motivated negotiative comparison. This assumption is validated by the ordinary fact that when each person says what he sees, each statement will be substantially different. The response must therefore be the starting point for the study of aesthetic experience.

In one sense, response has occupied this fundamental position for a long time. Aristotle, for example, defined tragedy as that sort of drama to which the audience's response is pity and fear, where such feelings mark the evaluative identification of the dramatic experience. By similar reasoning, the mere description of a work as comic or of a character as pathetic shows how response defines what we perceive. But because of the paradigmatic imperative to keep the symbolic object objectively real, the ensuing critical discussion is always characterized by the respondents' arbitrary shifts from their own responses to the assumed factualities of the object. Ultimately, regardless of the actual shape of the discussion, its conclusions are automatically taken to apply as if the symbolic object were a real object. But because such conclusions are always contestable, interpretatively formulated knowledge has less authority than mathematically formulated knowledge. The epistemological assumptions of the subjective paradigm equalize these authorities by conceiving any knowledge as having been deliberately sought and by relating its authority to the motives of those who seek it. More importantly, subjective epistemology is a framework through which the *study* of both response and interpretation may be actively integrated with the *experience* of response and interpretation, thereby transforming knowledge from something to be acquired into something that can be synthesized on behalf of oneself and one's community.

In spite of the considerable interest in the act of reading that the language and literature professions now have, there is uncertainty regarding just how to conceive a reader's response. Two recent essays—Cary Nelson's "Reading Criticism" and Eugene R. Kintgen's "Reader Response and Stylistics"—help articulate the problem.[1] Nelson poses the question by observing that in the prefaces to several important critical treatises, the authors present disclaimers or apologies for their strong voice, and he infers that this relatively unconscious convention shows that even the most accomplished critics are not certain about the nature and authority of the knowledge they are proposing. He traces this epistemological problem to "the collective professional illusion of objectivity" and proposes in his concluding remarks the abandonment of this illusion:

If we can forgo the collective professional illusion of objectivity and learn to be somewhat iconoclastic about what we write, the practice and evaluation of criticism will become unashamedly exciting. Both the reading and the writing of criticism will be energized by an inquiry into the dynamics of critical language. For the study of criticism is necessarily also the study of ourselves as critics, just as the study of literature is also the study of ourselves as readers. Those critics who can (or must) risk themselves in their writing not only give us a glimpse of their own inwardness, they also let us see ourselves from a new vantage point. Perhaps that self-reflexiveness, like the self-reflexiveness of this essay, can now be welcomed.[2]

1. Cary Nelson, "Reading Criticism," *PMLA*, 91, No. 5 (October 1976), 801-15; and Eugene R. Kintgen, "Reader Response and Stylistics," *Style*, 11, No. 1 (Winter 1977), 1-18.
2. Nelson, "Reading Criticism," p. 813.

In this formulation, Nelson seeks to enlarge the traditional purview of critical discourse by including, in subsequent critical efforts, the individual critic-reader's awareness of his own purposes, motives, and feelings. This is the principle of the "involved observer" which I explored in some philosophical dimension in Chapter One above. Pursuant to this principle, the critic-reader, instead of apologizing for the appearance of motives where they were not consciously intended, attempts to articulate his motives for knowledge as the rationale for his declaration of knowledge.

In answering responses to his essay, Nelson elaborates his own motives: "Though 'Reading Criticism' was motivated partly by a need to understand my own critical practice, it would be false for me to suggest I could have written it in some more overtly confessional form. In the process of reading, rereading, and writing about other critics, I learned a good deal about myself as a critic. This is one of the rewards of studying other critics: the benefits of pure self-reflection are not the same."[3] This passage brings out the complex difficulties in the problem of studying response. The personal need of the critic-reader for self-understanding is definitely a guiding factor in the search for knowledge; yet simply to "confess" one's own motives is not satisfying either to the individual or to others in his community. Thus, Nelson's work clarifies the problem of response to some degree: How shall subjective feelings and motives be converted into publicly negotiable issues, and what knowledge does this conversion yield?

Eugene R. Kintgen's essay discusses the connection between the problem of response and the study of language. Attention to language he points out, necessarily involves attention to style, which, in turn, cannot be understood without reference to the reader's perception of and response to language. He observes that "it is apparent that there may be no simple relation between the linguistic stimulus and our response to it, and . . . it is thus futile to attempt to account for response merely by isolating certain linguistic configurations." Furthermore, linguistic description may actually inhibit understanding of response: "It may be that the better a description is from a linguistic point of view, the less likely it is to reflect subjective processes."[4] Kintgen is one of a number of linguists who have begun to question whether formal linguistic description leads to the kind of knowledge demanded by many observers' intuitive experiences of language. He is relatively unique in this group in his tendency to understand the response to language and the response to literature as the same problem.

Kintgen's intuition of how to explain language is analogous to

3. Cary Nelson, "Forum," *PMLA*, No. 2 (March 1977), 311.
4. Kintgen, "Reader Response,", pp. 10, 11.

Nelson's of explaining literature and criticism. The intuition is that when a person uses language—either as a listener, reader, or speaker—the explanation and/or interpretation of such use is not an objective matter of formalizing a set of facts, but a subjective matter of becoming aware of how one's own participation in the study of language and literature shapes the construction of knowledge.

That the organized inquiry of the last few decades into literary response has emerged from the pedagogical community testifies that increasing numbers of literature students have intuited the inseparability of their knowledge from their experience. Yet the attempts of these students to develop some knowledge of response have met with repeated frustration, which can be ascribed to the inadequacy—or lack, in some instances—of the epistemological assumptions that prevailed in their work. Particularly, either of two main sets of assumptions were used. The first is largely objective, in that the response to a work of literature is isolated as an object of study and treated either as an independently analyzable item or as a member of a class of responses that is analyzed statistically. The second set conceives of response as the outcome of a relationship or transaction between a reader and a text, where the text is considered a real object. Although the results of both approaches have been problematical, the various research plans and their authors' judgments of their value suggest how subjective thinking may be most productively integrated into our present efforts.[5]

About twenty years ago, James R. Squire undertook to study the reading responses of fifty-two ninth and tenth graders because, "for the teacher of English, the study of literature must involve not only consideration of the literary work itself, but also concern for the way in which students respond to a literary work."[6] The rationale for Squire's work, as well as for dozens of similar studies begun at about the same time and still being conducted, is that attention to the text is not enough; attention to response is necessary. The atmosphere of this aim is pragmatic: textually oriented pedagogy was conceived as, in one way

5. The material that I am about to review will not include the contributions of the European school of *Rezeptionsaesthetik*, which has produced considerable work by Ingarden, Jauss, Iser, Groeben, and others. This work has been reviewed recently by Rien Segers in "Readers, Text, and Author: Some Implications of *Rezeptionsaesthetik*," *Yearbook of Comparative and General Literature*, No. 24 (1975), pp. 15-23. Most of the European studies differ in a fundamental way from those discussed here, for these European writers aim mainly at presenting models of the reader without studying specific responses of specific readers, and without inquiring into their own mental processes as readers. A study with purposes different from my own would probably provide a more suitable context to investigate this work in detail and to take into account its variety of theoretical formulations about the "aesthetics of reception."

6. James R. Squire, *The Responses of Adolescents While Reading Four Short Stories* (Urbana: National Council of Teachers of English, 1964), p. 1. The study was begun about eight years before it was published.

or another, ineffective. Many teachers believed that if they understood response, it would make the teaching of literature more successful, by whatever standards of success one applied.

Squire called *response* whatever a student said while he was reading a short story; he divided the stories into segments and recorded the remarks of each reader immediately after reading each segment. As a group, the resulting protocols were analyzed statistically. Each statement in each response was placed into one of the following categories: literary judgment, interpretation, narration, association, self-involvement, prescriptive judgment, and miscellaneous. The analysis showed that interpretations formed by far the largest group of statements. He further found that interpretive cogency was "generally unrelated to the intelligence and reading ability of the subjects."[7] Finally he saw that there were discernible correspondences between statements of self-involvement and those of literary judgment—that is, the same readers tended to have both sorts of statements in their responses.

Squire did not say why he thought interpretation was the predominating category, nor why he thought self-involvement and judgment seemed to go together. He did say that the independence of interpretive cogency from intelligence and reading ability reflected badly on the usefulness of the standardized tests he used to measure the latter two items. If, however, interpretation is conceived as a natural consequence of motivationally governed language experience, both its predominance as a reaction to literature and its independence of testable skills are explained. Interpretation is naturally motivated and is a more general and determining mental function than reading skill or test performance. Furthermore, if response is necessarily evaluative, deeper self-involvement brings with it more pronounced value judgments. In general, Squire observes, his statistical analysis suggests "that although certain group tendencies are observable in the reading reactions of adolescents, individual variation is caused by the unique influence of abilities, predispositions, and experiential background of each reader"[8]—that is to say, the reactions are subjective.

Squire directed part of his study toward this consideration. He investigated the personal backgrounds of thirteen of his subjects and obtained detailed information "through school counselors, conferences with teachers and individuals, and from a trained classroom observer who maintained a running anecdotal record of the behavior and comments of each student during his English class." Unfortunately, he felt unable to work with the results of this

7. Ibid., p. 51.
8. Ibid., p. 50.

investigation: "The case studies of 13 readers revealed certain additional evidence indicating ways in which personal characteristics influence literary responses. However, the complexity of the relationships and the individual variation tend to prevent any easy generalization. Moreover, the problem of obtaining clear-cut, easily interpreted evidence is compounded by the difficulty of developing precise measures both of the responses and of personal traits."[9] The epistemological standards of precise measurement and easily interpretable evidence prevented Squire from making use of the elaborate materials he had compiled. His intuitive attentions to response and its subjective character were ultimately inhibited by his sense that there was no way to extract conclusive knowledge from the natural sources and manifestations of response and interpretation. As a result, Squire concluded that "literary analysis" remained the pedagogical goal and response only a possible subordinate function.[10]

James R. Wilson's study of the reading of novels by college freshmen, conducted about nine years after Squire's, used the same research structure—fifty-four readers responding to three novels each, with the responses statistically analyzed using Squire's categories—but investigated more fully the depth-studies of nine of the subjects. The results of the statistical analyses repeated Squire's finding regarding the predominating role of interpretation in students' responses and further suggested that classroom discussion of responses increased the readers' interpretive fluency. Wilson's more consequential observations, however, came out of the depth studies. First, he says, although some responses "were unsophisticated or evasive, . . . fragmentary or partial . . . it would have been difficult to demonstrate that these interpretations were misinterpretations based on misreadings or on stock responses." This conclusion was reached in the course of Wilson's conscious attempt to test Squire's claim that his readers often misinterpreted and distorted the work. Wilson's finding was not ultimately contrary to Squire's; it was simply the result of closer study and less restrictive epistemological assumptions: "Even obvious

---

9. Ibid., pp. 15, 27.
10. Ibid., p. 54. Here is a specific sense in which Squire conceives literary analysis: "Techniques which enable the teacher to offer help in how to interpret at times when the interpretations are being made may increase the effectiveness of instruction in literary analysis. A teacher may read a portion of a story to a class, for example, and then ask students to predict the behavior of the characters on the basis of the segment presented. A comparison of the responses of students with the actual events in the remaining portion of the story could enable the teacher to deal concretely with such problems as plausibility and objectivity in interpretation." While this technique may be of interest, it remains no different from traditional means of teaching in its ultimate measurement of interpretive efficacy by assuming the psychological norm of the text. Thus, a student who did not guess the correct ending would have to consider his guess invalid, even though this guess might well contain an important degree of truth value for that reader.

misinterpretations caused by vocabulary deficiencies or by failure to finish reading the novel—and these were rarely found—involve complicated issues. On the one hand, what are the boundaries of valid interpretation? . . . On the other hand, is literature a 'structure of norms'? . . . An instrumental definition of interpretation might have bypassed these critical cruxes, but the findings suggested that an analysis of received responses was more useful.[11] Because Wilson was not certain what constitutes validity in interpretation, he was able to find complexity and value in a variety of readings and was even willing to allow the subjective source of failures of skill and discipline to enter as an ethically and psychologically legitimate aspect of a reader's interpretation. Attention to response, Wilson's work suggests, is therefore more relevant to literary study than the use of standards of interpretive accuracy.

Wilson's sense of the responses' significance led to his considering further Squire's observation regarding the connection between self-involvement and evaluative judgments. In discerning a "complex" relationship "between self-involvement and quality of interpretation," Wilson speculates that "an initial self-involvement is necessary for effective interpretational processes. Perhaps most subjects can begin to concern themselves only with questions which have personal importance. That is to say, interpretation may be a secondary predicative process, impossible without initial self-involvement." Although this is admittedly only a speculation, it accommodates Squire's observation, enlarges it to include interpretation, and thereby articulates the proposition discussed in the foregoing two chapters: interpretation is *predicated* on response. Wilson is generally less satisfied with the results of the statistical survey then was Squire, and seems to place more emphasis on the implications of the individuality of each interpretation. His protocols suggested that when there was what he deemed a "high degree of interpretational adequacy," "it seemed to unify rather than separate the processes of empathy and analysis."[12] By and large, in the context of Wilson's research, this last observation is anomalous, since it speaks against dividing the response into categories and in favor of viewing each response as a unified mental act describable mainly in connection with the respondent and only superficially in connection with other responses. More than Squire, Wilson is aware of the magnitude of this anomaly, but, again, because of the epistemological inhibition, his only recourse was to articulate it as a guideline or useful expectation for the college instructor of literature.

11. James R. Wilson, *Responses of College Freshmen to Three Novels* (Urbana: National Council of Teachers of English, 1966), pp. 39, 40.
12. Ibid., p. 38.

The work of Alan Purves, which began some years after Wilson's and still continues, proposes response study as the central feature of literary pedagogy in high school and college curricula. He has edited a series of volumes, *Responding*, which serve as texts for the response-centered curriculum he proposed some years ago.[13] The context of his proposals is the same as those of Squire and Wilson, namely, the intuition about the importance of any reader's response to literature and the creation of pragmatic plans to elicit response from and discuss it with student readers from the seventh grade through the university. Purves's epistemology is similar to Wilson's, but less responsive than Wilson's to the complexity of the issue, and thus less attentive to the subjective experience of reading.

The conceptual grounding of Purves's work is an elaborate system of classification originally designed to identify any element of all likely written manifestations of response to literature.[14] The system began as a refinement of those used by Squire and Wilson, but it became a categorical definition of the possibilities of response. The categories are engagement (or involvement), perception, interpretation, and evaluation. In the classroom, these become areas in which the teacher consciously seeks to improve student performance. Purves conceives of **engagement and evaluation as being regulated by the reader and his community, while perception and interpretation are regulated by the text**: "These two, the literary work and the individual who responds to it, can be used, I think, as the foci for any statements that that individual can make about a work, and these two theoretical foci could well serve as educational foci."[15] Toward the purpose of developing knowledge in the future. Purves suggests an analogous division of effort: "The next direction in research, thus, might well be exploration into the complex system of literary response. Such exploration might well employ the case-study technique of exploring many aspects of the responses of a few individuals. This technique should be combined with multivariate analysis, multidimensional scaling, partition analysis,

13. Alan C. Purves, ed., *How Porcupines Make Love: Notes on a Response-Centered Curriculum* (Lexington, Mass., 1972).

14. The classification system was first proposed in Alan C. Purves and Victoria Rippère, *Elements of Writing About a Literary Work: A Study of Response to Literature* (Urbana: National Council of Teachers of English, 1968).

15. Ibid., p. 64. Purves's conception of the text as a regulative norm may be seen in his view of the act of perceiving a work of literature: "When the student examines his statement of perception, he has recourse only to the text . . . and he can prove the validity of his statement by showing that the data are sufficient" (p. 61). As I have already discussed in some detail in *Readings and Feelings: An Introduction to Subjective Criticism* (Urbana: National Council of Teachers of English, 1975), a reader's perception of the text is of pedagogical interest far more in its idiosyncratic dimension than in its correspondence to the text, which can never be exact. I will further discuss this matter in Chapter Five.

and other more sophisticated statistical treatments."[16] In Purves's work, the attention to response is very great, while the conception of knowledge is unchanged from that of the Newtonian scientists; at best, in fact, there is no epistemology at all, as is manifested in the application of existing research techniques without a sense of how to use the knowledge they produce. For example, in order to use the four categories as developed, each class's response distribution has to be obtained, and then each category of response becomes an occasion for developing objective knowledge: presumably, a student sees that he is only involving himself but not interpreting, so that interpretation becomes the subject that he has to "learn." The pedagogical action in this instance is no different from that used when a student is required to "learn" literature. If a student should ask *why* he should now learn interpretation, the only answer he can get is that "studies show that response should (do, have to) include all four categories." Ultimately, the authority for developing knowledge is objective and prescriptive rather than subjective or self-generating. Correspondingly, organized research tries to collect larger, more statistically significant groups of responses and studies them with more complex mathematical techniques. Yet if individual response is not governed by actuarial findings, such findings serve no purpose: a reader's unique questions cannot be answered with statistical knowledge.

Purves's concrete proposals for classroom functioning show the consequences of the lack of epistemology. In the response-centered curriculum, he explains, "the teacher works to elicit the fullest possible response. At some points the teacher must be dogged about asking, 'Why?' 'What do you mean?' 'Tell us more.' 'I don't understand.' "[17] While these questions are consistent with attention to subjective response, the pedagogical issue is in the difficulty of dealing with the answers. Unless a teacher understands the kind of knowledge such questions can develop, there are no means of pursuing the discussion they begin.[18] The "fullness" of response is defined objectively, from

16. Alan C. Purves and Richard Beach, *Literature and the Reader: Research in Response to Literature, Reading Interests, and the Teaching of Literature* (Urbana: National Council of Teachers of English, 1972), p. 37.

17. *How Porcupines Make Love*, p. 48.

18. In the "Readers' Response to Literature" session at the November 1976 convention of the National Council of Teachers of English in Chicago, the presentation by Walter Slatoff was "On Responding to Readers' Responses," and that of Richard Adler was "They Read; They Respond. Then What?" As Slatoff's title suggests, his approach is informal; he encourages responses, but lacking any epistemological teleology, finds it difficult to integrate and define the authority he feels he has as a teacher; once he asserts this authority, the collection and discussion of response begins deferring altogether to him, and the class assumes a traditional format. Adler reported how he, by and large, followed Purves's technique and likewise defined his pedagogical authority in the traditional manner. It is particularly noteworthy in these two instances that epistemology is shown to be decisively tied to how each teacher conceives his classroom authority. The

the categories, rather than subjectively from the personality orientation of the reader at that time. The handling of a reader's efforts at self-knowledge, on the other hand, uses language that refers back to the motivational basis of the reading experience. Without such a language, the answers to the above questions can be perceived only as information-giving rather than as acts of personal synthesis. Purves's program represents the limit of what can be achieved in the study of response without revising the commonsense attitude that both the responding subject and the aesthetic object may be conceived as real objects.

In several efforts to study response, these assumptions have undergone important changes, though they have not involved a shift to a new paradigm. There are elements assignable to either paradigm in the studies, but they are better characterized as aparadigmatic because their attention is on the single anomalous experience of response, with a view toward discovering what it will take to understand it. This group of studies acknowledges the active role of the reader—his status as a subject rather than an object—in developing his response, and it conceives this response as the outcome, or expression of, the reader's relationship with the author or the text or both. The text is conceived as either a real object or a person, but not as a symbolic object. These assumptions represent a renunciation of the search for mathematically formulatable knowledge, but they do not embody an alternative epistemology.

About forty years ago, D. W. Harding proposed that the response situation is analogous to the gossip situation: "The playwright, the novelist, the song-writer and the film-producing team are all doing the same thing as the gossip. . . . Each invites his audience to agree that the experience he portrays is possible and interesting, and that his attitude to it, implicit in his portrayal, is fitting." Although in gossip, "the roles of the entertainer and audience are passed backwards and forwards from one person to another," the basic condition of the onlooker defines the listener in gossip and the audience in art.[19] In this way, Harding defines the response circumstance as overtaking a central aspect of a conversational circumstance.

Pursuing this line of thought about twenty-five years later, Harding articulated his proposal more exactly. He restates the original idea by saying that "the mode of response made by the reader of a novel can be regarded as an extension of the mode of response made by an onlooker

---

work of Fish, Elliott, and Jordan, discussed later in this chapter, helps to enlighten this issue.

19. D. W. Harding, "The Role of the Onlooker," *Scrutiny*, 6, No. 3 (December 1937), 257.

at actual events." Within this response (to art), two factors are
fundamental: "imaginative or empathic insight into other living things,
mainly other people," and "evaluation of the participants and what
they do and suffer, an evaluation that I would relate in further analysis
to his structure of interests and sentiments." Harding thus relates
cognition and evaluation as codefining features of response, as I
discussed earlier in the chapter. Harding then allows that the
correspondent of the gossip-reader is not a collection of real people
"but only *personae* created by the author for the purpose of
communication."[20] Therefore, rather than further defining response
by the symbolic character of its occasion, Harding returns to the
original gossip model and defines response as part of a communication
situation, this time with the author. Harding reaches the same
intellectual destination through his attention to response that Hirsch
reached through his attention to interpretation. Neither considers the
symbolic nature of the work of art as the factor that most determines
either response or interpretation. In spite of Harding's claim that
authors communicate their own satisfaction more than meaning, he
ultimately argues that "understanding in the reader and intelligibility
in the author are essential to literature and involve obligations in
both."[21] This view, like Hirsch's, diminishes both the psychological
range and the defining function of subjective action in response and
interpretation.

Like Harding, and at about the same time, Louise Rosenblatt tried to
reach a new understanding of response by reconceiving the reading
situation with special emphasis on the action of the reader:
"Fundamentally, the process of understanding a work implies a re-
creation of it, an attempt to grasp completely the structured sensations
and concepts through which the author seeks to convey the quality of
his sense of life. Each must make a new synthesis of these elements with
his own nature, but it is essential that he evoke those components of
experience to which the text actually refers."[22] Rosenblatt departs
from the views of Hirsch and Harding when, after acknowledging the
author's original creation of the text, she directs her attention to the

20. D. W. Harding, "Psychological Processes in the Reading of Fiction," *British Journal of Aesthetics*, 2 (1962), 147.

21. D. W. Harding, "Reader and Author," in *Experience into Words* (London, 1963), p. 173. In fact, Harding argues that the author's communication of his satisfaction depends on his meaning. This view of meaning is the same as Hirsch's: when "we depart too far from any meaning that the work could possibly have had for its author, . . . we lose the possibility of sharing in his satisfaction with the finished work" (p. 168). If, however, the reader's satisfaction and his meaning are not identified with the author's, the range of possible experience from reading is much wider and regulated by the reader's responsibility to himself and his community.

22. Louise M. Rosenblatt, *Literature as Exploration* (1938; revised and rpt. New York, 1968), p. 113.

reader's resynthesis not of the author's experience but of the meanings denoted in the text. The idea she uses to conceptualize this process is the literary transaction, which she explains in this way: "*Transaction* is used . . . in the way that one might refer to the interrelationship between the *knower* and what is *known.*" She is thus led to the distinction between "*the text,* the sequence of printed or voiced symbols, and *the literary work (the poem, the novel,* etc.), which results from the conjunction of a reader and a text."[23] This definition of the work is the keynote of Rosenblatt's basic outlook, which includes the idea of communication between author and reader but considers it only a subordinate function of the reader's subjective action—the knower's synthesis of the known.

She points out in this connection that many facts—social, biographical, formal—may be adduced as knowledge about literature but "all such facts are expendable unless they demonstrably help to clarify or enrich individual experiences of specific novels, poems, or plays." Meanwhile, the reader defines this experience by bringing "to the work personality traits, memories of past events, present needs and preoccupations, a particular mood of the moment and a particular physical condition. These and many other elements in a never-to-be-duplicated combination determine his response to the peculiar contribution of the text."[24] Each reading of a text, according to these considerations, is actually a different poem, a term which "should designate an involvement of both reader and text." A reading experience is an involved transaction, and this constitutes the work. Therefore, if we seek to "know" a poem, "we cannot simply look at the text and predict" it; rather, "a reader or readers with particular attributes must be postulated: e.g., the author-as-reader as he is creating the text, or as he reads it years later; a contemporary of the author with similar or different background of education and experience; other individuals living in specific places, times and milieus."[25] These formulations amount to the claim that no work even exists unless someone is reading it, that no matter when a text is studied it has to be conceived as a function of some reader's mind, and that, inversely, it cannot be described "without reference to the . . . reader."[26] As an operational principle, this is one of the bases of subjective criticism.

Rosenblatt's thinking represents the formulation, for the first time, of an intellectual attitude that can accommodate response, in its full dimensions, in the organized study of literature. Her proposals, like

23. Ibid., p. 27n. These views are also discussed in "The Poem as Event," *College English*, 26, No. 2 (November 1964), 123-28.
24. Rosenblatt, *Literature as Exploration*, pp. 27, 30-31.
25. Rosenblatt, "The Poem as Event," p. 127.
26. Rosenblatt, *Literature as Exploration*, p. 29.

those of Richards and Harding, were first presented several decades ago, but they only began receiving attention less than a decade ago. In the intervening years, a different outlook prevailed, that of the highly objectivist New Criticism. This history strongly documents the existence of the thought-paradigm developments that I discussed in Chapter One. Only after the objective paradigm had run its course in critical and literary study did the subjective forms of thought become viable.

Rosenblatt's work, informed though it is by subjective attitudes and interests, is most problematical in its exclusive conceptual attention to literary matters. Because, for her, the special connection between a reader and a text is not given as a local manifestation of a general paradigmatic shift, the basic rationale for recognizing this connection is pragmatic. The main authority she claims is moral—it is for the good of the student to inquire into his indiosyncratic literary experience. While this argument is acceptable, it is also rejectable because many believe the contrary—namely, that on a purely pragmatic basis it may be just as important to read carefully as to respond fully. In fact, Rosenblatt believes this latter argument, since in many phases of her discussion she cautions against straying too far from the "experience to which the text actually refers."[27]

The idea of a transaction between reader and text entails, in her treatise, an equal respect for both. She argues that as the reader's response develops, it is successively altered and limited by the text rather than by a new perception of it. The assumption behind this argument is the active nature of the text. It is true that there is often an illusion that a text acts on a reader, but it can hardly be the case that a text actually does act on the reader. The subjective paradigm, in emphasizing the distinction between real objects, symbolic objects, and

27. See note 22 above. Throughout Rosenblatt's treatise, there are formulations that imply an objective distinction between adequate and inadequate interpretation: "The attainment of a sound vision of the work will require the disengagement of the passing or irrelevant from the fundamental and appropriate elements in his response to the text. What was there in his state of mind that led to a distorted or partial view of the work?" (p. 79). As soon as there is a sense of "sound vision" or "distorted" perception, the ideal of objective correctness is implicitly invoked, and any student knows this. Rosenblatt subsequently speaks of the need to attain "an undistorted vision of the work of art" and argues that "the student should be led to discover that some interpretations are more defensible than others" (p. 115). I think that students already know that they can defend certain views better than other views, and that their task is to come to terms with the niggling suspicion that the teacher's interpretation is somehow always more defensible than their own. The universal facts of perceptual distortion and idiosyncratic interpretation come across in Rosenblatt's argument as immoral or inadequate features of mental functioning rather than definitive features that seek conscious cultivation in school. The idea of "transaction" is a rationalization for the contradiction between the habitual belief in objective interpretation and the new-found sense of the reader's defining activity. I will discuss this matter further in connection with both Rosenblatt and Norman N. Holland.

subjects (i.e., people), holds that only subjects are capable of initiating action and that the most fundamental form of that action is the motivated division of experience into those three classes. The distinction a subject feels between himself and the symbols he uses is the basis of sanity and conscious functioning. Symbols are the subjective correlatives of experience, just as the name *myself* is the symbol of the feeling and awareness of self. Because the reader is actually dealing with his symbolization of the text, knowledge of the reading experience has to begin with that subjective dialectic. The most that a reader can do with the real object, the text, is to see it. Readers of the same text will agree that their sensorimotor experience of the text is the same. They may also agree that the nominal meaning of the words is the same for each of them. Beyond these agreements, the only consensus about a text is on its role as a symbolic object, which means that further discussion of this text is predicated on each reader's symbolization and resymbolization of it. These two actions by the reader convert the text into a literary work. Therefore, discussion of the work must refer to the subjective syntheses of the reader and not to the reader's interaction with the text.

The issue of how to conceive the act of reading if major importance is attributed to response is most recently discussed in the work of Norman N. Holland. Although his view of the problem is different from Rosenblatt's in several key aspects, his underlying conception of reading is very similar: "Literary criticism . . . takes as its subject matter, not a text, but the transaction between a reader and a text. . . . The true focus of criticism has to be the relation between oneself and the text."[28] Holland claims that his formulations differ from Rosenblatt's because "she simply concluded that the text's causal role in the transaction equaled the perceiver's." But while Holland does not use the idea of causality to explain the role of the text,[29] he nevertheless claims that its

28. Norman N. Holland, *Five Readers Reading* (New Haven, 1975), p. 248.
29. Norman N. Holland, "The New Paradigm: Subjective or Transactive?" *New Literary History*, 7, No. 2 (Winter 1976), 345n. Rosenblatt did not discuss causality either, and she reached the same conclusion Holland did, but considerably before him. Rosenblatt did not invoke an epistemological paradigm; Holland did not either before Professor Ralph Cohen invited the essay cited above in response to my essay "The Subjective Paradigm in Science, Psychology, and Criticism," which appears in the same issue of *New Literary History* and is reprinted in revised form as Chapter One above. Holland claims his paradigm to be that "one cannot separate subjective and objective perspectives" (p. 339; italics in original). This circumstance cannot be paradigmatic because it *states* that no paradigm is in effect. Holland conceptualizes the aparadigmatic state by claiming mental life takes place in "potential space," as I discuss in the text. This space is the same as the one-year-old's "transitional space," which the infant has not yet divided up into objective and subjective perceptions. Applied to adult life, this idea denies the obvious and fundamental fact that one can systematically vary one's perspective from objective to subjective and that one does this as a matter of everyday behavior. From the standpoint of the subjective paradigm, any perspective as well as the

objectivity is significant: "Every reader has available to him . . . the words-on-the-page, that is, the promptuary (a store of structured language) . . . which . . . includes constraints on how one can put its contents together."[30] Under the subjective paradigm the epistemological role of these constraints is trivial: they function as any real object functions, since they can be changed by subjective action. For Holland, they are not trivial, as can be seen from how he derived the idea of transaction.

Holland says that a literary work is the same as a "transitional object," as first defined by D. W. Winnicott. Reading is the handling of such an object: "Reading provides us with a potential space in which the distinction between 'in here' and 'out there' blurs as we ingest the external world into our ongoing psychological processes. The world of things and people presents itself to us as transitional objects that are

---

possibilities for new perspectives are determined by subjective capacities for perception and cognition. The claim for inseparable perspectives amounts to a declaration of the chaotic nature of the human mind; epistemologically, our demand is to distinguish sensibly among perspectives, rather than to deny the problem by declaring no distinction possible.

Heinrich Henel ("Forum," *PMLA*, 91, No. 2, March 1976, 293-94) has a similar view of Holland's formulations. He first observes that Holland's essay "UNITY IDENTITY TEXT SELF" (*PMLA*, 90, No. 5, October 1975, 813-22) "is so full of hedges, equivocations, and contradictions that it is difficult to take issue with him." After detailing these difficulties, he concludes: "What actually happened is that Holland's objective criterion, which he mentions only to brush it aside, triumphed at least in this instance." Although my overall viewpoint is not Henel's, I agree with his perception of Holland's work. I believe there are so many hedges and so many evidences of the "objective criterion" because there is an out-and-out rejection of the whole epistemological question: "one cannot separate" the two perspectives. The hedges appear when Holland contradicts his declaration, and then arbitrarily and silently separates his perspectives and retains the right to claim an absolute objective perspective for himself. In my discussion of Holland's research format (later in this chapter), I indicate how I think he invokes this right.

30. Holland, *Five Readers Reading*, p. 286. Earlier, he had explained: "Yet the words can't be just anything. Miss Emily [in "A Rose for Emily"], we have noted, cannot be an Eskimo—at least not without doing violence to the text. The writer creates opportunities for projection but he also sets constraints on what the reader can or cannot project into the words-on-the-page and how he can or cannot combine them. The reader can violate these stringencies, of course, but if he does so, he loses the possibility of sharing with others and winning their support for his lonely and idiosyncratic construct" (pp. 219-20). This argument is identical to Hirsch's with regard to the author's determinate meaning. It is not a matter of dispute or interpretation whether Emily is an Eskimo or a salesgirl. But if someone *says* Emily is an Eskimo, this is an act of interpretation that can easily have meaning to an Eskimo. Holland is assuming that Emily *is* this or that; there are interpretations of *Hamlet* which *say* Hamlet is a woman; everyone understands that such interpretations are given over and above his putative designation as a man, since no one disputes the nominal designation. From a subjective standpoint, there is truth value in any such seriously-given reading, and to moralistically claim violations of the text is only an attempt to say that one's own objectification is more authoritative than someone else's. At the same time, the text cannot thus be understood as constraining, except in a trivial sense. The prior agreement by a community of readers to accept *this* text transfers all constraining action to the community and its motives in handling its language.

both found reality and created symbol."[31] The transitional object is Winnicott's conceptualization of the blanket, teddy bear, or similar item an infant becomes attached to as he makes the transition from sensorimotor intelligence to representational intelligence. Sometimes this object clearly represents the child's self; at other times it is a "friend" or something "objective." Emotionally, such objects are always very important to the infant, and they are usually not susceptible to the same treatment other toys get. Whatever the "essence" of such objects, they seem to play a major role in the child's development of the capacity for symbol-making; this might have been the role played by Helen Keller's two dolls in her acquisition of language. The objects are said to exist in "potential space" because it is usually not possible to observe exactly what they mean to children at any given moment. According to our perception, the object could be subjective or objective, or both, for the child; but the main fact is that an observer cannot tell. Thus, the general term *potential space* becomes useful simply to denote the phenomenon for discourse.

With regard to reading, however, the concept complicates our thinking unnecessarily. While reading, the reader converts his sensory perception of the words into an imaginary context or system that is clearly within the purview of his own subjectivity. Unlike the transitional infant, the reader already has a well-established sense of just which objects are real and which are symbolic. The words are real, but the thoughts in his mind that bear those words are symbols or conceptions. Neither a reader nor an observer of a reader can confuse the reader's conception of this experience with any real object. There is no need, therefore, to define a special space in which to locate the "union of reader and text." [32] The symbolization of the text and the interpretive resymbolization, if any, are both located in the reader's mind.

A two-year-old knows the difference between reality and "pretend." That is, he knows how to alternate his perspective from objective to subjective. From that age onward the instances are extremely rare when a person cannot thus alternate his perspective; it can happen during inebriation, delirium, or psychosis. But except under such circumstances, the condition of being conscious is identical with being able to alternate perspectives. The defining difference between the consciousness of a linguistic person and a prelinguistic infant is that in the former there is never a blur between real objects and symbolic

---

31. Ibid., pp. 287-88. The idea of the transitional object was invented to make a distinction between infantile and adult mental experience. To say, as Holland does, that experiencing in general takes place in this way cancels the understanding that Winnicott originally brought.

32. Ibid., p. 290.

objects, or between either of these and people (subjects). There is no sane, conscious person who does not make a decisive distinction between "things and people," or between what is in his imagination and what is not. When there is doubt, as when one hears noises of uncertain origin, special attention is given immediately to remove the uncertainty. Finally, at any moment during the watching of a film or the reading of a book we are capable of deliberately switching our perspective from "I am watching Donald Duck" to "I am watching a picture of "Donald Duck." Because the distinction in me between "in here" and "out there" is as clear in mind as ever, I know that the "text" of Donald Duck did not amuse me, but my way of perceiving and understanding it did.

Considerably more than Rosenblatt's, Holland's way of conceiving the reading and response experiences aims, as did Whitehead's, to "struggle back to some sort of objectivist position." In this cause, Holland observes that "Whitehead properly understood" supports the principle that "one cannot separate subjective and objective perspectives."[33] Holland presents the idea of subjectivity just as Whitehead did, as an instance of solipsism where the mere existence of tables and chairs is denied. The palpability of ordinary real objects is Holland's main argument that subjectivity and objectivity are merged not simply in the reading experience but in all experience. This means that Holland takes the standard of reality to reside in these real objects. He thus believes that this reality is "added" to subjective experience, though he no longer believes that subjective experience can be "subtracted" from objective reality.[34] The ubiquitous potential space is the result of this addition, and the "real" reality is where the two perspectives are inseparable. The experiential consequence of this fusion, he argues, is that one no longer need trouble to distinguish between what we say is objective and what we say is subjective, since all experience, in potential space, is "transactive." For Holland, the mentation involved in the way we relate to stones, books, and people is identical: we transact them. In Holland's view, verbal meaning in a text constrains response in the same way that a stone constrains one's foot; the objectivity of each is recognized as independent and *then* it is "added" to oneself. From the viewpoint of subjective epistemology, there is a different sort of motive at work when we handle these three types of experience, and in each instance the motive is located

33. "The New Paradigm," pp. 342, 339; italics in the original.
34. Terms like *add* and *subtract*, as well as the mathematical metaphors of function he uses in the essay cited above, further suggest the objectivist orientation of Holland's thinking.

unambiguously in the subject or in the community of subjects. The idea of potential space as Holland conceives it is similar to Whitehead's "self-transcendence": it is artificial conceptual baggage crafted to reduce the sense of psychological loneliness produced by the special responsibilities of subjective thinking.

The formal circumstance in which Holland tried to develop knowledge about literary response suggests his implicit view of such knowledge as objective. He began his effort with traditional assumptions about knowledge and therefore devised an experiment in which he would try to predict readers' responses from his own psychological analyses of short stories and his understanding of the readers' personalities as obtained in psychological tests such as the Rorschach and the Thematic Apperception Test. The readers were taken from a group of undergraduate literature majors who volunteered as paid subjects for the experiment. The responses were given by the readers during taped interviews in which Holland asked various questions aimed at evoking a full discussion of as many aspects of the stories as possible for each respondent. After he transcribed and studied the interviews, Holland saw that the "responses proved far too idiosyncratic" to be explained as the predictable result of a fixed stimulus, the story. But when he conceived the responses as the result of each reader's having "added" the story to himself, he tried to develop what he thought was a satisfactory explanation of the particular reading experiences, and he tried to formulate principles about how, in general, readers read.[35] In confronting the uninterpreted responses, Holland conceived his choice to be between two ways

35. *Five Readers Reading*, p. 289. Holland gives his own version of this change in his point of view in "A Letter to Leonard," *Hartford Studies in Literature*, 5 (1973), 21. He writes:

Schooled as I am in the objectivity claimed by twentieth century criticism, I had the same kind of resistance to this [subjective] solution [to the problem of explaining varying literary responses] that you do now Leonard, even though it had been strongly urged on me.

For some years, David Bleich had been trying in conversation to persuade me of "the primacy of subjectivity." He had written three cogent articles dealing with reader responses, the earliest of which you yourself published. Now, the ms. of *5 Readers Reading* elicited a highly detailed 13-page response (whimsically dated "Flag Day, 1971") raising over and over again the difficulty of basing an analysis of subjective responses on an ostensibly objective analysis of a text.

I received many other detailed commentaries from friends and colleagues, and, having other projects afoot, I resolved to put both manuscript and suggestions aside. I did not begin revision for six months, and even then it was not until March 1972 that suddenly one day looking for the I-don't-know-how-manyeth time at Dave's commentary, I realized with the proverbial shock of recognition that he was, quite simply and astonishingly, right!

I don't believe that a work actually transforms anything. Only a person can transform something. If you say the author makes a transformation, then I agree. And likewise for the reader. For better or for worse, a work is never independent of a person, and I find it hard to pretend, in the new critical tradition, that it is ever independent.

of viewing the juxtaposition of reader and story—the traditionally objective way (Holland calls this "stimulus-response") and a newer subjective way whose dimensions he sees as transactive. Not included among the choices was a consideration of the responses as a function of the experimental and interview situations. In either of the choices that Holland entertains, he is the observer and the reader is the observed. The relationship between himself and the readers whom he paid to participate in interviews with him was, first, not considered, and later, *ruled out* as a salient factor in the creation of the response. In this way Holland conceived of his research situation in traditional objective terms. The key principle of subjective epistemology—the necessity for the observer to include his connection with the observed in his proposals of knowledge—was not integrated into either the research situation or into the logic of Holland's interpretation of the results.

In trying to explain how and why his respondents viewed the stories as they did, Holland stipulates that all readers have the same general motive, namely, to re-create their own identity with the materials provided by the story. He proposes that in order to explain someone's particular "reading," one first infers that person's "identity theme," which is a personal "style permeating all aspects of an individual's life,"[36] and the reading is then conceived as a particular manifestation of this style. The explanation of any reading experience is the demonstration that it conforms with the preexisting personality style or identity theme. The epistemological questions raised by this means of explanation are whether and for whom it produces new knowledge, and whether the explanation be fruitfully applied to any—or, at least,

---

A story is a thing, and it is then processed by a person. The peculiar nature of symbols is their dependency on people. People *render* things symbols by using them in certain ways. A symbol does not really exist beyond its creator and its respondent.

The reader is the one that makes a text psychological by the simple act of reading. The act of internalizing a text renders it a subject of psychological study. But the new critical approach of objectivity renders a text ineligible of psychoanalytical inquiry.

This all seems to me direct and commonsensical. Texts do not, after all, have fantasies—people do. Literary works do not defend or adapt—people do. I also found this approach led to a much more straightforward and economical explanation of the responses my five readers had given. . . . No matter how you put it, though, it seems to me you have to give the subjectivity of the reader, as Bleich put it, "primacy." Only in that way can I account for the amazing diversity of people's responses to texts that seem to embody clear-cut psychological processes.

Holland's point of view changed in that he "added" my point of view to his own, even though the foregoing account gives the false impression that he adopted my point of view. As a result of "adding" subjective primacy to his continuing traditional objectivity, he came up with the "paradigm" that one "cannot" separate the two perspectives. Because of his attempt to retain his former point of view about reading and my own point of view, Holland's work gave Henel, me, and others the impression of hedging, equivocation, and contradiction.

36. Ibid., pp. 128, 61.

to most—reading experiences.

The idea of an identity theme is not new, but Holland conceives it as it was rearticulated by Heinz Lichtenstein.[37] In treating a particular patient, Anna S., Lichtenstein observed that the many relationships in her life, when viewed from her own perspective, could be described similarly as "being another's essence." When her original complaint was removed or eliminated—when she stopped wanting to be a prostitute—her real love relationship could also be described in the same way. Thus, after prolonged therapy with this patient and on the basis of considerable familiarity with her reports of life experiences, Lichtenstein conceptualized what he thought was her personality style, a denotation which represented both disharmonious and satisfying feelings and experiences. He further speculated, though he adduced no supporting evidence, that in each person a permanent personality style is transmitted by the mother to the infant by the time the infant reaches the stage of representational intelligence in the middle of the second year. In this way, identity becomes a motivational principle explaining all subsequent behaviors and experiences of any individual. The most basic and general motive for human behavior would therefore be the motive to maintain this identity.

Within the therapeutic situation, an identity theme has explanatory power in two respects: first, it is developed in retrospect of a great many of the individual's relationships and experiences, and second, a patient's acceptance of a particular statement of it constitutes a motivated act of self-enhancement in consequence of his therapeutic relationship. In other words, an identity theme cannot be defined objectively or quickly. The individual has to be motivated to articulate such a theme for himself or to accept the articulation of someone else in an appropriate relationship with him to do so. At the same time, it can come about only with a maximum perspective of one's own life history. Even if one assumes, which I do not, that a mother transmits an identity theme to an infant, the articulation of such a theme can come only in retrospect, like the interpretation of a dream, but in this case within the wide perspective of a great many personal and interpersonal experiences.

Holland's relationship with his reading subjects is not therapeutic; it is, perhaps, experimental, but it is mainly a contractual relationship, in which the subjects freely agree to behave in a certain way in exchange for pecuniary compensation. Furthermore, compared to the therapeutic relationship, these relationships are very brief. The basis for Holland's articulation of his subjects' identity themes is *Holland's*

37. Heinz Lichtenstein, "Identity and Sexuality: A Study of Their Interrelationship in Man," *Journal of the American Psychoanalytic Association,* 9 (1961), 179-260.

*research motivation*: none of the subjects' motives, by the contractual arrangement, enter into the construction of the theme. From the outset, the relationships are defined by the subjects' objective status; they only provide "data" and do not participate in the development of the theme. Therefore, the knowledge denominated by these themes was derived neither transactively, nor interactively, nor intersubjectively; it is presented as simple objective knowledge in the traditional sense.

Conceivably, it is admissible to use the materials from projective tests and informal response as contributions to the development of an identity theme, but it can hardly be enough if the idea of an identity theme has the same meaning it had for Lichtenstein. But conspicuously absent from Holland's materials yet prominently present in Lichtenstein's was a report of the subject's array of interpersonal relationships and personal history—parents, siblings, friends, lovers, vocational aspirations, religious and ethnic backgrounds, and so on. These items rarely appear in the materials Holland presents as representing his subjects, and they never enter into the conclusions drawn about the responses. If an identity theme has the far-reaching explanatory power Holland claims for it, it cannot possibly be developed from so brief and superficial a knowledge of an individual. But in any event, because the subjects themselves did not develop the identity theme, and because an identity theme is above all a motivated conceptualization of *oneself*, the only sort of response it might be said to explain is the sort collected in just the experimental circumstance used by Holland, where the subjects are, operationally, objects.

There is thus considerable doubt that an identity theme can be explanatory at all in the study of response. Here is an instance of how Holland presents its explanatory function:

> To ask how these factors [the factors that make up the readers' psychological condition at the time of response] affected what they said, however, is to proceed from the same cause-and-effect, stimulus-response model that we have already found inadequate. That is, the story did not "cause" their response—they did. Similarly, the interviewer and the interview situation did not "cause" their response. Nor did the current crises in their lives. But any or all of these might have—no, must have—entered into what they said about these stories. The point is: what "caused" what they said was their own inner style of creation and synthesis of everything they were experiencing at that moment.[38]

The word *caused* is consistently in quotation marks to indicate that the explanatory action of the identity theme is not causal in the traditional sense. The theme is a kind of shorthand for all the factors that Holland

38. *Five Readers Reading*, pp. 62-63.

sees about the subject as "converging" to that theme; these factors include the tests, Holland's informal observations, and the responses. Thus, if the interviewer does not matter, and the current life crises do not matter because all such factors have been assimilated to the preexisting identity theme, there is no context that can establish the generality of the identity theme and hence its explanatory authority over the response. Since the theme is derived mainly from the responses, it qualifies as a form of explanation of those responses within their own context. But then the theme no longer applies to the reader's "own inner style of creation and synthesis" and has none of the generality in Holland's discussion that it has in Lichtenstein's. Therefore, unless a personality style is carefully developed in the full way described by Lichtenstein, it cannot be a principle of explanation in the study of response. And there is no context of literary response that can actually work up a full therapeutic definition of each reader's identity. As a matter of epistemological principle, knowledge about response cannot be derived through use of identity themes.

While corresponding to a functional principle in each person, the identity theme, in Holland's thinking, is also an abstraction of four psychological functions which may be used directly to understand any response. When a reader reads, he brings to the work

a set of characteristic expectations, typically a balance of related desires and fears. The perceiver adapts the "other" to gratify those wishes and minimize those fears—that is, the perceiver re-creates his characteristic modes of adaptation and defense (aspects of his identity theme) from the materials literature or reality offers. He or she projects characteristic fantasies into them (and these fantasies can also be understood as aspects of identity). Finally, the individual may transform these fantasies into themes—meanings—of characteristic concern (and again, these themes and transformations can also be understood within the individual's identity).[39]

In addition to being a descriptive statement, this is a procedural instruction. Regardless of the form or context of a response, the standard means of analysis proposed is a definition of the reader's psychological expectations in terms of wishes and fears, a discovery in the response of characteristic modes of adaptation and defense, a similar definition of the fantasies and how they are characteristically transformed into characteristic meanings. The epistemological problem is the same in the attempt to use these analytic categories as it is in trying to explain instances of local behavior with the identity theme. Unless one has a reliable sense of just what is characteristic for each reader, the same aspects of a response may be read either as fantasy or defense, while no aspect may be understood as expectation.

39. Holland, "The New Paradigm," p. 338.

As a descriptive statement, the passage may well be applied in the context suggested by its language—orthodox psychoanalytic therapy, or perhaps Holland's objective context of response study. But as an attempt to use known psychoanalytic categories of behavior to explain every reader's response, the procedure is simply devoid of its normal form of authorization—the negotiative relationship between the subject and the interpreter.

By ruling out the interpreting relationship as a key determinant of response, and by converting the psychological categories into an objective formalism, Holland precludes explanation of perhaps the most familiar feature of aesthetic response—affect. He says that he did not try to understand it because "there is no satisfactory theory of affect in any circumstances, real life, literary response, dreams, or inner tensions."[40] In the appendix to the main treatise, he suggests that affect is probably a scalar item, varying from positive to negative, depending on the relative strength of the fantasies and defenses in the response. Yet given even this relatively narrow and quantitative view, a special theory of affect is not needed to understand it as a part of response. If response is conceived as an initial and largely peremptory symbolization of a reading experience, its affect is a visible form of valuation that cannot be separated from the perception or the uncensored rendition of this perception. The valuation itself cannot be scalar (though affect does vary in intensity), since its name—like *love* or *jealousy*—refers to a cognitive perception and therefore has a specific shape for that situation. If there is no way to measure the strength of fantasies and defenses, there is no sense in viewing affect as the difference between the two strengths. Viewed by itself, the affect "disgust" can be called negative.[41] But is it also a negative feeling if the reader enjoyed it, or if it appeared in a larger context of enjoying the work? Feelings appearing in response to aesthetic objects are frequently not to be taken at face value, since feelings of pathos or fear are commonly the motive for our perceptual initiative. Therefore the affective part of response is as directly subject to resymbolization as all the other parts, and a special theoretical structure for affect would be inapplicable.

40. *Five Readers Reading*, p. 292.
41. One of Holland's readers, Sam, said of the wedding night he imagined in "A Rose for Emily": "You're kind of loath to think about it, because it's kind of disgusting" (ibid., p. 297). It is very difficult for me to call this a negative affect or even, as Holland says, a "denial" ("Sam denied the wedding night"). Anyone who has uttered Sam's sentiments must have thought about it and felt disgust thinking about it. Is it either true or useful to say that Sam defended against it? And is there any sense in which there is enjoyment in a feeling of disgust? If affect is conceived in quantitative or scalar terms, it is no surprise that there is no "theory of affect." If a complex statement like Sam's is to be conceived only as a defense, then Sam is considered an objective patient rather than a subjective reader.

Consistent with the functional shrinkage of relationships, motives, and affect as defining features of response in Holland's work is the general dynamic conception of it as a reiterative process; the "one overarching idea" that sums up the four principles is "style seeks itself."[42] The basic motive for any response is the person's need to replicate his personality style. Holland claims that as a matter of epistemological principle, "tenacity, not negotiation, is the human style, for we use the ideas we hold to re-create our very identities."[43] This attitude is as defensible as any other sort of conservatism: there is sense in declaring the inertial character of personality, and there is sense in understanding certain behaviors as features of this character. But in which context is this sort of understanding appropriate? In the act of declaring that "style seeks itself," Holland defines the context of its application as any one where it appears that style does not seek itself. Thus, when a person perceives an experience as, in some important way, a departure from the normal run of experience, he would, if he accepts this principle, have to understand the new experience as a repetition of previous experiences: the act of resymbolization would be consciously directed toward denying the novelty of the experience. The idea of novelty loses its meaning altogether.

But there is a more serious consequence than the loss of novelty. If the act of self-enlightenment is only an act of self-replication, the idea that consciousness is an organ of self-enhancement has to be discarded. The defining characteristic of consciousness is its ability to take deliberate initiatives to improve the lot of the individual. This involves a continuing series of complex alterations of one's self-image and the conscious pursuit of experience that will facilitate greater psychological and social adaptability. If a person decides that he will begin a regimen of jogging, for example, it does not constitute an explanation of this act to say that it replicates his identity. But it is an explanation to adduce a motive for his attempt to *change* his preexisting self-image or lifestyle. By the same reasoning, it can hardly constitute an explanation of a new reading experience to translate the new configuration of perceptions, feelings, and interpretations into the ever-present identity theme. The search for an explanation is, to begin with, an act motivated by the desire to enlarge or enhance the sense of self at that time, and not by the desire to retain that sense exactly as before; in fact, the continuing process of growth defines any new act of ideation as a contribution to that process. The motive for perceiving the self-replication of certain behaviors appears only in therapy, where

42. Holland, *Five Readers Reading*, p. 113.
43. "The New Paradigm," p. 342. This claim is about as consequential as the familiar religious ones which say that man is basically good (or evil or guilty or sinful) and then derive ethical imperatives from the claim.

the experience of past disharmonies has produced a painful present that needs alleviation. But the ordinary engagement of self in new experiences has not such therapeutic motive; it proceeds from the natural impulse to articulate a new sense of self more commensurate with the most recent life circumstances. Style seeking itself, like the identity theme, cannot be a principle that explains response.

Early in this chapter, I claimed that the study of response and interpretation and the experience of them are part of the same activity. My discussion of the epistemological problems in the various approaches to response study held this claim as an implicit evaluative standard which proceeds from the subjective principle that the observer is part of the observed while the observed is defined by the observer. In his recent work, Stanley Fish reached the same standard by following established critical and pedagogical assumptions to their logical conclusions, just as Bridgman reached a subjective viewpoint by logically extending operationalism.

Fish began by considering the familiar question of how to understand and teach literary style. His normal habit of study was that taught by New Critics—scrupulously close reading of literature. The first important fact that he came upon was that every time he read another word in a poem, or another group of words, his *whole sense* of the poem changed. Although at first tempted to say that this change is to be understood as an action of the text, he soon conceived the source of the action as his own linguistic and literary experience. He thus observed:

The objectivity of the text is an illusion, and moreover, a dangerous illusion, because it is so physically convincing. The illusion is one of self-sufficiency and completeness. A line of print or a page or a book is so obviously *there*—it can be handled, photographed, or put away—that it seems to be the sole repository of whatever value and meaning we associate with it. (I wish the pronoun could be avoided, but in a way *it* makes my point.) This is of course the unspoken assumption behind the word "content." The line or page or book *contains*—everything.[44]

In his awareness of his own language as well as of the accepted language of criticism ("content"), Fish shows that when we symbolize a symbolic object as a real object, the result is an illusion. This passage also implies what I would state explicitly—that the motive for maintaining this illusion is the comfort in the palpability of an item which, in its definitive functions, is imaginary. Fish does suggest parenthetically that "perhaps literature is what disturbs our sense of self-sufficiency, personal and linguistic." His conviction about the

44. Stanley E. Fish, "Literature in the Reader: Affective Stylistics," *New Literary History*, 2, No. 1 (Autumn 1970), 140.

authenticity of this circumstance leads to the decisive shift of attitude: "I would rather have an acknowledged and controlled subjectivity than an objectivity which is finally an illusion."[45]

The subjective assumption was necessitated by several considerations regarding the nature of language. One of these is the widely accepted distinction between literary and ordinary language. Among critics, Fish states, literary language occupied a special position as intrinsically other than everyday language. Among linguists, everyday language was taken as a common denominator the explanation of which in terms of formal rules was believed to describe any manifestation of language. But because semantic aspects of any language system are "a motivating force in that system," whether literary or ordinary, the "objectively descriptive language unattached to situations and purposes that was traditionally at the center of linguistic philosophy is shown to be a fiction."[46] Language as a separate phenomenon cannot be so investigated because it necessarily includes the "realm of values, intentions, and purposes,"[47] the sources of which are always in the users of language:

Literature is still a category, but it is an open category, not definable by fictionality, or by a disregard of propositional truth, or by a statistical predominance of tropes and figures, but simply by what we decide to put into it. The difference lies not in the language but in ourselves. Only such a view, I believe, can accommodate and reconcile the two intuitions that have for so long kept linguistic and literary theory apart; the intuition that there *is* a class of literary utterances, and the intuition that any piece of language can become a member of that class.[48]

The openness of linguistic categories places the authority for their definition in subjective initiative. With regard to symbolic objects, intuitions are definitive, in that a shared intuition objectifies the literary status of, say, *Hamlet*, but the lack of such sharing withholds this status from *Captain Marvel*: "All aesthetics, then, are local and conventional rather than universal, reflecting a collective decision as to what will count as literature, a decision that will be in force only so long as a community of readers or believers (it is very much an act of faith) continues to abide by it."[49] Fish's affirmation of the intuition that sees

45. Ibid., pp. 147, 146.
46. Stanley E. Fish, "How Ordinary Is Ordinary Language?" *New Literary History*, 5 No. 1 (Autumn 1973), 50.
47. Ibid., p. 51.
48. Ibid., p. 52. I would put the argument thus: since language and literature are, when objects of study, symbolic, their status depends on semantics, values, intentions, and purposes; therefore, the principles of subjectivity and motivation, rather than those of objective explanation, are to be used.
49. Ibid. If we understand *aesthetics* to mean "knowledge of language and literature," this statement describes the intersubjective negotiation that develops such knowledge.

language and literature as commonly rooted in subjective choice over the intuition that separates the two as different objects results from a crisis in the development of knowledge. In both criticism and linguistics, the dependency of knowledge on varying degrees of communal faith had, under the influence of positivism, been devalued. The subjective assumption renders both areas of knowledge responsible to each other and mainly, to the fact that language governs all forms of ideation in these disciplines.

Fish portrays the crisis of interpretive knowledge in criticism as originating in the objective indeterminacy of verbal meanings of key passages in many prominent works. Any word available to multiple contradictory meanings "transfers the pressure of judgment to us."[50] The functional role of an interpretive problem in the act of reading is to produce awareness of the equivalence of reading and interpretation. Even though the occasions which instigate such awareness do not occur at every word read, they nevertheless imply the generality of the reader's constructive action in any form of interpretation:

What I am suggesting is that formal units are always a function of the interpretive model one brings to bear; they are not "in" the text, and I would make the same argument for intentions. That is, intention is no more embodied "in" the text than are formal units; rather an intention, like a formal unit, is made when perceptual or interpretive closure is hazarded; it is verified by an interpretive act, and I would add, it is not verifiable in any other way.... intention is known when and only when it is recognized; it is recognized as soon as you decide about it; you decide about it as soon as you make a sense; and you make a sense ... as soon as you can.[51]

In this view, any literary judgment has to be understood as part of the critic's definable perspective. Thus, only two readers who agree that there will be such a thing as an extractable author's intention will perceive this intention. The authority for such a perception lies only in the influence of that interpretive community which claims that perspective, which is its accepted way of making a sense of what it reads. Aside from this community's choice of perspective, there is no authority for claiming the objectivity of the author's intention in the text. For any community, "the choice is never between objectivity and interpretation but between interpretation that is unacknowledged as

50. Stanley E. Fish, "Interpreting the *Variorum*," *Critical Inquiry*, 2 (Spring 1976), 468. The implication of this transfer is that "it is the structure of the reader's experience rather than any structures available on the page that should be the object of description" (p. 468). To change priorities from the text to one's own experience of the text is a consequence of the shift to the subjective paradigm. If this shift is not made, we are in the contradictory positions of both Rosenblatt and Holland, which affirm the objectivity of both the text and the reader's experience, and the experience becomes just another text. But if this experience is a *priority*, then the subsequent knowledge has a new character altogether, as Fish claims.

51. Ibid., p. 478.

such and an interpretation that is at least aware of itself."[52] Thus, Fish shifts the standard of interpretation from illusory objectivities to communally declared awareness. This means that interpretations can be authorized by subjective resymbolization and intersubjective negotiation, and by nothing else.

Although Fish believes that this is the only view of interpretation that can be held with full integrity—that is, with no illusions or other superstitious claims—he suggests two problems which follow from it: first, there seems no way to "prove" that one is a member of a particular interpretive community, and second, one cannot finally identify the object of interpretation. From the perspective of the subjective paradigm, these are not problems, however. Fish actually solved the first problem himself. He says, "You will agree with me (that is, understand) only if you already agree with me."[53] This is the definition of a community—people who already agree with one another—and this fact is immediately obvious to a third party. Proof does not enter the question. On a less immediate level a community is founded on similarities of *concern*, where agreement is not always necessary except on what is of common interest. If this is not obvious, it is always negotiated until it is; if the negotiation is unsuccessful, the community dissolves. Conversely, the sheer continuance of the community means that negotiations have thus far been successful. In any case, the simple "knowing" that one is in a community on the part of two or more people defines that community.

The second problem is solved by conceiving interpretation as resymbolization of the interpreter's *response*. Although the fact of response is implicit in Fish's understanding of language, it does not enter into his conception of interpretation. If the object of interpretation is thought to be either the text or nothing, then it is not possible to name that object. But response, like a text, is a symbolic object and may be understood to be the text as immediately and evaluatively perceived. Fish indicates his own tendency to give special attention to line endings, and his subsequent reasonings accrue from this perceptual habit.[54] Therefore, it is no contradiction of his argument to say that he likes to interpret his perceptions of line endings in seventeenth-century poetry. I identify Fish's symbolization of his texts—his perceptual stress on line endings—as his response, and I identify his resymbolization of his response—the judgment that ambiguous line endings make a special demand on him the reader—as his interpretation. He then interprets his interpretation in the ways I have just discussed. The immediate motive for the interpretation is the

52. Ibid., p. 480.
53. Ibid., p. 485.
54. Ibid., p. 479.

response; however, to propose a motive for the response requires a more personal interaction with Fish. In the present context, this latter motive is not germane. Fish's logic of interpretation is consistent with the logic I outlined in the previous chapter. Fish's conception of interpretation is consistent with the present understanding of both response and interpretation as instances of subjective symbol-formation. To include response in the general notion of interpretation is to establish a means both to acknowledge and control the subjective perspective that is now needed for further thought.

The consequences of this orientation of thought, which has governed my own efforts over the past decade (as well as, in part, the recent work of Fish, Kintgen, and Nelson) are suggested in studies by Susan Elliott and Thornton Jordan of their own responses. These two inquiries aim less to produce "insight" in the traditional critical sense than to document how a proposal of knowledge about language and literature may be systematically authorized through deliberate attention to response. As with the work of Squire, Wilson, Purves, and Rosenblatt, the work of Elliott and Jordan grew from the increasing difficulty of using New Critical insight in pedagogical communities. The general result of the subjective attitude makes knowledge seem more reliable because it is not conceived as a real object or "thing" and because it allows each community to authorize its own knowledge with its own experiences.

Susan Elliott's study "Fantasy behind Play" (1973)[55] is an examination of the critical reaction and her own responses to Harold Pinter's *The Birthday Party, The Caretaker,* and *The Homecoming.* She explores reviewers' and scholars' comments about these plays and takes special note of their complaints that traditional literary comprehension is usually frustrated by study of the plays. Counting herself among those readers with the same complaint, Elliott presents and discusses her own free-associative response statements with the aim of further defining for herself the emotional character of, and reasons for, her general attitude toward the plays. Her detailed analyses of both the criticism and her responses produce the conclusion that her involvement in each play yields a similar feeling in her—the "odd man out" syndrome, in which she feels socially ostracized and sexually impotent. These feelings, in turn, explain her sense of intellectual frustration. That is, because she peremptorily sees the plays as occasion in which she is ostracized and impotent, she objectifies these feelings by saying *the plays* are irrational, incomprehensible, or absurd. Insofar as other readers are rendering similar judgments, sometimes with similar personal justifications, Elliott is proposing knowledge about the

55. Diss. Indiana University.

community of Pinter readers *to* this community, and she is authorizing her proposals by presenting her responses in detailed, organized forms.

In the conclusion to this study, Elliott reports the following observation, which she calls a "most amazing experience":

> In the midst of seeing Pinter's most recent play, *Old Times*, for the first time in
> . . . 1971, I felt myself powerfully rejecting it and saying in great disappointment, "Pinter didn't make it this time. How awful this is!" I felt terribly depressed after seeing the production. After hours of argument with my husband about what it was about, I suddenly recognized my problem. On the surface, the play had me stymied; I was puzzled. This had never before occurred to me so long after an experience of Pinter. Usually I had it "all figured out." I say that I was puzzled "on the surface" because later, after setting down some thoughts that came to mind about the play, and reading it once it was published, I understood some of my essential identifications with the characters and my emotional involvement in their situations. To be brief, they recalled some rather painful and disturbing associations to adolescence and made quite evident to me a recurrent theme of my responses to the plays studied here, the "odd man out" syndrome in my psychic life. Since that recognition of my subjective relationship to the play, I have re-read it several times, taught it to three undergraduate classes, seen it in two more productions, and enjoyed most of these experiences immensely.[56]

It is of particular interest in this report that Elliott's experience of the new play appeared to her at first uninfluenced by her previous lengthy involvement in the other plays and in Pinter criticism in general. Her knowledge of her patterns of response to the previous plays could not predict the response to the new work. On the one hand, it was "predictable" that Elliott would be puzzled by the new play as she had been by the others; on the other hand, it was also "predictable" that she would *not* be puzzled, owing to her awareness of how she had responded in the past. Her remark "Pinter didn't make it this time" suggests that she was significantly aware of her previous Pinter experiences as she watched this play. This fact strongly implies the determining influence of the respondent's *current* state of mind. The evaluation of that state begins with the recording of the response—"setting down some thoughts that came to mind about the play"—and then considering them in retrospect, which, in this instance, did involve reading the play as well as viewing it. The subsequent decision that she perceived the play in terms of a previously known psychological syndrome—the "odd man out syndrome"—is not a revelation about the inevitability of a certain response to Pinter in Elliott, but a formulation of how she understands her present concern with this author's work. Both the character of the response and Elliott's

56. Ibid., p. 542.

subsequent comprehension of it are local and must be understood by the rest of us not as a definition of her character but as a statement of her commitment to this group of works and to the community of those similarly committed.

Once the interpretations of Pinter are grounded in this psychological perspective, the proposals of how others understand and react to Pinter's work are authorized for negotiation. Instead of proposing a thought in the form "This is how Pinter is," Elliott says, "This is how I see his work." The former statement constitutes "an objectivity which is finally an illusion"; the latter is an "acknowledged and controlled subjectivity."

Thornton Jordan's use of a similar epistemology in the study of his response to the Joseph story in *Genesis* suggests certain consequential connections between language and interpretation and makes it possible to conceive of alternatives to the logical analyses of language currently used by linguists. After recording his perception of, and feelings about, the Joseph story, Jordan's retrospective analysis of his work yields the following observations: "The sense of double emotions, often ambivalent, is the dominant emotional chord of my response. . . . I let my ambivalent feelings influence my estimation of Joseph. . . . While I see his anger as a source of strength, I judge his patience, obedience, and sense of duty as 'inhuman.' " Jordan observes that in general, when he likes Joseph, it is for strengths Jordan claims for himself, and when he rejects him, it is for weaknesses he eschews in himself. He traces these feelings to his handling of his ongoing relationship with his father: "My sense of mission towards my father was founded on the double feelings of sensitive concern for his feelings and my own guilt for my mother's death."[57] These formulations of the motives guiding the response as a whole then become an explanatory principle for a prominent language pattern in the response statement: specifically, "ambivalence is characteristic of my style in this particular paper, as in the following examples":

(1) Joseph is envied *not only* because he is the favorite *but* because he is a tattletale, and he reveals his dream of superiority to his brothers.

(2) *On the one hand*, his retention of anger is a source of strength; *on the other*, his patience and obedience are inhuman.

(3) As I attempted to run away from home, I was *both* scared *and* angry.

(4) I chose my career *partly* from desire, *partly* as a gesture of anger.

(5) There were two motives for my choices: *one to pursue* a career on my own terms, *the other to bring my father* to recognize me.

(6) In emotional exile I felt the *double feeling* of resentment and longing.

(7) *I was angry and pained* at my parents' decision, *but* I characteristically. . . .

57. Thornton F. Jordan, "Report on Teaching Subjective Criticism of Literature," unpub. essay, Columbus, Ga., August 1976, p. 23.

(8) *I felt like* an alien . . . *but* did well.

(9) *I recognize* the advantage of Joseph's withholding resentment, *yet* I resent it.[58]

As an objective set of sentences bearing a semantic pattern, this is not very different from the hundreds of analogous ones extracted from novels and studied in the scholarly literature of stylistics. But the epistemological status of this set is considerably different because it was written by Jordon in one motivational context and then interpreted by him in a subsequent context, itself created by the first one. The succession of motives defines Jordan's interpretive authority in much the same way as Freud's interpretation of his own dreams became authoritative: the meanings for the sentences are defined, not in the act of writing them, but in the process of interpretation. The sentences have a nominal meaning independent of Jordan's judgment, but only in the sense that other speakers of English identify them as English sentences. Any view of a language sample beyond trivial functional identification must involve interpretation and, therefore, the motives and subjectivity of the interpreter. To propose a meaning for this set of sentences is to propose knowledge about Jordan and his community of cosubjects. Such proposals are more satisfyingly understood in psychological, rather than logical, formulations.

The doubleness Jordan indicates in the nine sentences quoted above appears in a variety of grammatical forms, sometimes through the juxtaposition of clauses, other times in two parts of the same predicate. As studies in stylistics have repeatedly shown, it is practically impossible to draw conclusions about language from a direct comparison of syntax and semantics, even though the intuition persists that they are systematically related.[59] Jordan's psychological considerations, however, help to validate this intuition. His idea of doubleness is derived from his knowledge of ambivalent feelings toward his father that are connected with his conception of himself and his perception of Joseph. In their varying grammatical forms, the sentences reflect these feelings. If the sentences are analyzed logically, the same value would be applied, say, to all main clauses. If they are analyzed motivationally, each articulation of doubleness is the primary psychological initiative that determines how the structure of each sentence is defined. Sentence 4, for example, is made up of two parts: "I chose my career," and "partly from desire, partly as a gesture of anger." The two parts of sentence 5 are on either side of the colon. Sentence 6 divides into two

---

58. Ibid., p. 25.

59. Kintgen (note 2 above) has reviewed some of these studies, as has Stanley Fish in "What Is Stylistics and Why Are They Saying Such Terrible Things about It?" in *Approaches to Poetics*, ed. Seymour Chatman (New York, 1973), pp. 109-52.

parts between "felt" and "the." Each of these pairs is a semantic, as opposed to grammatical, predication. The pair of ambivalent feelings in the semantic "predicate" is a personal comment on a variety of local topics. In sentences such as 2, 7, and 8, the predicate appears by itself as an instance of a full-sentence presentation of what Jordan considers the main feeling of the response. Because there is a prior psychological subject for these predicates, they are similar in psychological import to sentences 4, 5, and 6. In these latter sentences, the phrases "I chose my career," "There were two motives for my choices," and "In emotional exile I felt" presuppose an analogy between the speaker and Joseph. This analogy, which may be provisionally formulated as "the fact that I identify with Joseph" or "I perceive myself as I perceive Joseph," is the prior psychological subject for sentences 2, 7, and 8. Furthermore, the phrases "Joseph is envied" in sentence 1 and "As I attempted to run away from home" in sentence 3 are also specific new instances of the main prior psychological subject.

This prior subject is Jordan's *perception* of the text, or the text as he perceives it. Each full sentence written in response to this perception represents a different psychological initiative taken with the main perception, a different resymbolization of the original perception of the text—the original symbolization. Jordan's thoughts at the time of response concerned an analogy between this story and his own experience with his father and the extent to which this analogy is tenable for him. Accordingly, the response may be understood as a subjective dialectic between Jordan's identification with Joseph and his identification with (or distance from) his father. When the subjects and predicates of the sentences are understood as discussed above, each sentence manifests this dialectic, which, in turn, constitutes the meaning of the sentences most relevant to Jordan's context of presentation. The advantage of understanding the response this way is that the interpretation is immediately seen as a subjective presentation. There is no need to claim that the Joseph story is "about" ambivalent feelings of sons toward fathers, since it is obvious that this describes *Jordan's* experience of the story. More importantly, however, the language of the presentation is not subject to arbitrary confusion. The variety of predications given by each of the nine sentences are different dimensions in which the basic response motive is the organizing principle of self-expression for Jordan, and a principle of interpretation for his cosubjects to use, even with individual sentences and phrases.[60]

60. Although it is obviously necessary to advance a proposal such as this in a full-length discussion, the purpose here is to distinguish between two epistemological attitudes. Particularly, I understand the epistemology of formalist criticism to be the same as the

Undoubtedly, Jordan's sentences are describable with transformational rules to some extent; semantically, they do not seem obscure. The epistemological question is, How explanatory can logically formulated rules be in a consequential, knowledge-making context such as this? Even if every detail of the nine sentences is accounted for formally, it will not explain how or why *Jordan* made these sentences. Logical explanations have been most convincing in coping with mechanical phenomena and least convincing with psychological events. Alternatively, motivated behavior cannot be explained by finding a way to deny the presence of motives either in the behavior or in the explanation; behavior that always involves a subject—in this instance, language behavior—is most easily understood through motivational or subjective explanations.

Most of the sentences used to demonstrate the operation of linguistic rules are specifically stipulated to be unmotivated—that is, unrelated to the speaker and to his context of utterance. These sentences—such as the well-known "John is eager to please"—have only a trivial semantic: the nominal meaning is never in doubt. The concept of competence defines sentences by their formulation alone and thus defines out of consideration the only contexts in which language has any consequence to begin with—when individuals use it to deal with one another and with themselves. In the so-called steady-state functioning of language, the abstract form of sentences is shared by two or more speakers to the extent that this form is simply not a factor in the sentence exchange; it therefore cannot constitute an explanation of the language events. If the concept of competence is conceived as "capability of performance," it is determined by perusal of the range of sentences everyone already speaks, and nothing has been explained. If *competence* refers to "permissibility of performance," *permissibility* can only mean "that which the speaking situation permits," since each speaker is perfectly capable of changing rules arbitrarily and saying what he pleases. Speaking situations constrain speech to certain formalities and habits in order that we may isolate the unique and personal features of each contribution. The mutual perception of one another's unique contributions is the matter to be explained in any language situation. If this is the case, the formal abstraction of each speaker's sentences must be a subfeature of the motives which define the teleology of the speech situation, and the motives cannot be a

---

epistemology of transformational (that is, formalist) linguistics; if the epistemological paradigm is shifted to subjectivity it is much easier to see how the study of literature and the study of language involve the same forms of thought and the same criteria of explanation. Both require an epistemological principle that *explains both experience and explanation as one shifts attention from one to the other.*

subfeature of the abstractions.[61]

The practice of formulating response statements is a means for making a language experience (hearing, speaking, reading, or writing) available for conversion into knowledge. A response can acquire meaning only in the context of a predecided community (two or more people) interest in knowledge. These are the circumstances in which Jordan reached the knowledge he claimed. Aware of an identity element in himself as a teacher, Jordan entered class with the conscious purpose of reading and responding in cooperation with the others in the class. He collected a group of response statements, one of which is his own. It is not immediately clear what he or anyone else has learned, nor is it obvious how to coordinate the responses with one another. At this point, the subjective conception of language and interpretation governs the procedural options by posing the question "What do I, Mr. Jordan, a member of this pedagogical community, want to know?" To develop knowledge, the first step is not to consult the data, like an empiricist, or to consult an abstraction, like a rationalist. Rather, one *decides*, as in everyday life, what one would like to know. Jordan's attempt to characterize his own self-knowledge, like Elliott's, then makes it possible for the classroom community to negotiate that formulation in a direction of common interest. Jordan proposed both interpretive knowledge of the reading experience—knowledge of his own language habits in that response—and provisional knowledge regarding the connections between response, interpretation, and linguistic style. The main point is that response cannot be one particular object or thing that each person produces as just another learning activity; rather, it is an expression of, and declaration of, self in a local context reflecting a set of local choices, motives, and interests in knowledge.

Most of the negative receptions to response studies can be traced to an abiding sense that *any* means of making subjective experiences public necessarily leads to psychological danger, intellectual disarray, and pedagogical anarchy; some proponents of subjective pedagogy have even supported a certain degree of anarchy as a valuable principle.[62] Yet it seems obvious to me that such pitfalls are the common risks of any social initiative that involves new thinking.

61. As George Greenfield has argued (unpub. essay, Department of English, Indiana University, April 1977), unique phenomena are, as a matter of principle, not susceptible to either of the traditional rationalist or empiricist forms of explanation. This is one of the reasons both aesthetics and language have eluded systematic explanation. If it is accepted that both art and language (in their common status as symbolic objects) are, in experience, unique phenomena, then either no explanation or subjective explanations apply.

62. For example, Barrett John Mandel, *Literature and the English Department* (Urbana, 1970), describes the sense in which a completely open-ended classroom can be successful:

The connection between knowledge of language and literature and the formation of interpretive communities originates in the common social purpose of pedagogy. Kuhn has suggested that the usual conception of science as a monolith of truth was created by the transformation of scientific knowledge into textbook knowledge, which stresses unambiguous presentation of accepted formalisms. This fact points less to a defect in the establishment of knowledge than to a normal circumstance of its use and, more importantly, to its origin in personal and interpersonal motivation. In addition to its undisputed utilitarian function (say, of healing the sick), knowledge formation is a natural psychological function, and it takes place in the minds of young people and adults regardless of whether they go to school. Like the infantile process of language acquisition, subsequent contexts of knowledge formation are always communal, even if a particular individual forms knowledge in opposition to his community. Part of the communal contribution to new knowledge is to facilitate the dialectical process that leads to this knowledge. The activity of developing knowledge is as phylogenetically founded as the formation of new families.

When knowledge is no longer conceived as objective, the purpose of pedagogical institutions from the nursery through the university is to synthesize knowledge rather than to pass it along: schools become the regular agency of subjective initiative. Because language use and the interpretive practices that follow from it underlie the processes of understanding, the pedagogical situations in which consciousness of language and literature is exercised establish the pattern of motives a student will bring to bear in his own pursuit of knowledge. For the development of subjective knowledge, motivation has to become a consciously articulable experience, and the configuration of classroom relationships—between student and student and between teacher and student—themselves have to motivate such articulation. This involves a definition of the purpose, authority, and scope of the subjective classroom.

---

there are no set meeting hours, no exams, no set reading lists, and every item of work is initiated by students. Only pragmatic objections to such procedures are admissible; but these objections—such as a range of applicability, class size, existing requirements, teaching motives of the instructors, and so on—have to be summarily denied if Mandel's proposals are to go into effect. Mandel does successfully deny them, but the problem of how to authorize knowledge remains untreated, except in individual student reports that they "learned something important."

# Chapter Five

# THE PEDAGOGICAL DEVELOPMENT
# OF KNOWLEDGE

A classroom is any place where two or more people gather for the conscious purpose of developing new knowledge. When this place is used to disseminate information, it is not a classroom, but an ungainly bulletin board, unless such dissemination is a necessary subordinate function of the interpretive task. Also secondary to this task is the common fact that one person is the teacher and the other the student. The important fact is that two people with a common purpose have created a new relationship in pursuit of their purpose. Each person participating in the relationship naturally brings his own needs and motives. The pedagogical question is whether these personal tendencies and the common purpose may be made to serve one another. If the classroom situation is conceived in this way, its function has to include the means for reaching an acceptable common pursuit and also for disclosing and then interpreting each constituent's subjective contribution. This means that knowledge cannot be reached simply through discussion or even discussion of the text, but that personal motives for membership in the classroom have to be translated into motives for knowledge. That is, what each person *wants* has to be reunderstood as what each person *wants to know*. Unless each person in a pedagogical relationship knows what he wants to know, he will not be motivated to develop knowledge, and this is the case even if subsequently developed knowledge differs substantially from what the individual first decided he wanted to know. Knowing what one wants to know is the first conscious motive for developing knowledge.

Few people entering a classroom as formal participants know what they want to know. Sometimes they are motivated only to participate in a ritual activity. If knowledge is considered objective, the problem is not pedagogical, and in most circumstances it is ignored. This sort of knowledge may then be justly measured with an examination. Even though complaints about this system have been steadily increasing, the dangers perceived in more subjectively grounded alternatives have been decisively inhibiting. It is becoming difficult to separate pedagogy from epistemology and psychology, however, without replacing mental functions and motives with motor functions and skills. All the while, the long-standing interpersonal character of almost any classroom situation suggests that pedagogical institutions are readily adaptable to a responsible integration of subjective thinking into the development of knowledge.

While reading activity and pedagogical relationships are to be explained with different sorts of adult motives, both sets of experiences grow from interpersonal language contexts of early childhood. From this perspective, reading and knowledge about literature can be understood in predicative relation to one another. These more complex adult functions are psychologically shaped on the example of early syntactic predications: topic and comment. The infant's first language relationship, with his mother, is largely governed by the mother's telling things to the child. The child may then emulate (through assimilation of conversational forms—that is, conceptual imitation) his correspondent, and conversational activity begins. Obviously, other infantile forms of interaction do not disappear, but language is the main regulating principle in the relationship. By the middle of the third year, language functions have converted the child's sense of the parent's greater strength into a sense of *authority*; the child *understands* that the parent may prescribe behavior verbally. (The child may have cooperated with such prescriptions earlier, but he first understands it at this age.) Conversational fluency and the comprehension of parental authority make it possible for the child to be told a story. The schema of "telling" is mutual, but the child also knows that the parent "tells" better and that this can be a good experience for him. In this way the parent is the child's first author.

Because the child understands the active nature of telling, he is aware of the active nature of imagining in response to telling. Thus, a storytelling is frequently interrupted by demands for clarification from the "author," for other sorts of commentary, or for simple rehearsal of parts or all of the story. These requests for comments on the topic represent the child's efforts at consolidating his response to— his first symbolization of—the story. The response is his own first comment, which completes his rendering of the listening experience into an act of predication. The parent's role in this act is pedagogical in an operational, rather than a moral, sense. The child's learning was self-motivated, in the regard that his own initiative appropriated the relationship for his mental activity. The story experience thereby acquires cognitive stereoscopy as the child has divided it, in his mind, into perceptual and reconstitutive processes. Very much as the child had earlier learned to make the parent's language his own and enhance the relationship in that context, the story's narration becomes his own, while his own response enhances the new "literary" relationship with the parent. Insofar as the parent's authority plays a key role in the new relationship, it represents the child's first pedagogical experience. For most children, the capacity for this sort of experience permits them, at this age, to enter a nursery school situation for the first time.

I am conceptualizing the child's mentation in the storytelling situation as a *subjective dialectic* which means, informally, that the child can "talk to himself" and get answers. More abstractly, it represents the prototypical circumstance for subsequent forms of complex *reasoning*, which, in turn, may be described as the internal manipulation of two different *language systems*. Sensory perception—say, hearing the story from the "author"—is one system, while imaginative response is the other. The dialectic between the two systems may be explained in terms of the motives the child attaches to the perceptual system and those in the response system. The juxtaposition of perceived motives and inherent motives produces an experiential motive for symbolization or resymbolization. The story as heard in a new language system has its own series of predications. The child's own language system responds by symbolizing the new system, the result being his own evaluative sense of the story which he immediately objectifies as "the story." Subsequent responses to this imaginary object are resymbolizations, or interpretations. Unless a subjective dialectic were taking place in the child's mind, he could not interrupt the storytelling for comments and clarifications. The interruptions are motivated when the child's active translation of the motives in the perceived language system into the motives in his own system gives rise to either frustration or other sorts of subjective disharmony. Finally, the subjective dialectic is validated and promoted by the child's motive to further his real-life relationship with the storyteller through this new context or activity. At the same time, the dialectical actions help develop the child's subjective autonomy—his independence of the parent-author—just as predicative language did earlier in infancy.

A subjective dialectic is a complex means of developing a new predication; the two or more language systems involved are analogous to the two schemata the infant reciprocally assimilates in his acquisition of representational thought. The outcome of the dialectic is the same in basic form as any of the early syntactic constructions and *is motivated into existence in a like manner*. A child's knowledge of a story is analogous to his having learned a new word; early story experiences are acts of identification and iterations of such acts. An interpretation is also a predication, since the identification is then identified with something else. The motives involved in these predications lend them their aspect of being "alive" or "human" as opposed to mere formal equations. If a child identifies a giant with a parent, the identification makes sense only in view of the child's own feelings and motives for making it; otherwise it is formulaic knowledge applied rather than subjective knowledge developed. Each person's subjective dialectic eventuates in a motivated piece of new knowledge that is observable as a predication.

Because language activates and defines consciousness, a new experience enters consciousness as a new language system. The "language" of many experiences is sensorimotor and therefore does not result in complex symbolization, as in the salt-passing behavior discussed in the previous chapter. The important experiences are the ones which do enter the dialectic and undergo further symbolization. Symbolic objects and persons are experienced as language systems that automatically undergo motivated resymbolizations. The regulating principle for symbolic objects is usually subjective, while the corresponding principle for persons is intersubjective or *negotiative* pursuant to each individual's subjective value of the relationship. A reader's repeated returns to the text are subjectively motivated, while a person's pursuit of a conversation is intersubjectively guided. Although the resymbolization of a text is usually a fully private affair, it is always done in reference to some communal purpose: either the interpretation is a kind of "practicing," based on previous communally derived knowledge, or it is a conscious, active contribution to an ongoing communal effort. Moreover, in childhood, the subjective dialectic is developed from an interpersonal negotiation of language systems; and subsequently, in knowledge-seeking situations, it is governed by analogous, though more complex, sorts of communal negotiation. The activity of reading is therefore always a pedagogical undertaking motivated by the demand for knowledge.

Language systems are always finally related to individuals. For example, while it is possible to read a single poem, and then, say, go swimming, there are two possible results which do not involve forgetting the reading completely. The reading experience may be fully integrated into one's own language system, thereby enlarging or improving it; this effect is real regardless of what activity follows the reading. The poem also may be objectified as a language system. But the only context in which such objectification has meaning is in relation to other work by the same author. The author's literary productions comprise his language system; in fact, any recorded language acts by that author belong to his language system. The explanation of this system is of necessity motivational, insofar as remaining documents can establish such motivation to the satisfaction of the interpreting community. In any case, the symbolic object has no function except in the contexts of either the author's or the readers' language system.

In order to convert reading experiences into knowledge, the pedagogical relationship has to determine what common knowledge the constitutents want. The negotiated establishment of common motives involves an agreement on common items in each person's language system. Suppose, for example, that in Stanley Fish's classes, the constituents agree that line endings are important and that knowledge will be sought by negotiating the perceptions of the line endings. Although such agreement on motives and procedures may seem a small matter to begin with, the ensuing negotiations reveal its complexity; and only the gradual disclosure of perception, response, and interpretation on each reader's part can maintain the discipline of an acknowledged subjectivity that can develop trustworthy knowledge capable of being held in common. The resulting predication that names this knowledge is made up of two elements—the common purpose and the subjective dialectic of each reader. In this case, the predication would be something like "The importance of line endings is the sense of multiple verbal meanings I am able to develop that I would not be aware of if I did not specifically attend to these endings." It could also be "The importance of line endings is that they show me Milton's love of ambiguity," knowledge that would result from the earlier agreement to view the poetry as part of Milton's language system. If such knowledge is reached by Fish's *students*, it was made possible by their having taken over as their own, through respect for Fish the person, an element in his language system. Knowledge may also be reached through more conflictual motives—for example, in opposition to Fish's proposals, or in partial opposition and partial acceptance. In either case, the pedagogical relationship uses interpersonal motives as the groundwork for the development of new knowledge.

I would like to show now in some detail how this principle works in one of the more complex instances I just mentioned, where the motives of both student and teacher were not those of simple agreement and easy respect for one another. The work of the student I am considering did emerge from conflicting motives in regard to the class's purpose, which was to report and study a series of responses to reading experiences. The student did not think he could accept this easily, and thus he did not think he could do the work the course seemed to require. Of particular interest is the fact that the purpose I proposed came out of the pedagogical considerations in the present discussion. Both Mr. P, the student, and I came from the course with new knowledge made possible the negotiations in our relationship.

Mr. P appeared to me an intelligent, personable, well-dressed, mature student. He told me he was in my course because these were his last three credits needed for graduation. He was married, about three years older than most seniors, and he reported that he had an unusually good job waiting for him when he graduated. He had not gone straight through school, but had been out for a few years and had then returned with much increased motivation. After handing in four of the six short essays the course required, Mr. P asked to speak to me about a serious matter that was causing him some worry. It seemed that one of the conditions for his graduation was his receiving all A's in his courses that semester, but in this course he feared, because of justifiable criticisms of his work, that he would get only a B. He believed that getting a B would actually deny him the job he was expecting. According to my usual policy in courses that study response to literature, the response essays are not graded, but each student's work is discussed in class. The stipulation is that students doing all the work with reasonable conscientiousness will get a B, while students who in my judgment, showed some sort of special achievement would receive an A.[1] Mr. P felt he was unable to do any better than he was doing and wanted me to allow him to do extra work in order to insure an A in the course. I told him that it would not be possible to guarantee that grade with more work, but that I would spend extra time with him to solve what he perceived as a serious problem. I also explained to him that I did not think it was fair of him to imply that only a special dispensation from me would determine his graduation and a successful start to his career. Mr. P attended every class, participated fully and sincerely in each, and generally behaved in a spirit of mature good humor.

I had cited Mr. P's first essay as one which impressed me a great deal, and one which, in my view, was a poignant and significant personal statement. I did not have such a high opinion of the subsequent three essays, however, and he agreed that these essays did not reflect the same level of serious self-examination. The difficulty was that he could not, or did not, explain the inconsistency, and he seemed convinced that there was no hope of more satisfying achievement for him in future work. My view of this circumstance now began to include the possibility that Mr. P had not written the first essay by himself and that this could be the cause of his despair.

1. In my monograph *Readings and Feelings* (Urbana, 1975), pp. 105-10, there is a more detailed discussion of this system of evaluation. Essentially, it is a compromise between the existing grading system and the inapplicability of grading in a subjective classroom. Since I am proposing a new activity in the study of literature, most students find it easy to accept my declaration that "it takes this much work to do this job right," where "this much work" is about the same as in other courses. I also get the fewest complaints when I explain my distinctions between what is adequate and excellent as subjectively determined and negotiable, rather than being the result of a uniform application of objective standards.

For the first essay students were to choose one of six topics I had suggested in the concluding section of my short book *Readings and Feelings*. The purpose of the first essay was to explore what each individual considered to be an important feeling in his life. Mr. P. picked the following topic:

Try to remember your earliest feeling of love. Was it directed toward a parent, an animal, a baby sibling, or a food or a toy? When you felt love, then, how would you describe your "loving" behavior? How would you describe your relationship with the beloved object? How much did you have power or authority over what you loved, and how much did it have power over you? How much did you depend on what you loved, and how much did it depend on you? Do you love what you need or need what you love? What is the connection between how you loved as a child and how you love now?[2]

In his essay, Mr. P stuck relatively close to the issues here suggested; many of the questions are specifically answered, and the implicit psychology of the questions is also significantly engaged. In discussing the essay, I will try to understand it both as Mr. P's expression of his feelings about himself and about his relationship to me, the teacher. Here is the essay:

(1) In 19—— I was five years old. That was the year that I started to kindergarten, had my tonsils removed, and discovered my father. He had always been there and yet he had been just another part of my environment that was taken for granted. I still have no recollection of the circumstances surrounding this discovery. I can remember no certain actions or event that triggered these feelings. Even to this day, I don't know why or how it happened but at age five I fell in love with my dad.

(2) I suppose that this love manifested itself in the form of respect and admiration. Suddenly, this man who had just been "around" was the center of my attention. He was the strongest, bravest, smartest, and most handsome man in the world. I must have told this to everybody I knew—except him. I can never remember telling him that I loved him. He must have known, though. Wearing his hat and shoes around the house, pretending to shave, and trying to imitate his pleasantly low voice must have tipped him off.

(3) I don't know that this phenomenon radically changed my behavior. I could still be exceedingly good or exceptionally bad depending on my mood and, of course, whatever the situation called for at that time. However, it was just about this time that I can remember feeling terribly guilty and ashamed at times. This has to have tied in with the respect that I had for my father. The times that I felt the lowest and most ashamed were when I did something that embarrassed him in front of others.

(4) It was about the same time, too, that his way of handling me started to change. Suddenly it was no longer necessary for him to always raise his voice or spank me when I had done something wrong. The clincher was when he would lower his head and just walk away as if there was no hope for me. No

2. Ibid., pp. 98-99.

amount of whippings or evenings spent in the corner hurt quite as much as this did. However, this kind of power that he had suddenly developed over me was a funny thing. It seemed that the more influence his actions had on me, the more mine had on him. I don't think that it took me long to discover this. Even here I emulated him. I got him with his own weapon. Those sad quiet looks worked better than any type of crying or pleading. Today, I compliment myself by saying that the reason for this is because we are so much alike in many ways.

(5) I still don't think that I have ever told my father, point blank, that I love him. However, the older I get, the more I think about it. I look back to more and more memories of days spent with him when I am in need of a happy thought or an encouraging reason to accomplish something. I probably could not count the times that I told him that I wanted to grow up to be just like him. If I told him that today, I am sure that he would tell me to aim higher. I would settle for his height any day. It is foolish to think that the words on this piece of paper could in any way approximate my feelings for my father. However, writing them down makes me look at them with a different perspective. I hope that some day I will get around to telling my dad how much I love him. He must know, though.

That this essay answers my initiating questions comprehensively is one narcissistic reason I liked it, and perhaps why I considered it psychologically authentic. But on the basis of my early perception of Mr. P and my more involved subsequent interactions with him, I feel even more certain of its *psychological* truthfulness. Of special interest is Mr. P's emphasis that the important feeling described at the beginning and at the end of the essay cannot be told.

In a way, the feeling *is* told, but to me instead of the father. Mr. P does say at the end that writing down his feelings affects his attitude toward them. Thus, describing an important early feeling was a contribution to Mr. P's handling of the feeling at present. I, the teacher, was now participating in his emotional life at his invitation. On entering the course, Mr. P suspected that he might need my help in making the transition from college to professional life, and this help was not only in the form of a high grade. It was more significantly sought as a confirmation of the success achieved until that point and as an encouragment for the future. But Mr. P felt he could not come to me, a total stranger, and announce that he needed help because, I think, he felt it would be unmanly to do so. But he could follow my instructions and be like me as much as possible, express his feelings carefully in the "assignment," and thus demonstrate his positive attitude toward our relationship. Just as he shrewdly appeals to his father's self-esteem through imitation and emulation to gain his love and attention, he similarly appealed to me for my professional endorsement. His satisfaction was very great when I cited his essay in class as an excellent example of how to relate one's feelings. Mr. P was able to demonstrate his need for "love" without announcing it explicitly or risking embarrassment through disclosure of his presumed dependency or vulnerability.

Sometimes, I thought I could see that Mr. P was deliberately controlling hostile feelings toward me, not out of compulsion but from a conviction of their inappropriateness, as when I expressed my annoyance at being asked to permit more work for a higher grade. I think the essay also contains a subdued strain of hostility and aggression, but the control of it appears to be much less conscious. Mr. P reports that his behavior could embarrass his father, and this would incur painful punishments, either corporal or psychological. On three occasions in the essay, however, the language suggests a more violent dimension in his feelings for his father. In paragraph 1, he says that he remembers nothing specific that "triggered" his feelings of love. The sentence semantically denies the "triggering" effect, but it metaphorically compares the love feelings to the suddenness of a gunshot. In paragraphs 2 and 4 he describes the change of his perception of his father and his father's new "power" over him as happening suddenly. In paragraph 5, he says, "I still don't think that I have ever told my father, point blank, that I love him." Here, the phrase "point blank," a less ordinary metaphor than "trigger," compares telling his love to shooting, though this time it is Mr. P who is the active party rather than the passive one who was caught by the love earlier. In paragraph 4, Mr. P describes the process of emulation and how he learned to win his father to his own point of view with "sad, quiet looks." He characterizes this emulative technique of persuasion as "I got him with his own weapon." Finally, in the last paragraph, Mr. P reports that if he told his father that he wanted to be just like him, the father "would tell me to aim higher." Such fusillary imagery describes expectable feelings in relationships between fathers and sons, but in this case it seems related—even verbally, as in the "point blank" sentence—to his inhibition about telling his love. Furthermore, a father's telling a son to "aim higher" could be a gesture of love and admiration by the father, or an instruction not to "shoot at" him, or a gesture of self-effacement, or a rejection of the son's excessive admiration, or all or some of these at the same time. I think that for Mr. P in this essay, the first meaning is the main one, while the others are feared or suspected.

Mr. P does not explore the other possibilities on the conscious grounds that he need not confront his father with his feelings because, anyway, Father "must know." He says that he tried to "tell" his father through emulation, but even today, he is still wondering if this is enough. Mr. P describes a relationship in which one of his motives was to tell without articulating directly. I think this was also the classroom motivation in turning in this essay—to tell me his needs, without articulating them directly, by fully cooperating with the class's work. This is one reason I began to think that the essay could represent more "imitation" than is obvious. In the last paragraph, Mr. P says: "It is foolish to think that the words on this piece of paper could in any way approximate my feelings for my father. However, writing them down makes me look at them with a different perspective." I am thinking that they may not approximate his feelings because they are not all his words, but I also believe that regardless of whose words they are, they reliably express Mr. P's classroom motives as well as, probably, a degree of frustration in his relationship with his father. The pedagogically important matter—just in this essay—is my perception of the connection between the words and Mr. P's motivational situation in class.

My perception is this: Mr. P has some aggressive feelings—he would like to be able to just snatch away his A, graduate, and go on to his good new job. At the same time, he wants to earn this achievement; to do it right; to write honestly, learn from the experience, and emulate what he thinks is my ability and authority; and he wants the grade to represent this authentic experience. But the first essay expresses his problem as his impulse to *suppress* his true feelings and *imitate* rather than *announce* the feelings and *emulate*. His solution to the problem—in the essay, again—is the announcement, with a certain degree of aplomb and diplomacy, that the authoritative figure "must know." As the course proceeded, it became clear to Mr. P that I, at least, did not "know," that his fears had to be announced, and that my initiative had to be enlisted.

Other essays in this course, whose authorship I never doubted, contributed to this perception of Mr. P, and further show the kind of knowledge both of us were able to develop from our relationship. Just after Mr. P told me of his problem, he wrote an essay on the most important line in "The Love Song of J. Alfred Prufrock." The line he wrote about was "It is impossible to say just what I mean!" His final comment on the line and on the hero of the poem is this:

Then again he is forced to face the sting of reality. That reality is having so much inside to say but finding it impossible to say what he means. That one line ties the whole poem together for me. He knows what he wants to say and yet he rationalizes that he doesn't. He knows who he wants to address but doesn't because he rationalizes that they will misunderstand what he is trying to say. I suppose each of us has been in this situation at least once in our lives. I cannot imagine how frustrating it would be to feel that way every day of my life. I think I too would want to scream, "It is impossible to say just what I mean!"

In the traditional pedagogical situation, this paragraph would represent an interpretation that others in the class could test for truth. The issue would be whether the poem is "about" a man who does not know how to say what he means. But viewing the paragraph also as a subjective expression gives us a sense of its authority. I think that one important experience which authorized this judgment of the poem was the conversation with me in which Mr. P felt as he now sees Prufrock feeling: he felt misunderstood, especially when I implied, through my somewhat impatient tones, that it was not ethical to request special treatment just to secure an A. What he "meant" was that he only wanted to finish this course and achieve excellence in an honest way. I think he felt it "impossible" to express his fear of the consequences if this did not happen. In Mr. P's first essay, he rationalized not telling his father because "he must know." In this essay, he sees the exclamation of inarticulability as itself a rationalization, and he expresses relief that he does not feel this way very often. Therefore, the motive for the knowledge about the poem in this paragraph is similar to the motive for the first essay, but now there is an additional classroom experience that has made the first motive more immediate and given it a new form: there was a personal frustration in negotiating his relationship with me pursuant to his larger motivation in the course. His emotional inhibition and the inhibition of his language system are identical. Yet, when his attention is on the poem, he is able to articulate a statement that exactly expresses his own feelings about himself at the time of writing. By assimilating the reading experience to his own language system, he is able to reduce his frustration through articulation of his knowledge of "the poem."

Earlier in the course, Mr. P wrote an affective response to Yeats's poem "Crazy Jane Talks with the Bishop." He speculates that perhaps it is the bishop who is "crazy." He considers, though, that this may not be so, because the bishop "obviously did not reach his level of professional achievement without a certain degree of shrewdness." He then characterizes the bishop as trying to con Jane into sexual submission. He understands her as a whore but admires her because "the only thing she has left is her professional self-esteem"; she has "wisdom in her heart" and "even in spite of her wretched condition, she does not compromise her values." Both the bishop and Jane are "professionals." Because the bishop is professionally successful, he must be shrewd; Jane's uncompromising stand is also related to her professional self-esteem. Both remain, however, shady characters. If there is success, there must have been shrewdness; if there is integrity, the profession itself is corrupt. Because this reading considerably enlarges the poem's verbal meaning, I consider Mr. P's view imaginative. The source of his view was his personal preoccupation with his own ethical values in his professional undertakings—one of which was his work in this class. Jane is his heroine (a familiar interpretation of this poem), but in the special terms that he defines (a highly unique interpretation). Again, Mr. P created knowledge by assimilating his reading to the motivational shape of his language system at the time.

Mr. P's final essay in the course immediately followed the "Prufrock" essay and was written while he was still uncertain of my ultimate evaluation of his work. Mr. P wrote about what he thought was the most important aspect of Henry James's *The Aspern Papers*. This is his third paragraph:

> What causes us to compromise our values? If this question could be answered, life would be a lot less complicated because we would know our limits and be able to deal more rationally with the different stimuli that weave in and out of our lives. Unfortunately, the question cannot be answered because different things and events affect us differently at various times. It has been shown that even the most respected people among us are subject to this flaw in our makeup.

In his concluding paragraph, he writes:

> This [the compromise of values] is not an unusual theme in either literature or in everyday life. The story brings to mind times that I have compromised my values to gain personal ends. However, just as important as the actions taken by the characters and the motives behind those actions is the ending to the story. Each one compromised values they knew to be correct and good and each one lost. I think this is pretty much true of life.

Mr. P synthesized a moral meaning for James's tale. Without giving particulars, he reports that there is a personal dimension to this meaning. Mr. P also knew that I would be the principal reader of this essay; therefore, it is a communication to me of his personal and literary knowledge in the same statement. It is hard for me to avoid seeing something confessional here, especially in the second sentence of the last paragraph. But here, too, there is a rationalization: the "most respected people" are vulnerable to this "flaw in our makeup." This is a common rationalization younger people use when they try to do something they know in advance is "wrong:" "You parents and teachers do it; why shouldn't we?" In fact, part of the motive for such behaviors is emulative; it is as much a means of identification as rebellion. Mr. P's final knowledge of the story, as of the principle, is that "each one lost" when he compromised his values.

I obviously do not know what took place in Mr. P's mind in this latter part of the course; I only know that part of him that participated in a relationship with me and the rest of the class of seven students. Yet if his work, and the various pieces of knowledge that constitute it, is understood as a response to a pedagogical relationship, it is also possible to discern motives at work in the formulation of knowledge. Attention to these motives lessens the importance of what might otherwise be an inflammatory situation—my doubt about the authorship of the first essay—for my knowledge of our mutual motives would be much the same regardless of the authorship, whose historicity, like the exact factual past of a patient in therapy, or the exact cause of a dream, is a matter secondary to the productive handling of an ongoing relationship. A relationship defines a purpose, and a purpose defines a relationship. I think, in this relationship, Mr. P developed knowledge of his reading experiences, while I developed knowledge of my teaching experiences.

For reasons associated with the epistemological issues I have already discussed, it is difficult for most current pedagogical relationships to include mutual awareness of motives in the development of knowledge. No doubt, the development of such awareness would involve significant changes in the relationships and in the institutions which make them possible. While I believe these changes are necessary in view of the new sorts of knowledge we seek, I also think that most existing pedagogical situations can accommodate the changes without a revolutionary impetus to feverishly destroy the old and establish the new. In many ways, my relationship with Mr. P was a traditional one for a university community. The main pragmatic differences between my pedagogical relationships in this course and those usually occupying a college classroom were this course's announced purpose of studying subjective factors in literary interpretation and its regular conversion of essay assignments into *response statements*. How these documents were solicited, written, and negotiated in class enacted the principles I have heretofore explored, suggests the pedagogical basis for the formulation of interpretive knowledge, and represents the main pragmatic contribution of subjective criticism.

Knowledge in the subjective classroom is finally presented in fairly traditional forms—as *judgments*, a term which attaches the element of decision to acts of interpretation. The context, however, in which judgments are reached, is quite untraditional, in that the response statement, in addition to the unrecorded reading experience, is consciously used in the ideation which leads to the judgment. Which judgment is to be sought may be decided at any time during the response process, though usually, in a named course, one decides in advance the type of knowledge proposed, whether interpretation, historical significance, or generic status. In either case, it is an entirely different procedure to embark in search of a judgment without an intervening response statement than with it. It is a new sort of mental act to interpose the response into the more familiar procedures for reaching a judgment. Nevertheless, this form of interposition is necessary in order to make an interpretive judgment at all authoritative. The nature of the resulting judgments will be different from what they have been even though the principle of making judgments is retained.

Most of the rationale for this procedure has already been presented: the response, not the text, is the symbol that the interpretation resymbolizes. It remains to discuss how the *recording* of the response is a useful and emotionally honest way of dealing with response in a class or other community. For example, it is not obvious just how Mr. P's various statements are to be construed, relative to his motives. A written response is different from a transcribed spoken response, which, in turn, is different from, say, a videotape of a response conversation that is not otherwise transcribed. Each means of recording response requires its own contextual justification, which is derived from the motives and possibilities of the pedagogical relationship. I will confine my discussion to explaining the purpose and use of the written, essay-length response statement. Subsequently, I will suggest how the statements may be used in the formulation of judgments.

A response statement aims to record the perception of a reading experience and its natural, spontaneous consequences, among which are feelings, or affects, and peremptory memories and thoughts, or free associations. While other forms of mentation may be considered "natural and spontaneous," they would not be so in this context. Recording a response requires the relaxation of cultivated analytical habits, especially the habit of automatic objectification of the work of literature. When this is done, we become aware of what we know happens anyway—an affective evaluation that accompanies perception. Normally, the act of objectification inhibits awareness of response in the service of continuing to read. But to the extent that we decide to become aware of our response, the reading might be interrupted in the service of recording knowledge of our experience. These pauses are similar to a child's interruptions during storytelling. And just as the child's sense of the story is enhanced by the interposed commentary, so our own sense of the reading experience is more fully anchored in our self-awareness. At the same time, it is not necessary to interrupt the reading to record the response, and we may just as soon wait until the reading is completed and then record what we remember as moments of special attention. Whether we interrupt our reading is less important than deliberately becoming conscious of the affective evaluations that mark the reading either in experience or in memory. Essentially, the response statement tries to objectify, to ourselves and then to our community, the affective-perceptual experience, rather than the story.

The recording of a perception with just that aim in mind will not appear affective or evaluative even though the mere linguistic translation implies a change in those directions. If a whole series of perceptions is recorded, however, it will become clear that the mere selection of textual features to note represents at least an affective evaluation, but in any case stands for "the story *I* read." Admittedly, the actual reading experience is as unsusceptible of recording as the actual dream; neither can an actual memory be recorded. The record of such a memory is inevitably a symbolization of it, and there is no choice but to allow that the bringing of a reading experience under conscious scrutiny requires its translation into verbal language. Therefore, it is possible to argue that the recorded perception of the story does not correspond to the experiential perception. But at this pass, the defining authority of the pedagogical relationship will *declare* that the recorded perception will be communally objectified as "the story this reader read," with the proviso that the reader may subsequently revise or otherwise alter "his story." There is no other practical way to share a perception with others except to tell what the perception is. Furthermore, language has its maximum authority in its presentation of the mind of the user. Therefore, if ordinary language is to be used at all in the study of itself and literature, the starting point has to be the speaker's (reader's) presentation of his experience, the most rudimentary form of which is the perception.

When language is used denotatively—in this case, to report perception—we are not usually aware of its evaluative or affective cast. But the mere review of what we have said will make us aware of the feeling animating our statement. For example, if I remark, "Look at that big boat," and then stop and consider my remark, I become aware that I *like* the boat's size and that this probably motivated my statement to begin with. The new awareness coming from the review is now part of my response, so that I now know my response and can report it in addition to just having it. In the same way the affective evaluation of any perceived literary unit can be observed and recorded. Our peceptual disposition determines whether we see a character, a scene, a paragraph, or a word; but in each instance it is possible to know what we see and how we feel about it. The act of articulating a perception creates a motive to articulate the motivating feeling. The aggregate of these feelings constitutes the affective component of the response statement and, like the series of perceptions, becomes another subjective perspective on the reading experience.

While each reader may be able to share the idea of jealousy as an affect, its meaning in the language system of each is different. The meanings of commonly held words necessarily vary from person to person. For example, for a person growing up in a family of many siblings, the meaning of jealousy may have been developed from the problems of dealing with these peers, while for someone growing up as an only child, its meaning was more likely determined through relationships with the parents or other adults. Because the word *jealousy* is common to both of these people, it is easy to assume that the word "means" the same thing to both. Yet there is good reason to suppose that although a language is shared by a great many people, every individual has his own idosyncratic language system determined by the relationships in which his language developed. By allowing peremptory memories and thoughts to enter our minds in response to our having named a feeling, the private etymologies of these feelings are brought to consciousness.

The cultivation of formal "expository" discourse habituates young people into articulating only "objective" meanings—that is, meanings that have no reference to particulars, the best instance of which is dictionary definitions. Regardless of the formulaic meanings a person may know for a word, the one that carries the most weight in his own language system is defined either by his having heard the word in important interpersonal contexts or by his having used the word in such contexts. Even dictionary definitions first attain certitude in our minds when we recall familiar circumstances in which the word applies; this recollection is the effort to integrate the new word into our subjective language system. Conversely, the dictionary is consulted when authoritative support is sought for personal meanings. The functional meaning of a word is rarely the dictionary definition, which is almost always invoked as the solution when a dispute had originally posed it as the problem. Any time a word is used anew, there is a slightly new meaning for it; and in many instances, a major new meaning is being proposed. Insofar as the shared meaning of a word is not a matter of attention, it has little functional meaning; when the functional meaning is a matter of serious attention, as it is in a response statement, it is necessary to record the subjective etymology of the words—in this case, of the affects that are named.

The relative ease with which affects are noted or identified is due to the emotional importance of the situations in which they are first learned. For example, a child may habitually try to throw his baby sibling out of the crib; it is possible to say that, undoubtedly, this child feels jealous. But the child cannot identify his feeling until someone else tells him that he must be feeling "jealous." Thus, not only did the *feeling* originate in an interpersonal situation, but the *knowledge of that feeling* began in one also. As the number of occasions in which the word may be applied increases, the normal capacity for objectification makes the word seem an abstraction one of whose purposes is to develop a *sense* of linguistic autonomy identical with the sense of personal autonomy or self-awareness. The subjective construction of that meaning is thereby removed from consciousness just because the mind cannot function if it is aware of everything at once. But when the word appears in a motivated context defined by the writing of the response statement, the subjective definition needs to be disclosed in order to fully identify one's response to the reading experience.

It is not obvious that peremptory memories and thoughts following the recording of an affective response are the subjective definition of that response. If the associations are actually free, any number of them can appear in one's mind, and many of these thoughts appear unrelated to the affect under scrutiny. However, the mental act initiating free association is not prescriptive; it is only an attempt to abandon customary habits of abstractive definition and replace them with a relaxed imagination. Functionally, this means that the familiar social constraints of conversation are revoked and one can say what one thinks without censorship of ordinary ethical deportment. Presumably, when one is talking to oneself, there is no need to save or make "face." On the other hand, unless an unconscious mind with motives of its own is assumed, the freely given thoughts are not necessarily related to the affect. Therefore, the only other way to use these thoughts is just the way they are used in dream interpretation, as I discussed in Chapter Three. When the thoughts appear, the conscious mind will test through simple acts of memory to see if the new thoughts do symbolize the named feeling. A subjective dialectic is begun in order to resymbolize the affect in terms of its perceived historical role in personality. The germane associations will be the ones which the respondent feels best define the feeling. If both affect and the language that expresses it originate in interpersonal relationships, as I claim they do, the associations will name these relationships and

3. For some time in the past, it had been a matter of dispute between Norman Holland and me whether associations which allude to relationships are more germane in the study of response than others, regardless of their content. He had suggested, following the psychoanalytic tradition, that all associations were equally germane. But in transferring his thinking to a pedagogical context, he changed his mind and followed the logic I have just outlined—namely, he urged his students to "try . . . for three things: feelings, associations, persons" ("The Delphi Seminar," *College English*, 36, No. 7 March 1975), 790). The instruction alone is inadequate, however, if the principle of explanation continues to be identity themes, since they cannot be determined in a pedagogical situation and apply mainly to long-term clinical relationships, if at all.

This issue is related to a danger in subjective criticism I discussed in *Readings and Feelings* (pp. 12-13). That is, any inquiry into personality poses the risk of clinically articulated intrusions into personality. To reduce this risk, I have drawn an important distinction between the negotiation of a *particular response statement* into knowledge and the analysis of response based on a purportedly full or general conception of the reader's personality. The latter technique, which the use of the identity theme presupposes, is altogether clinical and, in my judgment, inappropriate as well as inapplicable in the thus complete the subjective definition of the affect.[3]

The fundamental act in the recording of response is shifting the mind's objectifying capacity from the symbolic object to one's self, the subject. Relative to the community in which this act takes place, the knowledge represented by the statement is private, in that it is a reader's knowledge of his response. But the synthesizing of communal knowledge cannot begin without the substrate of individual subjective knowledge. Within the pedagogical relationship, the response statement is negotiated with the commonly agreed-upon purpose. For each responding individual, the purpose is the opening topic, which, when placed in context with the person's subjective comment, is the predication that constitutes the new knowledge. For example, a traditional judgment of meaning, presented as a proposal of knowledge would be of this form: "The meaning of *Hamlet* is that man must learn when to think and when to act." The subject of the sentence, the topic, is the purpose, namely, to think of *Hamlet* as "meaning" something. This particular critic translates *meaning* into a statement of the form "man must . . ."—that is, a moral precept. Which moral precept the critic develops comes from his resymbolization of his response—or the community's resymbolization of it with him—which is then joined in the predicative relationship with the original topic to form a new piece of knowledge that the community again has to validate. If the knowledge is considered objective, this process is trivialized: to wit, the teacher *says* whether the interpretation is good or bad, right or wrong, and assigns a grade accordingly. This is the same process as the negotiative one I am suggesting, except that the rules of the negotiation are defined by the preestablished authority of the teacher to pass judgment and to give grades as a consequence. Often the linkage of ordained authority with objective knowledge is so strong that a teacher feels he need not give reasons for his evaluation of a judgment: the *authority* is automatically objective, which is authoritarianism. But if the knowledge is not objective, then the authority cannot be objective, and the communal negotiation may proceed on the grounds of each constituent's response-and-resymbolization efforts. Even after a negotiation is completed, though, the final knowledge is only a judgment, whose authority may grow or diminish depending on how the judgment fares in ever-larger communities.

---

classroom, even though I may trust the clinical competence of the teacher. One of the functional issues in any classroom, to begin with, is the extent to which a student *wishes* to engage his personality in the group, as well as the kind of engagement he seeks. The classroom seeks to develop a certain part of the personality to synthesize a new element of self-awareness, and to work, thereby, with what the reader is willing to contribute, and not with a preestablished, fixed conception of personality.

There are two important advantages—one local and one general—to conceiving knowledge as a negotiated judgment rather than an ordained law. The local one is that a negotiated judgment facilitates full personal involvement in the development of knowledge, and small classes and communities need not feel overborne by such authoritarian truth-making establishments as "the critics." The general advantage is the abiding understanding that no knowledge is absolute, no matter how it is formulated. The concept of gravity has, to me, a distinctly different character if I think of the *fact* of gravity rather than the *law* of gravity. Awareness of the adaptational function of knowledge provides a natural means of deciding which knowledge to seek, as opposed to seeking knowledge "for its own sake." "Laws" of nature and God have the same origin and purpose as laws issued by kings or enacted by legislatures—to provide a stable framework for social functioning. Just as legislation has increasingly shifted to communal contexts, the establishment of reliable cognitive regularities is a matter for pedagogical communities to judge rather than for designated authorities to declare.

If the pedagogical development of knowledge is founded on the conscious search for judgments, the prior question has to concern the grounds for deciding what each person, class, or community wants to know or explain. In one sense, any established discipline of knowledge already reflects what various communities wanted to know. But if the development of knowledge is paradigmatically determined, the nature of the search for knowledge changes within a new paradigm. To understand criticism—the study of language and literature—in the framework of the subjective paradigm requires a translation of existing forms of knowledge, like the translation of the swinging stone into the pendulum, and a definition of grounds from which new questions are posed.

Over the past ten years or so, in my work collecting response statements in classrooms and other informal groups, and then negotiating these statements from various standpoints, I have recast familiar areas of literary inquiry into four contexts for reaching subjectively based judgments. Although each of these contexts may represent an independent inquiry, most interpretive and/or critical questions involve combining two or more of these contexts in the formulation of the judgmental purpose. The contexts, or general cognitive purposes, are (1) judgments of taste and of changes in taste; (2) judgments of meaning (in Hirsch's term, "significance"); (3) judgments of the author as a historical figure and as a symbolized one in the reading experience; (4) judgments of common interests and the classification of texts.

JUDGMENTS OF TASTE AND CHANGES IN TASTE

An act of taste is a more consequential form of a local value judgment. I had earlier discussed how evaluation is a natural and automatic feature of perception and is especially prominent in the perception of symbolic objects. When such an evaluation is rearticulated with the purpose of making it public—that is, within a pedagogical relationship—it becomes a judgment of taste. Whenever such judgments come under extended scrutiny, however, they appear to be seriously problematical, with the difficulty growing from how we should understand their authority. If the judgments are considered purely personal, they are therefore "only" subjective and have little claim on anyone else's belief; if they are judgments of the "objective value" of the work of literature, there are no objective standards to prove this value. It seems that, ultimately, only the personal reputation of the critic can create authority for a judgment of literary taste.

In *Principles of Literary Criticism*, I. A. Richards acknowledges these dimensions to the problem, as I outlined in Chapter One. His solution, while not announced as such, is subjective, namely, that the critic's social function is to be declared by the community as a judge of good and bad in literature. But because Richards does not think of this solution as subjective, he is forced to claim that experts in matters of taste are in better psychological condition than everyone else; good critics and good authors may each boast psychic economies which have minimized "waste" and have thereby maximized both expressive and communicative capabilities.[4] The objective standard of value has switched from the work to the critic or author.

In conceiving a judgment of taste subjectively, the elements of personality which are adduced in that judgment are taken as explanatory rather than authoritative. The act of taste is first understood as a declaration of personal preference: the previously implicit statement of any value judgment—"I like this"—is made public. This feeling will always appear as part of the response statement and is elaborated by the associations. The intersubjective motive for rearticulating this response in the form of a judgment is to *identify oneself literarily* to one's community. Any discussion of literary value cannot proceed unless the readers articulate and document the value perspective in which they are reading on that occasion. At the same time, to say simply, "These are the books I like, and these I don't like," does not authorize one's taste—it only announces it; but to include response statements to particular works which define one's

4. I. A. Richards, *Principles of Literary Criticism* (1925; rpt. New York, n. d.), p. 52. Particularly, the idea of waste refers to either excessive self-discipline or excessive indulgence in terms of pursuing the satisfaction of appetencies.

taste is to provide consequential personal explanation for the configuration of taste at that time.

As elements of communal self-knowledge, judgments of taste are not easily arrived at. It is possible, for example, for each member of a class to submit and document his taste for a single work of literature. That class will then have at its disposal a variety of subjective authorizations for new judgments that each member might want to make. Yet if the class wants to conceive its taste as a group, a new inquiry has to be undertaken. (I will further discuss such inquiries under "Common Interests and the Classification of Authors and Texts.") Meanwhile, if the idea of personal taste is to have consequence within the self-concept of the reader, he needs to investigate a series of readings and responses in order to understand taste in terms of ranges and values; an important validation of one's taste for one particular work is knowledge of one's taste for other works. The authority for any individual judgment of taste is increased to the extent that it is part of a knowledge of one's *range of tastes.*

Furthermore, because one is always growing and changing, the range of taste is even more fully defined relative to earlier tastes, say, during childhood, adolescence, or youth. For most people, knowledge of these tastes can come only through memory or through interrogation of parents or siblings. Yet almost every reader will well remember a book from childhood, the circumstance of its reading, and the atmosphere it represented in his mind. Although it is probably not possible to recover original historical circumstances, if the memory of such events has lasted, such residues have important truth value and demonstrable relevance to current, conscious tastes. In pursuit of childhood tastes, the peremptory associations brought forth in the response statements can bring insight out of their original context. Through the reader's interest in knowing his change of taste, the investigation of his personal and interpersonal history becomes part of the pedagogical task, but in terms of ordinary self-enlightenment rather than in terms of therapy, cure, or moral sanitation.[5]

---

5. The conception of children's literature usually taught to prospective elementary-school teachers is tied to principles of moral sanitation. Such courses, which have been taught at my university for a long time, suggest that criteria of whether a book is good or bad for the child are more important than whether the child will like the book or not. At the same time, many surrounding communities strongly support such approaches with lists of censored children's books. Obviously, these coercive moral preoccupations are no different from those in academic criticism, and the source of the criteria is, again, the traditional religious alliance between objectivity and moral authority. Although the problems of teaching children's literature require a detailed discussion, I can now claim that if the subject is taught from considerations of taste and, especially, the nature of the child's changes of taste, it begins to look like a new subject altogether. Most enlightened colleges of education offer many courses on child development. Rarely are such courses systematically linked to the study of children's literature, though it reflects the

Tastes also change much more locally than in long-range comparison to those of one's childhood and youth. In classroom situations, tastes almost always change under the influence of knowledge derived from the extended pedagogical relationships. It is of interest to any reader to know how his reading attitude has changed after spending time with a particular teacher. Again, this cannot be done by announcement: the responses in the first part of a course can be compared with those, perhaps to the same works, in the last part. Both the terms of taste and the judgments of taste probably have changed. Personal experiences have intervened; instead of these experiences being brought forth at the end of the semester as excuses for poor performances on final examinations or late essays, they may be productively seen, in subjective classrooms, as either contributors to, or inhibitors of, the development of new knowledge. In principle, any period of time may be set aside as a framework for the study of the change in taste, depending on the kind of knowledge that is sought. It is just as important to learn how and why one's taste changes as it is to know the range of taste at any moment. But unless either sort of knowledge is pursued deliberately through response statements and communally negotiated judgments, the claimed knowledge will have neither authority nor explanatory power.

In proposing a series of pedagogical contexts for the extended study of taste, subjective criticism tries to parlay natural evaluative habits into occasions for knowledge. These occasions require the same dimensions of attention as more traditional school subjects—extensive preparation by the teachers, curricular open-endedness, background readings of prevailing thought, especially work in personality development and relevant psychologies, but most of all, belief in the importance of such knowledge to oneself.[6] If it is unimportant to each reader to understand his taste, there is no point in pursuing these activities, for

---

characteristic concerns of each developmental phase in childhood. If one observes how children choose books and how they respond to the books they choose, and relates these responses to the known psychological preoccupations of their developmental stage, it is easier to understand the connections between subjectivity and taste than if one makes similar observations of an adult. Yet, the principles of taste development are the same in child and adult. From the nursery on, the exercise of taste, when it is not used as an occasion for moral suasion, is a rudimentary pedagogical impulse. I will discuss this matter further in the second part of Chapter Seven.

6. The continued widespread use of Dr. Spock's book on baby and child care shows that most people's psychological awareness does not come from years of course work, though it is necessary to inform oneself about current thinking in child development. Mothers understand what Spock says because they are highly motivated: the demands of the child have to be met immediately. The habitual demands of an infant produce habitual understanding of the possibilities of what these demands might be, even though each demand is signalled in the same way—by crying. In this way, mothers are motivated to understand, in general, their own motherhood. The same motivational logic applies to the study of taste: one is naturally motivated to understand one's own tastes.

they are curricular in scope—they are not just a local unit or an activity to provide spark for dull classrooms. If the importance of taste and its change is accepted, there is enough latitude for classes of many orientations and persuasions to decide for themselves how their own tastes may be defined and understood.

### JUDGMENTS OF MEANING OR SIGNIFICANCE

A judgment of meaning is an act of interpretation governed by a social or pedagogical motive. In discussing the logic of interpretation in Chapter Three, I emphasized its subjective motivation and its spontaneous appearance in the routine handling of symbolic material. An interpretation is judgmental when it functions as intersubjectively developed knowledge. When judgments of meaning are purely explicatory—that is, unrelated to an independent system of thought like Marxism, psychoanalysis, or structuralism—they assume a moral character. The text is conceptualized as a Biblical sort of repository, where the interpreter applies his own subjective standards of right and wrong in human affairs. Consider the following instances of explicatory meanings given by senior undergraduate students for D. H. Lawrence's *Lady Chatterley's Lover:*

(1) The only meaning I can get out of this novel is that the only way to escape the pressures of society and petty life is through complete love. Lawrence gave an ugly view of the rest of the world. The only beauty that was in the novel was when Mellors and Connie were together in the hut. When you get right down to it, man's attempt to better his society always fails. He is at his best just in the act of love. . . . Here is the only beauty in life.

(2) The book shows the finding of sensuality that is more than mere sensuality, though I won't call it love, in a very sterile world. The world of the passions finds a place in the world of cold intellectuality. Connie goes through stages of trying to maintain intimacy in different ways, coming to the ultimate conclusion that tenderness is best.

(3) In *Lady Chatterley's Lover*, Lawrence seems to be proposing his theory of how to save man from his concern with materialism. Lawrence feels that man is heading for his own destruction because of his desire for money and success—the bitch goddess. He hated cold lovemaking. Although I like his attitude toward sex, I don't see how Lawrence thinks that this will save the world and man from destruction.

(4) Man's only salvation is in what is left of his instincts, his passions. For a woman to experience the fullness of being woman she must not deny herself the same pleasures as man, but her role is a passive and submissive one.

(5) Although "men despise the intercourse act, and yet do it," (i.e., despise themselves for being such insistent, insatiable, dog-like beasts), there remains a ray of hope that man will be able to accept himself as such a beast and still let the spiritual oneness of two lovers follow its natural course notwithstanding.

The hope rests on the fact that neither exceptional lover attached societal values to his actions. They merely let their own hearts guide them. Mellors's final letter to Constance suggests that there will be a real, honest, and lasting love between them either because of in spite of their sexual relationship.[7]

In traditional pedagogical situations, such statements are tested for their degree of correspondence with the "text as objectively perceived." This is possible because all members of the community with an explicatory purpose tacitly accept that any explication will uncover a text's moral imperative. Frequently, this imperative is assumed to be identical with the author's presumed intention to tell the rest of the world how to live. I will discuss such attributions briefly in this chapter and in some detail in Chapter Nine, so let me now only call attention to the moral flavor of the meanings proposed by these five respondents.[8]

If these statements are conceived as objective meanings—in the dictionary sense—Lawrence's novel is to be understood as an allegory of salvation. Perhaps man will be saved from society through "his instincts, his passions," or man is "at his best . . . in the act of love," or "tenderness is best." Similarly the world is headed for destruction, or there is a destructive world of cold intellectuality or a "very sterile world" outside sensuality. It is not obvious to me that a story about Connie Chatterley and Oliver Mellors in England can be unequivocally translated into an allegory of man in the world. But in the absence of any other preannounced language of interpretation, this moral language expresses "meaning," or something more or larger or greater than the particulars of the reading experiences. While I may be able to translate each of these meanings into the particulars of my reading experience, I also observe that respondent 1 speaks of bettering society; respondent 2, of combatting "cold intellectuality"; respondent 3 of overcoming materialism; respondent 4 of the sexual roles of men

7. These respondents were seniors at Indiana University participating in a seminar in the study of response. In a project to understand what ordinary critical meaning is, I asked the students to write down a meaning for this novel, as they understood *meaning* from their previous study of literature. No other instructions were given.

8. Some will probably suggest, in reading these meanings, that their moral cast is proof that Lawrence's work has, objectively, a moral cast. Insofar as many in our community do think this about Lawrence, I suppose these statements can be *viewed* as proofs. It depends on what we would like to know. I would like to know how readers propose meanings in our interpretive community. So I compare these meanings to other interpretive works I read, classroom lectures in graduate school, and hundreds of statements by authoritative critics and scholars. In my experience, the resemblance between these five statements and the hundreds of critical meanings is more important than the correspondence between the moral statements in the meanings and *someone else's claim* that Lawrence's work has this moral cast. Furthermore, I may propose another subjective context that will test, through my response, whether   Lawrence's novel has meanings related to the salvation of man. But this is another issue. Now I am exploring whether meanings are proposed in this moral way.

and women; and respondent 5, of overcoming one's own sense of bestiality. These are different perceptions, different concerns, different language systems, from my own and from that in the novel. Yet in no instance do these meanings report the particulars of the reading experiences which led to the meanings. At the same time, there was no announced pedagogical purpose of formulating the respective reading experiences in moral terms. Rather, the purpose was only to state a meaning, as each reader understood the term. While individual moralities differ from reader to reader, the tendency to announce interpretive judgments in moral terms is probably a cultural habit, enforced by traditional pedagogy and ratified by the link between religious thought and objectivity I discussed in the Introduction and in Chapter One. One need only survey modern New Criticism to verify the moral tendentiousness of the presumably context-free explications of literature.

In subjective criticism, morally formulated explication is one possible pedagogical purpose—or, in Fish's language, one possible interpretive strategy. By deciding on such a purpose in common and in advance, and by then pursuing this purpose in dialectic with the response statement, the knowledge developed is understood as one sort among many likely interests of each reader. In this frame of mind, the meanings will lose their homiletic character, in consequence of the recognition that moralities vary from reader to reader. The ethical precepts formulated from the dialectic between the reading experience and one's own life experience represent genuine, usable, consequential knowledge, as opposed to ritual locutions or sanctimonious declarations of having discovered the true moral purpose of the author.

Judgments deriving from other purposes—say, the needs to view literature from Marxist or structuralist perspectives—similarly gain an explanatory dimension when they are articulated in conjunction with a response statement. Used without response, they are always vulnerable to dismissal as the formulaic application of received dogma to literature. A response statement particularizes known systems of thought and gives a motivational ground to a particular reader's understanding and use of that system. For example, because of the personal background given by Frederick C. Crews in his discussions of psychoanalytic criticism, I can understand the sort of authority he sees in it and claims for it, and I can understand his use of it far better than I could before he gave this background in his recent book.[9] Few critics

---

9. Frederick C. Crews, *Out of My System* (New York, 1975). I appreciate Crews's candid announcement that this book represents his continuing intellectual struggle between "rebellion and caution" (p. xiv). This personal dimension in his study allows me to view more sympathetically his effort as an attempt to distinguish between a point of view and a dogma.

have taken the trouble to discuss, as Crews has, the origins and growth of their intellectual views. In a pedagogical situation, the response statement establishes a regular social forum for including the motivational substrate of interpretive judgments about language and literature.

Because literature is a symbolic object, its normal function is to create interpretive occasions: there is no such thing as an autonomous literary work. Any discussion of literature will assume a standard for translating the work into "meaning." From the standpoint of subjective criticism, no existing standards are necessarily right or wrong, and the question of their absolute correctness is irrelevant because the response statement is a means for personal and communal validation of standards at the time of use. Both the interpretive judgments and their criteria of viability are intersubjectively renegotiated when they are proposed anew. Established knowledge, in this context, is communicated in conjunction with its paradigmatic framework and is itself implicitly available for renegotiation. This may mean that interpretive knowledge is less stable than knowledge in general was heretofore conceived. Yet unless the stabilizing machinery rests unambiguously and self-consciously in the community of students, the knowledge is idle and of no consequence.

### JUDGMENTS OF REAL AND SYMBOLIZED AUTHORS

As I have suggested in my discussions of Richards, Freud, Hirsch, and Harding, any reading experience, at some points, in some degrees at least, is marked by the reader's feeling of communicative involvement with the author. Many people are originally motivated to read by the desire to immerse themselves in what they consider important literary and emotional authority; many reading experiences are spontaneously oriented perceptually around "what the author is saying." When knowledge is proposed on the basis of such perceptions, the grounds on which the reader symbolizes the author are susceptible to easy dispute. Sometimes the reader's image of the author is based entirely on his reading, while at other times it is based on the reading combined with communally accepted and biographical information. While it may seem like common sense to carefully separate in our minds biographical facts from perceptual inference, most criticism, as a matter of course, formulates interpretive judgments and other types of knowledge as if they were deliberately intended by the author, as respondent 3 above does—"Lawrence feels," "Shakespeare is telling us that," "Milton believes," and so on. The subjective perspective suggests a wider rationale for understanding such usages and for allowing them more commanding claims on our belief.

A symbolic object becomes meaningful when it is understood from any subjective viewpoint or language system. The reader has one language system and the author another; the object is also meaningful with reference to the language system of a specified community past and present, and I will discuss this situation shortly in this chapter and in some detail in Chapter Ten. On the stipulation that an author's language system may be assumed because the author is or was once a real person (a subject), a community may then seek meaning in the relationship between a text and the author's language system as it is manifested in his biography and in the rest of his work. Although the authority of such meanings is rooted in the community which synthesizes them, the relationship between a text and its author's language system may be understood, consistent with the subjective paradigm, as an objectification motivated by the demand for that kind of knowledge: readers would like to know, to one degree or another, how and why this author wrote this work at this time. This demand is analogous to the common interpersonal demand to account for one's behavior in important matters. In meeting the literary demand, however, we shall always have to rely on facts determined probabalistically and by consensus, as Hirsch discusses in his treatise.[10]

Thus circumscribed, biographical criticism is an integral part of subjective criticism. If the concept of the "author's intention" is taken seriously, and is not viewed as something easily inferred from perusal of the text, it can be understood as motivation (as discussed in Chapters Two and Three); and the work may be conceived as a highly complex predication which came about as a result of the author's effort to enlarge or consolidate his sense of self at that moment and at that developmental phase of his life. Admittedly, such knowledge will never be available about many authors because the most relevant documentation is either lost, destroyed, or never existed to begin with. For many others, however, especially those more nearly our contemporaries, biographical investigation has proved extremely enlightening. Often, the simple accumulation of rudimentary facts— marital history, parental difficulties, financial dealings, travels, personal illnesses and habits—has placed major individual works in a new and credible motivational perspective. As long as such knowledge is understood to be probable and tentative, it has the salutary function of extending inquiry and discussion. For some authors, like Henry James and Hart Crane, so much biographical material is available that, at least for me, biographical understanding becomes the starting point for response, interpretation, and other forms of literary pedagogy. To assume only that an author "intended" what he wrote may make sense,

10. E. D. Hirsch, *Validity in Interpretation* New  Haven, 1967), pp. 173-207. I have discussed the epistemological difficulties in this viewpoint in Chapter Three.

but intention is then understood differently by each reader. Yet if biographical material is presented as what is now believed to have motivated this author to write this text, the initial acts of perception and response are that much more integrated with the natural communal interest in the motives that it can associate with the symbolic object.

It may seem that the pursuit of biographical fact proceeds independently of response. The sheer disclosure of documents and information need not be tied to a reading motive; however, it is obviously related to other sorts of motives deriving from the nature of the biographer's membership in his interpretive community. This membership, in turn, derives from the biographer's biography, but more particularly in the present consideration, from the biographer's attraction to his subject. Leon Edel is given to characterizing his efforts as "detective work,"[11] and, as I have detailed in *Readings and Feelings*, I felt able to overtake his sense of his work, translate this sense as applying to James in his work and then resymbolize it as applying to me and my work. Reading, pedagogy, and biographical research have greatly enlarged importance when they can be understood as deriving from a common motive. This motive originates in the pedagogical relationship, which defines and then negotiates the types of knowledge that it and its surrounding community wish to pursue. To the extent that a community accepts certain motives as the author's, the motives have been objectified and represent knowledge the community synthesized for itself. The community, however, is the only and final arbiter of this knowledge, and it is therefore subjective.

To an individual reader, knowledge inferred about the author from the reading experience also seems objective, since it seems to the reader that the author is actually speaking to him. (As I discussed in the Introduction, we first feel, in a conversation, "I believe *you*" rather than "I believe *your words*.") If this assumption is replaced with the more nominal one that "I am reading a book," thoughts about the author are better understood as symbolizations growing from the normal perception of language. If the reader is already familiar with the author's language system—his biography—the symbolizations are governed, in part, by this knowledge. To the extent that a reader is unfamiliar with the author or his language system, however, he will *invent* an author as part of the normal activity of response and interpretation. The symbolization of an author is as much a perception of the text as the isolation of formal or thematic units. Increased concentration on the symbolized author serves many familiar psychological functions: localizing one's own feelings and thoughts in someone else; providing a human, motivational origin for novel

11. The first time I heard Mr. Edel use this phrase was in his class, in 1962. Since then I have heard him use it repeatedly in personal conversations.

imaginings; bringing authority into one's reading experience; and so on. Sometimes the cultic reputation of an author is part of the original motive to read his work. In a pedagogical situation, however, unless there is a deliberate separation of the individually symbolized author from the author synthesized by communally accepted documentation, negotiations between private perceptions and public knowledge cannot proceed. In the next chapter, I will suggest how some responses, by maintaining this confusion, can bring the pedagogical dialectic to a halt.

Each reader's symbolized author may become an occasion for communal negotiation and research concerning the historical author. In the reading experience, the symbolized author may be motivationally explained, just as other aspects of response are. In either case, attention is fixed on a subject—the historical figure, who all agree existed, or on the readers in the present community, whose existence is absurd to debate.

## COMMON INTERESTS AND THE CLASSIFICATION OF AUTHORS AND TEXTS

Any reader reads in relation to his communities and societies, and all authors write within the same relations in their own time. Symbolic objects, in many of their palpable, real features, are often similar to one another in spite of their having been produced in different periods of history. To declare that a person or a symbolic object is part of a group or category, is to propose knowledge. Every community will take some degree of such knowledge for granted—for example, that Shakespeare is an *Elizabethan* playwright, Keats a *Romantic* poet, *Paradise Lost* an *epic* poem, the Wife of Bath a *comic* figure, Brooks a *new* critic, or a poem with fourteen five-footed lines a *sonnet*. The community will also take certain groupings within itself for granted— for example, undergraduate English majors in a university, people under twenty-two, United States citizens, and the like. As in the case of biographical criticism, interest in other communities is related to communal self-interest. For example, a widely accepted justification for the study of history is that "we can better know which mistakes to avoid in the future." Although it is obvious that knowing why Rome "fell" will not necessarily prevent America from "falling," the interest of American civilization in maintaining itself is a motive for historians to study Rome; public institutions pay the salaries of those engaged in this study. In language and literature, the analogous logic is "If we understand how people used language in the past, we will better understand how we use it now." This originological tendency is derived from Darwin, who proposed the explanatory nature of origins and whose classification of living things is given in an originological framework. The classification system is an explanation of man, while knowledge of man's connection to other species is given in the service of man. Since Darwin, the pursuit of humanistic knowledge has generally followed this motivational logic.

When dealing specifically with symbolic objects, as opposed to the development of living things, systems of classification do not work in the same originological way. Symbolic objects are related to one aspect of one species; to treat such objects as having an independent history would be something like trying to systematize the development of dog food from carrion to Alpo without reference to the dogs' general living conditions. Just as it is impossible to recover an author only by reading his work, it is impossible to gauge the group most works belong to by comparing topical features. To say that three works 500 years apart from one another all manifest the same myth is the kind of knowledge that can be understood only in the light of the present community's motives for declaring this knowledge. As a piece of objective knowledge, it is about as consequential as knowing that classic Greek plays, Elizabethan plays, and modern plays all have about the same performance time. While it is conceivably important to have such facts, they are usually presented as if their value were self-evident—that is, unrelated to specific communal purposes.

When classification is explanatory, it views a work in terms of the motives of its community or society. For example, to say that a novel is Victorian is to suggest that the work is a manifestation of Victorian motives where *it is assumed that these motives are accepted as such by the present community.* Yet Victorian motives are as variegated as its language system, which can be objectified only from the perspective of our own community; and our own community, in turn, has long omitted pornographic literature, for example, as one of the contributions to the language system. If pornographic literature also turns out to have contributed to the author's language system, the present objectification of "Victorian motives" is altered in that light. At the same time, unless these motives are proposed as relative to our own to begin with, we shall not be able to perceive their individuality. Therefore, a concept like "the Victorian mind" is meaningful only in connection with a locally defined, present-day pedagogical purpose. Placing a work of literature in that category does not make sense except when we are aware of our purpose for doing so.

Similar reasoning applies to proposals for generic classification. Insofar as "tragedy," for example, is more than a topical identification of literature, it is defined by our present language system. In traditional literary forums, it is considered important to decide whether *Death of a Salesman, Hamlet,* and *Oedipus Rex* are all instances of tragedy. From our subjective standpoint, we can maintain that the community which uses the term to define the genre declares something in common between itself and the original communities from which the plays come. Those who do not want to use the term for all three plays simply understand the plays differently from those who do apply the term. But to debate the issue as if a final, objective genre of tragedy will finally be discovered and solve the problem is idle. Acceptance of the term as used by all three communities involves developing a meaning within the language systems of those communities and then negotiating that meaning with our own. I establish my own meaning by testing my conception of tragedy against my response to the plays under consideration. In this way a predication involving my conception and my response is produced, where the knowledge is of interest to me and my interpretive community.

Most questions of genre are subtler and more consequential than this, since, as Hirsch argues, knowledge of the author's use of genre can suggest which literal verbal meaning the author had in mind: the genre might be able to tell whether the same words refer to parting lovers or to a dying man.[12] Undoubtedly, there are occasions when such knowledge will act just as Hirsch says it does. Since the concern is the relative certainty *in our minds*, however, as long as the connection between the genre and the words is probable, we are reliant on our interpretive resources. An author's use of a known genre is just as often motivated by his wish to transform it as it is by the aim of making his words conform to it. Usually, there is no way to establish intention in such terms, and it makes the most sense to view the author as not necessarily caring whether he is transforming or maintaining a received genre. From our own perspective, we may observe the relative prominence of several genres in a particular society in the interests of determining shared values. But once we think that shared values create interpretive necessities in our own reading, there would be no way to understand how genres from past times are given new meanings by new generations. Especially in cases where the conventional usages are unclear, the question of indeterminate past fact can be productively translated into the definition of present values disclosed in the response statements of those in the pedagogical communities.

For a group to define itself as an interpretive community is perhaps the most difficult task of subjective criticism because the longevity of the community depends on each member's motivation to identify himself with it for an indefinite period of time. A classroom has a fixed expiration date; a school of thought requires nothing of its members except public announcement of membership. It is doubtful that any interpretive communities exist at this time as organized, ongoing forums for the development of specific new knowledge outside the

12. Hirsch, *Validity in Interpretation*, 68-126.

quantitative sciences. Yet, as a matter of social and psychological fact, almost every person considers what others think to be important. Outside a pedagogical relationship, knowledge of what others think comes to us through informal and nonauthoritative means—hearsay, newspaper reviews, cocktail parties, and so on. The most decisive manifestation of the motive to affiliate oneself with a group usually can be seen in such behaviors as the purchase of stylish clothes or the viewing of hit movies. The extent to which an individual actually depends upon authorities and peers and uses his knowledge and his tastes to create relationships with others is rarely conceived as one of the fundamental facts of pedagogy.

A classroom in language and literature is especially conducive to inquiring why we wish to belong to a community at all. It is a place where young children are aware for the first time that because others speak differently from them, these others also think differently and *are* different in surprising ways. This early perception of varying language systems is an obvious means to begin to ground pedagogy in language awareness. At the same time, language awareness is a basis for disclosing common purposes of this group: common language defines common interests. When a person is motivated to make another's language his own, he is entering into community with that person; the community is similarly suggested if we identify ourselves with others' tastes and ideas. It is of interest to each person to know how and why he assimilates other people's language and thought.

Certain authors and certain types of literature attract groups, of various sizes, of students and followers. The traditional means of trying to understand the popularity of authors like Shakespeare and Dickens has been to seek out some element of "greatness" in their work as an explanation of their continuing appeal. But this is not a motivational explanation; a motivational explanation would, rather, look for shared motives in the assenting group, society, nation, or historical period. To explain Shakespeare's popularity from a subjective viewpoint involves defining elements of Western civilization that need to hear Shakespeare or that need to think of him as "great." Shakespeare's work has become a common language in our civilization, and the understanding of his popularity lies more in how and why this language has been so widely appropriated than in some essential objective feature of his work. To a large extent, this appropriation must be due to the prevailing psychology of literary authority as it has been passed through generations. It is conceivable that Western civilization and languages might develop in such a manner as to reject the greatness of Shakespeare, which is, in principle, as ephemeral as the absolute truth of Newton's laws of motion.

In any case, such questions cannot be raised on an abstract level. The first step in this inquiry has to be a pedagogical community's awareness of the intradependence of its members, particularly, of the ways in which prevailing linguistic habits and literary popularities represent communal self-definitions. When tastes are publicly presented on the basis of response statements, it is possible to distinguish between tastes based on motives for compliance or for self-satisfaction. If the latter motives are taken seriously in public, the principles of public taste-formation are altered, since the element of compliance is significantly reduced. The investigation of the nature of popularity in this way is likely to change what is considered popular. But regardless of what is popular on any level, the pedagogical community can, by directing attention to common interests in language and literature, begin, in the most elementary situations, to make our natural dependencies on community functions occasions to produce new knowledge.

These four contexts for the pedagogical pursuit of knowledge about language and literature are not prescriptive; and they are each, and as a group, derived from the subjective paradigm. The first two contexts concern what I, the subject, feel and think; the third concerns what I do with what you or the author says; the fourth, with how I negotiate what I feel, think, and do with communities larger than just you-and-me, and how I perceive such communities of the past. Although I will discuss each context more or less independently in Chapters Seven through Ten, their independence is just one pedagogical option for developing subjective judgments. For example, judgments of taste frequently concern the choice of one author over another, or one genre or one historical period over another: many professional commitments are founded on such judgments without awareness of their motivation. For certain readers, construing the author may depend on their awareness of meaning, as it did for Freud and Hirsch; however, for each, the connection between intention and meaning was different. For other readers, the good and the popular are the same; and for still others, the good and the popular are opposites. The choice of contexts for seeking knowledge is not limited in any objective way. Following the logic of the subjective paradigm, the contexts are determined by our capability of publicly defining what we want to know. Even if a solitary student carries on private research, his subjective dialectic follows the language systems of his previous pedagogical communities—and of his family—and unless he is a hermit, the dialectic is geared toward eventual reentry into a community.

I prefer the essay form of the response statement mainly because of my success with it in the classroom situations that I face. Although I am not comfortable with it, electronic recording equipment probably can also be used to provide a document for the review and study of response. But no matter what sort of symbolic objects are under scrutiny, it is not likely that the development of subjectively grounded knowledge can proceed without a verbal document and its verbal negotiation. Writing a description of one's feelings is not easy: it demands habituation based on belief in its value. But I do not see another choice because, of all forms of symbolic expression, language requires the *least* special interpretive skill: its subtleties and strengths are available to more people than any other symbolic capacity. Most importantly, our language is, after all, both the subject of interest and the means of investigation. The response statement is a symbolic presentation of self, a contribution to a pedagogical community, and an articulation of that part of our reading experience we think we can negotiate into knowledge.

# Chapter Six

# THE RELATIVE NEGOTIABILITY
# OF RESPONSE STATEMENTS

In principle, any statement that a reader considers a response is, in one context or another, negotiable into knowledge. Within any pedagogical community, response statements vary in character according to how each reader considers himself a member of that community. The common purpose in each group determines the relative negotiability of the individual response statements. For example, an informal study group that meets voluntarily and carries no university credit may more easily be able to vary its purposes to accommodate responses than a formally constituted classroom with purposes that fit into a larger curricular framework. Or, a group with an announced therapeutic purpose may see a learning opportunity where a pedagogically oriented group may see obstructing inhibitions. Regardless of the group's purpose, some response statements will always seem more susceptible to public discussion and potentially more enlightening than others, and such standards of negotiability have to be commonly understood before the group can function.

My discussions of response statements in Chapter Five and in *Readings and Feelings* suggest what these standards might be in university classrooms. By understanding perception, affect, and associations to personal relationships as a natural unit, I am claiming that responses including that unit are more negotiable in a pedagogical group than others. Given the purposes I outline, it is easier to develop knowledge from those responses than from responses which do not include this. I consider these latter responses as inhibited in some way from optimum participation in the group. It is true that what I judge as less negotiable someone else may judge as more so; other classrooms may be better able to make adjustments to response contingencies that I consider inhibiting. Nonetheless, as long as a group has a common purpose, all response statements are not equally negotiable relative to that purpose. It is not possible to avoid a group's evaluative judgments of an individual's work; the only course is to turn these judgments to mutual advantage.

A negotiable response statement facilitates the development of knowledge about a reading experience, as opposed to about the reader or about some "reality" outside the reader. Knowledge about the individual alone is clinical, while knowledge about reality based only on a response statement is religious. The analyses of response statements in this chapter are oriented around this distinction. Central attention to the reading experience keeps the class's pedagogical purpose in the forefront and establishes a conceptual restraint on the tendency to discuss each reader's personality problems or the moral imperative one imagines the literature to give.[1]

Although I will try to make my analytic judgments of the response statements as persuasive as I can, these judgments were originally made relative to the class in which the students participated, and relative to my ability to work with that class at that time. It is quite possible that if the statements now appeared in my class, under circumstances in which I feel more certain knowledge about response processes, I would reach different judgments. In classes which now deal with response statements, however, the distinctions in negotiability I am proposing are the same. The way these distinctions are used has to depend on the constitution of the class. Although I will indicate the nature of the classroom situation in some of the response discussions in subsequent chapters, the main purpose now is to demonstrate a pragmatic distinction in negotiability in actual response statements.[2] I will discuss three types of response and the terms of their

---

1. In note 3 of Chapter Five, and in *Readings and Feelings*, I indicated the danger and inappropriateness of clinical judgments in the classroom. If a teacher succeeds in controlling his own tendency to make such judgments, there is then the task of recognizing and controlling the students' same impulse. I have found that my advance warnings do not prevent even the most highly motivated students from publicly deciding that this respondent "has a father problem" or "seems to be a very insecure person." Formulations in received critical terminology of the author's "moral meaning" are similarly motivated by what is partly an innocent zeal to sum up the author. Conceptual restraint in this regard means viewing each response as the expression of a local reading experience and as a contribution to a group effort, and not as a reflection of illness or even of character. The definition of a pedagogical community implies the *decision* to stress knowledge about one's own mentation over knowledge of cosubjects' illness or moral stature.

2. These responses were collected in seminars where each person, including me the teacher, presented his own responses. I had stressed the necessity of such a situation in *Readings and Feelings* and in Chapter Four above. My relation to the responses I discuss in this and subsequent chapters is not that of an objective observer, but that of another observer of the group I was in reporting my observations and making claims about them. My only claim to authority in this regard is experience in the kind of situation I am describing, a situation which I initiated to begin with. In Chapter Five, above, I indicated,

negotiability—(1) reader-oriented, (2) reality-oriented, and (3) experience-oriented—where the last is viewed as more negotiable than the first two, though once a class is experienced the first two become increasingly negotiable.

### READER ORIENTATION

#### The Response Statement of Ms. B to More's *Utopia*

(1) Utopia . . . When I was younger and read a lot, I frequently created for myself alone different worlds. It was something like the picture in *Psychology Today*, the one that's always there—the girl in the attic with the light coming through the one window, but minus the American flag. This picture is both of the world I was in and the worlds I insisted on creating. But I was always the only one in these worlds; I could never figure that out but I rather liked the fact at the time if I remember correctly.

(2) My worlds never were clear or concrete; they were always vague and dark, but pleasantly so, like the picture of the girl in the attic. And they always had one point of emphasis, different ones at different times but always only one at any given time. Although I never tried it at the time, I feel sure I could have never created other aspects of my world to go along with the basic obvious ones which were emphasized in the beginning of my vision. To move in and try to focus on my world would have made the picture go away, I feel quite sure. I could not have possibly come up with eating habits or economics systems of the other people in my worlds—nor would I have wanted to at the time, or presently. But I know for sure that my worlds were more real and more wonderful than this Utopia.

(3) With this Utopia and tales of early founding, More should have been a Roman. Utopus—Romulus and Remus—Octopus. It all makes equally as much or as little sense as you wish. Even the "God forbids" fit into the Roman scheme—for what that's worth. I envision all my old Latin professors coming to life if only to give their nod of approval to Sir Thomas More for his profound thoughts and grand style before fading back into oblivion to discuss some obscure technicality in Caesar.

(4) The streets are twenty feet wide. If only in the complex world one needed to worry about such trivia. A friend of mine had a wreck on the street since they were unable to make it to the scene of the accident due to the

---

with the same exemplary purpose, how my relationship with one of my students did progress. Subsequently, I will discuss my own responses and one or two instances in which my relationship with readers was germane to understanding response statements and developing knowledge from them.

Of the three statements I discuss in this chapter, I consider only the third typical of a seriously motivated reader. I have not often encountered responses in the first two categories, but I think they represent habits of thought that appear in many more usual responses. Such habits are exhibited by linguistic predilections—certain verbal usages, juxtaposition of sentences, citations of the text—that I suspect may be systematically connected to motivational inhibitions. Since I first collected these responses, I have been discouraging less-motivated readers from writing responses at all, and have urged them instead to expend their energies on work of more manifest conscious concern to them.

weather conditions [sic]. If from the measurements the street appeared to be a four-lane highway then my friend was obviously the one at fault. If it proved to be only a two-lane highway then the other party involved was at fault. A group of us used this as an excuse for a party and spent the evening measuring the street at various times. I have no idea how the thing turned out.

(5) We have a song about trivia—it has only one word, "trivia," of course, and we use it to indicate that we feel that the person to whom it is directed is avoiding the issue at hand, clouding the discussion, or attempting to avoid intimacy by tossing out trivia. I find myself spending a lot of time bluntly telling people I find them superficial or, I guess, telling people I find that most other people are superficial. It's like a mad drive and desire for almost continual intimacy on my part. It scares me sometimes—most of the time, in fact. More has his syphogrants—we have our syncophants—and I just have people who offend me with their lack of depth. How More could have praised and gloried in this I absolutely cannot understand.

(6) I have a "thing" about being a real human being and depth of experience. That makes me think of *The Prophet*, where Gibran speaks of tears hollowing out the soul so that it can hold more joy. To me this is important. A person who has not known true sorrow cannot know true joy. Yet persons easily aroused by trivia to one or the other are not experiencing true emotions of any sort so that their depth of experience and thus their depth of feeling is quite small. So small in fact that they cannot even comprehend other things with true depth when exposed.

(7) I have tried to explain to one of the people I am forced to live in close proximity to what I mean by depth of feeling and how it comes from depth of experience, which one does have some control over. But it does absolutely no good. She insists on smiling in her usual insipid way, accepting and yet not accepting and not understanding what is said to her just as she does most of the time. Oh, for the man too easily made glad. That's from somewhere—and probably comes in some other form.

(8) It was the same way with our speaker the other night. He had something profound to say—he could have taught each of us what it's like to wonder who you are and where you are going and to realize that each of us has the power to control what we become. But the group in their usual profoundly stupid way was able to turn the discussion into a trivial gripe session all carried on with the biggest of words and most profound of expressions. And the Dianes of the world fall for all that—it makes me ill . . .

(9) The joy and wonder of gazing at a star. I guess there's hope after all. There are other people who spend their time gazing at stars. Wollam has a poem if you can call it that:

caterpillar . . .

cocoon . . .

butterfly . . .

can there be no miracles?[3]

3. The discussion of this response, which follows in the text, is based on the problems I

In this statement, there are no allusions either to basic family relationships or to love relationships between Ms. B and some peer. In paragraphs 3 and 8, there is mention of authority figures, the Latin professors and "our speaker the other night," the former in a pejorative context. Also in paragraph 3 there is an implicit disparagement of More, the author. Peers seem to be mentioned specifically in paragraphs 4 and 7, and in the latter instance in a negative light—"the people I am forced to live in close proximity to" (these are not her parents or family). In general, important relationships do not inform these associations, while the other relationships are or have been rejected by Ms. B.

There are no formulations articulating an affective response to the reading experience. I infer that Ms. B was relatively impatient with this book, but only from the critical statements she makes through her associations. Affects are reported about the items in her associations and about the generalized "people" such as those in paragraph 5 "who offend me with their lack of depth." In paragraphs 1, 3, 4, and 5, there is specific mention of items in the work; those in 1 and 3 are citations of the work in general, while 4 notes the street width and 5 the syphogrants; for these last two, there are brief associative elaborations, but no description or discussion of what was perceived.

This response can be negotiated if, in each of the three aspects, new and more elaborate information about the *material already in the statement* can be obtained. For example, in order for those of us who read the statement to develop knowledge about Ms. B's taste for this work, she would have to explain to us more about the Latin professors, her relationship with them, the people she lives with, and her relationship with them. Similarly, Ms. B can be asked to say explicitly what her feelings were about what she read, and then she may be asked to say more about the aspects of the work she has noted already. The other readers can, without judging the adequacy of the response, just request further information. This means that a large part of the negotiation would be concerned with simply getting a response for subsequent negotiation. If, however, I were to respectfully request Ms. B to indicate if any family relationships came to mind as she read, or if I pursued any of the other aspects with a similar implication of the inadequacy of this response, I might well create further inhibition and preclude the chance of any negotiation at all. On the other hand, if Ms.

thought I had when I first received it along with a group of others to the same work. I had to choose which responses to discuss in class; and although I distributed this one along with the others and did comment on it, I thought it would be too difficult both for Ms. B and for the rest of the class—who were just beginning their acquaintance with response study—to understand the response in the dimensions I am suggesting now. Ms. B's participation in the seminar after submitting this response was marginal.

B is responsive to these further requests, even more time is spent just listening to and recording Ms. B's fuller response, which she could just have easily recorded to begin with. If it could not have been recorded, and Ms. B actually depends on a public discussion to bring out her response, that means that the negotiation of the response into knowledge is put aside in favor of all other readers helping Ms. B to respond. The net result is that Ms. B the person has become the topic of public attention, rather than Ms. B's reading experience. This is one important respect in which Ms. B's is a reader-oriented response.

Suppose, however, that no time at all is spent encouraging Ms. B to fill out her response, and the group elects to negotiate what is already written. The substantive material in the statement falls into two areas—the private worlds she constructs and her sense of the emptiness in most other people. It is fair to say that these worlds are a symbolization of the world she perceives in the *Utopia*. But there is no way to know that her perception went any farther than the title or received information about the book. The response enters these worlds—which were "always vague and dark" and "always had one point of emphasis," and were "pleasant" because of the vagueness—and for the most part remains there. Most importantly, she "was always the only one" in these worlds. Although the worlds had no laws or economic system, they were "more real and more wonderful than this Utopia" (2). The fact that her "pictures" were more private, simpler, and completely her own is the motive for the reduced subjective dialectic between perception and response. The affirmation of self is substituted for the dialectic with the reading experience, and the implicit judgment of taste is that the reading is to be rejected because it is *not her world*. Therefore, there is no motive for negotiating the reading into knowledge through interaction with other readings that are not her own.

The contemporary world which appears in most of the associations in the second half of the response seems to be a symbolization of the trivial details she sees in the Utopia, starting with the width of the streets in paragraph 4. She juxtaposes her own sense of depth, profundity, and real humanity with the trivial superficiality of those she lives with. In this half, as in the first, it is difficult to estimate the role that perception of the reading experience plays in the response, because the main attention is in coping with the offense given Ms. B by the "triviality" of those around her. Indirectly, she associates herself with the authority of the "speaker," whose potential for profundity she might have helped realize had it not been for the trivial interests of the rest of the audience. Earlier, and more directly, in paragraph 6, she cites Gibran in order to say that "true depth" comes from "true joy," which is founded on having hollowed out one's soul with tears. This could be taken as an intimation about her own sense of depth having come from sadness, but since it is not a direct statement, we cannot be sure. Also cited as a kind of antidote to the triviality around her is the thought of star-gazing and the "poem" about the transformation of the caterpillar. I cannot feel sure of the status of these allusions or why they appear; the only thing that seems clear about the statement in general is the decisive rejection of the reading perceptions and of almost all those people around her. The reader's perspective, *independently of the reading experience*, is the main concern of the response and will necessarily be the topic of negotiation if the statement is taken as given.

Although the language of this response is marked by several repeated usages, it cannot be interpreted independently of motives. For example, in the early parts the word *always* appears three times, *never* four times, and the adjective/pronoun *one* seven times; the terms *only* and *if only* appear prominently, as do the terms *vision, picture*, and *world*. In the second half of the response there are similarly habitual uses of words like *true, depth*, and *profound* in varying forms and combinations. By themselves, these patterns mean little; under the assumption of the respondent's strong self-orientation, they become descriptive of that orientation. I therefore characterize, preliminarily, and only on the basis of this statement, Ms. B's motive with regard to the group as the desire to keep herself apart from it. This may or may not be true of Ms. B; it may or may not be conscious in her. But this motive will explain the relatively reduced negotiability of the response statement. Functionally, Ms. B was not motivated to negotiate—or share—with herself or anyone else her reading experience.[4] The public submission of this response is her declaration of the kind and degree of her membership in this pedagogical community.

I had earlier claimed that this and most similar responses are nevertheless negotiable in principle. I can publicly accept Ms. B's motive and then view her statement as a description of *my* reading experience. I can see her work as an interpretive judgment saying that More's *Utopia* is concerned with trivialities and is itself trivial because More is "really" the only figure in the work. As students of utopian literature are aware, this is a familiar criticism of utopian visions, one of which occurs in *The Tempest* when Antonio derides Gonzalo for wanting

4. This judgment is based not only on the considerations outlined in the text but also on my larger experience with Ms. B in this seminar. In every instance where responses are collected, they are necessarily perceived in the context of a face-to-face relationship. It is useless to try to avoid seeing a response independently of one's image of and relationship to the respondent. And it is a definite disadvantage to ignore such knowledge in the negotiation of responses into sharable judgments. In this instance, my judgment is based on the fact that Ms. B did *not* share very many of her responses with the rest of the class. I think some of the features of her response statement help explain behavior, just as her behavior helps explain her response.

to be king in a land where he has just proclaimed "no sovereignty." Although it makes a difference whether the reader is offering this judgment as such or whether I am deciding that a response is a judgment, the latter decision is useful when the fuller dimensions of a reading experience are not accessible to the community. Ms. B might sit out such a discussion, or she might be invited into it by the simple recognition shown her response by the discussion. In either case, a personal response statement is the occasion for negotiation and interpretation, and this encourages the motives of many readers to come into conscious action in the development of knowledge. If a group is resourceful, almost any form of inhibition can be converted into a knowledge-producing effort.

## REALITY ORIENTATION

The second direction a response statement may take does not appear to be inhibited. Yet as a negotiable statement it is both inhibited and inhibiting in ways similar to Ms. B's.

### The Response Statement of Mr. J to Hawthorne's *Blithedale Romance*

(1) Coverdale displaces his attention from the reality of the external world in favor of recent memory. The Veiled Lady is a placebo for his actual encounter with the real "enigma" of the present moment. My imagination transports me beyond reality into a creation of my own making. With reference to real events, new occurrences are conjectured. I sit and watch the movement of people and allow all that my senses detect to be felt inside me. The "stir and hubbub" of the world is not under my authority. Everything is as it is from moment to moment. I don't think anyone can be "freakish," for who am I to dictate structures of life upon another. How could I be a free spirit, if I do this? I reminisce as does Coverdale. How else may I satisfy my imagination?

(2) "There can hardly remain for me . . . so cheery." I think of "cherry," and my shock upon hearing a whispered remark from a classmate in my Freshman composition course. He made a dirty out of my words. He said something evil out of my innocent reference to an "open girl." The "frosty bachelor" may have had girls in the past but time is running out. (Sex is fun.) The "chill mockery of a fire" yields "withered leaves" reaching out for an "imaginary warmth." The better world dreamers usually waste their energies in ineffectual attempts to impose their own life style concept upon an indifferent universe. All good life thoughts beyond the necessity of satisfaction of minimal needs can lead to the seeking of trivial luxuries. "In quest of a better life" he corrupts all simple thoughts and acceptance of limitation. Nourishment which ego pretension demands. There is no greater heroism than to carry out the dreams you have. Yet if dreams are acted out, they should never be rebellious ones. We seek "better air" that is cleansed of "falsehood, formality and error." I can find no ultimate hope in the rejection of present reality. If I feel that something such as a particular life style is better than the

old way, I should not look backward but continue toward my own creation without referral to antecedents (still memory is an inescapable part of the directions in which I move). "The churl" who knows the bitter wind for its effect upon his body, is not about to bother with the amenity of greeting. I applaud this passing stranger. Who does this Coverdale think he is? He thinks himself better than others, and that is why he seeks a better life. I know him as a pretentious fool, as are all leaders.

(3) "True" is "strong" and "natural" is "sweet." The poet feels he knows what the actual manifestations of these abstractions are. I have respect for certain persons more than for others. The qualities which compose these persons' characters have special appeal to me. Common in all of these persons are characteristics which I consider out of the ordinary . . . They will attend to their determined chores. Coverdale equates woman's work to that which "chiefly distinguishes artificial life." Men think they are superior because of their work. Actually woman is closer to life, since she spawns it and protects it . . . "ordinary intercourse" (means sexual intercourse). Total feeling and ecstasy comes from the stimulation of sex exchange—the best kind of give and take activity. Coverdale thinks he has left behind the "rusty iron framework of society," but he hasn't. The "established system" is "intolerable" since we never achieve full personal independence . . . Pride is not cast aside, when concern remains for "advancement of our race." I want to be as unselfish and humble as my Christian heritage tells me to be but I need to realize that these outward expressions will be revealed in my activity only when I feel the highest degree of trust in my own selfhood. "Pigs!" "The swinish multitude" "The outside barbarians"; Coverdale depreciates the worth of others to elevate himself. All of us do this to a greater or lesser degree. Zenobia mysteriously withholds something, and that is that her presence causes Coverdale to see their "heroic enterprise . . . like an illusion." I think that women are mysterious. They hold life within their bodies. I can never experience this.

(4) Coverdale admits his condescension . . . The light through the window is a welcome beacon to the travelling stranger. The poor young girl is thought to be a stray cat of the philanthropist Hollingsworth, and they hesitate to welcome her into their closed society. We keep others apart from us. They are unknown strangers, and can't be trusted. Self-protection from the uncouth. Preconceived standards make evaluation of other persons nothing more than matching their behavior to the proper abstraction. ("Behaving less like a civilized Christian than the worst kind of ogre.")

(5) Stupidity of worshipful adoration of one person for another. It seems to affect us all. Probably it results from our antiquated familial system of child-rearing. The boy identifies with his father, and the girl emulates her mother. The parents become figures to which the child extends affectional interest. Child is chattel to his parents. We become slaves at the earliest age, and we never seem able to escape our servitude. Blindly we seek out a marriage prospect to replenish the system-of-supportive-others. We depend upon our love objects. They serve to enhance our meager selves and see us through. Marriage is another of the abstract forevers. The foolishness of "transcendental purpose." "love . . . one can conveniently dispose of." Love in the abstract makes it uncomfortable for those who seek it. . . . "nature . . . the

awfulness that really exists in its limitless extent." We attach ourselves to such as is most convenient for reinforcement of the fortress of self. Our shelters are built by our own hands. To each of us is given a "little parallelogram of sky." "Perpetrating some huge sin in his proper person, and examining the condition of his higher instincts afterward." I feel a compulsion to transgress the highest law. By committing the most unpardonable sin, I might free myself from all desire and temptation . . . Quarrel about alternate names for Blithedale (a rose by any other name . . .) "How cold an Arcadia was this!" He needs Zenobia's woman's warmth, but his masculine ego will not allow him to receive it. Never will he possess the warmth of a woman. The place he really wants to be is back in the womb. The quest for peak experiences can only be a defense for the real wish for total regression.

(6) "patient Job himself." The intellectuals cannot understand the existence of suffering if the world were actually created by a benevolent and forgiving God. They confuse their own mortal meanness with the unknowable. We are afflicted with the hypochondria of Coverdale's illness. Fever of mind and heart . . . Hollingsworth had "something of the woman in him" . . . "what is best in them." So Coverdale actually believes what I do. That is very interesting. "hither verge of life." The nearer to death one gets the more he recognizes life as "an unsubstantial sort of business." This "hither verge" expression also appeared in Coverdale's original description of Zenobia. The words at first reminded me of "hither parts," i.e., the sexual equipment of Zenobia. "In due time, I remembered what he said." When the time comes we remember what we want to remember. I remember those past experiences which seemed in their occurrence to be beyond anything I had felt before. I recall my dream of the nubile young girl (I was eight at the time). She is reclining. Suddenly her budding breasts are transformed. Her right breast develops beautifully, but her left breast is replaced by a chick which hatches from an egg . . . "She made no scruple of oversetting all human institutions." That beautiful dancing lady, Isadora Duncan. She adopted the motto: "truth is beauty, beauty is truth, this is all I know, and all I will ever know." Zenobia's flower recalls an expression I learned as a child whereby a woman between two men is described as a "rose between two thorns." . . . Marriage as "the great event of a woman's existence." This is a great delusion of men and all too many women. Actually women don't want to be subject to ceremonial commitment any more than do men . . . Coverdale's conjectures about Zenobia reveal that old prejudice for the unspoiled virgin on the wedding night . . . Coverdale seeks more than the "mystery" of Zenobia's life, he wants to be given access to the inaccessible mysteries.[5]

Unlike Ms. B's statement, Mr. J's includes wide-ranging and copious citations of what he read. Although there are many adverse judgments

5. Mr. J was in the same seminar as Ms. B. Unlike her, however, he did not withdraw from participation; on the contrary, he was relatively resilient when his responses were criticized by others and enjoyed discussing his and others' responses. But although there did not appear to be a strong inhibition to response, the usual result of discussing Mr. J's responses was that he became the object of attention, since most inferences about his reading experience had to be checked with him first.

of the characters, Mr. J is reporting directly on his perceptions within the reading experience. But while Mr. J's reports imply many feelings and affects in his experience, he never records that he feels thus and so *about* this figure, sentence, or piece of fictional behavior. Many of his observations can conceivably be construed as either in sympathy with or opposition to what he thinks is in the novel, but in order to ascertain such feelings, we would have to ask him. Furthermore, there are only two thoughts in this statement that can be called associations. In paragraph 2 he reports the incident in his freshman composition course, and in paragraph 6 he tells a dream he remembers. In neither of these associations does he speak of his relationship with other people, and there are no such allusions in the rest of the statement.

Perceptions of the text constitute the "reality" around which this response is oriented; awareness of subjective experience is a relatively less prominent feature. As with Ms. B, Mr. J's wider subjective background for the response may be made the topic of negotiative interest, but this will mean that Mr. J, rather than his reading experience, is the item of study. On the other hand, if the perceptions and Mr. J's judgments about them are the topics of interest, their "objective" validity will be debated, since there is little subjective authorization for them. This kind of discussion usually takes place in traditional formalist criticism, where ever more textual "evidence" is gathered by opposing opinions without consideration of the motivated character of each opinion. The text has thus become the final reality which is viewed as an arbiter of validity in interpretation. Since the text really cannot judge anything, the teacher becomes an "official" judge of its objectivity. The reality-oriented response treats the symbolic object as a real one, and the response is a contribution to the reiteration of objective thinking. Mr. J's response shows the direct connection between objective-reality orientation and the presentation of interpretive judgments in moral terms.

In the second paragraph, Mr. J observes, "The better world dreamers usually waste their energies in ineffectual attempts to impose their own life style concept upon an indifferent universe." Particularly of Coverdale, he says, "He thinks himself better than others, and that is why he seeks a better life. I know him as a prententious fool, as are all leaders." If judgments like these followed a personal presentation of Mr. J's sense of the "indifferent universe" and of the pretentious foolishness of leaders he has known, they would sound less sanctimonious, because I know I have had similar thoughts. But I did not write them in a response; perhaps I confided them in a private conversation with people who would tell me if I was too sanctimonious for their taste. Objectively, such judgments have no meaning; in order to give them meaning, Mr. J may be asked to authorize them further with subjective etymologies of the terms he uses, like "ineffectual" or "pretentious." Because Coverdale is a symbolic object, his reality can be understood only in subjective terms. Mr. J takes for granted the objective sense of the phrase "I know."

The perception of Coverdale is presented in the context of the relation between men and women and Mr. J's opinion about what this relation really is. In paragraph 3 Mr. J first says that while men think themselves superior because of their work, women are "actually" superior. The conclusion of the paragraph elaborates this thought: "Coverdale depreciates the worth of others to elevate himself. All of us do this to a greater or lesser degree. Zenobia mysteriously withholds something, and that is that her presence causes Coverdale to see their 'heroic enterprise . . . like an illusion.' I think that women are mysterious. They hold life within their bodies. I can never experience this." While I may combine the first two sentences of this citation with Mr. J's earlier announcement in paragraph 1 that he identifies with Coverdale and then conclude that Mr. J is elevating himself by castigating Coverdale, the words do not say this literally: Mr. J admits only to a *general* confession: "all of us do this." He likewise admits that Zenobia is an element in "all women," the "mystery" of whom relates to holding life in their bodies and points out his own inability to experience this. Because the novel's language and characters are Mr. J's only language in this response, it becomes a universal or objective language: he, Coverdale, and "men" are the same; Zenobia and "women" are the same. There is no dialectic between the novel's language and his own.

A similar effect occurs in paragraph 5, where Mr. J discusses marriage and children. This topic follows a perception of "worshipful adoration" in the work. Since the child is "chattel to his parents," "we never seem able to escape our servitude." Through this generalization, Mr. J *implies* his sense of his own enduring childhood, but again, does not announce it in personal terms. It is also not clear if Mr. J is identifying the adoration of lovers with the child's feeling for his parents. If he sees himself as Coverdale, with both having a "masculine ego," the last part of this paragraph presents both as wishing for "total regression" but being prevented by the masculine ego, which wishes for "peak experiences." Although this may represent an important facet of self-knowledge, Mr. J's language hides it from himself and from those who read the response: the face value of the language is objective—a judgment about how Coverdale and Zenobia represent men and women in general. The language cannot be negotiated without making Mr. J, the person, the object of attention.

This response, like Ms. B's, is marked by habitual superlative or totalistic constructions: "He corrupts all simple thoughts"; "I can find no ultimate hope"; "total feeling and ecstasy comes from the stimulation of sex exchange"; "all of us do this"; "it seems to affect us all." Without guessing the psychological reasons for these habits, it is enough to say that they are part of a nondialectic presentation of self—a self identified with the perceptions of the text. The language system of self as developed through affects and associations has been inhibited so that it is available neither to the reader nor to the community.

In his first paragraph, Mr. J announces this mental condition. The "recent memory" which he sees Coverdale choosing is for himself the recent memory of the reading. By reminiscing "as does Coverdale," he re-reports the text. He says that this is how he satisfies "my imagination." The external world is "not under my authority"; only the imaginative reading world is, and that is what he says he is presenting. The concluding association in paragraph 6 gives another product of his imagination, a dream of the "nubile young girl" which comes in the context of his discussion of Zenobia's "hither parts." Both here and at the beginning of the second paragraph, where he sees a sexual pun in the word *cheery*, female genitals are part of his thoughts—but Mr. J, by presenting these thoughts as puns on the language of the text, stops his presentation at that point and does not elaborate with his own language. Earlier, he had characterized his and Coverdale's regressive wishes as aiming toward "the" womb, rather than toward any particular womb as he knows it. At first, the imaginative language and sexual thoughts are presented not as his own, and then, as his dream's, whose elements are neither explained nor associatively elaborated.[6]

In spite of the important inhibitions in this response, it, like Ms. B's, may be negotiated. To do this, I accept the identification of Mr. J and Coverdale, and I entertain the *interpretive judgments* that, for example, Coverdale envies Zenobia, perhaps her mysterious "hither parts"; that all leaders are "pretentious fools"; or others, as I choose. To the degree that I assimilate these propositions to my reading experience, I can develop knowledge, perhaps in negotiation with the rest of the community. Or I may ask to what extent I, like Mr. J, become fully caught up in the language of the book. In other words, do I share with Mr. J the things that I see in his work? Yet in these latter instances, the negotiative path is more circuitous than if the statement had presented somewhat more of Mr. J. Ultimately, though, there is no objective reason why the longer path is less productive than the shorter.

6. This dream is typical of the difficulties raised by Mr. J's response statement. The dream easily becomes a point of attention in the discussion of the response; however, since there are no associations, each person wants to guess at its "meaning," while Mr. J evaluates each guess. Due to the understandable class interest in this project, the study of the reading experience is subordinated to undirected dream interpretation: Mr. J is playing "guess my wish" while everyone else plays along.

### EXPERIENCE ORIENTATION

The experience-oriented response statement has elements of both the previous two types, but in it the reader's subjective dialectic between the perceived language system and his own is much more apparent.

### The Response Statement of Ms. R to Lawrence's *Lady Chatterley's Lover*

(1) My initial reaction to *Lady Chatterley's Lover* is one of disappointment, just because of the book's reputation for being so lewd and its actual lack of pornography. I remember when I was younger, in the sixth or seventh grade, I used to babysit for some people, the Mungers, whose bookshelf's top shelf was filled with DIRTY books. After I got the kids to bed, I used to leaf through them and look for the dirty parts, and I distinctly remember that I could never find any in *Lady Chatterley's Lover*. During this reading, in my senior year in college, I had the same impulse to find the nitty-gritty stuff, and I can now understand why my earlier efforts were so futile! Wow! What an overrated book!

(2) It's a strange thing about *Lady Chatterley's Lover*; I think it will always be a classic to kids of my age, because we were just learning about sex when the big obscenity trial took place. The Mungers once more return to my mind. Their oldest child, Milton Munger, Jr., was only two years younger than I, and he was fat and puffy and wore horn-rimmed glasses—a really repulsive specimen, who looked just like his father. Mrs. Munger was really sort of pretty, too; I always felt sorry for her having such an ugly son. I remember I used to hate it when Mr. Munger took me home; I think I entertained some notion that he would turn rapist or something, because I figured he and his wife couldn't possibly *still* do that mysterious and terrifying thing. They also had prints around the house—I think they were Gauguin's Tahitian girls with bare breasts—and these only served to add to my schoolgirl fantasies. I was terribly curious about sex and very naive about it. I was also an "early developer," which didn't add to my cause at all.

(3) The aspect of the book that stands out most in my mind is Lawrence's descriptions of Connie's relationship with Michaelis. He describes how she would hold out until after he had achieved orgasm, and then she would make him wait until she had eked out her own little pleasure. This description really conjures up ludicrous images in my mind. It reminds me of squeezing the last little bit of toothpaste out of the tube. When I was a small child, I remember my father always telling me to squeeze the tube from the *end*, but I always forgot and squeezed from the middle, and consequently there'd be a lot of wasted toothpaste and a lot of end-squeezing to get the last available bit out.

(4) This quirk of Connie's also reminds me of the talking Lawrence detests so much in the book. This affair seems like physical talking, with Michaelis expounding and Connie giving short answers! It's really a ridiculous affair when you think about it—there sits Connie, the former Emancipated Woman, in an old house with her crippled and impotent husband, listening to his friends talk, talk, talk, and she finally gets the chance for a little fun—spice in her life—and she holds out on herself. Michaelis reminds me of a rodent, sort

of swarthy and sneaky. I must confess that my picture of rodents comes mostly from the cartoons I saw when I was a little kid. The ugly old mice were always beating up the cats, who were only following their instincts and trying to catch the little creatures. Michaelis is sort of like a cartoon mouse.

(5) I was also particularly impressed by the description of Connie living in a world which was really only a dream, and "she herself was a figure somebody had read about, picking primroses that were only shadows or memories, or words. No substance to her or anything . . . no touch, no contacts." Her sister notices that she is losing weight, and she admits that she is getting bored. I can really identify with Connie in this respect. I remember as a child, I would often feel withdrawn like that, especially at adult parties (before which, Mother always was saying, "Now when you meet them, say 'how do you do?,' not just 'hi' "). Lots of times I'd suddenly get a headache and have to leave.

(6) I'm still the same way. At social gatherings I'm prone to getting suddenly very, very sleepy, even when I'm not consciously bored. I especially hate the kind of cocktail party or similar gathering where I meet someone who immediately decides to pick my brain. I remember one time in particular when I was a junior in high school, I'd gone to a prom week-end at a boys' boarding school in the boondocks. I didn't know my date very well, and as soon as I got there, he started pursuing me with questions. He was trying *so* hard to be profound, and I was *so* bored. It's no wonder the incessant talk around Wragby Hall lulls Connie into a stupor. The funny part about the whole thing is that in her relationship with Mellors, she tries to pick *his* brain. I find myself doing that too sometimes.

(7) The character of Mrs. Bolton is another part of the book that I can associate to my own personal experience. As I read the book, I kept picturing her as looking just like the lady who lived next door to us when I was a small child. We called her "Tonney." Tonney was soft. That's the only word for her. She had soft coloring and soft skin and a soft laugh. And enormous grandmotherly breasts. I can remember how comforting just the touch and smell of Tonney was whenever I was upset. She was an utterly feminine person, always cooking great meals and homemade pastries, and knitting and sewing. It would have really been easy to become dependent on her the way Clifford did to Mrs. Bolton.

(8) I must add that as Mrs. Bolton's influence over Clifford becomes greater, I feel less and less sentimental about her. Her attachment to Clifford becomes so perverted—her regarding him as a big, overgrown baby and his returning slowly back to the womb, or at any rate, the breast, yuk. She sort of kneads the crippled man into what she wants him to be, her child, who is absolutely and totally dependent on her, and by doing so, she sort of sets herself up as the Perpetual Mother. In this semi-Oedipal situation, Connie becomes the mother's competitor for the son's love, and true to her role, Mrs. Bolton never warns Clifford about Connie's infatuation with Mellors . . . she lets it happen, and thus gets her satisfaction from Clifford's reliance on her. I think I had one of my strongest visceral reactions to the book in the scene where Clifford starts crying and finds comfort in touching Mrs. Bolton's breasts. It's just like finding comfort in Tonney's breasts, I suppose, but the picture of a 35-year-old man grabbing hold really turns me *off!*

(9) As I think about it, Clifford himself turns me off, and yet I feel strangely sorry for him. In the first place, it must be a major drag to be stuck in a wheelchair all your adult life, not to mention being impotent. And *then*, to top it all off, he listens to that blasted radio all the time. I remember as a youngish child, ten or eleven years old maybe, visiting my grandfather. About five years before this, my grandmother and my cousin (Grandfather's favorite grandchild) were killed in a fire. All his life Grandfather had been one of those tremendously active people; he enjoyed his work as a lawyer and his hobby as a farmer. He always used to get up with us children and take us for long hikes in the morning so we wouldn't wake my parents up. Well, anyway, after Grandmother and my cousin died, Grandfather seemed to get old—too sick for walks, only strong enough to spend a little amount of time at the office every week. But I remember him sitting there in the music room of his house listening to Harry Carey broadcasting the St. Louis Cardinal games. His radio was old—big and brown—and the reception was lousy, and I always got fidgety and bored and would leave. It made me sad, those awful baseball games; they meant no more evening walks with Grandfather. I guess that's why Clifford and his radio hit me so hard—it was sort of the final acknowledgement of his being a cripple—the life being drained out of him.

(10) The scene with the wheelchair made me laugh at first, but it really isn't all that funny, when I think about it. Poor Clifford, it's *so* frustrating when you really want to do something by yourself and you find you just can't—so embarrassing and humiliating. I'm like that and so is my father. When I was in about the fourth or fifth grade, I was determined I'd learn how to knit. Someone taught me, but I'd get confused and make mistakes and my handiwork would be a total abortion. I'd get mad and frustrated, and I'd rant and rave and throw things and slam doors before I'd ask for help. I try to curb this tendency in myself now, but it's not all that easy. But it's so ironic— Clifford, who has suggested to his wife that she have a baby by another man. Poor pathetic creature.

(11) Connie and Mellors make me laugh. This idyllic naked-in-the-spring bit really gets me. And who would seriously sprinkle flowers in somebody's pubic hair without cracking up! Mellors seems honest—in a fairly ridiculous way. Right after he makes love to Connie, they have a conversation that really slays me:

> . . . "And are you sorry?" she said.
> "In a way!" he replied . . . "I thought I'd done with it all. Now I've begun again."
> "Begun what?"
> "Life."
> "Life!" she re-echoed, with a queer thrill.
> "It's life," he said. "There's no keeping clear."

Really, how ridiculous. When I was a senior in high school, I got to know a guy who was trying to finish his senior thesis so he could graduate from college before he went into the Marines. Peter was a strange guy, and at first I was really attracted to him. He said "beautiful" things, and was always talking about souls and spirits and stuff. When I finally started listening to his words, however, I realized most of what he said was so fatuous. He sounded exactly as Mellors sounds when he says "this is life."

(12) I started pulling for Connie and Mellors, though, after a while, but it was the same kind of cheering I do for soap opera characters. If life is reduced to good and bad, meaningful or meaningless, then it's easy to root for one or the other. Mellors gave Connie meaning, so, okay, I hope things work out for them. Except I was surprised when they did work out. I must be too realistic or something, but after a while, I thought I was floating through a flower-soaked fairy land. "Float along with Connie and Ollie!"[7]

The feature of this statement which renders it more easily negotiable than the other two is that Ms. R objectifies her reading experience; the topic of discussion is announced in the first paragraph as "my . . . reaction." Subsequently, there are judgments about the book, about particular characters, about general aspects, passages, and words, but in each instance Ms. R's comments place them in the context of her experience of them. The verbal articulation of the response is a complex symbolization of some of the mentation that took place in the original reading. As such it records the enlargment of her own language system as a result of its subjective dialectic with the perceived language system.

In almost each instance where Ms. R records a perception, it is elaborated into affect and association. Also, her response to the whole reading experience is given affectively and associatively. After reporting, in paragraph 1, that she was initially disappointed with the work, she says at the beginning of the next paragraph that "I think it will always be a classic to kids of my age, because we were just learning about sex when the big obscenity trial took place." The affect is defined in terms of her own history of sexual enlightenment, a part of which is given in the Munger associations. By and large, the affect comes from the dashed expectations of pornography, a feeling she reports having as a girl and now, in the present reading. This affect appears at the end

7. Ms. R's "negotiable" response did not simply happen, since she, like most other readers, had no way of translating the vague idea of "response" into an actual document without first discussing the matter. It came, rather, after a few weeks of practice in class. One of the main purposes of *Readings and Feelings* was to set out a pragmatic procedure for recording response statements in a larger rationale for literary study. Many of the considerations presented in that work and in this derive from my actual experience of workability of Ms. R's type of response. I was able to decide on the negotiability of her response only after I saw how it was negotiable. I did not know in advance that hers was any more negotiable than Ms. B's or Mr. J's.

Of course, many sorts of conclusions may be drawn from the careful examination of this and the other response statements. It may be possible to articulate even more decisive knowledge of each reader's experience. On the other hand, there is no reason to delve deeper here, since my aim is only to set out the problem of public negotiability. Reaching more important knowledge about reading experiences is reserved for contexts in which a common knowledge-seeking purpose has been established.

of the response in her characterization of the work as producing the same feelings in her as "soap opera characters." (12). She admits sympathy for the two principals but understands this feeling as more juvenile and less "realistic (12) than she might now have, presumably, about real life. The explicitness of the general attitude precludes the need for further interrogation about it and permits the communal attention to settle on its pedagogical task of developing knowledge. That is, we may now consider to what extent the attitude is a reflection of her larger taste, of her judgments of meaning, of the tastes of her peers, and so on. The response is ready to be reunderstood in conjunction with matters of common group interest.

Such negotiative resymbolization of the response into knowledge is possible, however, only in view of the relative depth of and frequency with which the associations in the response define the affective attitude in terms of personal relationships. The more significant ones are those she had with Tonney, her grandfather, and her father, and then with her mother, Mr. Munger, and two of her dates. Each of these relationships—and, indeed every figure mentioned—is cited in terms of some disappointment Ms. R had with them, though the feeling in each case first appeared in the reading experience and the associations suggest that sometimes the disappointment is with herself.

Tonney is cited in connection with Ms. R's perception of Mrs. Bolton. She admires Tonney's femininity, but when she reports her disappointment with Mrs. Bolton's increasing influence over Clifford and the strong rejection of its infantile character, Ms. R cites her susceptibility to the same kind of dependency. Her adult perspective helps her reject this susceptibility. The feeling more germane to the present experience, however, is the visceral rejection of Clifford's "grabbing hold" (8). This is a disappointment both in the masculine sexual failure and in Mrs. Bolton's cultivation of the failure. This feeling relates most directly to the general response—the reading disappointed Ms. R's readiness for sexual experience, and both the male and female figures, in her eyes, have let her down. During the Munger discussion early in the response, she cites her early puberty as one of the dimensions of her sexual consciousness; the Gauguin paintings in the Munger household also betoken to her Mr. Munger's hidden sexuality, which, she imagined, would emerge violently as she was being taken home from babysitting. As instruments of sexual power, the breasts she is aware of do not seem to do what her imagination expects of them. Even insofar as she identifies with Connie, she seems to find no path to sexuality. In paragraphs 3 and 4, her attention is on sexual frustration. Connie and Michaelis are "eking" out their satisfaction, and then she sees Connie as holding out on herself. When Connie does fulfill herself with Mellors, then Mellors is the ridiculous figure, and the whole relationship is too sentimental for her taste. Ms. R is disappointed because she does not find the articulation of sexuality in the work adequate to her present sense of sexuality.

In paragraph 5, where Ms. R says "I can really identify with Connie," she considers herself limited by her mother's instructions. Although she gets bored with "brain-pickers" (6), her identification with Connie tells her that she too can be a brain-picker. In the toothpaste episode with the father, it is uncertain who is making whom squeeze out the last bit of toothpaste. This association is to the question of sexual priority and initiative in the relation between men and women. While one cannot conclude just what Ms. R believes on this issue, there is a sense in which her disappointment is related to the frustration that seems to follow her own imaginative sexual initiatives. In paragraph 4 she identifies Michaelis with the "ugly old mice" in the cartoons; but Ms. R is on the side of the cats, "who were only following their instincts and trying to catch the little creatures" (4). On both a social and instinctual level, Ms. R describes frustration in what to her are normal feminine expectations and initiatives. Most of the time, she feels the frustration as a result of a masculine shortcoming.

That this shortcoming is also partly her own was suggested earlier in her analogy between Clifford's dependency on Mrs. Bolton and her own dependency on Tonney. Later responses to Clifford bring out a further, if oblique, identification with him. In paragraph 10, she understands his frustration with the wheelchair; her own frustration is similar when her handiwork turns out to be "a total abortion," and she suggests that she is like her father in being thus vulnerable to such frustrations. While distinctly identifying the frustration as feminine ("abortion"), she sees it as part of a masculine identification. Toward her grandfather, in the previous paragraph, she is both sympathetic and impatient—symmpathetic with his plight, impatient with his passivity, and noncommittal in her response to the death of her grandmother and cousin ("Grandfather's favorite grandchild"). For whatever reason, Grandfather is not to her what she would like him to be. Both paragraphs 9 and 10 suggest forms of disappointment in herself that are related to disappointments first in Clifford, then in her grandfather, but perhaps offset through identifications with her father.

Ultimately, to Ms. R, the feeling of disappointment is objective in the sense that she does not seem to have any doubt about it. She objectifies the novel as a document of early adolescence; and all her perceptions, affects, and associations bear this out. The seriousness with which Mellors views lovemaking with Connie, cited in paragraph 11, is "ridiculous" to her, even as Connie's affair with Michaelis conjured up "ludicrous" images of toothpaste squeezing. The novel seems to describe for her what gauche teenage boys do to impress teenage girls. In her response statement, these feelings were brought out, and she rejected them on various grounds. She did not, however, reject the whole reading experience; rather, she *identified* it both in general terms and in terms of her own emotional vocabulary. The relative success of this symbolization rendered the reading experience negotiable even though her opinion of the book was not very high.

In order to further distinguish between degrees of negotiability, consider the following two passages from Ms. R and Mr. J, respectively: "Her attachment to Clifford becomes so perverted—her regarding him as a big, overgrown baby and his returning slowly back to the womb, or at any rate, the breast, yuk" (8); "Never will he possess the warmth of a woman. The place he really wants to be is back in the womb" (5). I can make only one substantive distinction in the negotiability of these two observations: Ms. R's insertion of the word *yuk*. Without this word, the two judgments about Clifford's and Coverdale's actions have about the same authority, and they are susceptible to the same kind of debate. Ms. R's expletive identifies her judgment as subjective, as perhaps a perception more than a judgment. As a perception it is more negotiable than it would be as a proclamation. The lexical content of the statement is unchanged by the addition of the word, but as a result of that word, we perceive the meaning of the whole sentence differently from the way we perceive the meaning of Mr. J's statement. We would have to *ask* Mr. J just how objective he intends his statement to be; one would not have to ask Ms. R. The process of negotiating Ms. R's statement with our own may begin immediately; Mr. J's statement has to be further clarified. There is no need to debate whether Ms. R believes that Clifford is "really" headed for the womb—Ms. R settles for the breast, as described in the novel—but there is a need to determine just how metaphorical Mr. J's statement is to him.

Ms. R's statement makes a more decisive separation between her own language and that in the novel: *womb* is her own; *breast* is in the work. Ms. R juxtaposes them within her own language system. Yet "the breast" is also defined by Ms. R through several important associations, just as Mrs. Bolton and Clifford are defined through citation of relationships. For Mr. J, Coverdale is not thus defined, and neither is *womb*, except through relatively superficial puns. In almost every citation of the work. Ms. R describes how that passage made her think, feel, associate; for example, "the scene with the wheelchair made me laugh at first" (8). At the end of his third paragraph, Mr. J writes: "Zenobia mysteriously withholds something. . . . I think that women are mysterious." He does not say that Zenobia's withholding *makes him think* that women are mysterious. We can infer such causality, but to do so responsibly requires us to check our inferences with Mr. J. We need not make such weighty inferences, by and large, in understanding Ms. R's language, which is superordinate to the novel's language.

In this linguistic dimension, Mr. J's statement is similar to Ms. B's: there is no way we can tell if the language of the work occasions Ms. B's thoughts. For the most part, her language stands alone, and our inferences about it have to be validated in the same way as our inferences about Mr. J's. In each case, it is difficult to discern a dialectic between language systems. While it may be clear that both read the works, it is much less clear how we may develop knowledge from their responses without making the readers themselves the primary objects of investigation.

I claimed earlier that Ms. B's and Mr. J's statements are negotiable in principle but that a statement like Ms. R's is more easily negotiable. This claim is grounded on the argument that language behavior is best understood in motivational terms. Through her fuller presentation of perception, affect, and association, Ms. R. speaks more directly and more variably of her own motives than do the other two; her statement is thereby more responsible to the purpose of developing knowledge in common. It presents more of herself as "given" to this purpose. If we other members of her community now reconceive her response as, for example, a judgment of taste or meaning, more of the subjective grounds of reconceptualization are available from the statement, and the role of the respondent is more that of a participant in this mutual process and much less that of a regulator of inferences or a supplier of new information. Should the issue be whether taste for this work depends on our residual adolescent feelings, the discussion will center, not on whether Ms. R really feels this way, but the extent to which this dimension of taste is shared by the rest. Of particular relevance is the fact that to this community, "adolescent feelings" is not simply a one-sentence claim but a carefully documented statement of how these feelings have appeared in one reader. Similarly, if the pedagogical question turns on whether this novel "is" an expression of adolescent feelings in the England of the 1920s, or in D. H. Lawrence's mind, the respondent is an equal participant in the search for historical or biographical materials to enlighten the question; she has already been the means to define the question.

Of course, no response statement is complete, and each reader will alter his sense of the reading experience as negotiations proceed. Such alteration, however, is a separate occasion for knowledge. Within the given statement, there are enough subjectively documented perceptions and judgments to render them provisionally responsible to a common purpose. The regulating principle of negotiation is the assumption that each new public perception or judgment is given in its subjective dimension and that each new pedagogical purpose is considered acceptable by the community. Without such regulation, public discussion could be fun but would be irresponsible, or lawless, in that any claim would be permissible. There is no advantage in giving all statements equal weight or value if there are no common principles of validation. *The use of perception, affect, and association as means of determining interpretive responsibility is rooted in the normal function and psychology of language.*

Relative negotiability has long been an implicit principle in the proposal of many sorts of knowledge. At the same time, this principle has been as silent as the paradigmatic determination of knowledge. Once it becomes explicit, it is consciously variable according to what knowledge a community demands. Such variability is especially necessary, at this time, in the development of language-based knowledge. The study of literature in particular has been subject to *ad hoc* applications of different modes of thought without regard for communal interests or for normal subjectivity. The purpose for developing critical knowledge has customarily simply been assumed: it is obvious that one needs to know the phallic symbolism in *Macbeth*. By similar reasoning it is obvious that one needs to know the weight of a bowling pin in order to bowl. Both are conceivably knowledge, but to what end? While I have argued that the purpose for any kind of knowledge determines its nature and authority, this view is most obvious in the study of literature. Determining the negotiability of response statements is part of the communal definition of its purposes and part of the delineation of individual responsibility within the group. I have tried to suggest possible purposes and to outline a minimum individual responsibility. It remains to discuss and to show what sorts of knowledge may be developed under these circumstances.

# Chapter Seven

# ACTS OF TASTE
# AND CHANGES OF TASTE

In Chapter Five I proposed that an act of taste is a literary value judgment reconceived pursuant to the subjective paradigm. Traditionally, when an authoritative critic distinguished between the good and the bad, his judgment was accepted as knowledge presumably derived from principles of evaluation. While the judgments often held sway, however, the principles did not. From the standpoint of subjective criticism, principles may still be related to acts of taste, but now they act in the subjective dialectic with perception to produce the act of taste. The response statement, or several response statements, of any reader documents the action of that reader's principles at the time of judgment. When the reader announces his taste, its subjective origin is not merely assumed but available for public scrutiny and further negotiation. In this way, a judgment of taste is a proposal of knowledge that can gain public authority in the same way as most other forms of knowledge—through its sharability and its subjective efficacy for other readers and communities.

A judgment of taste cannot be simply a statement of preference or a similar informational announcement. As a proposal of knowledge, it is given under the assumption that the community wishes to know the dimensions of its constituents' tastes. But just as important as the knowledge of what the tastes are, are the means of authorization for that judgment; these means are actually part of the judgment.

Earlier I indicated that subjectively conceived acts of taste may be negotiated into knowledge in a variety of contexts, such as for an author, a genre, a period, and even for individual works on isolated occasions. Similarly, many forms of group tastes can be understood as knowledge. Just as widely applicable is the fact that taste always changes in one respect or another. Thus, my two main categories of thought are the act of taste and the change of taste. In this chapter, the discussions of particular response statements are aimed at showing only one instance of each category. It is assumed that analogous reasoning will apply when acts of taste are proposed in different contexts.

The following response statement of Ms. M to Henry James's "The Turn of the Screw" is relatively long; following it, Ms. M gives her analysis of the response, showing how she arrived at her judgment of her own taste for the story. This analysis is of special interest as a clear demonstration of what subjective knowledge looks like, but also because it was developed independently by Ms. M, without coaching or training. Furthermore, it articulates the act of taste as something that grew from prolonged consideration of both the reading experience and the response statement, where the latter was a contribution to the formation of a more satisfying judgment for Ms. M.

### The Response Statement of Ms. M to James's "The Turn of the Screw"

(1) My response to "The Turn of the Screw" begins with uneasiness when Douglas's promise of a "dreadful" story is followed by an enforced period of waiting. I hate waiting. I will never forget waiting for my second child to be born—she was three days overdue; undoubtedly the three longest days of my life. I had just begun my first course at the college and everyone looked at me rather cautiously, as though I was a bomb ready to explode, which wasn't really unreasonable because that was how I felt. The worst part of it was the feeling of no control—there was absolutely nothing I could do. The sense of waiting is one that continues and increases for me throughout the story. Waiting also makes me think of my parents and their passive, waiting approach to life. If something goes wrong, or if they really want something they consider prayer to be the answer. They don't seem to see themselves as willing things to happen—God does that. As far as I can see this is nothing but a loser's attitude. It opens the way for putting up with almost anything because it is "God's will" and because life is an endurance test that one must wait out for vague rewards later on.

(2) Douglas's description of the governess's visit to Harley Street makes me very angry. The governess is described as a "fluttered anxious girl" and of course her future employer is "gallant," "splendid," "handsome," "bold," etc. etc. etc. So what happens? She goes off to the country to a boring and isolated job where she can become more fluttery and anxious and he buys off his responsibility and presumably continues being gallant etc. It's the old double bind situation—exactly the kind of thing a woman encounters being "just a housewife." On the one hand there is this incredibly efficient social sales pitch that assures her that what she is doing is completely worthwhile, necessary and fulfilling. And, on the other hand there is the attitude of the children's uncle, which characterizes the attitude of many men, "she should never trouble him, never, never." In other words, "I have more important things to do, leave me alone." Douglas calls this a "strange" condition. It's not strange; in fact, it's so typical it makes me sick.

(3) When it is suggested that the governess was in love with the children's guardian I feel skeptical and somewhat put out by what seems to be a lack of consideration of the circumstances on Douglas's part. Since when is "I was carried away" accompanied by a laugh equal to beautiful passion? It reminds me of last week when I was at the dentist. To counteract boredom I tried to concentrate on an essay I'd been writing—then gave that up and started counting holes in the ceiling tile. Needless to say, this wasn't exactly stimulating activity. Anyway, since the dentist was only five inches from my face and since he is rather good looking, I started thinking about him in a lazily sexual kind of way. It was a more pleasant way of filling the time than staring at the ceiling but hardly what one could call "beautiful passion."

(4) During the governess's drive to Bly I want to tell her to stop and go somewhere else, anywhere else, while there is still time. She has no idea what she is getting involved in. At the same time I know she really has no alternative and I feel angry again. Given the conditions of her times, becoming a governess is probably the only way that she can support herself. The same month that I turned eighteen, I graduated from high school and got pregnant. I suppose I equate the governess's lack of alternatives with my apparent lack of alternatives at that point.

(5) The kind of isolation that exists at Bly terrifies me. It makes me think of the place we lived in when we were first married. Our apartment was in the basement of a large older house. The people upstairs were gone all day and everything was so horribly quiet . . . it was also very cold. Our windows were small and large bushes grew in front of them blocking the light. Sometimes the landlord worked shifts and was home in the daytime. Then he would spend hours practicing the scales on his trumpet. I felt as though I was in the middle of some illogical dream . . . there I was . . . not at university as I'd planned but sitting in a damp basement with either deadly silence or scales on the trumpet. Actually, the isolation continued when we moved to the middle of an apartment complex. Since I never joined the coffee-klatch rat race, the majority of my conversations were with babies or my mother. Mrs. Grose's tendency to use clichés reminds me of the way in which my mother often speaks. The governess seems determined to make her situation interesting. I can understand why but in isolation insignificant details can become obsessions. When my husband used to get home from work I would squeeze from him as many details of his day as I could. I suppose when you think of the governess's implied love for the guardian as a product of boredom and isolation it is understandable.

(6) The governess is never called by name. How appropriate! The only way I can refer to her is by a title that defines her relationship to the children. For a long time that was the only way I could define myself . . . the fulfiller of incessant demands . . . a mother . . . not only the real demands of the children but the stupid, unbelievable societal demands as well. A mother must be permanently available and unceasingly patient. While dealing with whining, crying, shitty diapers and days filled by talk with two-year-olds she is to be loving, understanding, selfless, and above all she must smile—she is being fulfilled. I remember reading over and over again that my failure could result in anything from juvenile delinquency to schizophrenia. And Freudian

psychology—what a boon to motherhood—I could do it all before my children were five. I felt as though I was trying to run with a huge ball and chain attached to each leg. Maternal instincts? I doubt it. I remember when I first started verbalizing the absurdity of the whole situation. One evening we had several friends over for dinner and I became involved in a heated discussion about women's roles. Afterward, I tried to explain how I felt to my husband. He suggested that perhaps I needed psychiatric help.

(7) The first time the governess sees Quint—when I am not sure whether he is a real person or not my initial reaction is: "Oh Christ, not this routine again—the male rescuer and reliever of boredom . . . the Prince here to rescue Rapunzel from the tower." I am glad when Quint doesn't turn out to be a rescuer. It makes me think of the Sesame Street version of Rapunzel, which I prefer to the traditional one. Rapunzel is calling from the tower. The Prince, on his way to rescue her, is a complete and utter dud. He can't find his horse, he can't even remember what he is supposed to do. Kermit the Frog, reporting the event for Sesame Street news, has to remind him. When the prince finally gets around to calling "Let down your hair" Rapunzel can't hear him. He has to repeat his message several times, and each time his voice sounds a little testier. Eventually she answers, "Are you sure?" "Yes," he yells back (by this time slightly hysterical). "O.K." she says, somewhat doubtfully, and throws down her wig to the ground. "What do we do now?"—Rapunzel is bald. Without waiting for an answer, she mumbles something about a pizza and says she is getting out of there herself. The prince goes back to looking for his horse. That's more like reality. Waiting in towers is useless; if you want to get out you have to do it yourself.

(8) I really enjoy the governess's description of her third meeting with Quint: "We faced each other in our common intensity . . . dread had unmistakably quitted me and there was nothing in me unable to meet and measure him." She is not really weak at all. I like that kind of strength. For some reason this scene makes me think of my father. My father is a person who not only shouts a lot but whose ordinary speaking voice is usually louder than anybody else's. When I lived at home this didn't matter all that much in discussion with him because his definition of "talking back" was so broad that replies were seldom possibly anyway. I remember being "grounded" not for the words I said but for the tone in which they were spoken. Now that he can no longer keep me in on a Saturday night if he dislikes what I say, he uses a different power tactic. He simply shouts his own opinions while I'm speaking. He's become like his own father even though we all used to laugh about the way Grandfather "discusses." Grandfather is French and deaf in one ear—a rather effective combination. When he disagrees with my viewpoint (or anyone's) he pretends either that he can't hear or that he can't understand the words being used. I like to see the governess counteracting Quint's power with a power of her own. If the ghosts are imaginary (as I believe they are) then Quint's power *is* the governess's power. Perhaps, then, the situation is one of the governess not realizing the extent of her own strength.

(9) I rather enjoy the sexual aura about Quint. The vague and frequent references to his sexuality make him rather intriguing . . . I feel very curious about him. This is something that I did not readily admit to myself—perhaps

because of his implied connection with evil. It is somewhat similar to the
constant warnings my parents used to give me about the evils of sex—which I
always had trouble equating with my idea of it as fun—and which led to the
conclusion that fun is usually wrong but that goodness (by their definition)
must be boring. I think I always suspected that they were not so concerned
with protecting me as preventing me from enjoying myself. Since I had six
younger brothers and sisters I felt justified in wondering about the consistency of their logic.

(10) Throughout the story I feel male and female forces set in opposition to
one another. Even little Miles's maleness becomes an issue toward the end
when he objects to being "with a lady always" because he is "a fellow . . . who's
getting on." I can understand what he is saying but I detest the patronizing
note in his voice both when he says this and when he addresses the governess
as "my dear." It reminds me of the way my husband often reacts to my anger—
in a very cool, condescending way that makes me feel like a poorly behaved,
slightly demented child. I had a close (but very annoying) friend in high school
who used to constantly interfere in my life while assuring me that he was
looking after my welfare and that he had brotherly feelings for me. I think
that these kinds of occurrences are why I get so much enjoyment from the
governess's direct and equal confrontations with Quint.

(11) I realize that although I maintain that the ghosts are imaginary I
continually respond to Quint as if he was real. This is comparable in a way with
my efforts to deal with the after effects of my Catholic upbringing. I had 18
years of indoctrinations in the wondrous ways of saints and spirits. My parents
used to bring a newspaper home from Church. When I was about ten it
contained a spurt of enjoyably terrifying accounts of possessions by Satan. I
remember one story in particular in which a nun was supposedly possessed.
She was reported to rise out of her pew into the air in the middle of the mass
mouthing obscenities. The article continued with a long and detailed of her
exorcism. Those were stories to rival Henry James. Anyway, even though I
now consider myself an atheist, there are times (always at night) when I have
nagging suspicions that I could be wrong. Not long ago a friend with a similar
background and I spend a hilarious evening mocking heaven, hell, rosaries,
novenas, purgatory, etc. etc. etc. Driving home, though, I knew it was
ridiculous, I had the distinct feeling that I was about to encounter a horrible
and sudden end—struck by lightning or something equally dramatic. When I
was about twelve I used to give God chances to prove his existence . . . "If you
really exist, God, make it start hailing at ten to one." In a somewhat similar
way, I look for proof of Quint's existence but find more proof of his non-
existence.

(12) I feel very upset when Miles steals the governess's letter to Harley
Street. Maybe, if she'd been able to communicate to someone outside Bly, her
actions wouldn't have had such a disastrous outcome. The whole story is
plagued by ineffective communication. Why does the guardian not say why
the governess is never to bother him? Why doesn't the school give exact
reasons for Miles' dismissal? Why doesn't the governess speak more directly to
the children? I realize that the story is built on the assumptions that these
questions generate; nevertheless, they frustrate me. The stolen letter reminds

me of a dream I've had more than once. I am sitting alone in the living room of our apartment. Gradually I become aware of movement in an apartment in the building directly across from me. There is a large group partying there—my husband, some friends and a number of people whom I do not recognize. It suddenly becomes very important to me to communicate to them what seems to be a crucial message. I am never sure of the exact content of the message . . . I only know that it is crucial. I gesture frantically at the window and eventually experience tremendous relief when I catch their attention. Desperation quickly builds up, however, as my attempts to make them understand me fail. They watch intently for a while but as my gestures become more wild, one by one, they become bored and move away from the window. Still convinced of the urgency of my message, I find a pen and some paper. Now I have no trouble making my message understandable. I write on and on, page after page of beautiful prose that clearly conveys what I must tell them. But, when the letter is finally finished and I look up at the other apartment—everyone is gone . . . it's too late. Actually, although the letter attempt at communication fails for the governess, she shows incredible verbal skill that fascinates me in her relationship with Mrs. Grose.

(13) Miles's death completely devastates me . . . I feel winded . . . somehow responsible for what happened. For the first time in the story, I try to think of what is happening from the children's point of view. All along I've been thinking about myself and ignoring or disliking the children. I have difficulty separating in my mind the consequences of my own negative feelings about motherhood and the awful consequences of the governess's behavior. The tight feeling in my chest is similar to the one I feel in my periodic bouts with guilt about putting my children in daycare. Every so often, I lose sight of my carefully worked out reasons for not being at home and am plagued by doubts. "Maybe this isn't the right thing to do." Miles's death seems to confirm these kinds of doubts . . . I evade my responsibility and something terrible does happen. The sexual tension I feel during the story climaxes in the governess's final encounter with Quint but the satisfaction is short—Miles's death distorts it and makes it a different thing entirely. It is rather similar to the way sex was like a game for my husband and me until I became pregnant, which put it all in a new and far more serious perspective.

### Ms. M's Response Statement Analysis and Judgment of Taste

(T1) I first read "The Turn of the Screw" during the semester break when I had been at home with my children for three weeks. In that time I had become frustrated and bored not only with caring for the children, but with the way in which my marriage had quickly slipped back to the way it was when I was permanent housekeeper and babysitter. I associated reading the story with my unpleasant feelings about motherhood and with the guilt accompanying those feelings. Until I began writing this response I was not really aware of the ways in which I reacted to other aspects of the story, and would have said, on the basis of my frustration and guilt that I disliked the story. But, upon reviewing my response in its entirety, and taking into consideration the fact that "The Turn of the Screw" has stayed with me for several months, I have come to the conclusion that fascination, even satisfaction and enjoyment are more accurate terms for my judgment of taste.

(T2) First of all, there is the matter of my identification with the governess, which begins before her narrative when she is described as anxious (the way in which I see myself) and when it becomes apparent that it will be her responsibility to care for two children (also my responsibility). The identification becomes enjoyable when the governess does not really turn out to be anxious at all but strong and powerful. My personal associations with the isolation at Bly allow me to continue the identification and thus feel a potential for strength and power within myself.

(T3) The difficulty that arises in identification with the governess is that Henry James was a man. Initially I thought that I had solved this problem by ignoring it. When I review the persons with whom I associate power and control, however, it no longer seems adequate to assume that this is really what I have done. The awareness in my response of "maleness" and "femaleness" makes it unlikely that I was successfully able to say "The author was a man but doesn't matter—I'll forget it." The experiences that the governess's power brings to mind involve my father, my grandfather, my husband, and my friend in high school—all males. Perhaps by establishing a bond between myself and the governess I am attempting to align myself with the power that I see socially ascribed to James as a male.

(T4) On the basis of my reading in *Readings and Feelings* and as a result of the lectures I am also aware that James had doubts about his own masculinity and tended to see himself as a young female. This makes identification with James (through the governess) easier and more comfortable because it allows me to combine the elements of femininity that I enjoy (e.g. sex) with the traditional elements of masculinity (e.g. strength) to which I aspire. The associations I describe are incidents in which power seems also to be linked with communication. The times when I feel most powerless—when I was home with the children, when my father kept me in or now when he shouts at me, in my dream etc—are also the times when my attempts to communicate what I think or feel are ineffective or unsatisfying.

(T5) I think there is an enjoyment—self-punishment antithesis present in my response. I obviously enjoy talking about my own feelings, ignoring the children, yet later punish myself with guilt. Pregnancy and motherhood come across as punishments for enjoying sex (despite what my parents said) and the fear that God might really exist for enjoying mocking the religion I was brought up in. But the response also seems to show that such self-punishment is functional for me. I do not experience constant guilt for putting my children in daycare, for example, but "periodic bouts" that allow me to continue enjoying leaving them. I think this is particularly clear in the final paragraph when I describe experiencing guilty concern for ignoring the children's feelings and go on to discuss, not the children's feelings, but the guilt.

(T6) As far as motherhood and religion are concerned it could be that I avoid directly confronting the personal conflicts they present by converting them into larger social concerns. I can feel less responsible, for example, for my failing as a mother, or maybe even as a Catholic if I see faults in the institutions and not myself.

(T7) "The Turn of the Screw" becomes satisfying, then, in that it allows me to identify with strength, purge some guilt and perhaps displace some personal responsibility. There are likely more elements to explain in my response but in attempting this analysis I have had to work on the premise that the elements I am able to pick out are the most meaningful aspects of my response. I found that the procedure of response analysis required a high degree of objectivity—i.e. treating my response as though it belonged to someone else—before I could subjectively evaluate it. The most difficult part of the analysis was avoiding the temptation to rationalize rather than understand the response. I think that I responded to many of the same aspects of the story that I would have chosen to discuss in a traditionally "objective" paper. The essential difference between the two critical methods is that through a subjective approach I accept responsibility for focusing on particular features of the story and attempt to understand why I have done so.

The knowledge Ms. M developed from this reading and response experience, given in the first sentence of paragraph T7, outlines the dimensions of her taste for the tale. The terms of this description suggest that liking or disliking is not enough to articulate taste; rather, she tells of specific psychological premiums that accrued to her as a result of her work. That sentence, furthermore, is only a shorthand for what she described earlier in her analysis; this analysis, in turn, is a resymbolization of the response statement, which was, in its turn, a symbolization of the reading experience. The motive behind this recursive process was just to develop knowledge, though at first the knowledge seemed other than what it finally was: at first she did not like the story, but as she thought more, she became more satisfied with it. Only when she understood her response, however, could she say that there was *knowledge* of her taste; before, there was just a feeling or a sense of it. The articulation of her *judgment* of taste brought new knowledge.

Ms. M observes in the concluding paragraph of her analysis that to understand her own subjectivity, she had to have "a high degree of objectivity." This shows how the natural capacity for objectification enters into the formulation of subjective knowledge. Instead of objectifying the story's semantic, she objectifies her perception of the story. In full deliberate consciousness Ms. M temporarily thinks of her work as belonging to another person. Of course, this is a fiction and it works *only* because it is a fiction. This means that there is no confusion between subjective and objective and that the response is not both. It is subjective but Ms. M objectifies it to discover knowledge of her taste. Self-objectification in the development of knowledge is the adult form of infantile self-enhancement during the learning of new words and the synthesizing of new sentences.

In paragraph T4, Ms. M indicates her awareness of the pedagogical situation in which the response study was undertaken; this included the class and the course and its purposes. Ms. M's cordial relationship with me and her cooperative attitude toward the ideas I proposed obviously contributed to the kind of knowledge she formulated. She had read my book, heard my discussions of it, and heard my remarks about Henry James and my report of what Leon Edel wrote of James. Among various levels of acceptance of response study in the class, Ms. M's was higher than most. The response statement was not written for public distribution, and Ms. M thus knew that I would be the only one to read it in that class at that time.[1]

In the few conversations I had had with Ms. M prior to her writing this essay, we discussed women's rights, and I expressed my skepticism sometimes in teasing, hyperbolic language. It is unlikely, however, that our half-serious dispute had an adverse effect on our pedagogical relationship. Rather, Ms. M's concern with women's rights became part of her response and her analysis. I think the relative prominence of this subject in the response is partly due to its relative prominence in our conversations. This is one of the means through which Ms. M was able to synthesize new knowledge: her essay was a contribution both to her own enlightenment and to mine; after that it was a contribution to the issue of women's rights and to subjective criticism.

The response statement does not have an independent logic or meaning. As complex as it is, each statement and each buildup of thought was retrospectively resymbolized by Ms. M in her analysis, with the aim of defining what her taste for the story was at the time of analysis. For example, the material in paragraph T3 concerning her awareness of the author's gender may be given any number of meanings. It could be an element in Ms. M's fantasy of the author and in her research into what the real author was like; it could be a motivational element in an interpretive formulation of the story as "about" the power confrontation between the sexes. On the other

1. Ms. M's response and her analysis of it was written in an introductory course in subjective criticism and related thinking on literary interpretation. Each student had the option of doing a response study—either of his own response or of mine (which had been presented to the class and discussed)—or could write an essay on another related topic of his choice. In conferences with Ms. M prior to her writing this essay, I did not see her response or know what she would record. We had no private discussion of James's novel; as she reports, I had discussed it in a lecture, and I had discussed my remarks about it in *Readings and Feelings*. Thus, the statement and judgments her statement presents were not negotiated with me. My discussion of it here may be viewed as a further contribution to my pedagogical relationship with Ms. M.

It is significant that this essay was articulated solely on the basis of materials presented in the classroom—Ms. M undertook no technical outside reading and had received no special training. The main explanation I have of its success is Ms. M's serious motivation. I also think, however, that this essay can be a reassurance to those who are skeptical about subjective criticism because they think that it requires special psychological knowledge or belief in one form of psychology or another. This statement, and others in subsequent chapters, show that only traditional amounts of reading and patience are required for the successful practice of subjective criticism.

hand, many who oppose this kind of criticism will easily pick out the narcissism, and concentrate on how little anyone else cares whether Ms. M is aligning herself with James or not. They will insist that a statement like this indicates that subjective criticism is only therapeutic. Thinking according to the subjective paradigm, however, prevents such premature categorization. Even in the context in which Ms. M's response statement was offered—my class in subjective criticism—its meaning may be construed and reconstrued with an indefinite number of aims. As linguistic acts, the statements are to be explained first in reference to the motive for their synthesis, and then generally in reference to the motive for their public, pedagogical use. Many readers may not care what Ms. M thinks, but finding out what Ms. M thinks is not a search for final, authoritative responses and judgments. These same readers care what Mr. Big thinks in order to decide what they themselves think. We commonly read the work of others in order to know our own minds. There is no objective authority in anyone's formulations.

The issue of authority is one of Ms. M's strong concerns in this reading; it appears in many forms in her response and analysis and is part of her interest in the pedagogical relationship. In paragraph 8, Ms. M finally saw the governess exercise strength in facing down Quint. In paragraph 12, she is fascinated with the governess's "incredible verbal skill," this observation following a report of a recurrent dream in which she feels strength, though along with frustration, in being able to communicate through writing. This issue is related to whether she can identify with James, the masculine author. It might also relate to the question of how to deal with the masculine teacher—which may not be clear because of my skepticism about this very issue of "sexual" politics. A less prominent theme in this connection concerns her residual feelings about Catholicism, whose authority she related to Quint's in paragraph 11. She remarked at the outset of that paragraph that she knows Quint is a ghost but that she responds to him as if he were real. Her solution is to take over the "strength" of the ghost. She says toward the end of paragraph 8 that "Quint's power *is* the governess's power." The "strength" of communication is her way, on this occasion, of feeling what she sees as masculine strength—the author's and the teacher's. The need to communicate was a motive in writing this essay. I think Ms. M "believed" many of the claims I made in this course—about reading and about James. Yet it is clear from the response and the analysis that she made my authority her own; she is fully responsible for her own formulations and feels this way.

In the last paragraph of the response statement, she speaks of concern for her children as she realized that she had not looked at the tale from the children's point of view. This raises the issue of responsibility—about caring for her children now, and about how much of it she had when she and her husband were much younger and sex was only fun (her pregnancy "put it all in a new and far more serious perspective"). The analysis says that part of her satisfaction in the reading is that it allowed her to "displace some personal responsibility." In the last sentence of this paragraph (T7) she sees this essay as an occasion for accepting responsibility for her perceptions of the tale. In part, she must feel that part of her child-rearing responsibility is "displaced" onto the importance of finishing at the university. But the child-rearing responsibility is just as soon understood as *replaced* by this more personal and more public kind of responsibility to her own development and to the pedagogical relationship that she takes seriously. Better communication at home and in school ratifies this transformation of duties and restores a sense of strength.

At the beginning of her analysis, Ms. M reports (T1) that she first read the tale at a point when the duties of motherhood had become irritating. According to the discussion in this paragraph, the earlier parts of the response statement may be construed as reflecting Ms. M's mood when she first read the tale, several months before she recorded the response. Between the first reading and the writing of the response, her taste for the tale had changed. After the first reading, there was only the affective feeling, "on the basis of my frustration and guilt," of dislike. After she records the response, there is at least fascination, and "perhaps satisfaction and enjoyment." Over a relatively short (in developmental terms) period of time, and in view of several salient experiences, the qualitative form and the substantive content of her judgment changed.

Ms. M emphasizes that her recording of the response was the agency of change. Earlier in this course, she had submitted another essay—not a response inquiry as this was—which I had cited publicly for its excellence. Also, she read my book and talked things over with me, as I have indicated above. I suggested in Chapter Five that a change in taste is an instance of growth, in which the individual enlarges his sense of self through the stereoscopic evaluation of then versus now. It is possible to view Ms. M's change as an achievement in the service of her growth stage.[2] When she first read the tale, she felt "isolated";

2. I am referring here to the eight stages of growth into which Erik Erikson divided the human life cycle in *Childhood and Society* (New York, 1950). In an extended study of taste and other forms of interpretive judgment, an awareness of age-specific predispositions becomes increasingly important. In studying children's responses, for example, one can establish different emotional preoccupations for two respondents of, respectively, three and six years of age. Likewise, one may expect differences between two readers of twenty years old and forty years old. Ms. M is in Erikson's "intimacy/isolation" stage (between

subsequently she felt "intimate"—perhaps with herself, with the class, with a friend, family, or just the reading experience; or, she felt strength, instead of weakness, in isolation. It is not necessary, however, to apply Erikson's concept of growth stages rigorously; there is a more specific or local sense in which growth may describe the change in taste. As Ms. M describes it, her domestic concerns have to do with one sense of herself, while domestic plus university concerns have to do with another sense. Ms. M is in the midst of making the second, larger sense prevail. As the response statement shows, this involves negotiating what was taught by her parents, and so on. Regardless of these larger considerations, though, the manifest statements in the analysis claim an enlargement of the sense of self, particularly in her greater awareness of responsibility. This sense is not of the form "I must be more responsible," or "I have been irresponsible," but rather, "my sense of responsibility depends in such-and-such a way on my domestic situation and in this other way on my pedagogical situation; the reading experience of this story made this clearer than it was before." In other words, Ms. M better identified the role of responsibility in her life at this time. This makes sense to her as an explanation of her change in taste and as a definition of her taste to begin with. It cannot be determined how far-reaching this knowledge is for her; but it is clear that it took place at least in the context of this pedagogical situation and had at least local consequence.

Unless one studies one's taste from month to month and from year to year, one cannot say that knowledge developed at this moment has permanent application; it does have present value and may have value in the future. But a longer-range perspective may be invoked in the attempt to understand how one's taste has changed. Since we did not record our responses from many years back, most of us have only the memory of childhood reading experiences to compare to our present perception of the same works. Especially when the memory of a childhood reading is strong, it is likely that comparing this memory with a new response today will yield a different, but equally important, piece of knowledge. Both the ways our taste has changed and the ways it has stayed the same will produce significant knowledge. To this end, consider two response statements by Ms. H to Lewis Carroll's *Alice's Adventures in Wonderland*, the first statement a memory of the childhood response, the second the present response.

---

about twenty and the mid-thirties); hence, her long exploration of isolation and its persistence in spite of her motherhood, and perhaps even because of it. But in general, such judgments should be reserved for the discussion of children's responses on the one hand, or for face-to-face negotiation of response statements on the other. It is not very enlightening to draw conclusions about how the statement relates to the growth stage on the basis of the statement alone.

The Remembered Response of Ms. H to
Carroll's *Alice's Adventures in Wonderland*

(1) When I first read *Alice in Wonderland* I was ten or eleven years old. No one was present while I read it; I usually tried to find a quiet place, where no one was around.

(2) As I read the story I remember thinking Alice's reaction to her situation very odd. She never expressed any real fear towards anything that happened to her. When she saw the white rabbit, she only reacted with curiosity. I also felt curious; a rabbit with a waistcoat and watch, who could talk, was very intriguing. I approved of her following the rabbit, but when she jumped down the hole after him I felt she was being too hasty. At this point I began to lose interest or probably the ability to identify with Alice as a real girl.

(3) I especially found her detachment disconcerting; the nonsense she talked as she slowly fell, and her picking objects off the walls and putting them back, was very eery, like she was out shopping. I knew I would have been afraid and would not have had time or the inclination to observe what was on the walls. Especially as I fell to what was possibly my death.

(4) The slow motion of her fall was like a bad dream, where everything has a lingering quality; every intricate and excruciating moment is magnified. When she did finally reach the bottom, she merely fell with a thump, just like she had fallen off a chair, nothing more. Alice did not seem to be disoriented; here she has fallen to a place she may never get out of and her main feeling is curiosity. I am sure to have been terrified and would have immediately started to cry. But Alice is calm, though a little puzzled and looks around with interest at her surroundings. And what does she find at the bottom of a tunnel—well nothing more than a glass table. This piece of furniture was the last object I would have imagined to be found there. I would have expected there to be slimy and creepy things. So I was puzzled as to how this table could have gotten there. But Alice was not a normal girl, Her reactions were to me too adult and measured out. An adult mind trying to think like a child. If I found a bottle that said "Drink Me" I would probably have drunk it as well. Though I remember thinking how nauseating the contents sounded; cherries and turkey mixed together is not very appetizing.

(5) I also became confused with her many transitions from big to small. I grew impatient with the whole story. I could not understand how she or what she had eaten to make her shrink to four inches high. Or why she was so polite to all the odd creatures that gathered around her. What I felt particularly unnatural in this episode, was the mouse taking leadership, while another queer animal suggested a race to dry themselves off where no one won. The logic appeared to be all backwards. There were no references to the normal, ordinary world in which I lived. But I suppose the state of normalcy can be argued as relative in certain experiences. In the case of a child, the only reference he or she has is from family and peers and Alice's world is the reversal of that.

(6) Another episode I recall with distaste is when Alice confronts the Duchess. I really became afraid, not only of the violence but of the grotesque drawings of the Cook and Duchess. Their appearance and manners were terrifying, especially the horrible way in which the Duchess sang to her baby,

while the Cook threw dishes everywhere; it was total madness. I could not relate this mother to my own; never in my wildest moments of childish frustration could I believe my mother like the Duchess. Though I did have fears of my mother turning into a werewolf. Could this horrible image of the Duchess be such an association? I knew if my mother did turn into a werewolf, she could also turn back into her better self. But with the Duchess there would be no such leeway; she was the embodiment of unreasonable and constant punishment. It is something a child would not let himself think of; a perpetually cruel mother is hard to conceive of, when you have a mother who is kind and almost too permissive. Therefore my fear was unmotivated.

(7) The other creature that evoked everlasting fear in me was the Cheshire Cat and I love animals, especially cats. But this fearful cat was out of a nightmare; was far from my idea of a warm loving companion. Its grin was too human for an animal, too cynical, grinning in the midst of violence. At this period in my life I still sucked my thumb, and the only one I felt comfortable doing this in front of was my cat. Therefore the grinning cat meant a betrayal to me. Ridicule from an area in which I had grown to believe was impartial and unchangeable.

(8) I remember another experience associated with the Cheshire Cat. During the time I read *Alice in Wonderland* my family lived about a mile away from school. One route I had, took me past the house where an old couple lived. This particular day as I was passing their house I noticed them standing or they may have been sitting looking out of the window—straight at me. They were very close together and only their heads were showing from behind the curtain. What was curious and frightening were the heads, which were perfectly round and grinning as widely as the Cheshire Cat. The resemblance struck me instantly and reinforced my dislike of the story even more.

(9) Another part of the story that I recall having strong feelings about was at the Mad Tea Party. The nonsense they talked was beyond me, and I do not remember or understand what they said. But I do remember vividly how the Hatter and the Hare tormented the poor Dormouse who was always falling asleep and who finally was put into a tea pot. This passive and gentle character was my favorite of all the animals in the story. Maybe because it was so harmless, and always being victimized, it evoked complete empathy from me. I could really identify with its situation. I was the middle child, between an older brother and sister and a younger brother and sister. I became the go-between and sometimes victim of the older ones and baby-sitter of the younger ones. I saw the Dormouse in this light and felt Alice had abandoned him to a bad end. Her total calm and unconcern for him made me dislike her even more.

(10) I only felt frustrated with Alice remaining so impartial; even when she got exasperated with some of the characters, like the Caterpillar, she did in such a polite sociable way. She remained totally calm and gracious to the Queen of Hearts and her cruel croquet game, where the balls and mallets were hedgehogs and flamingoes. While the whole time the Queen is rushing around yelling to her guards to cut off someone's head. It was insanity, though not as mad and terrifying as the Duchess. Therefore when Alice finally loses her temper at the end and says the whole bunch of them are only a pack of cards, I felt she finally asserted herself and I finished the book with a sense of relief.

(11) I was very glad to find that Alice had merely dreamt all that had just happened to her. I did not want to believe that such things could really happen outside of a dream. Though to even have dreamt such an experience would have left a traumatic effect upon anyone.

(12) *Alice in Wonderland* left many distorted images with me. I have associated only the bad experiences of my childhood with it. This may be attributed to the style and subject of nonsense that has led me to parallel it with the most unhappy times of my childhood. Therefore I would generally say *Alice in Wonderland* is not children's literature. Its imagery is too confusing for the child's mind, leading only to derogatory comments and memories when considered in retrospect. Which is unfair treatment to such a masterpiece of nonsense.[3]

Although there is no way to be sure of what actually happened in Ms. H's mind when she read this book at age eleven, this response statement makes frequent distinctions between what she definitely remembers, what she supposes must have happened, and what may or may not have happened. These distinctions came from the conscious effort to remember the past; her sense of her previous response seems no less authentic than would be anyone else's memory of events that took place fourteen years before. Following Novey's reasoning (discussed in Chapter Three), this memory is synthesized now, and Ms. H has separated the memory from the response she recorded after rereading the book. Ms. H's subjective dialectic between the memory and the present response is the issue of interest.

Ms. H says that her childhood distaste for this work came from the "odd" or "eery" aspect of many things in it, probably, she lost "the ability to identify with Alice as a real girl" (1). In paragraph 4 she notes that Alice's responses to things were "too adult and measured out" and that there were many "unnatural," "queer," and "backward" items which baffled and frightened her.

Ms. H says that she was particularly fearful of the Duchess (6) and the Cheshire Cat (7), and her associations suggest the nature of her fear. After first saying that she could "never in my wildest moments of

---

3. Ms. H's responses were submitted in a course in children's literature that I taught with Michael Steig. There was only a bare minimum of discussion and explanation of response statements. The work options included research in children's literature, study of one's own childhood and present response to a single work, and collection of recorded responses of young children to their favorite books. More emphasis was placed in this course in evaluating what could be significant in the response statements of adults and children than on consciously developing knowledge. Our primary concern was only in discovering just what happens during adults' response to children's literature. Ms. H's second statement was discussed in class.

One of the issues I raised in connection with *Alice* and similar works of nonsense pertained to the kind of comprehension young children actually have. At what level are they entertained by it, and is their interest similar to adults'? Ms. H wrote her second statement after participating in discussion of other nonsense works, but before discussion of this one.

childish frustration" believe her mother like the Duchess, she allows that she feared her mother's "turning into a werewolf." She then "reasons" that if Mother did so transform herself, she would be able to resume her normal self again; but this thought is also attenuated by the observation that Mother was "almost too permissive." Finally she says, most likely from the perspective of the present, that "my fear was unmotivated." This paragraph reports a distinct childhood response, but in retrospect it does not seem explainable to Ms. H.

The Cheshire Cat was fearful because it also seemed to her a transformation of a loving being—her own cat. This fear is of being aggressively discovered or watched in her privacy. That she sucked her thumb was a secret between her and her cat; the grinning cat, like the grinning old couple on the way to school, seemed like "a betrayal" to her. In the first paragraph, she reported reading this work in complete privacy; encountering such treacherous observers also helped reduce the emotional premium of the private reading experience.

Ms. H responded sympathetically to the "poor Dormouse" (9) because he was a "passive and gentle character." As a middle child this was how she felt in relation to her four siblings. Alice, in her "impartial" (10) character, "abandoned" the mouse "to a bad end." Finally the moments of sympathy were far outweighed by the fearful feelings, and Ms. H felt only relief in finishing the book and learning that it was all a dream anyway.

Ms. H seemed glad of the opportunity to inquire into this childhood experience, especially in a context whose announced purpose was to develop knowledge about how childhood literary experiences contribute to adult tastes. In her response to the adult reading, further associations from childhood and later emerge; and it is possible to distinguish Ms. H's change of taste as it relates to a part of her maturation.

The Present Response of Ms. H to
Carroll's *Alice's Adventures in Wonderland*

(1) Upon re-reading *Alice's Adventures in Wonderland* I find my present response to be more favorable than I expressed in my childhood experience. Though I still have an aversion to many of the characters such as the Duchess and the Cheshire Cat, I now see other sides to the story which I had missed before.

(2) One passage that greatly affected me: "How she longed to get out of that dark hall, and wander among those beds of bright flowers and those cool fountains, but she could not even get her head through the doorway." The garden represents a glorious imaginary place where ultimate peace exists. The need for peace and love causes us to constantly reach out for it; we must always be expanding ourselves and our principles to achieve it. Alice is searching for a way into this haven when she drinks the liquid in the bottle

marked "Drink Me"; the need to reach that garden makes her repress any fear of its being poison.

(3) When she finally does become small and she can fit through the door,"... alas for poor Alice! when she got to the door she found she had forgotten the little golden key." When she eats the cake marked "Eat me," hoping to grow large again, she forgets that she will again be too big. These ups and downs of Alice's seem very typical of my life and probably of everyone else's. When you really want something, in many cases, you have to overcome certain barriers to get it.

(4) Alice's adventures could be said to be her initiation into the frustrations of adulthood. She becomes very confused with the continual changing from large to small, causing for her an identity crisis.

(5) I have suffered similar crises recently, when one after another I received blows to my ego: personal assaults from people close to me and in my academic work. Failure to understand the reasons for suffering creates confusion and disorientation. I previously had a well-rounded image of myself which came tumbling down, leaving a very bruised ego.

(6) For instance, until recently I have maintained a fairly good average in my academic work, but since I began upper level work I have fallen into a slump. With help from my teachers I am beginning to work my way up again, but such incidents are very frightening. Therefore I can readily identify with Alice's confusion and her tears of frustration and fear in the dark tunnel of having changed in the night.

(7) Another side to Alice which I overlooked in my childhood response was Alice's constant reference to her cat Dinah. I love cats and my affection is much the same as Alice's. Like her I miss the companionship of a cat, as Alice says, "She is such a dear quiet thing . . . and she sits purring so nicely by the fire." How nostalgic I become with this image. Both of us love our cats for the security and contentment they embody.

(8) When Alice finally does find the way back to the little door, she had grown in experience with the world of nonsense. She realizes that the only way to deal with a world with no rational sense is to keep her temper and follow their rules.

(9) Upon opening the door she says, " 'Now, I'll manage better this time,' " and then methodically makes herself the right size in order to get through the door. Alice's action of making herself small is similar to what I, and a lot of other people, tend to do when amongst strangers. To ingratiate myself with them, I try to dilute my opinions and therefore make myself more acceptable; in other words, become a hypocrite. Even when associating with some of my relatives I find myself being this way, especially my grandmother, who is very nice but can be very disapproving if I contradict her.

(10) Therefore Alice's final emergence into the garden could be viewed as another step in her initiation into the adult world, which can be very nonsensical. But her garden that was her main goal from the entrance into the dark tunnel, turns out to be just as irrational as the rest of Wonderland.

(11) The Queen of Hearts is one of the irrational inhabitants of the garden. I do not find her as threatening as I did in my childhood response. She now appears pompous and ridiculous whereas before she was a frightening

mother-figure with the authority to cut one down to size with merely a shouted phrase, "Cut off her head." My mother never shouted at me; she is still a quiet, even tempered, loving woman, whom all her children love very much. Thus my childhood dislike of the Queen was prompted by her unmotherly behavior which her title Queen of Hearts indicates.

(12) I also noticed that the people playing croquet are like squabbling children. "The players all played at once without waiting for turns, quarreling all the while, and fighting" to get the attention of their mother and her approval. I do not recall having to fight for my parents' attention. My mother was mainly in the background when I was a child and our father would always give us the attention we wanted. We could jump all over him even when he was relaxing and play games; he enjoyed every minute of it. I never really knew my mother until they got a divorce and I became a source of support for her during this trying period of her life.

(13) The one character I still have a great deal of aversion for is the Duchess. Her transition from a violent sadistic mother figure to a smiling friendly person in the Queen's garden evokes in me a suspicion of hypocrisy on her part. Worse than that she engages in subterfuge to gloss over her previous behavior. Especially when she says, " 'You can't think how glad I am to see you again you dear old thing!' " and then she tucks her arm "affectionately" into Alice's she gives me the same feeling an old school teacher of mine did. Like the Cheshire Cat she always wore a smile on her face, even when she was angry. I never felt I could trust her, as I would never trust the Duchess. Especially when she says to Alice, " 'I dare say you're wondering why I don't put my arm around your waist.' " This seems to me a very intimate proposal an acquaintance to make. Though this may have been an acceptable manner of expressing friendship in Victorian days, it must surely have been reserved for very good friends. The Duchess is being very presumptuous in suggesting it to Alice, who reacts with distaste in any case and makes an excuse to avoid having her ugliness near her. I recall feeling repulsed when my mother sat too close to me when I was in my teens. It bothered me a great deal to have my mother lean on me when riding in a car, though this was a phase I got over as I grew older. But in the case of the Duchess I do not feel I am over-reacting when I say there may be something sexual involved in her suggestion. I was relieved when the Queen came and ordered the Duchess away.

(14) In the last part of the story, during the trial, I felt the same relief when re-reading it as I did in my childhood response, when Alice finally asserts herself. She has learned to stand up for what she believes in. Even when the opponent is a person of authority. The last reversal of logic Alice could take was when the Queen said, " 'Sentence first—verdict afterwards.' " Alice would not stand by and let this irrational statement go unchallenged; she had to say something. She had previously accepted rebukes from many of the other creatures but now she was physically superior and unafraid. Though it would have been more courageous of her if she had spoken up when she was still small. I remember trying to stand up to authority; it was in my first year of school. I was reprimanded by my teacher for cheating. I felt this unfair since I was merely daydreaming. But she did not believe me and sent me to the corner for punishment. Similar episodes caused me to fail the whole year. Thus my

experience with authority figures makes me sympathetic with Alice's final triumph when she woke up to realize her own personal worth. Though her triumph is short, she rejects the irrational adult world of Wonderland and escapes back into her childhood and to safety.[4]

At the end of her remembered response, Ms. H observed that although this work is a "masterpiece of nonsense," its "imagery is too confusing for the child's mind." In the later response, she feels more favorable toward the work because "I now see other sides to the story which I had missed before" (1). In finding that her taste is now more commensurate with her belief that the work is a masterpiece, it changed in the direction she thought it should. Her more favorable opinion is related to new perceptions and subjective definitions of them. Both the memory and the new response are functions of the respective growth stages—prepuberty and young adulthood—in which they occurred. The later statement suggests that Ms. H is still susceptible to some of her juvenile fears, but that the appearance of adult concerns and outlooks help her to understand these fears in a way that reduces their strength and thereby changes her overall taste for the work.

In the first statement, Ms. H sees Alice as "odd" and "not normal": Ms. H feels a definite fear in response to the Duchess and the Cheshire Cat and does not see why Alice is not also fearful in this unusual world. Her specific concern is whether her mother can become fearful and maliciously intrude on her privacy, which is the scene of her reading and her surreptitious thumb-sucking. She may be embarrassed by an adult's discovery of her pleasurable and vaguely autoerotic activity; it is odd to her that Alice is not comparably concerned. In the second statement there is a fairly detailed discussion in paragraph 13 about what seem to her homosexual advances toward Alice by the Duchess. It is noteworthy that after she entertains the thought that this may be a normal Victorian mannerism, she decides that the advance is sexual anyway. This perception is related to her memory of her mother's physical closeness during her adolescence, which was part of her mother's dependency on her after her parents' divorce. The distasteful element in the Duchess's advance is due partly to the latter's "ugliness" and partly to Ms. H's perception of her deviousness and insincerity. The unnatural sexual elements are bound up with the fearful

4. In the earlier parts of this statement—paragraphs 2 through 4—Ms. H uses some of the same language habits that appeared in Mr. J's response in Chapter Six. (For example, "the need for peace and love causes us constantly to reach out for it.") In this statement Ms. H's identification of her own feelings with "everyone else's" is quite local, and as the response proceeds, it stops. The relative negotiability, in the sense of more explanatory affects and associations, increases from the middle of the statement on toward the end, where there is a forthright discussion of her parents' divorce and its personal consequence for her. In the process of writing the response, Ms. H seemed to overcome her inhibitions and assert herself, as she does against the Duchess and in support of Alice.

emotional potential in the Duchess. The sexual dimension of her fear that was relatively latent in the first statement is relatively overt in the second; although there may be many sources for this exposure, at least one is that Ms. H now thinks and speaks a more sexual language as a result of normal growth.

The new language allows her to see Alice as more of a normal girl: she mentions new parts of the work, particularly Alice's confusion at the outset, that render her less adult and more like Ms. H remembers herself. In paragraphs 2 through 9, she understands Alice's feelings more fully and perceives more girlish emotions in her. In paragraph 10, she views Alice's entry into the garden as "another step in her initiation into the adult world." For Ms. H, the initiation into the adult world made greater sense of the fears brought out in both readings and made greater sense of both readings in general. In paragraph 14, she elaborates her identification with Alice's final self-assertion, but now she notes Alice's "physical superiority" as part of the reason for her new strength. She further relates the physical strength to the moral strength and courage needed to "stand up to authority," which includes teachers and her grandmother (9). Wonderland, instead of being just a strange place, is now viewed more articulately as "the irrational adult world" from which one can escape to childhood and "to safety." Rather than being fearful about her childhood privacy of daydreaming, she is angry at its having been mistaken for cheating. Such feelings are in contrast to the predominantly helpless ones she reported in her first statement.

Ms. H observes that part of her present, stronger attitude comes from having experienced and overcome difficulties in school. She reports having felt victimized as a child by her teacher. In paragraph 6 of the second statement, she reports being able "to work my way up again" with the help of her teachers. The course in which these responses were written was part of this working her way up; the chance to inquire into her responses thereby relates to a difficulty that she reports overcoming in the statement. The change of taste between childhood and the present is also a change of attitude taking place entirely in the present; it is not possible to distinguish between the motive for the long-range change and for the more local one taking place now. In each case, her desire for self-enlightenment is related to the attempt to deal less hypocritically and more courageously with family and pedagogical authority.

In the present statement, certain of Ms. H's usages are more abstract or intellectualized. In addition, she sees some of the material in the work metaphorically. For example, she calls the Queen of Hearts a "mother-figure"; she considers Victorian mores a possible explanation of the Duchess's behavior; she sees "irrationality" instead of oddness or insanity; she sees Alice's changes in size as emotional as well as physical. Such forms of thought result in part from the discussions of children's literature that took place in the six weeks between her first statement and her second. Ms. H adopted some of the language of both teachers in this course. I take these usages to be more authentic than compliant because the presentation of her affects and associations was enhanced and not inhibited in the process. The language seemed particularly helpful to her in reducing the fearful quality of some of the inhabitants of Wonderland. By judging the Duchess's behavior as sexual, for example, Ms. H renders her behavior less fearfully vague; just after this judgment (in paragraph 13) she remarks that she grew out of the "phase" in which she felt uncomfortable with her mother's physical closeness.

Ms. H does not say whether, as a result of the later perspective on the reading, she still considers the work unsuitable for children. But a parent or teacher with the kind of knowledge developed in the second statement can conceivably ameliorate a fearful reading experience by guiding response in some of the directions of identification with Alice reported by Ms. H. To Ms. H, Alice "is" different from what she "was" in her childhood reading; she is a girl learning and reasoning instead of a detached "adult." The key feature of the new perception is that it is part of a different orientation, which is what the child reacts strongly to in the pedagogical situation. Like Ms. M in the previous response, Ms. H is more analytical in the second statement, with a corresponding decrease in the moral view of the work's unsuitability. Understanding taste in subjective terms reduces the tendency to communicate it in moral terms.

Articulating a longer-range perspective in one's own taste minimizes the number of negative value judgments one can make.[5] If both the fact of change and its principle can be known, the reader will have documented the relativity of his judgment. He will have demonstrated to himself the variability of perception and the operation of various motives that influence the normal flow of likes

---

5. I am frequently asked if I think there is such a thing as a negative value judgment. My answer is that, no, I don't think there is. In principle, and except to make local feelings clear to others, I don't see any sense in saying, "This is a bad book." I have found that, placed in a perspective suitable for me, the "worst" book can provide great interest. When I do not like a work as a "good yarn" or a great thought or a moving lyric, it usually becomes just as engaging as a biographical document or an object of mass appeal. If literature were a machine, its quality would be determined functionally. Since literature may reasonably be the subject of an indefinite number of mental functions, there is no way to say that it is intrinsically disfunctional, only, that some readers in some contexts do not like it, while others in other contexts do. When the development of taste becomes a disciplined activity, one finds mental benefit in an ever-increasing variety of works; knowledge of one's own taste greatly increases its versatility. Knowledge of how Ms. M made her negative judgment helped bring her to a more favorable one; the case is similar, though less consciously directed, with Ms. H.

and dislikes. Rejection of a symbolic object is a kind of self-censorship, since one is actually rejecting one's resymbolization rather than the object itself. When the object is considered real by those in authority, rejection turns into public censorship. Although there has been considerable sentiment against book-banning for several decades, it continues in many quarters in connection with children's literature. If Ms. H had left her childhood judgment without further inquiry, it would have remained as the ground for withholding the work from children, "for their own protection." Adult censorship is usually justified by the same dubious altruism. When there is no organized censorship, teachers' subjective predilections are presented as objective value judgments, and young readers gradually abandon their desire to choose and their responsibility for what they do choose. It is easier to choose nothing that to be accused of bad taste.

One of the main proposals of subjective criticism is that the organized study of taste is a natural starting point for language and literature programs. While it may seem like common sense to teach a course in "great books," such courses communicate to students that unless they like these books either to begin with or ultimately, their taste is deficient. Once they discover that it really makes no difference whether they like these books, they become skeptical of pedagogical purposes and can barely use the classroom to their advantage. If taste is understood as an expression of subjectivity, its cultivation depends, first, on identifying it as fully as possible and, then, on testing it on works that may not be "great" in the eyes of either Leavis or Freud. Those teachers who believe that this pedagogical aim is preferable, however, usually have no language to speak of taste in nonprescriptive ways; in doing the best they can with what they were taught, they bring back the great books, though in a more modest presentational atmosphere.

The regular use of response statements will obviously change the traditional notions of taste from something that *may* be developed to something that *can* be. Instead of one's taste being a fixture of personality, it becomes an instrument of self-enhancement and self-possession. Becoming aware of literary and linguistic predispositions is necessarily a cumulative project. Ms. M's and Ms. H's essays only suggest how such cumulation works and show how the issue may be broached within the limits of a single course. Nonetheless, because important growth goes on from year to year in each reader and because, in the university, vocational preoccupations heavily influence intellectual effort, personal concerns will enter consequentially when the inquiry into taste is coordinated with the slow development of these concerns. This is the rationale for the programmatic investigation of taste, for the need to reinquire into one's taste regularly in new pedagogical situations. One of the likely results of long-term study is that many will discover that they just do not have a taste for literature. Many college majors in this and other subjects cannot say either to themselves or to anyone else why they are enrolled in the program at all. From a subjective standpoint, it is a pedagogical responsibility to articulate the subject in a way that facilitates knowledge of one's involvement in it. It is less and less possible to study almost anything without commanding one's motives and directing them on one's own behalf.

A judgment of taste is as much a psychological constituent of the development of knowledge as of the choice of food, clothes, or friends. The pedagogical interest is in just how conscious these judgments can become. It is not likely that they can become much more conscious than they are now for most readers, without disciplined inquiry into local and developmental response processes.

# Chapter Eight

# THE CONSTRUCTION
# OF LITERARY MEANING

Interpretation is an explanatory activity that is itself explained by the principles underlying the acquisition and use of language. Linguistic articulation—naming and identification—is the symbolization of experience; interpretation is a resymbolization motivated by the demand that the knowledge thus symbolized be explained, or converted into a more subjectively satisfying form. In this way all explanations are interpretive and may be understood as the construction of new knowledge.

The view that knowledge is constructed rather than discovered proceeds from Piaget's explanation of the development of intelligence. He sees his own work as having shown the constructionist foundation of human knowledge-making.[1] Significantly, the history of literary hermeneutics suggests a similar conclusion from a much different perspective. This history documents how the *same questions* about literature are posed and reposed with each new generation and epoch. These questions seem to admit only of local solutions. For example, although *Oedipus Rex* has been the same work for millenia, it remains legitimate to formulate new meanings for it at each new reading or performance. Meanwhile, Kuhn's reconceptualization of the history of science argues that, similarly, scientific knowledge amounts to new local solutions for enduring questions (while the habit of viewing this knowledge as absolute truth likewise derives from local, communal motives).

---

1. Piaget's conception of knowledge, while not subjective in the sense I have been discussing, derives from observations of infantile development which demonstrate the knowing subject's activity: "To my way of thinking, knowing an object does not mean copying it—it means acting upon it. It means constructing systems of transformations that can be carried out on or with this object. Knowing reality means constructing systems

This understanding of knowledge-making is a direct consequence of the fact that the same psychology governs both hermeneutics and linguistic functioning. Because language has had, over the span of human phylogenetic development, the same adaptive role, it follows that demands for knowledge are to be explained by local manifestations of enduring adaptive motives. New knowledge is created when intellectual efforts make subjective concerns serve new conscious purposes.

Most generally, the interest in literary meaning grows from the desire to make knowledge from experiences with symbolic objects. Of particular concern in the present context is that the symbolic objects are themselves linguistic. It would appear to be only common sense to begin thinking that a verbal configuration such as a poem or a story *already had* meaning in it, in contrast to a piece of music or sculpture, which do not seem to be semantic language systems. Literary interpretation would thus seem to be a process of extraction, either on the assumption that the words themselves contain the meaning, or on the assumption that the author's special version of these words hold the meaning. From this (objective) viewpoint, it appears that literary interpretation finds, rather than makes, knowledge.

The discussion in Chapter Three proposes why actual interpretations are most productively understood as having been made and not found, even when the dreamer participates in the interpretation of his own dream. Also, as I indicated briefly in Chapter Five, and as I discuss further in Chapter Nine, if a literary work is deliberately associated with its author, its proposed meaning is still validated by the reader and by the prevailing standards of knowledge in his interpretive community. The issue of present interest is how the inclusion of response statements in the formulation of literary meaning permits the disclosure of motives for knowledge and the public use of motives in the pursuit of knowledge. In the discussion to follow, the response statements are to be understood as the readers' peremptory perceptual identification of the work, which is then resymbolized by the meaning formulation. Neither of the two formulations under scrutiny represents a conscious attempt to relate the reading experience to a system of thought such as Marxism, psychoanalysis, or structuralism; rather, the abstractions each reader developed are largely moral and perhaps somewhat psychologically oriented, with primary attention to some en-

---

of transformation that correspond, more or less adequately, to reality. . . . Knowledge, then, is a system of transformations that become progressively adequate" (*Genetic Epistemology*, New York, 1971, p. 15). Subjective considerations imply that when the criterion of adequacy is applied to knowledge of symbolic objects, it is not possible to consider such objects "objective." That is, the knowledge constructed will not appear to be adequate unless it is thought of as knowledge of a subjectively constructed object.

during generality of the human condition. In this regard, I assume that these readers are more representative of nonprofessional respondents, and that their interests are not governed by adherence to a particular ideology or intellectual language. Nevertheless, the explanation of more ideologically governed meanings rests on similar principles.

The two interpretive efforts I am discussing were prepared differently from one another, and this difference is of both pragmatic and conceptual consequence—pragmatic because different pedagogical practices are involved; conceptual because different types of knowledge are constructed. The response statement of Ms. K to Hawthorne's *Blithedale Romance* was recorded during the actual reading of the novel. When she finished reading, she reports that she switched her mind, so to speak, into the familiar interpretive gear that she had learned in undergraduate literature courses. Her meaning was therefore formulated without systematic conscious reference to the response statement, and, in a sense, *as if* the response statement had not been given. Ms. A, on the other hand, wrote her response statement after two readings of Kafka's "Metamorphosis," and the formulation of meaning, as is clear from the statement, came as a result of conscious review of the response. I will return to the significance of this difference once the motivational substance of each effort has been proposed.[2]

The Meaning Statement of Ms. K for Hawthorne's *Blithedale Romance*

(M1) *The Blithedale Romance*, like so many of Hawthorne's works, seems to be dealing with the fundamental problems of the roles and nature of man and woman, so often enveloped in Hawthorne's stories within the veil of Original

---

2. Ms. K's statements were given in a seminar whose announced purpose was to study the contributions of response to the process of interpretation. The prior stipulation for each participant was to at least try to separate the meaning statement from the response statement, and to prepare the response statement first. The class in which Ms. A prepared her statement had a similar purpose, but there was no stipulation, one way or the other, with regard to separate preparation of response and meaning. Ms. A's statement thus represents her choice of how to present and explore her interpretive processes. Except as it is relevant to these preannounced purposes, the classroom negotiation of these statements is not part of my discussion in this chapter, though I believe in each case my relationship with the particular student was important. Although both readers presented highly negotiable statements, each had a distinct and serious belief in objective interpretation, and each was suspicious, in a friendly way, of the value of collecting response statements. At the time, I thought both were competitive and achievement-oriented and were correspondingly relieved that grading would not apply in these courses in the traditional way. I think that as a consequence of this relief, a fully internal standard of accomplishment came into play in that both were eager to write a "good" response in the interests, among other things, of distinguishing themselves as students. How such motives come into play in literature classrooms is obviously of considerable interest, and this is partially explored in Chapter Five in connection with Mr. P. The present discussion, however, will concentrate on the relatively local issue of how individuals formulate interpretive judgments in a nonprofessional and nonideological circumstance.

Sin. Here we see four people, each of whom is dominated with distinct views and feelings toward their roles as men and women and toward the roles of the other men and women in their lives. We see all of them both clearly expressing their feelings, while at the same time, all are trying to defend their other interests against these feelings, with the exception of Priscilla.

(M2) I feel that the key to the whole story is found in Chapter XIV. This conversation at Eliot's Pulpit, surely an appropriate enough place for the truth to finally come out, is one of deep emotion on the part of all four characters. Here Zenobia, in defense of Hollingsworth's overpowering hold on women, states her conviction on women's rights. Here also, however, we see Zenobia reduced to utter helplessness under Hollingsworth's influence. Zenobia is in every way a woman, except for her refusal to accept her proper role as subordinate to man. This subordinate role was indeed within her, but she fought against it to the point of death.

(M3) Hollingsworth possessed all the important qualities of man except for his devotion of all his being to his own purpose. This was perhaps a quality which might better have been possessed by Zenobia. If she would have dedicated herself to Hollingsworth with the dedication with which he dedicated himself to his plan for criminal reform; if this one quality, which accounts for the "femininity" often associated with Hollingsworth, would have been transferred to Zenobia, both characters would have been able to accept their roles and would have "lived happily ever after."

(M4) Hollingsworth and Priscilla are the two characters which accept their natural roles as man and woman. It was inevitable, then, that they should finally become the couple to be married. Priscilla's desire, indeed her *need*, is to be domineered by Hollingsworth's masculine strength. The tragedy seems to be, however, that once Hollingsworth has achieved his goal of finding someone submissive enough to become completely swayed to his mind, he loses his initiative. This seems to have been the result of Zenobia's death, for which he felt responsible. His efforts to win submissiveness could lead only to the death of the strong-willed Zenobia and the ultimate realization on Hollingsworth's part that his single-mindedness was indeed an evil and destructive quality (i.e., in a man).

(M5) The most interesting aspect of all this is the conflicting qualities within the nature of man and woman. Despite the hopelessness of Zenobia's and Hollingsworth's characters, they certainly were the most admirable characters of the novel. What perhaps is most frustrating about the novel is the realization on the part of the reader that women are meant to be Priscillas, not Zenobias.

(M6) Coverdale is a hard nut to crack. I'll simply say that he does mainly fulfill the role of the Chorus as he himself says. The "confession" that he loved Priscilla came as no surprise. In the Eliot's Pulpit chapter earlier alluded to, he defends Zenobia's feminist argument, but this was, just as Zenobia's argument had been, merely a defense against his real feelings. His continual references to his futile attempts to win the affections of Priscilla which he always saw directed to Zenobia and Hollingsworth clearly show that he desired her simple, womanly affections far more than he wanted the love of Hollingsworth or Zenobia, by whom he would have ultimately been crushed.

(M7) Like Hawthorne's "The Birthmark," the flaw of the woman cannot be removed. She must maintain it, or cease to be a woman. The natural birthmark of the woman is her submissive nature to man, and her role of wife and mother. Zenobia refuses to accept this, and Hollingsworth does not realize what his singlemindedness is doing until he sees the potential wife and mother destroyed by his desire to possess her in the wrong way.

Ms. K's interpretation of *The Blithedale Romance* is that it defines the role of women. The actual interpretation, best summarized in the sentence "The natural birthmark of the woman is her submissive nature to man, and her role of wife and mother" (M7), is a subordinate clause in the implicit predication "The novel means that. . . ." This predication is assumed in the conventions through which interpretive efforts are communicated, and this assumption is identical to the one which holds that words have meanings or that any symbol has a meaning: it is the assumption that the confrontation of a symbolic object will result in the formulation of a meaning for it. The implicit public assumption is "The novel means," which is the "topic," and the new meaning is the "comment"; the resulting predication is the basic resymbolization. Just as in infantile speech, the two parts of the predication need not be grammatical in the traditional noun-verb sense; rather, the grammar of the resymbolization is defined by its purpose, which is to create a relationship between "the novel means" and some other linguistic formulation.[3]

The statement of central interest is the "comment." *Both* parts of that predication are proposed by Ms. K—namely, that the topic of the novel is "the natural birthmark of the woman" and the comment is "her submissive nature." In a context where objective interpretation is the assumed standard, topic, comment, and their proposed relationship are tested against the "objective" text with the aim of showing that in all three categories, Ms. K has recovered original meaning. By and large, in her statement of meaning, Ms. K tacitly assumes the objective standard; this permits a second assumption that the meaning of this work will be similar to the meaning of other works by the same author. She invokes this assumption in the opening sentence of the statement. The functional result of the second assumption is that an assumed meaning of "The Birthmark" becomes the meaning of *The Blithedale*

---

3. At the complex level of functioning where interpretation takes place, the subject-predicate breakdown of all sentences will not necessarily add up, through transformational calculations, to the fundamental judgment. But if the phrase "the novel means" is *considered* a predication (with *means* an intransitive verb), that sentence corresponds to the community's purpose of finding meaning for novels. Which predicative structure will define the formulation of knowledge is a matter of choice and not grammatical logic. The cascading of predicative structures toward an authoritative formulation is obviously not explainable by the logical structure of language but by the motives brought to bear by those involved in the negotiation.

*Romance*; this shift seems objectively plausible on the grounds that it is commonly expected that separate works by the same author partake of the same or similar meanings. Most of Ms. K's discussion, however, presents material in the novel. The final meaning in paragraph M7 is the result of combining the "objective" meaning of another story, that of Hawthorne's work in general, and a series of perceptions of this novel in particular.

It is usually admitted in criticism that none of these standards of knowledge are, in the final analysis, certain or objective; but even assuming they are, there are so many other statements in this interpretation that are obviously subjective judgments that it is foolish even to try to justify them as pieces of objective secondary knowledge "proving" the conclusion about the role of women. In paragraph M2, for example, Ms. K says she "feels" the key to the story is the conversation at Eliot's Pulpit; in paragraph M5 she says that the "most interesting" aspect of what she previously discussed was that the roles of man and woman were themselves "conflicting." In the same paragraph she observes that the reader's realization that women were "meant to be" Priscillas "is most frustrating about the novel." In this last judgment, if we take it literally, the tacit assumption is that any reader reading this novel would have to come to the same realization and feel the same frustration. Of course, most critical readers would not take the judgment literally and would simply allow this as Ms. K's subjective judgment; but as such, it has no authority, since there is no way of understanding the subjective meaning, to Ms. K, of "women are meant to be Priscillas." Almost none of the statements in this interpretation, regardless of their forceful and confident tones, can be objectively authorized, and none are subjectively authorized. Yet the language is coherent, eminently intelligible, and communicates Ms. K's dominion over her judgmental processes; it seems to have a logic of its own, rooted in familiarity with the reading experience and with the traditional concerns of critical reading.

I think that the public interest in this interpretation is just this subjective quality. For example, the topic sentence in the concluding paragraph remains technically ambiguous, even if the word *in* were inserted after "like." Yet the main clause of the sentence is clear as a piece of knowledge Ms. K associates with this reading experience. Of critical interest is just how Ms. K attributes this claim to Hawthorne or to this work, and just what "the flaw of the woman" means in her subjective vocabulary; similar sorts of questions apply to the opening sentence of paragraph M3. Although we may have an intuitive sense of the meaning of "all the important qualities of man," Ms. K's subjective meaning would authorize this knowledge and make it more available for our assimilation.

The great majority of the judgments in this interpretation were constructed from the vocabulary of motives that Ms. K brought up in her response to the original reading experience. The explanation of the style and meaning of this interpretation cannot, therefore, be found by measuring it against our own perception of the same novel; each of our reading experiences would bring up a different perceptual and motivational configuration. Rather, because each interpretation is to be understood as a resymbolization, Ms. K's symbolization, or her peremptory perceptual identification, becomes the document of explanatory relevance, since it will suggest the array of subjective references for both the secondary and concluding interpretations.

### The Response Statement of Ms. K to Hawthorne's *Blithedale Romance*

(1) "These characters, he [the author] feels it right to say, are entirely fictitious." I recall here the ending of the old "Dragnet": "the names have been changed to protect the innocent." It was about this time in the program when the inevitable battle between me and my parents began over my going to bed. I used to *hate* to go to bed and was always thinking of stupid excuses for staying up as late as possible.

(2) Veiled Lady—the veil is "white with somewhat of a subdued silver sheen."—reminiscent of an Xmas book I had as a child in which the pictures of angels and cherubs sparkled. I thought the book was incredibly precious. I looked at the beautiful picture over and over again and felt that there was something very special about the sparkling pictures.

(3) Coverdale "really getting to be a frosty bachelor, with another white hair, every week or so, in my moustache"—I used to have a great fear of seeing my mother get old and used to sit on her lap and try to pull out all the gray hairs on her head.

(4) Description of snow scene. Terribly excited by snow. I always had snowball fights with my father, and was always delighted when he built up a tall, smiling snowman for me.

(5) "We grown-up men and women were making a play-day of the years that were given to us to live in." This reminds me of "playing house" with the girl across the alley. I was very bossy about the games and insisted on playing my own way. If I played the "mommy" I always played a very cruel character and was as mean as possible to my "daughter." When my playmate protested I defended myself by saying that that was the way my own mother always treated me. This wasn't true at all, but it was a means of justifying my rules of the game.

(6) Zenobia's description of Hollingsworth as "a great heart"—calls to mind a childhood repulsion towards Catholic "bleeding hearts,"—how could anyone pray to anything so horrible?

(7) Bothered by Zenobia's superior attitude towards criminals as being "beyond help." I usually reject despairing attitudes.

(8) Priscilla's fear of storm—my own fear of thunder and lightning when small used to make me physically ill, nauseous. This was mainly due to my grandmother's insistence on closing blinds, unplugging everything, etc. as if

the storm was really a threat.

(9) Coverdale overhears Hollingsworth at prayer. How embarrassing! It should be the most private of activities.

(10) Hollingsworth somewhat repulsive—"establishing himself as my nurse." "But there was something of the woman moulded into the great, stalwart frame of Hollingsworth." Coverdale pictures Hollingsworth as a priest. Despite my being bothered by Hollingsworth's femininity, I tend to agree with the suggestion that he be a priest. This seems strange because priests have always seemed very masculine and domineering to me.

(11) Zenobia—"that she had always a new flower in her hair." My grandfather always grew beautiful flowers when I was very young and used to go to his house to stay for weekends. He was always very good to me, even too good. He never got angry and always gave me anything I wanted: I remember how he used to give me "horsy-back rides" when I came to his house. I used to hide from him in a closet when I saw him coming up the walk from work, and I'd giggle uncontrollably when he'd come in shouting, "Where's my sweetie?" He was able to grow the most beautiful flowers, but hated having cut flowers in the house. He liked seeing them living and blooming outside "where they belonged." A cut flower was a dead flower.

(12) Priscilla—the "strange maiden had set herself diligently to work and was doing good service with her needle." "Needle" makes me think of hypodermic needles, which I was deathly afraid of. Whenever I became ill when young, I used to throw horrible tantrums whenever the word "shot" was mentioned. I once got spanked for having kicked a nurse who was trying to give me a shot. I got her white uniform all dirty from my shoes. My mother is also a nurse, and I put up the same fuss whenever she gave me shots. I was usually punished for this behavior.

(13) "In the midst of cheerful society, I had often a feeling of loneliness." Throughout my grade school days I had few friends. I was never "popular" and was often laughed at and scorned by my schoolmates. All this stemmed from my lack of concern for fashionable clothes or for particularly well-combed hair, and also because of my general laziness which kept me from getting "good grades." This led to a complete scorn for all the popular kids and to a state of despair. I was lonely, but kept telling myself that I didn't need their kind of friendship which I felt was based on false values of popularity. If they didn't like me, then I didn't like them either.

(14) "To endeavor to save Priscilla from that kind of personal worship which her sex is generally prone to lavish upon saints and heroes." If only someone would have saved me from this. I've worshipped heroes and saints for as long as I can remember, usually based on very irrational stimuli. I see a movie or read a novel and I find myself madly in love with the hero—be it Christ, Thomas Becket or Davy Crockett. In my younger years (and to some extent now) I found myself transferring these heroes onto the actors representing them. I'm extremely ashamed of this, but am still unable to totally escape the nostalgia of childhood daydreams. I think that if, ten years ago, I'd met Charlton Heston, then Moses to me, I probably would have fallen down and worshipped him as if he were God. These thoughts are blasphemous and I'm totally ashamed of them. Yet, I still find myself struggling to overcome them. I

seem to feel a necessity for having someone real and tangible, yet someone very high and noble, to cling to. That may explain why I've chosen actors—they're real men, yet portraying high and noble ideals.

(15) In reference to those whose idealism led them to Blithedale—"I seldom saw the new enthusiasm that did not grow as flimsy and flaccid as the proselyte's moistened shirt collar. . . ." I've always been this way myself. Even in grade school, I would jump up enthusiastically to volunteer for special projects, plays, extracurricular activities, etc. I always started out with a bang, and always ended up either never completing what I started or else finishing it in the quickest slipshod way possible. I meant well, but unfortunately for me, meaning well is as far as I ever got. This was and is by far my greatest fault. I will do well on something only as long as I'm enjoying what I do. It's great to make plans, but it's something else to do what's necessary to put them into practice. I feel very guilty when I plan things that I don't finish. I've often simply wanted to give up trying to do anything constructive.

(16) Coverdale's forest hideaway—like a place I used to visit when an adolescent. I always wanted a place that I could consider my own secret place. I found this wooded place one summer where a [sic] felt at peace which made me become oblivious to any other existence. Call it what you will—a transcendental experience, the presence of God (as a [sic] prefer to call it)—I felt no relation to worldly problems and never wanted to leave that spot. I've asked myself ever since, was all this a worthy experience, or merely a result of my own desire to escape from reality?

(17) The picture of the veiled lady and Theodore seems to represent a sort of wedding with the girl in the white veil and the wedding kiss which the groom refused.

(18) "Slept beyond all limit, in my remoteness from Silas Foster's awakening horn." Oh, how I hate alarm clocks and how much I love sleep. It's my chief means of escape. When I was in grade school I used to have horrible times getting out of bed. I hated school anyway and much preferred to remain in my sleepy dream-world. I remember how aggravating it was to have my mother wake me up from a dream about Roy Rogers or Flash Gordon for the highly unpleasant activity of dressing, and going to school to be bored and yelled at. Coverdale's pleasure in sleeping late is so very easy for me to appreciate.

(19) Coverdale's homesickness is something I have trouble understanding. I always had a very easy time in being away from home. I remember my first day of kindergarten. A lot of the kids were crying at being left there by their mothers, but I distinctly remember simply telling my mother goodbye as she went out the door. After school, I was exasperated to find my father waiting for me outside the school. I cried hysterically—I was big enough to walk home by myself! I put up such a fuss that my father walked home a different way so I could walk home alone.

(20) Coverdale looks at Zenobia through windows. We live just across the driveway from our neighbors. As children we used to spend our evenings talking across to each other from our bedroom windows and used to get up in the middle of the night to talk and send secret messages. As the neighbors had a girl and boy about my age, the location of the windows led all of us to many instances of Peeking-Tomism—very embarrassing.

(21) Discussion of mystical experiences at performance of veiled lady—used to be horrified at ghost stories and movies. At one Saturday afternoon ghost movie I got so scared that my father had to take me out of the theater. I tried to scream when I got scared, but no sound came out of my mouth. My father took me downtown to look at the store windows until I got back to normal. He kept telling me that there was "no such thing" as ghosts. This all seems sort of funny now, because I now believe strongly in ghosts.

(22) The masquerade party—I went to one at Halloween when I was in second grade. I was wearing a big clown suit that had a big pocket in the front. One of the other kids had won a picture puzzle in a game that I wanted to have. While another game was going on I stole the puzzle from the table it was sitting on and put into my big pocket. When I got home I told my mother that I'd won the puzzle. I played with it for a short time, but felt increasingly guilty over having stolen it. In what I considered a legitimate penance, I threw the puzzle in the garbage can. I felt I had made up for the theft by depriving myself of playing with it any longer.

(23) Silas Foster when searching for Zenobia's body—Reminds me of the gravediggers' scene in *Hamlet*. Before I ever knew anything about the play I'd seen pictures of the man holding the skull and fancied that the story was about a graveyard. I was shocked to find the morbid humor involved in the scene when I finally read it. The humor was offensive to me as it is here.

Although Ms. K begins her meaning statement by announcing the general issue of the "roles and nature of man and woman" (M1), her attention turns in paragraph M2 to Zenobia's role, to the degree of "femininity" (M3) in man and woman, and ultimately, in paragraphs M5 and M7, to the nature of womanhood mainly. Ms. K implies that she views Hawthorne's works in general and this one in particular as defining women through the "flaw" of submissiveness; however, it is not clear from the meaning statement whether Ms. K thinks Hawthorne defines women this way or whether she thinks he is expressing in his fiction something really true about women, and this ambivalence is present in the last as well as the first paragraph. In the meaning essay, moreover, the main emphasis seems to be placed on Zenobia, Hollingsworth, Priscilla, and Coverdale, in that order. It is therefore of interest to ask why the response statement deals most prominently with Coverdale.

Although it is not clear from the meaning statement why Coverdale is "a hard nut to crack" (M6), the response sets forth a complex series of feelings associated with Ms. K's perception of him. These feelings, marked by both masculine and feminine identifications, originate partly from Ms. K's identification with Coverdale pursuant to her spontaneous involvement in the reading. The result of the conflict between masculine and feminine feelings in the reading experience is the relatively unambivalent definition of femininity in the meaning. Ms. K used the process of objectification in the meaning to reformulate the *novel* in a way that greatly reduces the complexity of the response. Ambivalent feelings about Coverdale appear both early and late in the response. In paragraph 3 he is associated with Mother: Ms. K is the daughter who wants to keep Mother young by removing her grey hair. In paragraph 5 she describes playing like Coverdale, where, in the playing she is the mother. While the two statements show different authority roles for Ms. K—child and parent—they each show Coverdale being associatively translated into a feminine figure. In the last two-thirds of the response, beginning at about paragraph 13, Ms. K identifies either with Coverdale's feelings or with the object of his observation and feels that she is correctly described by Coverdale's judgment. In paragraph 13, she recounts how she coped with loneliness in a cheerful society; in 16, she tells of her own forest hideaway; in 18, she sleeps late like Coverdale; and in 20, she looks through windows at sexual scenes—like Coverdale. If these four instances are viewed as a sequence, they move from loneliness to a secret religious communion with "God" in the forest to fantasies of Roy Rogers and Flash Gordon and finally to an actual association of "Peeking-Tomism." Both the religious experience and the dream imagery are forms of "escape." Similarly both the window-peeping and prayer-peeping (in paragraph 9) are "very embarrassing." Complementing the masculine intrusive watching is Ms. K's identification with Priscilla (through Coverdale's judgment of her) in paragraph 14, with the impatient idealists in paragraph 15, and indirectly with Zenobia in paragraph 20 as the object of Coverdale's peeping. She is "ashamed" of her worship of mythic heroes and movie actors (14); she is "guilty" of overzealous planning and noncompletion (15); and she is "embarrassed" at participation in the peeping activities (20). She thus perceives herself through Coverdale in passive and active terms, masculine and feminine, judging and judged.

The parts of the response which identify with what Coverdale judges subsequently appear in the meaning statement. Ms. K's identification with Priscilla as Coverdale responds to her (paragraph 14) is found in the meaning as the "reader's" realization that women "are meant to be" (M5) Priscillas and not Zenobias. The associations in paragraph 14 suggest the nature of Ms. K's identification with Priscilla: "I think that if, ten years ago, I'd met Charlton Heston, then Moses to me, I probably would have fallen down and worshipped him as if he were God." In this observation about herself, Ms. K relates the mythic figure, the religious leader, and the real actor to her own habit of feeling religious and sexual attraction in the same way. The object of worship is "someone . . . to cling to." The shame she feels in these impulses could be related to the two typing errors in paragraph 16, where the article *a* is substituted for the pronoun *I* in her description of the "secret" meetings with God in the hideaway. In paragraph 15, where Ms. K identifies with the undisciplined idealists (as judged by Coverdale), she calls her habit of noncompletion "my greatest fault"; and she observes that this fault is true of her now as well as at the time alluded to in the association. In addition to reducing the complexity of the response feelings, the meaning statement reduces the shame, the guilt, and the fault by presenting them as a natural inevitability and implicitly including herself—the "reader"—as part of that inevitability.

Almost entirely absent from the meaning statement is the train of aggressive feelings Ms. K reports in responding to Coverdale and to other aspects of her reading experience. In paragraph 19, she rejects Coverdale's homesickness in favor of autonomy in the outside world: she made her father walk home alone so that she could also go alone. In paragraph 6 she is irritated by the intimation of generosity in Hollingsworth, and she tentatively identifies with Coverdale's pejorative suggestion that Hollingsworth should be a priest (10). Paragraphs 11, 12, and 22 suggest a more precise definition of these aggressive feelings. Ms. K's admiration of the flower in Zenobia's hair is defined by her memory of the exciting times with her grandfather— the rides, the giggling, and the fact that "he always gave me anything I wanted" (11). By implication, however, she could not get from him a flower for her hair, since he did not believe in cutting the flowers: "A cut flower is a dead flower." Relative to Ms. K's remembered relationship with Grandfather, the flower in Zenobia's hair represents something extra and unavailable to Ms. K, even in terms of an exciting relationship with a beloved older man. Ms. K's associations to Priscilla's sewing needle suggest it as more of weapon—the hypodermic needle (12). Although she was "deathly afraid" of these needles, she was not defenseless, for she reports trying always to kick the assailant away— though finally failing and being punished. Priscilla's passive needle is peremptorily identified in much more active and aggressive terms, and with her mother as the other participant in the battles. The implication of these two paragraphs is that there is something especially *feminine* about having a flower in one's hair and wielding a needle: feminine *and* aggressive. The puzzle in paragraph 22 is analogous to the flower and the needle: while "masquerading" as a clown with a "big pocket in the front," Ms. K intentionally steals a puzzle from someone else whom she envied, hides the puzzle in her pocket, and subsequently renounces the stolen item. This is the only association in which she reports guilt other than the discussion in paragraph 15, where she announces her "greatest fault." In both instances, the guilt has to do with pursuing things she cannot or should not get—with wanting too much, with taking a trespassing initiative. In paragraph 22, and subsequently in the meaning, Ms. K renounces these initiating impulses. In the response, the renunciation is characterized as a deprivation; in the meaning, it is a statement of what women are "meant to be."

Several associations suggest that Ms. K perceived her experience in terms of childhood aggressions as well as feminine aggressions. Hawthorne's announcement of the fictitious status of his characters (1) suggests a crime drama to her and calls up the memory of the domestic "battle" that followed the viewing of this drama. In paragraph 18 she reports that she was reluctant, also, to *leave* bed (the scene of Roy Rogers and Flash Gordon) to go to school to be "bored and yelled at." It is her mother who interrupts these latter dreams, much as it was Mother who wielded the hypodermic needles. The aggressive feelings seem to have been stimulated by the parental abrogation of Ms. K's watching importantly violent scenes; it seems that her perception of the author's claim of fictitious characters suggested to her the aggressive nature of the story about to be told, in that the claim would not have to be made if the characters did not in fact resemble real people. In this way, Ms. K responds positively to the thought that she is about to read a tale of aggressively watched aggressive behavior.

Insofar as her father is associated with aggressive feelings, his presence has a salutary effect. The snow scene alluded to in paragraph 4 suggests to her the pleasure of the snowball fights with Father and his making a snowman just for her. In paragraph 19, Father accedes to her "fuss" and grants the independence to walk home alone (while Mother did not thus accede and punished her for kicking to avoid the injections). Finally, in paragraph 21, Father is her companion in watching the ghost movie and, subsequently, the one who helps overcome her fright. Aggressive feelings associated with Father are more pleasant and supportive than such feelings in relation to Mother.

The material in paragraph 21 is particularly important to the overall response statement. The concluding sentence—"I now believe strongly in ghosts"—seems anomalous in its superstitious character. Regardless of its applicability to Ms. K as an individual, however, its function in that paragraph is similar to the function of the sentence in paragraph 15 where she describes her "greatest fault": it announces that the remembered feeling still exists in her today. The association describes how Ms. K believed in the reality of the symbolic scene in the movie to the point that she was unable to respond fearfully by screaming. The content of this association is related to several other observations in the response where Ms. K relates the importance to her of watching stimulating scenes, such as those in her dreams and in other movies as well as the window-peeping in paragraph 20. Here, the response is to the discussion of those watching the veiled lady perform. Ms. K's watching initiatives are related to an abiding interest in a *reality* represented by the veiled lady.

Her other associations to the veiled lady help define this interest. In paragraph 2 she is reminded of an "incredibly precious" book containing pictures of angels and cherubs—a religious and aesthetic memory. In paragraph 17, she understands the scene with Theodore as a wedding kiss rejected by the groom—a religious, social, and sexual thought, with emphasis on the sexual frustration. Paragraph 21 then contributes feelings of acute fear that are relieved only by Father's initiatives in showing her store windows in which the glass is a solid and distinct boundary between her and what she is watching.

In the meaning statement, Ms. K begins her remarks by observing that "so often" in Hawthorne's stories, "the fundamental problems of the roles and nature of man and woman" are "enveloped . . . within the veil of Original Sin." Insofar as the "ghost" represents the frightening aspect of the movie she is watching, and insofar as the claims to still believe in this frightening element today, and insofar as her "greatest fault" was present in childhood and remains today, it seems that the reading experience built up the sense of looking in on her own initiating sexual impulses, complete with their religious, spiritual, aesthetic, romantic, and finally, frightening accoutrements. If the language of the response is taken as an explanation of the phrase "veil of Original Sin," then Ms. K perceives women as being defined by the wearing of this veil; if the veil is lifted, as Ms. K tries to do metaphorically in her aggressive watching, she sees a frightening "ghost" or, alternatively, an unreachable godly being—perhaps a hero, an actor, a man, Moses, Christ, and so on. The reading experience was marked, through her identification with Coverdale, by exploration of both masculine and feminine affective experience ("the roles and nature of man and woman"). But in the meaning statement, the complexity of this exploration was ironed out, simplified psychologically and intellectually into just the role and nature of woman.

This simplification originated from both an abiding motive and the immediate motive created by the reading experience. The abiding motive is the need, at Ms. K's age, to define adult feminine identity. The reading experience contributed an awareness of the connection between this motive and certain experiences in childhood, such as the habit of noncompletion and the belief in ghosts. The general motive created by the reading experience is the sense of complexity of sexual identity—that, experientially, being a woman involves sometimes acting like a man, and being a man involves some culturally designated "feminine" traits, such as the generosity of priests and nurses. Particularly, the response suggests that the option of wanting and taking sexual initiatives, normally associated with men (according to Ms. K's preexisting cultural and religious thought habits), complicated

Ms. K's sense of femininity the most.

The meaning statement resymbolizes these complex experiences, recorded in the response, by declaring the role of woman to be that of a passive and submissive wife and mother like Priscilla. Although it seems that Ms. K attributes this view to Hawthorne and his work, the first sentence of paragraph M7 implies some doubts as to whether this is simply Hawthorne's view; perhaps it is a general truth about women. In paragraph M2, she says that the Eliot's Pulpit scene is the "key" to the story; there, it is shown how Zenobia's refusal to accept her "proper role" seems instrumental in her death. Yet in paragraph M5 she notes that the "conflicting qualities within the nature of man and woman" constitute the "most interesting aspect" of the whole issue. Accordingly, Ms. K has difficulty in working Coverdale into her overall construction of meaning: he is a "hard nut to crack" (M6). She accepts his taking himself out of the picture—he is a "chorus"—but she also sees him (in the meaning statement) as a traditional man who wants the "simple, womanly affections" of Priscilla. The source of Ms. K's difficulty is seen in the response statement, which shows how her identification with Coverdale disclosed conflicting sexual feelings in her. The local resolution of this conflict is a meaning which stresses womanhood and its necessarily "flawed" nature, with Coverdale receiving only passing mention. The meaning transfers the central emotional attention of the response into terms just as close to Ms. K's subjective concerns but less expressive of the conflict.

The terms of the meaning construction are fully pursuant to the pedagogical motive of presenting to the classroom community a clear idea of what Ms. K thinks are the cultural and intellectual issues raised by this novel. When the meaning is understood as a resymbolization of the response statement, these issues have a range, depth, and human authenticity that is not available from any purely nonpersonal discourse. But once the personal dimensions of literary meaning constructions are introduced, it is an utter necessity to discipline their presentation; the response statement makes responsible presentation of subjective materials possible.

Ms. K's meaning statement was not a conscious or deliberate resymbolization of her response. In order to determine how much difference it makes if the meaning is thus deliberately developed, let us examine the combined response statement and meaning construction of Ms. A.

### The Response Statement and Meaning Construction of Ms. A for Kafka's "Metamorphosis"

(1) Choosing to respond to the meaning of "The Metamorphosis" involved an attraction and a repulsion; like taking cod liver oil. Kafka is usually referred

to with a grimace, a shiver, or an unsavory eeriness. I had such expectations when I undertook to read it. My usual impulse is to avoid confrontations with personally violating situations, to retreat, and I consider this to be retrogressive. So, in a small way, encountering Kafka in his full grotesque regalia provided a challenge to dredge unsavory and generally inhibited elements in my mind.

(2) A multiplicity of feelings were evoked by the reading but they were all in the context of a pervasive mood of melancholy and general upset. The aspect that struck me hardest was the familial behavior of the Samsas. It reminded me too much of unsettling realizations regarding my own family during my younger years. It would be a gross distortion to correspond my family to the Samsas; however, the reading did summon up thoughts and feelings of familial regrets and grief. These centered around a lack of emotions, communication, and dialogue, and in fact, a suppression of them sanctioned by shame and embarrassment. Having a boxing glove heart was helpful in those days.

(3) I felt extreme sadness at the plight of Gregor because I identified him with Donald, my brother. Just as Gregor was insulted, defeated, and alienated by his family (primarily by his father), Donald underwent a similar humiliation owing to a fire and water clash between father and son. In the astrological sense, they were indeed Fire and Water, a bad combination. Like Gregor, Donald endured the unhealthy relationship and wanted to be accepted and loved, but our father, for some reason, wanted virtually nothing to do with him, and so, pretended that Donald did not exist at all. When I was younger, I was very ashamed of my family life, especially having had friends from the Russian community who are conversely very expressive, emotional, and loving. I envied them and enjoyed the generous and humorous affections of their parents. Hence I myself identify with Gregor, although imagining that he is Donald has more emotional impact.

(4) Gregor's death did not represent some form of nihilistic satisfaction, as it very well could have for someone else. Rather, it was a wrenching good-bye to someone who could not cope or compromise to the demands put upon him. Not unlike Gregor, Donald chose to kill his relationship with his family and soon after he reached working age, he moved far enough away and gradually disassociated himself with the rest of us, and the only affirmation of life is a generous Christmas gift to Mom and Dad each year. Why, I would not recognize him if I met him today and if I did, I would be very formal with him. These things were not resolved before he left years ago.

(5) The image of the dung beetle had a superb effect on me. I feel quite vulnerable confronting insects and other scuttling little creatures because I am never very kind to them. Insensitivity prevails, if not outright sadism. I feel that in this light, these creatures ought to hate me and would want to do me harm if at all possible. I was aware of nervous kinesthetic responses in many passages involving Gregor. He embodied a troubling thought that sometimes occurs when I squash out the guts of an ant or spider—just what is it experiencing? And here we have such an enactment in Gregor. The fact that my husband is fascinated by, and is kind to living things, plant or animal, deepens my guilt and fear of insects in a confrontation. This association plus

that of my brother to the dung beetle form of Gregor can help explain the attraction-repulsion involvement.

(6) Another reason for fascination and identification with Gregor is that I have felt like the equivalent of a dung beetle at times in my life. For instance, during my adolescence when physical appearance meant so much, I was endowed with a horrible pimple face. I felt at the time that it was the worst of possible things that could happen to me. I think that Gregor resignedly accepted the ghastly metamorphosis because it was simply par for the course . . . as he was at his lowest ebb to begin with, he just could not feel much the worse for what had happened to him. Despair equals despair in those terms.

(7) The image of Gregor with the "rotten apple in his back and the inflamed area around it, which were completely covered with fluffy dust" brought to mind a crippled girl I attended elementary school with. Without doubt, she was not charming. She had a terrible limp, unmanageable and ratty hair, mucousy eyes, bad hygiene, and match stick girl wardrobe topped off by a goofy expression. Josephine Murphy was heckled and taunted with "Murphy germs! Murphy germs!" by the nasty elements in the school and she tried to smile awkwardly through the torment. At one point, I wanted to ease my conscience of not sticking up for her and brought her home, wanted to be friends and fixed up her hair into a worse mess than she had started with. But it didn't last; I thought she was dirty and I didn't like her dirty house nor her zealously religious sister and generally chagrined by the whole situation. But the thought of her still hurts like the pathetic image of Gregor.

(8) I remained comparatively aloof from Mr. and Mrs. Samsa, as there was no substantial insight into their character or interaction with them on an emotional basis. I vaguely sense my mom in Mrs. Samsa to the extent that she reacted to my brother in a similar way—very concerned but not understanding, not having the capacity to understand. I expect that if Mrs. Samsa's character was further developed, she would have suffered the problem of a vacuous woman, like trying to live up to the ideals of soap opera values. If I have anything against my mother it is that she is not a responsible thinker and many of the values which she tried to inculcate upon us were based on banal social appearance. I did not want to displease her and yet couldn't live according to her standards.

(9) To carry out the identification of my brother to Gregor, it was tempting to equate Mr. Samsa to my father, but again he, too, strikes only light emotional chords. An attraction-repulsion conflict is my response to Mr. Samsa—repulsion for his treatment of Gregor, but attraction because he, too, is an individual with frailties and sensibility. I had a next-door neighbor "friend" who was treated like porcelain by her parents and was spoiled but reticent and obsequious. Something about her frail nature made me bully her and make her cry on several occasions until her father stepped in and put me in my place. But I've never been able to explain my streak of meanness towards her. As I got older, I simply grew bored with her and that was that. Is it this sort of irrationality that is behind Mr. Samsa's attitude?

(10) My double reaction to Mr. Samsa corresponds to similar antithetical feelings towards my father, disliking his repressed behavior while appreciating his underlying devotion (at least to my sister, myself and Mother)

and understanding his cultural and social circumstance of having largely lost touch with his Japanese heritage, not having fully assimilated to the Western culture, added to ugly memories of wartime internment by the country he called his own.

(11) I felt Grete was as irritating as a "Look Ma! no cavities!" commercial at a funeral. She was too normal and well adjusted amid the doom and gloom. If I could have forgotten about the pain and suffering that Gregor undergoes, I would have sympathized with Grete's final judgment of him; after all, that too was the result of an embittering experience with a parasitic horror. In any event, I felt like switching her off; after all I was undergoing an exorcism of sorts myself.

(12) I was similarly displeased with the conclusion because the impact of Gregor's death was still strong while the prospects in life for the Samsas were looking brighter because of the death. My sympathies for Gregor outweighed the happiness of the others in the family. There were, however, times when I felt Gregor was a snivelling wimp. For example, his perpetual lack of fighting spirit gets a bit difficult to sympathize with but my prevailing thoughts were that he had been caught in a choice between responsibility and loyalty to his family or rejecting them. Upon choosing his family and working to support them as a salesman, which was quite contrary to his nature, he finds himself a broken man and I think that he is irrevocably metamorphosed into a dung beetle, and he is, without choice, a weak, snivelling, wimp of a dung beetle. Under different circumstances, he may have been a butterfly.

(13) The maid and the three boarders were minor influences in the Samsa drama and much too impersonal to respond to individually, but they were so foreign and disentangled from the Samsa nightmare that they allowed me to step out of the Samsa family and breathe easily. The maid, in her breezy, burlesque manner seemed to be someone, at last, that was strong and sure, even if not particularly charming or kind. It is like being an awkward group of people when in walks a happy-go-lucky goof. His presence is a comfort and releases tensions. I was glad to have the maid aboard.

(14) The three boarders, although potentially harmful to the welfare of the Samsa family, are not particularly despicable, but tolerated in their fusty behavior. They point to the easily intimidated nature of the Samsas that borders on being silly and undeserving of sympathy. They caused me to wonder why I was so caught up in the silly melodrama of the Samsas because if one extricates himself from the suspension of disbelief, the Samsas really do not have any admirable or redeeming qualities. It is possible only to identify with them as victimized people, particularly in the case of Gregor. If the Samsas were at all times nasty and cruel while in this predicament, I would be hard pressed to identify with anyone in the book excepting the maid and the three stooges. In a sense, this is in keeping with the lives of most of us; we are at once victims and the victimized. I find it fits better with my conscience and psychology to identify with the victims. It seems I have arrived at a judgment of meaning in the "Metamorphosis." It is structured on the drama of the victim/victimizer dualism, where the two are inextricably bound together and it becomes impossible to discriminate between them. They are both victims of their desires and victimizers of people who serve to actualize their desires.

Gregor inhabits this absurd world where love is beset by fear and results in repression and perversion, finally, an escape into death. Prior to his metamorphosis, however, his family depended upon him and had little control over their own welfare. When Gregor changes, the situation reversed itself as his family slowly revitalized and strengthened.

(15) A state of tension caused by my inconsistency of attitudes to people in my associative responses disturbed me initially. However, they are manifestations of response to the climate of Kafka's novel that runs in variance with notions of justice, mercy, and order; the world is chock full of contradictions that are arbitrary.

(16) Notably, my responses are childhood recollections and I would venture to speculate that it was the period in which I most powerfully experienced the complexity of victim/victimizer and when I was least able to control these states, much less understand them. Certainly, these intimate recollections made the reading experience more meaning*ful*, in the fullest sense of the word. Indeed, upon a first reading, I did not have a rapport with any of the characters; my sense of equilibrium was disrupted and I simply fled to the finish line. The second reading was a more sensitive and rich experience because I succumbed and involved myself not on a linear race track, but in a new territory in which I explored and indulged myself. The difference in the two readings is characterized by the fact that without identification with Gregor *et al.*, the whole episode was uproariously funny, and the characters were insufferable fools. But upon involvement and sensitively experiencing the characters, it certainly was not comical in the least. I suppose that it points out the idea of human empathy and what it involves. I think that very often I am guilty of being in a stasis between the comic and the tragic.

(17) My link with the Samsas was a real experience, albeit not a pleasant one, and the sense of involvement was much more enriching than the usual jigsaw puzzle approach used for academic purposes. I certainly did not resolve in any melodramatic way anxieties underlying certain aspects of my familial relationships but the response has enlightened me further upon what my past has brought to bear upon me. In fact, it is a uniquely felt instance of the idea that the past and present do not have boundaries, but are inextricably intertwined.

The meaning Ms. A constructed for "The Metamorphosis" appears in paragraph 14; for her, the work states that the victim and victimizer are "inextricably bound together and it becomes impossible to discriminate between them." In the discussion just preceding the announcement of meaning, she observed that "it fits better with my conscience and psychology to identify with the victims," though in the lives of "most of us" we are "at once victims and the victimized." And before, that, she had observed, "I would be hard pressed to identify with anyone in the book excepting the maid and the three stooges." Ms. A began the paragraph by alternately seeing the Samsas as victimized yet not having any "admirable or redeeming qualities." The back-and-forth of this paragraph seems to be the instigation for the clearly articulated judgment. By pronouncing the alternation a "dualism," she objectifies her subjective dialectic, and this objective language finishes the paragraph.

In paragraph 15, she claims that the "climate of Kafka's novel" is responsible for producing in her the psychological tension manifested by "my inconsistency of attitudes to people in my associative responses." She then, in paragraph 16, reviews the responses in terms of the construction of meaning: she characterizes her childhood experiences as marked by the dualism, thereby retrospectively rationalizing (objectifying; making rational) the feelings which she reported as, e.g., "irrational" (9) and which occurred in her second reading of the story. In the first, she "did not have a rapport with any of the characters," her "sense of equilibrium was disrupted," and the "whole episode was uproariously funny," with the characters appearing to her "insufferable fools." Her more involved second reading was "not comical in the least"; however, the two readings seem to have in common Ms. A's lack of identification with any of the characters. Her observing that she is "very often . . . guilty of being in a stasis between the comic and the tragic" suggests her awareness of having remained "outside" the story regardless of the type of experiential involvement. The meaning she formulated is consistent with both readings and is as much a product of the "dualism" between the two readings as of the ambivalences she claims to have felt in the second reading. In the final paragraph, as she overviews the whole effort, she reports yet another dualism, namely, her awareness of how the past and present seemed to her "inextricably intertwined"; the term *inextricably* here repeats its original usage in the sentence that first formulated the meaning.

The response statement (that is, the first thirteen paragraphs) suggests that the feelings which led her to the meaning were not ambivalent at all, but that her feelings *about* these spontaneous feelings were ambivalent. For example, while she often describes her response as identification with Gregor, there is only one instance—paragraph 6—in which she draws a direct analogy between herself and Gregor. In all the other instances, Gregor is an object of her fascination, rather than identification.

In paragraphs 3 and 4, Ms. A sees Gregor in terms of her brother, who is the victim of her father's enmity. By implication, she sees Gregor's metamorphosis as an intentional act analogous to her brother's final departure from home: "Not unlike Gregor, Donald chose to kill his relationship with his family" (3). The pain Ms. A feels in this situation is shame that her family was not emotionally "generous and humorous." Father is not blamed for Donald's humiliation: rather, they just had opposing personality traits, and bad scenes at home made Ms. A envious of other families. In paragraph 9, Ms. A's associative definition of her attraction to Mr. Samsa is the description of her "streak of meanness" toward her "obsequious" neighbor-friend. When she moves on to her father in paragraph 10, it is not his bullying but his "repressed" behavior that she dislikes, and she justifies it by his having been wrongfully victimized during the war and by his "underlying devotion . . . to my sister, myself, and Mother."

In paragraphs 5 and 7, whose descriptive detail considerably outweighs that of paragraph 6, Ms. A indicates pleasurable feelings at being the bully. She is aware of the sadistic component of these feelings. First, the "image of the dung beetle had a superb effect" on her. Her feeling of vulnerability in the presence of "scuttling little creatures" is a consequence of her impulse to "squash the guts out of" insects and then wondering what they are experiencing. In paragraph 7, after once more identifying Gregor with someone else—her unfortunate schoolmate—and describing the girl in graphically negative terms, she tells how first, she did not "stick up for her," and then, when she tried to ease her conscience, she continued to be repelled by the girl, while in retrospect, the *thought* of the girl "still hurts."

When Ms. A returns again to Gregor in paragraph 12, she first reports in general terms that her sympathy for him "outweighed the happiness of the others in the family" at his death. Most of the paragraph, however, discusses and analyzes why Gregor appeared to her a "snivelling wimp." Although she says it was not his choice to become so, she observes that "his perpetual lack of fighting spirit" makes it difficult for her to sympathize with him. From all of these discussions of Gregor—and especially from the associations they evoke—Ms. A's sympathies appear to be a *reaction* to her spontaneous feelings of disgust and sadism. When she observes aggression and hostility emerging, guilt and fear follow immediately, producing her retrospective sense of ambivalence in her overall response.

Ms. A's responses to Mrs. Samsa, Grete, and the maid do not follow this same psychological path to ambivalent feelings. The material in paragraph 8 barely goes beyond the affective stage; paragraphs 11 and 13 are only affective. Her feelings about Mrs. Samsa, presented through comments about her mother, are accommodating of the latter's uncomprehending ignorance; while the mother's behavior is not inspiring, it also does not evoke conflictual feelings. The response to Grete reflects little ambivalence for a different reason: the irritation she seems to have caused is traceable to her appearing as a distraction from Ms. A's own "exorcism." The important feelings that arise from viewing the Samsa family in terms of her own do not concern Ms. A's relationships with the women. The maid, in a small way, is a salutary figure for Ms. A, in that even though she is a "happy-go-lucky goof," she is "strong and sure." In her ignorant certainty, the maid seems also to represent a release from inhibition, and hence from conflict. Her appearance in the course of the response—just before Ms. A announces her meaning—helps bring on the detached and objective frame of mind that formulates the "objective" meaning. In general in this response, detachment and objectivity are less problematical about women than about men.

Pursuant to Ms. A's observation that she envies more emotionally expressive families, she reports more difficult feelings when she does allow herself greater involvement—as in the second reading of the story. The reading thereby becomes an occasion to explore what she knew to be a long-standing problem. In paragraph 5, where she explores her sadistic feelings, she contrasts her impulses with her husband's greater kindness. The ambivalence is that greater involvement seems to imply greater aggression and meanness, a difficulty which seems to make sense to her only as the "attraction-repulsion" dualism, which is actually mentioned several times in the response. Ultimately, while she believes emotional engagement to be a "more enriching" experience in studying literature, she formulates its good effect as her having further understood the "inextricable" dualism of her past and present.

Relative to their respective responses, both Ms. A's and Ms. K's meanings perform a similar psychological function: they resymbolize the response statement in accordance with the demands of public presentation in the class and the critical community. Both readers translated their reading experience into a formulation that passes as interpretive criticism today. They aimed to objectify the private experience; in so doing, the act of reading became "the story" and their own feelings became the judgment about the work. The new predications—objectifications—thereby took the familiar form of "the work means this."

Ms. A's meaning for the work is ostensibly based on direct perusal of her response, in which she reports conflicting feelings; these become the "victim/victimizer dualism" in the meaning. This act of objectification deauthorizes itself as soon as it is separated from the response statement; the same is true of Ms. K's meaning for *The Blithedale Romance*. Ms. A's response shows a specific sense in which the dualism was developed—namely, her spontaneous feelings in her reading experience were bullying or sadistic, which were immediately followed by shame or guilt or both as soon as she became aware of her malign feelings. More specifically, she identified with the victimizers and was articulate on behalf of their behaviors. She was then victimized by her own conscience; paragraph 7 perhaps best describes this psychological action. Even though, now, the thought of Josephine Murphy still "hurts," she does not rationalize having rejected her even on the second effort. Her conscience is still victimizing her while she continues to indulge in sadism in her strong description of Josephine. This is the subjective meaning of the "dualism." Even though victim and victimizer may be inextricably bound together in her mind, the objective meaning does not portray the relationship between them that is developed in the response. Similarly, Ms. K's definition of femininity in her meaning statement does not reflect the complex sense in which she experienced it in her reading. Rather, both meaning statements actually *remove* the consequential psychological import which gives the meanings personal authority and public negotiability. Furthermore, the objective semantic of the statements makes the meaning seem to apply to the work instead of to the reader's experience of it. Both in abstracting the response and in making the abstraction apply to the work, the objective meaning deauthorizes itself and eliminates the reader's personal responsibility for it. Insofar as criticism encourages such depersonalization, it undercuts the compelling authority it might otherwise command. But when the response statement helps to define the meaning, its negotiation becomes an ethical undertaking rather than a mutual moralistic confrontation.

Although Ms. A's and Ms. K's meanings were both partly motivated by considerations of traditional intellectual hygiene, the different recording techniques used by each suggest the complex psychology involved in either technique and raise further epistemological questions for pedagogical inquiry.

Paragraph 14 of Ms. A's response tells how she felt she arrived at a meaning for the work. The meaning was formulated in retrospect of all the other material in the response, in addition to the actual reading experience. Part of the activity of formulation was the conscious attempt to let the response statement guide her thinking about the work's meaning. On the other hand, the fluency of the paragraph also suggests that the formulation of meaning was a spontaneous process, once Ms. A was aware of her own response. The only principle that can accommodate both of these situations is that Ms. A was *motivated* to arrive at the meaning she did. It is not possible to tell from the motives given in the response statement much more than that these motives existed on the reading occasion. These are the only motives of interest in the *present* discussion, however. They may be of continuing interest in my own further discussions with Ms. A. Pedagogical concerns do not demand that conscious and unconscious motivation be separated: all motives are retrospectively adduced; therefore they are conscious now, at least.

From my description of how Ms. K wrote her response and meaning statements, it is clear that she did not deliberately set out to formulate her meaning from the materials of the response. As conscious acts, recording the two statements resulted from two *different* purposes, where the second was understood to be independent, during its synthesis, of the first. It is therefore germane to consider why the response statement is nevertheless to be thought of as the symbolization on which the interpretation is based.

In Ms. K's effort the governing purpose was just as much to develop a meaning as it was in Ms. A's. The identical pedagogical purposes presuppose that the response and meaning statements will be related to one another as symbolization and resymbolization. It remains a question for local negotiation what sort of a difference it makes to use either means of response-and-meaning recording. For example, it is clear from Ms. A's statement that she simply was not in as close touch with the reading experience as Ms. K was. Yet her response was certainly "valid" by any nominal criterion, and definitely negotiable by the standards I discussed in Chapter Six. A difficulty did appear in trying to distinguish original feelings from feelings about feelings, though it seemed quite possible to do this in Ms. A's response. The point is that the process of judgment and interpretation is so peremptory that the longer the delay in recording a response, the more likely it is that a judgmental overlay will become part of what seems to be the response. Yet, within the process of developing the response, Ms. A becomes unambiguously aware that she has begun formulating a judgment in paragraph 14. And there is little doubt in my mind that writing out her response did procure that "quantum" shift of awareness, motivated as I described, of a new sort of mentation supervening on the response. Furthermore, it is of significant interest in general to be able to observe oneself coming to a judgment and to be able, retrospectively, to trace out its path. For Ms. A, this was in fact an important motive; her response suggests that the reading experience is more easily assimilable when she can find a way to detach herself more from it. One of the ways she did so was by *consciously* moving from the response toward the interpretive judgment.

Ms. K's response statement was a blow-by-blow effort; she recorded the affects and associations as she was reading. Obviously, she had the experience of setting forth her response partly in mind when she formulated the meaning, but she deliberately tried to write a meaning *for the novel*. The pedagogical issue then becomes the validity of my proposals of how the response is related to the meaning. These proposals were negotiated in the open classroom and were validated through discussion with Ms. K—for that particular occasion. In this sense, the pedagogical purpose of understanding the thought processes of each reader is the same for both Ms. K and Ms. A.

In confronting Ms. K's response-and-meaning, we do not need to stipulate the recovery of unconscious motives. In answering the question, Why do I find that the novel means this? there is no choice but to determine the most sensible—to Ms. K—possible connections between response and meaning. When these connections are called motives, Ms. K has explained the response and the meaning experiences to herself. Even though Ms. K—and Ms. A, for that matter, too—was not aware of subsequently adduced motives at the time of writing, it serves no purpose to assume that the source of these motives is an autonomous unconscious mind. The salient motives are all subsumed under the prevailing pedagogical purpose of the classroom. Just what role these formulated motives will play as knowledge is a matter for a subsequent decision. The knowledge can easily be brought to bear in a social or psychological context as well as the pedagogical one of interest in the present discussion.

Essentially, it depends upon personal and pedagogical preference whether the construction of literary meanings will proceed in the manner used by Ms. K or by Ms. A. The important matter is the understanding that any meaning is a construction whose topical fluency and objectivity need no longer deny its subjective origins and character. The objective form of interpretive formulations is not the product of illusion. The foundation of language is its continual development of new objectification. Subjective criticism proposes that when the object of attention is symbolic, the attempt to explain that object is necessarily a subjective (and intersubjective) reconstruction of our own perceptions of the object. To construct a literary meaning is to explain a spontaneous perception and the means of understanding it in the same act.

# Chapter Nine

# THE CONCEPTION AND
# DOCUMENTATION OF THE AUTHOR

On several occasions in this study I have alluded to the fact that when language is perceived, it is almost always associated with the person who originated it in that context.[1] E. D. Hirsch uses this standard of experiential common sense to claim that the most fundamental means of understanding literary language is to find out how its originators intended it.[2] Consideration of what is involved in the ontogenesis of human language suggests, however, that the mere perception of language is so complexly rooted in an individual's interpersonal history that the concept of intention is different in each language relationship in which it is sought. In nonsymbolic functions, such as waiting in line in the grocery, discovering intentions is a negotiative procedure: "Is this really the express check-out line? Are you in it?" To try to define intention where no negotiation is possible results either in a tautology—he did it; therefore he intended it—or in an imaginary fact—what he really meant was this. The substrate of factual reality associated with a work of literature is the individual author and his having created this aesthetic object. On the great majority of occasions, even this simple fact is not susceptible to knowledge with the same certainty that we "know" the grocery store manager. Furthermore the normal interest in identifying an author as fully as possible is the consequence of acquain-

---

1. For example, in the Introduction, in Chapter Two, and in Chapter Five.

2. One of the premises in *Validity in Interpretation* (New Haven, 1967) is that the search for the author's intention is justified on the same principle on which we try to determine a speaker's intention in a conversation: language must have proceeded from someone's mind. As Hirsch puts it, "There is no magic land of meanings outside human consciousness" (p. 4). The problem with this view is the author is not speaking to me, and I am not speaking to him. I am reconstructing a piece of language whose origin is permanently inaccessible to me.

tance with his work. The reading experiences produce the motive for learning about the author. Knowledge of an author can help explain these experiences and further motivate reading interests. Single specific intentions for either nominal verbal meanings or for the act of writing have no meaning independent of reading motives and local community interests.

In pedagogical situations where biography is not discussed directly, it enters interpretive discussion through unspoken assumptions: whatever meaning is attributed to the work is frequently assumed to be the result of the author's action. Often, interpretive inquiry turns in an undisciplined way toward what is the most likely logic in the author's mind that could have formulated this work with this meaning. It is taken for granted that the perceived logic corresponds with the synthesizing logic—with classroom discussion providing certain minor adjustments. But even if this correspondence is not silently assumed, traditional pedagogy has no systematic means of inquiring into the extent of its validity.

This inquiry may be conceived in terms of two issues: the reader's *de facto* conception of the author before and during reading and its role in his perception of the reading experience; and the kind of biographical documentation sought in consequence of this perception. I will discuss the first issue through consideration of two response statements of Mr. D to Joyce's *A Portrait of the Artist as a Young Man*, and the second through consideration of the kind of biographical documentation I sought for my conception of the author of James's *The Turn of the Screw*.

Mr. D's two response statements are longer than the others explored in this study.[3] They were formulated in the course of an independent study program Mr. D undertook with me on the topic of Joyce. The purpose of this program was to investigate what effect extensive biographical familiarity would have on Mr. D's conception of the author of *A Portrait*. The first response statement was recorded before the study program began; the second, after Mr. D had read *Ulysses*, Ellmann's biography of Joyce, *Stephen Hero*, and other works of Joyce. Mr. D came into the program regarding Joyce as one of his real heroes. He was especially sympathetic to Joyce's youthful struggles with religion, art, and sex; he felt he had gone through similar struggles and had thereby a special understanding of the pain a sensitive and articulate young man feels under the influences of parochial education and Roman Catholic values. Of specific local relevance to Mr. D was his then-

3. There is no optimum length for a response statement. The context in which it is used determines the most suitable length. Since Mr. D's statements were written during a relatively leisurely independent study program, he was able to indulge his natural impulse for detailed observation in formulating his responses.

current vocational quandary: he did not know if he wanted to be a teacher, a scholar, or an artist. For this reason also, he found Stephen's vocational concerns of particular interest. In general, it was an enormous comfort and pleasure for him to know that the world-famous artist James Joyce had had a boyhood and youth similar to his own, and that his analogous frustrations might well be the origins of great success.

The First Response Statement of Mr. D to Joyce's
*A Portrait of the Artist as a Young Man*

(1) "His father told him that story. His father looked at him through a glass: he had a hairy face." Vague remembrances of a whole flurry of things which happened to me with my father when I was a child are recalled to mind by this passage. When I was about four or five years old, my father would often take me out walking around the north side of Chicago where we lived. Sometimes we would come to the big concrete bridges which stretch over the river and I would run up to the edge to try and look over in order to see what was happening on the river. Because the concrete restraining barrier was usually taller than me, my father would have to lift me up on top of the edge. When he liked to tease me—which was often—he would lean me far over the edge and I would panic as though I thought he really would let go of me. I would start to scream and cry until he lifted me off and set me back down on the ground. It happened often and I still remember each of them, it seems, as though they had occurred just yesterday. I can still see the pebbled grainwork of the concrete and the murky waters of the river during the winter. I always wondered whether these experiences made me more trustful or more distrustful of people. It would seem the former since my father never let loose of his grip, obviously. But I'm scared it might be the latter, though I know it's probably nothing so simple as an either-or impression which was formed on me.

(2) Similarly, when I was about the same age, my father took me on roller-coaster rides which today I'm deathly scared of. I'll never forget the last time I was on something like one (any sort of carnival ride, just the slightest bit more daring than a carousel or maybe a ferris wheel strikes instant terror in my heart). I was in Dusseldorf, Germany during the city's annual summer festival and they had a carnival on the opposite side of the Rhine. I and a group of German and American friends went there one night to see what sort of rides and entertainment they had to offer. After walking the circuit once, we came upon a sky-mobile or space-flight ride (I don't remember the exact name of it any more). Everyone—except me of course—decided this was the ride to be had. So, they all paired up, since the ride consisted of two cockpits which fit two each—one in the back and one in the front like pilot and co-pilot. I was adamantly refusing to go, gradually withdrawing into the throngs surrounding the deal when the last unpaired kid—a fat German guy of about twenty—came up to me and tried to convince me to go. I said no, I wasn't feeling very well at the moment. He kept urging me to go on, saying it wouldn't be anything at all to upset me, it was a nice pleasant ride. Boy, it sure didn't look that way to

me. The two cockpits were affixed to opposite ends of an axis which in turn was connected to an arch-like bar which made the main axis and cockpit swerve all over the place which was complete with wild cries from whoever was in the cockpits. Nice ride. Anyway, he finally convinced me to go on it because he said if I didn't go with him he'll never get to go on since there were no longer any singles left to pair up with. So, I finally agreed, thinking it wouldn't be too bad if I could sit in the back in the co-pilot's position and close my eyes through the whole ordeal. So, we bought our tickets and waited in line. When our turn came, the guy I was with opened the cockpit and started to climb in the back seat. I told him I wanted to sit back there so I wouldn't have to look out the front, but he said it would be best if he sat back there because he was so fat he would make good ballast. I couldn't argue with that, I certainly didn't want us to flip over if the ballast, by sitting in the pilot's seat, would turn the damn thing over on us. So here I was getting in the front seat with my heart palpitating madly and they were closing the iron grill-like cover down on us. I never thought I'd make it through without fainting or vomiting or something. Not only was it bad enough that this thing would head straight up into the sky and then suddenly jerk downward, but it swerved from side to side when the arch-bar began to rotate upward. After we got going at full speed and reached the pinnacle of the arch, I was about ready to jump out of the cockpit regardless of the consequences when this damn bastard in back of me started to swing the cockpit back and forth screaming hysterically and joyously as though he were having the time of his life. I thought for sure it was all over then because the cockpit started shaking back and forth uncontrollably. I couldn't close my eyes because if we were going to crash I wanted to see it. Another paranoid fear of mine whenever I'm in those kind of things is I feel that the thing's going to break off from its mooring or whatever and go hurtling through the air into the concession stand or something. I usually can't go to sleep in a car either unless I really trust whoever's driving because if there's a possibility of a crash I want to be awake to scream. Somehow I made it through the whole thing, though I can't say I felt better afterward for doing it.

(3) Anyway, my seemingly irrational fear of such things I trace back to when my father used to take me on the roller-coaster ride at Riverview in Chicago when I was young. At first, I guess I didn't mind it, but then once I became sick or something and after that I was terrified of such rides. But, sometimes my Dad would buy tickets for it without telling me in advance and then say that I had to go on since he had already gotten the tickets even though I screamed that it was the last thing I wanted to go on in the park. I don't think he ever would have made me get on the damn things if he really knew how scared I was at the time.

(4) My father never seemed to know when I was just kidding or when I really was frightened to death of something. He also used to wrestle with me when I was about six or seven and sometimes grab a pillow and stuff it over my head and hold it. I'd always panic because I'd think I'd suffocate without him knowing it, so I'd scream and squirm, crying I want to get out. It was all in fun, but I don't think he ever realized just how much that terrified me. I also remember when he would rub his hairy face on my cheek so it would scratch a little and that's what "He had a hairy face" reminded me of.

(5) Stephen is walking with his father through his father's old haunts in Cork. A small midwestern farming town of about about five hundred people, now mostly all old people because anybody young moved out of the dying place many years ago searching for greener pastures than what the town had to offer. My father used to take me through the town when I was younger when he went visiting some of the people he used to know there. It was always so strange to me. Here were all these people like they were from another dimension of time or something that my father knew as a boy when he worked the strip coal mines in the region. Now there's nothing left of the town or its people because the mines gave out a long time ago leaving vast acres of reddened earth heaped up in barren mounds all over the place. These old barbers and farmers and retired old men aimlessly living a past life. It all seemed too alien, yet because my father had lived here as a boy and knew all these people I thought that I too should have some special feeling about them. But it all felt like some kind of dream in which I had to keep saying to myself, "This is not you. You're from the city where nobody's ever heard of this kind of thing or else doesn't talk about it at all." It was so foreign to me and yet seemed as though I could have lived it all that I had to jolt myself back into place somehow like Stephen when he says, "I am Stephen Dedalus. I am walking beside my father who is Simon Dedalus."

(6) "How foolish his aim had been. He had tried to build a breakwater of order and elegance against the sordid tide of life without him. . . . Useless." This is how I feel when things around me seem as though they're going to deluge me. I constantly try to maintain an inner control and stability against what is threatening to break in on me from all sides. Useless. Sometimes you just can't prevent what's destined to drown you in it. Like when I have a whole pile of work to do that's due soon. I try desperately not to let it get me down so I don't start coming apart at the seams or something. Inevitably, I go wild because I keep thinking about how I'm ever going to do all this shit in time. I get desperate and hysterical and pretty soon I find I can't even do what little I attempt without getting frustrated and thwarted at every turn. It seems impossible to keep order and direction in your life at times.

(7) "Now what is the meaning of this word *retreat* . . . ?" Wow, does that ever strike a bell. I remember too well the retreats we used to have when I was in Catholic grammar school and the seminary for one semester. They were never actually too bad. We never had a fire-and-brimstone preacher like in *Portrait*, just jovial fat monks with the knotted cords wrapped around their plump waists. We had to go through the "examine your conscience" routine but never in such an oppressive "the fires of hell are burning constantly" climate as Stephen has to undergo. Usually, we were just allowed to take nice long walks in solitude to think a while—something I always enjoyed just in order to have some time to think by myself. Maybe it was those long introspective walk-sessions I had by myself which convinced me to leave the seminary after a couple of months. I never did figure out why. The thing which I dislike about priests like in *Portrait* is that they always spoke as though your soul was in the most grievous danger of being damned because of some hidden heinous crime you've committed but failed to admit to yourself. "It was never too late," they would always say, "God will forgive even the most sinful of you as long as

you are truly penitent and love Him with your whole heart and soul." After a while you began to believe that you really were sinful and naturally bad and, so, would go to confessional to confess the pettiest thing you could think of, like you lied to this girl at school so you wouldn't have to walk home with her or else how you drank too much milk at lunch and thus were the most gluttonest of all gluttons who ever befouled your lunch room.

Mr. D's first reading of *Portrait* confirmed the feelings he had brought to his study of Joyce: he felt a more decisive identification with Stephen as a victim, a loner, and a rebel. In private conversation with me he indicated that he equated Stephen and Joyce. The elaborate detail of this response (and of the subsequent one, for that matter) is partially attributable to Mr. D's taking over the role of the confessional author; conversely, one of the reasons for his easy identification with Joyce was his own enjoyment of writing about himself and his eagerness to indulge in this pleasure. In this way, Mr. D's conception of the author helped to determine the character of the response statements.

In paragraph 7, where Mr. D is responding to Stephen's experience with retreats, his sense of sympathy is particularly strong, even though his own experiences were not as oppressive. The associations suggest that the actual source of the sympathy was that the advertisements for confession in Stephen's retreat and in his own life both encouraged a private sense of sinfulness out of all realistic proportion. The demand for confession ultimately produced ludicrous behaviors (like thinking himself the "most gluttonest of all gluttons who ever befouled your lunch room"). Much as he conceives Joyce to be doing in his novel, Mr. D uses the response to "confess" to sentiments he considers the opposite of sinful—namely, feelings of victimization, isolation, and justifiable quandary due to inexplicable circumstances.

The most predominant of these feelings are presented in the four long paragraphs of associations to Stephen's infantile perception of his father (paragraphs 1-4). This material records an important aspect of the overall relationship as recalled and as it seems to affect his feelings much later. The framework in which Mr. D and I originally understood his feelings was in juxtaposition with his basic identification with Joyce, the author-hero. The response statement implies, accordingly, that the subjective contribution of Mr. D's strong identification was the uncertain feelings produced in his relationship with his father. To identify with Joyce-Stephen was to overcome both the oppression of religion and the threats he sensed posed by his father.

The associations of paragraphs 1, 3, and 4 all portray the father's psychological aggression against Mr. D. He describes his father's teasing as seeming to give the father pleasure in the child's fear. Although, as in paragraph 1, Father never actually did him harm, Mr. D wonders if the bridge experiences compromised his sense of trust in people.

Similarly, in paragraph 3, he reports letting his feelings be known by screaming and his father going ahead with the rides anyway. At the end of both paragraphs 3 and 4, Mr. D says he does not believe his father would have persisted in his teasing if he "ever realized just how much that terrified me." But the graphic descriptions emphasize his deep fear and suggest that the father's nonobservance of this feeling was part of the teasing. Even Mr. D's memory of his father's hairy face involves the fact that it scratched his own—implying, again, something like, How could Father not know it was hurting me?

The long anecdote about the amusement park ride in Germany further portrays how the fearful feelings arose in an apparently innocent situation—a summer carnival, where his own generosity toward and sympathy with the remaining fat fellow led him to be victimized and terrified. Here, Mr. D is less restrained in characterizing the fellow who cajoled him into the experience he knew would be extremely fearful. At the height of the ride's violence, he describes how "this damn bastard in back of me started to swing the cockpit back and forth and screaming hysterically and joyously as though he were having the time of his life" (2). He concludes this story by observing that even when riding in a car, it is important that he "really trust" whoever is driving. It is noteworthy that while Mr. D feels the fat fellow's "hysterical screaming" to be particularly irritating, he had earlier portrayed his own screaming as an ineffective behavior with his father and then as a means of warning the driver of an imminent accident (2). Mr. D suggests that his only defense against a physically superior force, whether personal or mechanical, is screaming. In feeling vulnerable to masculine hostility, he finds a hero in Joyce-Stephen.

Paragraph 5 suggests a degree of isolation from Father even while there is an awareness of kinship. The experience in the farming town "was so foreign to me and yet seemed as though I could have lived it all that I had to jolt myself back into place somehow like Stephen" when Stephen identifies himself walking alongside his father. Most of this anecdote, however, stresses the alien nature of his father's boyhood home, and especially its moribund and barren atmosphere. Mr. D observes that he felt some obligation to connect himself with this past: "Because my father had lived here and knew all these people I thought that I too should have some kind of special feeling about them." The problem of wishing to connect with one's father's past and being unable or uninterested in doing so is partially ameliorated by the declarative identifications of himself and his father. In this instance also, Mr. D's identification with Joyce is of psychological help.

The knowing sympathy with Stephen when he criticizes his own aim in paragraph 6 brings to Mr. D, the son, the sense of authoritative self-control that improves upon dependence on father. Although the common realization between him and Stephen is of the sordidness of the "life without" them, the fact of commonality is itself a "breakwater" at the time of the response.

The first four paragraphs of this statement differentiate Mr. D from his father; the next two identify him with Stephen psychologically. The religious material in paragraph 7 is also an allusion to Mr. D's first vocational problem, as well as to an abiding concern with the values of his childhood. Insofar as the identification with Stephen in the paragraph includes Joyce, it ratifies Mr. D's rejection of the priesthood as a possible vocation and holds out the hope of perhaps more important success. The response statement, in its particular configuration of materials from childhood and adolescence, is mainly concerned with specifically masculine matters, and this concern helps to explain the unequivocally positive image Mr. D had of Joyce at the time. Moreover, the response presents the psychological complexities and idiosyncrasies in this instance of postadolescent hero worship: there are older men and younger men; and if this youth Stephen can become this great artist Joyce, then this is a reassuring fact. Mr. D's conception of the author is motivated by the need for such reassurance.

By the time Mr. D became familiar with more of Joyce's work and especially with his biography, the conception changed considerably. Although his vocational quandary did not significantly diminish, the terms in which it is expressed were greatly transformed. In one sense, the change in conception of the author rendered the problem even more complex, even if it seemed more individuated and specific. Mr. D's second response statement suggests that the only clear premium he derived from documenting the author's life was a greater knowledge of certain facts and a more satisfying sense of why he was interested in both the author and his work.[4]

### The Second Response Statement of Mr. D to Joyce's *A Portrait of the Artist as a Young Man*

(1) "The evening air was pale and chilly . . . he felt his body small and weak amid the throng of players and his eyes were watery and weak. . . ." Our apartment, when we lived on the north side of Chicago, was on the second story of an old wooden-frame house. The kitchen window overlooked the neighboring backyard of another apartment house. Because it was big and littered with junk, the kids of the neighborhood played there every evening.

---

4. My term "only clear premium" applies mainly to the context in which I am presently discussing the response statement. In our private conversations Mr. D acquired many sorts of knowledge, but the full construction of these insights could not be presented here in a convincing way. Each association had further qualifications and definitions; many details brought up in conversation referred to items in the text that were not mentioned in the statement. The aim of my discussion here is to outline as forcefully as possible the specific psychological components of Mr. D's "more satisfying sense" of his interest in Joyce.

Most vividly, I remember when it was late autumn it was already getting fairly dark toward suppertime and the bitter cold of winter already hung in the air. My mother could look out of the kitchen window and watch us play. I always felt some sense of security in that backyard because my mother's watchful gaze kept me out of the danger which the kids of our neighborhood were so susceptible to—like accidentally getting locked in a discarded refrigerator, which happened to one girl who was luckily found before she had been locked up too long. Also, as usual with rough lower-class neighborhoods, older kids could easily victimize the littler ones at any time except for the fact that our mothers were usually within eyes' glance in the evenings (once they had come home from work) to protect us from such bullying.

(2)While I must have played many times in that backyard in the evening, I really only recall one such cold autumn evening—which might, after all, be a collection of many similar times rolled into the same remembrance—when my mother came to the front porch and called out to me to come in for supper. It was like the "All in! All in!" cry that Stephen hears from a distance which was not an interrupting or saving pronouncement, but just comforting and warm. Like Stephen, "flushed and muddy" from the cold rain-soaked ground, I was "glad" to go in. I ran back to the warmth and bright light of our upstairs apartment from the quickly-falling darkness and the cold air of the neighbors' dirty, garbage-littered backyard. I have a lot of remembrances of our autumn and winter evening suppers at the kitchen in the middle of our large white-washed kitchen. Like Stephen, I used to sit quietly listening to my parents speaking about things over supper which I couldn't understand, but somehow it didn't matter whether I knew what they were talking about. It was warm and comforting just to be there among them glancing from the window which looked down over the (by this time) completely dark playground where I had been moments before back to my parents talking over the table.

(3) "His mother had told him not to speak with the rough boys in the college. Nice mother." Why, I don't know. And to this day I haven't asked my mother her motivation as to why she subjected me to a kind of fear-conditioning process when I was in my first few years of grammar school. She would tell me of stories (which were undoubtedly true) or else read newspaper clippings of brutal murders or kidnappings or else gang slayings. Sometimes they were so awful and gruesome that I would begin to cry. One such related incident I remember distinctly was about some teenage kid who killed his girlfriend or maybe it was just some girl he trapped, I don't remember that part exactly, and then hacked her body into pieces in a basement sink, wrapped the dismembered parts up individually in newspaper and then put them in some alley garbage cans. Someone discovered them somehow and he was caught. These stories would terrify me so much I would have horrifying nightmares and scream out in the middle of the night. I remember now that once I started crying during one of these "story-hours" and burst out, "Why do you tell me these things?"

(4) Oddly enough, I don't remember my mother's reply exactly, but it was something about not wanting me to grow up like some of the people she told me about. I remember that at this time my parents and aunts were really scared that I would grow up bad. In a neighborhood such as ours, I guess there

was little control a parent actually could have over his kids once they mingled with the "society" or their peers outside on the streets. Already at this time the teenage gang menace had grown to such a proportion in our district that they were terrorizing the neighborhoods so bad the police had almost given up trying to cope with it—just as they have done in the black ghetto sections of Chicago now. When Stephen talks of staring in awe and terror at Nasty Roche, a bigger, older boy who was the rebellious bully of Clongowes, I remember standing behind his counterpart at my grade school when we were in the lunch line one day. He was only one grade above me (4th) but had already spent time in a reform school for stealing cars. I remember staring at his big hands and thinking that he could beat me to a bloody pulp if he wanted to and there was nothing I could do about it. If he caught me on the playground at school after hours, there wouldn't be any nuns or priests around to stop the slaughter. Despite the fact that I was terrified of him, I—as well as my other friends—had a certain respect and worship of him. He possessed a kind of daring which we would have liked to emulate if we had half the guts he had.

(5) So, if we would have stayed any longer in that neighborhood than we did, I probably would have grown up to be exactly what my parents feared I would become.

(6) "There was a cold night smell in the chapel. It was a holy smell." I often went to the church at times when there was likely to be no one else there, during the late afternoon when the playgrounds were covered with kids playing ball and other games or during hot summer days when everyone was either at the swimming pool or else in the air-conditioned comfort of their homes. The vast hollowness of an empty church had a peaceful and soothing solemnity for me. It often served as a precious sanctity of seclusion from the blinding force of the sun and from the flood outside which threatened to wash over me before I could erect a bulwark against its fury and might. Was it that merging with the vast tide of others that was so frightening to me that I ran to the spiritual sanctuary of myself contemplating with the empty space of a lonely church? Did I think I was really praying to God? Or, was I seeking some direction in life through which I could find success (whatever that might mean) independently of those around me? None of my interests in grade school or high school were really dictated or influenced by my friends. Whatever I picked up as a hobby or interest I usually pursued it alone. This wasn't true all the time, but usually because my desire to practice or pursue something was so fanatical and indefatigable, I isolated myself from those closest to me.

(7) The pandybat episode and the theme of unjust punishment. I've been **trying desperately to come up with some kind of counterpart incident in my life to Stephen's punishment by Father Dolan, but I can't.** Only one association comes up and it persistently sticks to my thoughts, though it seems very trivial and why I should still remember it is incomprehensible to me.

(8) In second or third grade during our Christmas party in class we were running around these old wooden desks in the classroom playing some kind of game when I tripped over one of the black iron desk legs. I fell down and scraped my head and started to cry. The nun said I could sit down with my head on my arms on top of the desk like we would do when we took naps in the

afternoon. So I just sat there with my head buried deep into the pocket my crossed arms formed and stared into the blackness of the desk top. Somehow it was very comforting to seemingly be all alone like that while all around the kids were still running about playing games. It reminds me of *Ulysses*, the film, when Stephen is in the brothel and everyone is shouting and laughing. As though the boisterousness and confusion of the situation were too much for him, Stephen blacks out and finds himself in a dark room with only one dimly-lit light bulb. There he sees the faint outline of his mother's apparition and hears her mournful voice, for the first time since her death, call out to him. He swings blindly at the light bulb, enraged and horrified, and then awakes from his somnambulistic state. In contrast, I felt relief and comfort in the isolation afforded by my arms and the top of my desk. Like Stephen, I felt the flurry of events rushing around me but if I tried hard enough I could even blot out their sound and their entire presence. Every once in a while, I would peek out through the openings made by my crossed arms to see what was happening around me. The kids were now passing out candy to everyone. My head hurt but not as bad as I made it out to be. But I didn't feel guilty about overdramatizing the situation either, just content to sit there and rest with my head in my arms as though I had been seriously injured and had to remain quiet. As the kids went around passing candy out, they would stop by my desk and place some next to my folded arms. Sometimes they would leave a little extra because they felt especially sorry for me. I in turn especially enjoyed their pity. Unfortunately they let us out of school early so I couldn't enjoy my new-found haven as long as I would have liked.

(9) Chapter II. Stephen romanticizes a lot about the books he is reading when he is playing or walking alone through Dublin. It reminds me that I read a lot—an uncommonly lot—when we lived in Chicago because there was nothing else to do at home during vacations because both my parents worked and all my friends from the Catholic grade school lived too far away to play with. Out of loneliness and boredom, I turned to books and read anything and everything I could get my hands on. My mother would have to take me to the neighborhood city library every Saturday to get some new ones. The big treat was going downtown to the loop in Chicago with my mother because she would take me to the big main library by the lake. I would go sit in one of its large reading rooms next to the ghost stories and mystery thrillers collection and read all day while my mother went shopping. I would always try to sit next to one of the big picture windows which looked out on the lakeshore. They were nice quiet and pleasant times—times when I would just sit and read my book and stare out the window from time to time and wait for my mother to pick me up for lunch and afterwards take me back for a couple of hours again until she was ready to go home. Invariably, the days were always rainy and dark as I remember them. I liked that too because it made you want to sit inside where it is comfortable and warm and just read or stare outside.

(10) "He listened without sympathy to his father's evocation of Cork and of scenes of his youth . . ." It gradually dawns on me, but is really no surprise, as I'm recalling all these memories of my childhood in Chicago that my father is almost imperceptibly in the background of most of these scenes. There are such associations in which I picture my mother standing in the forefront of the

scene and my father is faintly visible to the rear. The whole thing seems like a painting of some kind—perhaps like one of those Rembrandt paintings of domestic life where the protagonists are unidentifiable and strangely silent, though staring up at you. When I picture my parents like that, I feel the need to call to my father to come up to the front and not hang there in the background where I can barely see him. But somehow the effort would be futile; they can't hear me for they're too far away or as though they don't know I'm there. It reminds me of a play I saw on T.V. when I was very small about the child of a family who died, but was somehow granted the wish of returning to earth to re-experience one particular day out of his past life. The only drawback was that the child would only be able to watch, not participate in what was happening. So, he returned to his family for the day of one of his birthdays when his family is preparing a surprise party for him. It seemed so undeniably sad and lonely to watch someone separated from those he loves by an impassable barrier which exiles him forever to an isolation of complete loneliness and emptiness.

(11) Stephen wanders into the red-light district. Just off the Reeperbahn, a long street in Hamburg filled with striptease joints, bars, moviehouses, "lokals" or discotheques where rock-bands play (the Beatles played in one before they became famous), is probably the biggest red-light district in the world. When I hitchhiked to Hamburg to see the university there, I stayed in a youth-hostel which was only a few blocks from the area, which was situated between the Reeperbahn and the hostel. My first night there, I met some other Americans and we went off to explore Hamburg's nightlife. It didn't take us long before we wandered into the red-light section where girls were hanging out of windows or standing on street corners trying to grab single guys and even guys who were walking with their girlfriends or wives into a door of some squalid house. There was one particular street which the police close off to anyone below eighteen. The whole street was a series of brothel-houses where the windows of each house were slightly above street-level. In each window a girl sat on a chair, beckoning to the passersby. In the narrow street were literally hundreds of people of all types—couples (guy and girl or wife) or groups of just singles—milling about, every now and then going up to a girl to talk with her or make the proposition. Mostly, though, everyone was just laughing at them or at those who went into one of the houses. Everyone was having a good time; it was like some kind of goddamned carnival. I couldn't help but feel sorry for the prostitutes. They seemed to be subjected to the worst kind of degradation possible. They probably had to sit in those absurd window-boxes every night while people walked past and laughed or hurled some kind of jibe at them. At the same time, though, there was something elusively attractive about them. They tried to be cold and aloof from the whole thing. They were sexy and appealing in the same way a good-looking girl who's arrogant and snobbish sometimes is. They were so cold and distant it was almost mesmerizing in a way that it wouldn't normally be with a non-prostitute. They created a kind of spell for me which was like the imploring, mournful songs of the Sirens for Ulysses. Yet, on the other hand, there was something crass and vulgar about their attitudes and mannerisms. I was intrigued by the whole scene, but never enough to want to go into one of the

houses. I just hung in the middle of the crowd and watched as though caught in a witch's spell.

(12) Chapter III—Stephen walks alone through the streets of Dublin. Sometimes I spend a lot of time walking alone through the streets when I'm troubled about something. Perhaps not so much now as I used to, but still on occasion I'll take to the street if I'm feeling restless and worried. My first two years of college, which I spent in two different towns, were restless unsettling years in which I spent a lot of time walking around the two cities externally exploring the area while internally trying to sort out my mind. When I was in Europe the summer following my sophomore year, I did a lot of idle wandering there as well. Sometimes I would just start walking in some unknown city and keep walking not even knowing where I was headed and keep going until I felt tired, then I would try to find my way back. Since I have a pretty good instinct for directions, I usually wouldn't have too much trouble getting back. Cities are like mazes to me: I love to get myself lost in their conglomeration of sights and sounds and their unknown streets and alleyways. It's difficult for me to get so absorbed that I completely lose myself, though, because all the while I'm walking, I'm trying to fit the streets and squares and bridges into a pattern, a formula, or grand scheme. Somehow an unknown city gradually puts itself together in my mind—all its disparate parts slowly but progressively begin to fit together like the innumerable parts of a great puzzle game. Sometimes this process is almost unconscious, as when I'm preoccupied with my own problems, walking absently around strange corners and down unfamiliar alleyways, and yet somehow I instinctively pick my way back home. It's as though I've solved my problems somehow if, after I've thoroughly enmeshed myself in the maze, I can find my way out of it. Some people say I have an analytical mind; maybe this kind of instinct is indicative of that.

(13) Once, however, I did get lost—really lost. I was in Brussels at night and I had been walking a long time when I decided to head back to the youth-hostel where I and my friend had been staying. After walking for some time in the direction in which I thought the hostel was, I realized I was beginning to walk in circles, yet I knew for sure that the hostel was in the general area but I couldn't find the side street which led to it. After some time, I wandered into a street which wasn't so deserted as the others I had been walking down. I could see several men walking aimlessly about, sometimes crossing the street to look in the window then crossing the street again to look in a window of another house. I thought, "What the hell is going on?" Then when I got to one of the windows which was dimly lit, I looked inside and saw two girls sitting on chairs staring back at me. It didn't dawn on me right away that they were whores and I was right in the middle of Brussels' red-light district until I noticed the next several houses in a row were the same way and some of the whores motioned for me to come closer to the window. It was the first red-light district that I'd ever seen, so I wasn't sure exactly what was happening at first. Once I realized it though, it was kind of exciting and frightening at the same time. It was as though my aimless wandering was destined to bring me here like Stephen's meandering through the streets of Dublin toward Nighttown is unconscious,

yet somehow internally directed to an appointed destiny. Unknowingly, yet by innate predilection, I had found where the concentric circles of Hell led, just as Stephen had done. But I wasn't so daring as he; I just walked from window to window and stared fixated and paralyzed by what I saw, but remained passive and motionless in reaction to their beckonings. I was more content to view my fantasies from a dirty, dark, rain-soaked street and into their dimly-lit windows than risk shattering my crystal dream image. I walked on and soon found my way back to the hostel. It had been a strange, but somehow momentous night.

(14) "The archangel Michael, the prince of the Heavenly Host, appeared glorious and terrible against the sky. With one foot on the sea and one foot on the land he blew from the archangelical trumpet the brazen death of time." In our old parish church in Chicago there's a plaster sculpture-like replication of this scene which is on the side of one of the side altars. Of all the statues and sculptured scenes which adorned the over-ornate baroque altars of the church, this is the one which fascinated me the most when I was small. It held my attention for long periods of time with a mixed feeling of terror and awe. The only difference between Joyce's description and the frescoe-like duplication in our church was that the land the archangel Michael was resting on was a piece of earth suspended over the fires of Hell and the sea was the sea of souls which were condemned to eternal life within those flames. His foot was suppressing those who seemed to be trying to climb out of the fire. He was indifferent to the suffering and anguish below him, for he was looking up, blowing the long heralding trumpet which blows the "brazen death of time."

(15) Perhaps because it was my (middle) namesake which was depicted, that I was so captured by the scene, but I think it was more the scene of the people seemingly screaming aloud in the flames of Hell trying to escape and being pushed back down again which held my attention to the scene. I remember sitting next to my mother and just staring at it while my mother was either saying the rosary or trying to follow the Mass. I think what frightened me most about it was thinking that at death I would be separated from my mother and perhaps condemned to perish eternally in a pile of writhing squirming bodies which would be fighting each other to get out of the flames only to be pushed back in again if they ever made it to the edge of the abyss.

(16) "I will not serve." Do I have the courage, the guts, the rebelliousness? I don't know. In some ways, I know that when I reach the point where the limits of rightful tolerance have been stretched too far, I will not serve. I know because I've done it already. Like Stephen, after a time, I refused to be a servant of the Church. I'm ready to blaspheme its name just as soon as the next person, but in my revolt I haven't as yet renounced God, just his earthly manifestations. God I have just pushed aside as irrelevant and distant. But just how far my rebellion stretches, I am still not sure. I know that I could never go as far as Stephen. While I might consider myself a free-thinker, I don't claim to be free: "Man is born free yet everywhere he is in chains." Some chains I refuse to defile. I would never do as Joyce did at his mother's death bed. I would sooner be a hypocrite and kneel down to a false god than refuse her.

(17) "The idea of surrender had a perilous attraction for his mind . . . "

Ditto. But what exactly that surrender constitutes I'm not exactly sure. Is it an attempt at complete and thorough debauchery and degradation—the kind which Stephen has partially gone through in the preceding chapter at the brothels of Dublin? I'm not sure; I don't think Stephen really knows. I know I don't. Sometimes I have the urge to surrender myself to the worst, to the most demonic and evil wishes of my mind, but I'm not even sure what those are. I can get stone drunk and/or screw a girl and that still doesn't constitute total iniquitous surrender. The idea is very fascinating and sometimes I think I almost yearn to find the door and I'll do it. Perhaps, "I will not serve" completely is it and as Stephen says, "There seems to be only one sense of the word to me."

(18) "He longed for the minor sacred offices, to be vested with the tunicle of subdeacon . . ." This pisses me off. Either I mistake Joyce or he wanted nothing less than the vestments of the celebrant as he served Low Mass (actually far more gloriously ritualized than High Mass) in front of a cathedral of the most important people in Ireland. I never entertained any megalomaniac aspirations like this when I thought about becoming a priest. I never assumed I would be anything but the average priest celebrating the Mass twice, three times on Sunday and at six-thirty Mass during the weekdays. It would be an inglorious routine, but still a sacred routine. Maybe I'm hastily judging Joyce. Perhaps, his wish for the lowest position on the altar steps is similar to his whoring: an attempt to attain a certain perverse kind of sanctity through degradation and enforced humility. Maybe this was the perilous surrender he was talking about: surrendering himself for the rest of his life to a vocation which would never exalt his being on the platform of public acclaim as he hoped publishing would.

(19) ". . . without regret of a first noiseless sundering of their lives. The university." What a transition. It's beautiful. I had no idea just how big of a transition from home-life to the university it was going to be when I first left home to go someplace where I didn't know anyone and do something I wasn't sure, especially if I could do that something successfully or not. The separation didn't bother me. After a while, I became depressed and lonely at college with its 900 beer-soaking frats and sorority sisters, but it wasn't because I missed home. It was the first recognition that I was directionless and alone in the world—I don't mean alone like there's no one physically close to you to comfort you and provide solace in your hour of need. It was rather the first awakening, the first cold touch of experience and not just premonitions of the fact that each person is really alone in an empty cold universe. A mother, a girl-friend, a lover, a wife, a close friend—these were all short-lived reprieves from the real struggle of making it alone, of wandering aimlessly without direction, of constantly being reminded that you alone with no one at your side are at grips with a vast void. You make with it what you can: the existentialist hero, alias poor shnook, creates out of nothing. He is his own god and he fashions his universe according to his own shape:

> His soul had arisen from the grave of boyhood, spurning her graveclothes Yes. Yes. Yes. He would create proudly out of the power and freedom of his soul. . . .

(20) Chapter V—"Dedalus, you're an antisocial being wrapped up in yourself. I'm not. I'm a democrat: and I'll work and act for social liberty and equality. . . ." There are two fiercely irreconcilable strains which run through my character and which force me to the brink of contradiction or else paralyze me in a hopeless and pitiable state of impotence. Within me are both the Stephen and McCann of *Portrait*: I am both the antisocial, introspective, ego-centered "artist" who is alienated from and embittered toward his fellow man and the socially-oriented, freedom-fighting advocate of people's rights. At times I'll refuse to join movements, sign petitions, or agree with popular opinions simply because my estranged soul feels called upon and duty-bound to rebel at being forced into anything, especially unity with other people. At such times, I feel the drifter and the misanthrope in me rise to the surface and rage with fury at whoever confronts me. Just the other day I shaped my protean image into the rightist conservative for a girl who was desperately trying to classify me as a weak-minded liberal or even more ghastly, a "young Republican." I could give a fuck about what she tries to label me, and yet I felt a faint inward glow of satisfaction at knowing I was involved in such things which she so carelessly harangued about long before she ever dared leave her bra at home, or thought of wiping her gooey make-up off her pock-ridden face. I can't stand pseudo-radicals, not so much because it rings so false in my mind but because it rings of desperation. There are always wild-eyed, desperate people who will pick up on the tail end of a movement, a feeling, a spirit and embrace it as their own and only their own, castigating any and all who don't think, act, breathe, and fuck like they do—and all without really knowing what it is they're calling their own.

(21) There are times too when I'm the opposite: I'm the "democrat" as McCann calls it. If I believe a cause or an issue is right, I may—just may—pick it up and pursue it as far as I can. Just when or why I will do this is still an enigma to me.

(22) There's always an inherent contradiction in the rebel's position. Stephen refused to sign the petition for world peace, yet he abhors violence and Joyce declares himself neutral to the Austrian government and moves to Switzerland. McCann, the confirmed "democrat" and advocate of world peace calls one and all to sign his petition, yet, he, like the Arab who says he wants peace but qualifies it by an "honorable peace," at the same time strives to fight for Ireland's independence regardless of the means or the consequences.

(23) "Is that called a tundish in Ireland?" While sitting at a table over coffee and pastry in Dusseldorf with my American friend and our German "brother," the latter turns to me in the middle of a discussion and says, what is "Angestellte" in English. How weird . . . he who knows English far better than I know German should ask me for a translation as though I knew the two languages better. Ironically, I knew. At times when I was in Germany, I felt I could have almost been born there or maybe even was. It was very strange to think that it was possible to have grown up in a place which seemed so foreign and so alien and yet somehow mystically familiar as though you had known it long ago. When I came back from Europe, I went through kind of a minor identification crisis. I wasn't sure what I was or who I was. Exile is a mental state.

(24) Stephen's theorizing about art leaves me cold. It's like trying to fit yourself into something to which you already half belong and are trying to draw the blueprints for getting the second half in. Too artificial. It also reeks of literary pretentiousness, something which was entirely in character for Joyce but which he was usually good enough at to escape derogatory accusation for.

This response statement gives several indications of Mr. D's changed conception of Joyce. In each instance the change is related to a reduced identification with Stephen. In paragraph 18, in responding to the possibility of a priestly vocation for Stephen, Mr. D cannot reconcile Joyce's personal ambition with Stephen's apparent modesty; he cites his own modest ambitions when he was considering the priesthood. On the other hand, he reasons, if Stephen-Joyce did not have lofty aims, the announced aim was only a "perverse kind of sanctity." He resolves the apparent contradiction of motives by observing that, for Joyce, publishing would fulfill the ambitions that the priesthood would not. Again, in paragraph 24, Mr. D observes that Stephen's "theorizing about art leaves me cold," but *Joyce* may have had enough artistic talent to justify such theorizing. The diminished identification with Stephen results in a more decisive objectification of Joyce—a greater understanding of him with no loss of respect.

In paragraphs 16 and 22, Mr. D is critical of both Stephen and Joyce. Although he sympathizes with Stephen's strong rejection of religion, he would not, if it came to an analogous crisis, disappoint his mother as Joyce did his. Joyce's move to Switzerland (22) seems contradictory to him in view of his rebellious attitude and his commitment to peace. Yet, because of his own enigmatic responses to public causes (21), Mr. D understands Joyce's position as more complex though not altogether admirable. His basic identification with Joyce remains in this response, but a sense of a greater distance between himself and his hero has been introduced.

The single most repeated source of this new distance is that Mr. D identifies himself more in juxtaposition to women than he sees Stephen or Joyce doing. This is the case in Mr. D's response both to Stephen the child and Stephen the adolescent. In the first five paragraphs, Mr. D distinguishes his own childhood frailty from Stephen's by portraying his analogously dangerous experiences as having occurred under the "watchful gaze" (1) of his mother. He describes at some length how the security and warmth of his home provided an ongoing protection against predatory behavior in his neighborhood. Even though he reports significant fear at the means his mother used to goad him into being careful (3), his association in paragraph 4 suggests his parents were justified in their fear and prudent preventive measures: he and his peers had had a "certain respect and worship" for the bully they all feared. What "would" have happened cannot be determined, but Mr. D, in the present perspective, says that had he stayed in the dangerous neighborhood, "I probably would have grown up to be exactly what my parents feared I would become" (5). The great detail of these associations creates his sense of the prominent role his mother played as a saving agent. The sentence he cites from the novel (3) is simply Stephen's mother's bland warning not to "speak" with the rough boys. These feelings also contrast with the presentation of the same feelings in the first response statement, where Mr. D's childhood frailty is defined in terms of vulnerability to his father's teasing. While feelings of bodily weakness are still present, the emphasis in this reading is on his maternal source of protection and security.

Mr. D's associations to Stephen's childhood religious experiences are memories of his own psychological resourcefulness rather than of his distaste or victimization. The church was a place for retrenchment and contemplation, and its loneliness is associated with the solitary pursuit of a private interest. In responding to the "theme of unjust punishment" (7), Mr. D indicates that he does not understand the tenacity of the one thought he can associate with that theme. The incident related in paragraph 8 is the exact opposite of unjust punishment: Mr. D had injured himself in an innocent accident and then gets more sympathy than the occasion warrants. His pain was "not as bad as I made it out to be," and he "especially enjoyed their pity." As he is writing the response, these events remind him of Stephen's experience in the brothel (in the film version of *Ulysses*), except that "in contrast" to Stephen, Mr. D felt "relief and comfort in the isolation afforded by my arms and the top of the desk." The apparition of Stephen's mother evoked guilt in Stephen, but Mr. D in the childhood scene gets only sympathy and "didn't feel guilty about overdramatizing the situation." In paragraph 7 of the first response, where Mr. D describes how his own retreat was less fearful than Stephen's, the emphasis is on the oppressive claims of the confessors in both the novel and his own life; here the emphasis is on the better circumstances in his own life.

In reaction to Stephen's "romanticizing" about books (9), Mr. D characterizes his own start in reading in terms of its physical situation and his mother's significant involvement. His reading, while a solitary activity, is marked by feelings of relaxation and security indoors, a certain excitement about the "big main library," and the attendance of his mother. The content of the books, not mentioned by Mr. D, is subordinate in this association to the importance of the psychological occasion, which, in both response and novel, is the end of childhood and the beginning of puberty. In this connection, the associations of paragraph 10 represent both a response to Stephen's lack of sympathy with his father's recollections of Cork and a review of the previous material in the response statement. The first statement showed Mr. D's greater identification with and confusion about a boy's removal from his father's childhood. In this paragraph, Mr. D again differentiates himself from Stephen by feeling "the need to call to my father to come up to the front and not hang there in the background where I can barely see him." The distance from father is there, but the stress is on the need for greater affiliation with him. His review of the whole statement—and the observation that Father is absent—is the first phase of the psychological individuation, relative to the earlier reading, that this response in general reflects. Once Joyce had become more of a person and less of an image or hero for Mr. D, he felt his own role more acutely in this formulation of the reading experience.

The feelings presented in paragraphs 11 through 18 draw a conspicuous distinction between Stephen's indulgence and aggressions and Mr. D's restraints and compassion in the handling of adolescent emotions. Mr. D identifies with Stephen's peripatetic impulses, but stresses that while the temptation was there, he was "never enough" intrigued "to want to go into one of the houses" (11). Mr. D's obvious fascination with and interest in the activities of red-light districts is limited to their influence on his imagination, and he claims that his pity and compassion as well as his sense of the vulgarity of it helped to override the temptation. Paragraph 13 seems to combine the associations of paragraphs 11 and 12. Here Mr. D suggests that it is not simply a sense of high moral character that inhibits his indulgence but also an instinctive homing impulse. On the one hand, he feels able to extricate himself from the most complex urban maze; and on the other, he feels led "by innate predilection" to the center of the "concentric circles of Hell." Once his "crystal dream image" was appeased, he found his way home. This phase of the response statement continues the feelings broached in the opening paragraphs: home is a source of strength and a salutary influence in his life. The relevance of this theme is not in its historical authenticity but in its definition of Mr. D's second reading experience of *Portrait*. Home and Mother are the locus of feelings called up in the service of distinguishing his own sense of self from his sense of identification with Joyce.

This emotional atmosphere precipitates the strong statement at the end of paragraph 16: "I would never do as Joyce did at his mother's death bed." Just prior to this declaration, at the end of paragraph 15, Mr. D described viewing the damned in Hell while with his mother in church; at the same time, the fearful quality of the scene is less attributable—he says—to his identification with the overbearing angel than to its suggestion of ultimate separation from his mother. He then reasons that he cannot go along all the way with Stephen's "I will not serve" because its final consequence would be offending and disappointing his mother at the moment of final separation.

This paragraph raises the issue that was of immediate concern during the period that Mr. D wrote the two responses: his vocational and psychological identity. Direct awareness of Joyce the person also enters the response at this point. First, Mr. D does not know if he has the "courage, the guts, the rebelliousness" to reject the Church altogether. On the other hand, he is "not sure" (17) if he is actually tempted by complete surrender as Stephen is. Drunken sexual activity does not seem to qualify. In college, he does not, like Stephen, regret having left home; however, "directionlessness" (19) is a struggle that goes beyond any succor that a beloved woman can provide. He quotes Stephen's jubilant affirmation, but it is not clear in paragraph 19 whether Mr. D identifies himself with it or whether he is skeptical about it. When he responds to the discussion between Stephen and McCann, he sees part of himself in both figures (20). He spends the most energy recording his supercilious feelings toward pseudoradicals, citing his own experiences with causes. Yet in spite of his present enlightenment, he claims no answer for himself and emphasizes the difficulties ("contradiction") in either position (22).

In response to the discussion of the "tundish," Mr. D cites his own surprising (to him) knowledge of German. But this paragraph alludes to a topic that receives a great deal of attention in this response statement: Mr. D's European experiences. Germany seems alien and foreign, yet "somehow mystically familiar" (23). Other European experiences were extremely important in his responses—the carnival in Germany and the amusement park ride, the red-light district in Hamburg, and the "momentous" (13) night in Brussels getting in and out of the red-light district. Mr. D repeatedly describes efflorescences of personality away from home—even reading in the downtown library—that are regulated by his strong attachment to home. He finally observes in paragraph 23: "When I came back from Europe . . . I wasn't sure what I was or who I was. Exile is a mental state."

This is the form of Mr. D's identification with Joyce at the time of the second response. Joyce said exile was a virtue and a weapon. But in saying it is a mental state, Mr. D is subjectively acknowledging it as a problem. Mr. D spends much time in the response showing that he does not affirm what he thinks Stephen and Joyce affirm: there are other factors in his life of a more domestic, compassionate, and benign nature. Mr. D's sense of separation from his erstwhile hero probably aggravated his vocational quandary—but this is a therapeutic matter, not the topic of our pedagogical inquiry. Our interest is Mr. D's identification of the knowledge he developed as the result of rereading

*Portrait* with a fuller and more complicated conception of its author. This knowledge could be characterized as pertaining to exile as a mental state—in himself. It could also be understood as knowledge of a certain taste, and as a detailed definition of this taste. But I would describe what Mr. D now knows as "Joyce, better than before," a familiar phrase which is given a specific meaning with the use of response statements.

Between writing the first and second response statements, Mr. D acquired a great deal of new information about Joyce and his work. The important matter is the effect of this new material on him. Of particular concern to him was his understanding that Joyce was extremely egotistical and ambitious, a feature of Joyce's personality that Mr. D had not perceived from his first reading of *Portrait*. Paragraph 18 of the second response shows the effect of this new image on the reading: he now understood Stephen's modesty as Joyce's false portrayal of himself. Seeing Joyce's artistic manipulations of himself helped to reduce Joyce's heroic stature in Mr. D's eyes. Mr. D relates this artistic detachment to his larger revised image of the writer as being cold and unfeeling, especially toward his parents. This new realization is largely responsible for the affection and sympathy Mr. D shows in the second response toward his mother, and to a lesser degree, toward his father. These feelings, in turn, must be the result of a revised *self*-image. Mr. D's biographical readings made possible a definition of himself as decidedly different from Joyce in items more psychologically germane than their childhood sensitivity and Roman Catholic upbringing. The occasion for the resymbolization of Joyce was the search for that knowledge motivated by the belief that knowing Joyce actually meant knowing himself better. This belief was ultimately justified, but in an unexpected way that left Mr. D feeling somewhat more alone. Significantly, even this aloneness is Joycean: "Exile is a mental state."

Mr. D's new knowledge helped him synthesize a new identity element as a less ambitious and more home-oriented person. Within the boundaries of the study program, this knowledge is relative to his new conception of Joyce; whether the knowledge of himself obtains in other contexts remains to be seen. It is also the case, though I am not exploring it here, that repeated contact with me, a teacher, helped to precipitate in Mr. D the shift of self-identification from author to teacher, a profession he subsequently followed. In any event, Mr. D's new conception of Joyce acquires meaning and consequence as a function of motives originating in subjective concerns at the times of reading.

It is customary in critiques of subjective efforts with literature to claim sanctimoniously that the "itness" of literature is lost. Mr. D's response statements suggest that this "itness" is a construct to begin with. Work formulated by another person is not an object. Its otherness is created by the subjective reader in the service of that reader's motives. Knowing Joyce, or Milton, or Shakespeare has never meant, in critical discussion, actually having known these people; the phrase "knowing Joyce" has always been figurative, its reference being to someone's having read Joyce's work and perhaps his biography. But this reference, if applied in more than a trivial sense, is ambiguous if one is speaking of two Joyce scholars. Do Bernard Benstock and William York Tindall each *know* something different about Joyce? Do they each *know* a different "Joyce"? Or, as I think it more responsible to claim, does each *say* something different about what *they think they know* about Joyce?[5] Each reader objectifies something about his experience with the author's work in terms of the author if that conceptualization is more suitable to him than, say, meaning or taste. Mr. D's responses show that the interest in the author to begin with can be directly understood as a subjective function; it follows that the way one conceives the author in a critical judgment is likewise subjectively governed and, more importantly, observable in oneself. For people with such interests, the locus of objectification is the author; the greater the familiarity with his work, the easier it is to conceive him as a distinct individual—to objectify him. But such objectification is idle, and even unfair, unless it represents the construction of the author out of the materials of one's experience with his work and other available information. "Knowing an author" means knowing one's own conception of the author.

Biographical documentation is sought in order to validate one's conception of an author. It is assumed that the documents and other historical artifacts used by a biographer to synthesize a portrait are the most authoritative basis on which to conceptualize the individual under study. No matter how full such a portrait may seem, however, and no matter how certain one is of the supporting artifacts, there is no final way to decide that a particular biographical formulation of an author's life or personality is objectively true. The formulation can be either more or less adapted to the biographer's community and to subsequent readers, and it can be appropriated as an influence in that community, but only to the degree that it serves subjective (and intersubjective) literary interests. I will explore this issue by discussing how my own use

5. The wordings are important. It is customary to think of different wordings as being superficial when epistemological assumptions are shared. Since I am proposing a different critical epistemology, it is necessary to emphasize that my different wording grows from this epistemology. When the epistemology assumes that Joyce is the object of knowledge the idea "say what they think they know" is a mere courtesy for "saying what is true of Joyce." But if the object of knowledge is one's own conception, the former phrase is a literal description of the subjective status of the proposed knowledge.

of biographical documentation becomes a function of my conception of one of the most fully investigated literary lives, that of Henry James.

In *Readings and Feelings* I presented a detailed consideration of why biographical documentation helps me to produce the most satisfactory understanding of my experience of *The Turn of the Screw*.[6] In my response, I claimed that I did not "know" the governess. But after reading Leon Edel's biography of James, I feel I do now know her as Henry James:

> I have thus gained the missing knowledge: I now know who the governess is. The full extent of my [imaginary] relationship with the governess has been exposed. I first identify with Miles as a strong little boy; I then replace this identification with an identification with the governess. The ambivalent feelings I have about this identification become wishes [motives] to *know* more about *her*, thus projecting her out of me and containing my sexual feelings. Finally, I translate my identification with her into an identification with Edel and James [a biographer and an author].

This last sentence means that *for the purposes of the reading experience*, I identify with my former teacher and become a biographer; I become an author by writing about this experience. There is an important difference between my biographically documented conception of the author of the tale and Edel's overall biographical portrait, but this difference is determined by different motives for knowledge and not by objective historical facts.

Edel writes that the major immediate psychological impetus for writing *The Turn of the Screw* was James's decision to move from London into Lamb House in Rye.

> In "The Turn of the Screw" James was saying, on the remote levels of his buried life, that Lamb House was a severe threat to his inner peace. It was haunted. It contained all the ghosts of boyhood—pushing, demanding governesses, Aunt Kate, his mother in her moods of severity. He could not be "a fellow, don't you see?" in such an environment. In the house of Family, Henry had always thought of himself as a claimant. . . . To establish his claim, to take possession, carried with it the certitude of punishment—the demanding ghosts would exact their price, and little Miles's . . . sacrifice has shown what—somewhere beyond rational existence—he believed that price would be.

> James wrote "The Turn of the Screw" accordingly on a theory of unexplained extra-human terror, that terror within himself that could not tell him why he had felt a sinking of the heart, at the simple daylight act of providing himself with an anchorage for the rest of his days.[7]

---

6. *Readings and Feelings* (Urbana, 1975), pp. 72-78.
7. Leon Edel, *Henry James: The Treacherous Years, 1895-1901* (Philadelphia, 1969), pp. 211-12, 214.

In describing James's state of mind in writing the tale, Edel emphasizes the ineffability of his fears. While Edel names the fear as one of irrational punishment for just trying to be a "fellow," he stresses that James did not name that fear explicitly to himself, and that it instead emerged through intuitive or instinctive forces acting during the process of creating the tale. On the basis of this reasoning, Edel identifies the writer's mind most centrally with the figure of Miles, since Miles's fate would then represent an expression of James's deep fear of punishment.

In his discussion of James's background associated with this tale, Edel characterizes an important feature of James's psychology:

> To be male was to risk (in the remote fantasy of childhood) such things as amputation like his father's; females seemed the most serious threat to his sense of himself, as a boy, and later—by disguises of the imagination, by thinking himself a little girl and by being quiet and observant—he could escape "amputations" and punishments. The strategem succeeded. His mother called him "Angel." He could be above all an observant exploratory young female. The disguise of femininity was necessary mainly when he was confined to "Family" and had to contend with his elder brother; in that relationship he always saw William as strong and active and himself as inhibited and passive.[8]

These observations are presented, not in explanation of the dramatic action of the tale, but as a contribution to the description of the fearful atmosphere in James's mind as he was about to move into Lamb House. Edel does not suggest a connection between the disguise of femininity in childhood and the feminine gender of the tale's narrator.

In my own conception of James, however, this is a vital explanatory connection. I understand James to have identified himself with the governess, who—by imagining a demonic sexual figure, Quint—"kills off" Miles, the masculine boy in James. The psychological premium of this disguise for James is *survival as an author*: and it is a successful one at that in respect to the listening audience within the tale and to James's reading audience as well, whom, at the time of writing, James was trying to win back after a slack period of his work. Even as Edel describes them, James's fears were not vague. At that period of his life, homosexual feelings played a greater role in his personality than they **had in the past: identification with women had a new meaning, even if,** as Edel documents, this impulse is traceable back to his childhood. At this point in his career, James is appropriating the literary and psychological "disguise" for the local purpose of reestablishing himself in maturity.

It is true that Miles is "sacrificed" and Quint is exorcised from him by the governess-narrator. But the governess's survival is more important

8. Ibid., p. 210.

biographically. In the tale, her story is actually being read by an unnamed third narrator (Douglas being the second) who was given the manuscript written by the governess and passed on to Douglas (now dead). At the end of the tale, this third narrator does not reappear: only the governess survives, if I speak only in terms of my reading experience. At the outset of the tale, this third narrator claimed to have a title for the story, but he does not tell what it is. Therefore, my solution to the namelessness both of the story and the narrators is to understand them to be named on the title page of the published work—"The Turn of the Screw" by Henry James. For me, the biographical meaning of the story is that the author is overcoming both long-standing psychological fears of sexuality and conflicts of domestic power as well as then-current professional doubts partially precipitated by the catastrophic failure of his play, *Guy Domville*,[9] and by the diminished popularity of his fiction. This meaning entails a somewhat different conception of the author than that proposed by the more authoritative reader, Leon Edel. But *my documentation is the same as his.*

Negotiating different conceptions of authors is an ongoing critical concern. What is or is not claimed about an author, however, is determined by either the biographer's community or the reader's demands for biographical explanation. For example, it is not an objective good in biography to aim for psychological portraiture over historical chronology; but strong public interest at this time may demand an analytical presentation of character, and many current biographers respond after the pattern of Lytton Strachey and Leon Edel. It is equally arguable that a chronological history gives each reader a better opportunity to formulate his own conception of the author. This subjective motive underlies the many attempts at biographies of the same author. Any biographical effort is necessarily interpretive—the biographer's motivated resymbolization of "the author." Leon Edel has already articulated this principle in his own reflections on what biographical effort entails:

The biographer must try to know himself before he seeks to know the life of another: and this leads us to a very pretty impasse, since there seems to be considerable evidence that he is seeking to know the life of another in order better to understand himself. The biographer's dilemma thus becomes double: he must appraise the life of another by becoming that other person; and he must be scrupulously careful that in the process the other person is not refashioned in his own image. This, in reality, is the subtle process involved. . .

. . . [The biographer] has taken into his consciousness a great many documents about another's life. And the book that will emerge will be *his* vision, *his* arrangement, *his* picture.[10]

9. Ibid., p. 201.
10. Leon Edel, *Literary Biography* (1959; rpt. Bloomington, 1973), pp. 11, 12.

The value of a biographical study lies in the kind of subjective interest the biographer has applied to his task. Some studies are important because the biographer hates his subject; others command interest because the biographer's point of view is unique. But to imagine that any single biography has actually set forth the objective life of the subject can only serve to inhibit further interest. Every reader's conception of an author is his own construction; even when a new conception is assimilated, it remains his own construction. The process of recursive reconstruction produces new knowledge. It often seems that scholarly documentation such as personal letters and testimonials are new facts about an author, and sometimes they do disclose new information. Yet regardless of whether such disclosure takes place, each new document is a *new point of view*, and each time another is read, the perspective is complicated and changed. Whether a reader reads biographies or original documents or both or neither depends on what kind of knowledge he seeks. The search is most productive when it is the consequence of knowledge of oneself.

The linguistic nature of a reading experience establishes the subjective dialectic, which negotiates the experience into knowledge. This means that when the knowledge sought concerns the real, but permanently unavailable, historical author, awareness of one's motivated conception of the author is a necessity for such knowledge. Mr. D's experiences show how the response statement greatly facilitates this awareness. My own search for and use of documentation of the author grew from the belief that biographical knowledge was necessary for my reading experience. Finally, any biographical interest, as Edel further observed, is "deeply intimate and highly subjective."[11] Knowledge of the language and literature of another mind rests on knowledge of the language of one's own.

11. Ibid., p. 9.

# Chapter Ten

# COLLECTIVE INTERESTS AND
# THE DEFINITION
# OF LITERARY REGULARITIES

One of the major reasons for the formulation of the subjective paradigm was the observation that subjectivity is an epistemological condition of every human being. It was not only that one or a few people decided that they were unalterably subjective and therefore decided that the same had to be the case for everyone else; rather, it was perceived that mutuality and collectivity made no sense without a prior awareness of individual subjectivity, and that mutual agreements and collective actions are predicated on the definition of common ground by a group of subjective interests. The difference between knowledge as the product of a collective subjectivity and knowledge as the discovery of autonomous and immutable facts is that the latter assumes a standard of true and false to exist independent of human and other life concerns. If there is no such external standard, collective interests are the highest authority, and knowledge depends ultimately on how individuals form groups and circumscribe the existence of other groups.

The term *group formation* may be understood in at least two ways. It can refer to a collection of people who *form themselves* into a group, or it can refer to a person (or a collection of persons) who form a group out of a collection of *things* (not people: if one person groups other people, those people accept themselves, provisionally, as things). Put another way, an individual can only join a group of "first persons" (in the grammatical sense); he can only *propose* that second and third persons are groups or parts of groups. Consequently, two sets of motives are of interest: motives for affiliating oneself with a group, or joining, or knowing what one has in common with certain others; and motives for cognitively distinguishing one's self and one's group from others by *defining* other groups in a range from "everyone else" to just "you" or "him." Through the idea of "person," all languages make either this distinction or analogous ones. Group definition is a natural result of the use of language.

In criticism, a collectively synthesized act of taste, in which whole societies hold certain authors in high esteem and others in lower regard, helps to delineate membership in that society. Complementarily, insofar as a society subscribes to a certain array of literary categories, that is *likewise an act of self-definition*. In a subjective framework of thought, the seemingly different phenomena of cultural prominence or popularity, generic classification, and historical periodization may each be understood as knowledge formulated under the aegis of collectively held motives. Each sort of knowledge discussed in the previous three chapters sooner or later finds itself, at least in part, under the authority of communal and societal motives. This authority is expressed by almost all university curriculums, which have the great majority of their literature courses arranged in terms of "major" authors, literary genres, and historical periods. Under the influence of objective thinking, these subjective societal choices are widely accepted as permanent categories of objective knowledge about literature. The minorites who have different conceptions of how literary knowledge is to be developed have affected these traditional curricular assumptions only marginally.

The use of response statements in the study of literature shows how subjective these categories are, suggests just what sort of truth value they can have, and provides a collective means of helping to establish categories more responsive to changes in local motives for formulating new knowledge. Two matters will be of primary concern in the ensuing discussion—collective self-definition expressed through the acceptance of a single author's cultural prominence and societal definition of a literary-historical period through the exercise of its own subjective values. I will assume that the reasoning proposed in this second issue can be analogously applied to generic classification. In both matters, the aim is to show how the response statement makes these traditional and linguistically rooted habits of thought instruments for exploring the complex fluctuations of the collective interests which define interpretive communities and other societal groupings.

Many in America regard Robert Frost as the quintessential American poet of our time, in contrast to T. S. Eliot and his cultural obscurities or Wallace Stevens and his difficult abstractions. An important reason for this acceptance is that schoolchildren are exposed to his work at a relatively early age, and for many he thereby comes to be identified with poetry. It is obvious that the plain language, the simple rhythms, and the "G-rated" subject matter are major factors in his high-school prominence. Frost, however, achieved prominence before he was anthologized, not afterward, so that the source of his reputation must be other than simple classroom familiarity. In some way, Frost's work must have defined a set of American cultural values in such a way that large numbers of people could say that he speaks for them. By speaking for people, Frost and his work defined a collective interest and value system. It is not clear, though, what Frost "says" when he speaks for those who affiliate themselves with him. In confronting this question, I will first present and discuss a sample of images of Frost collected in 1967 in an upper-level university classroom in order to suggest just how familiar this "popular" poet is to students who expect to teach English and literature in secondary school.[1] I will then compare this collective knowledge with the subjective knowledge one respondent to "Stopping by Woods on a Snowy Evening" records in her response statement. Finally, I will evaluate the extent to which the subjective knowledge also reflects collective interests that are customarily separated from the interests routinely announced as spoken for by Frost. Response statements disclose motives for collective interests that are usually not available and sometimes purposely ignored.

Images of Robert Frost by Twenty-one Undergraduate
Prospective English Teachers

(1) Frankly, being a person who dislikes poetry, I don't know very much about Robert Frost, since he is a poet. I have assumed, however, that he is a very distinguished poet since I have heard his name mentioned many times from the time I became a high school student until the present. Evidently, you [me, the teacher] have some feelings about him—either positive or negative—since you had us write about him.

(2) It was asked of me this morning why I would want to take this course. I asked myself this identical question upon glancing through the several books on Robert Frost which will be used during the course. Frankly, I must concede that my lack of interest in Frost is typical of my lack of enthusiasm for most of the poetry I have read. I know absolutely nothing about his life, and I am not familiar enough—or educated enough—regarding his particular style, or

---

1. The date is especially germane when a "popular" author is the subject of response. Frost had died four years earlier, and Thompson's biography (vol. I) had been out a short while. Thus few readers could have had occasion to demythologize or debunk any popular knowledge of Frost. On the other hand, it would be of interest to solicit a similar set of responses today; the reasoning of this chapter would imply that there would be no significant difference in the collective image of Frost, though scattered individuals will have learned more about him. There is a sense in which certain collective values inhibit the search for facts on their behalf, and there are motives to perpetuate the image irrespective of information. Images serve different motives than does information.

Each of these statements were given on the first day of class in a course whose main activity was to read Frost and report various sorts of responses to his work. The only advance knowledge of what this course would be came from the availability of the books beforehand. The students were asked to record in a time period of about thirty minutes everything they knew, believed, or felt about Frost.

technique—or whatever literary mannerisms distinguish his writing from that of his contemporaries—to opinionate. This situation, of course, lends itself to considerable improvement.

(3) I could write what little I know about Robert Frost in one sentence. He is an American male poet of the twentieth century. Other than this my knowledge is completely limited because I don't remember anything he had written and have never studied his works. Until mentioned in class, I didn't know he was dead. I wonder how long he's been dead. Although I've never seen him, he brings to mind a picture of a white-haired, bent-over old man. I wonder if he really *did* have white hair and really was bent over. I suppose he's one person an English major should know about. Guess I'd better find out.

(4) My geography lab instructor's name is Robert Frost. And he was a pretty cool guy. Any connection? The names are the same. But my lab instructor doesn't have billowing white hair. In fact he's kind of bald. And I don't know if he's written any poetry. But I doubt it. He doesn't seem the type.

What is the type? Why is one Robert Frost a poet and the other not? Why does one talk about snowy woods and it's called poetry while the other talks about snowy woods he's referring to the latest weather report? Maybe it's their backgrounds. The poet's mother probably told him to write down what he saw and the weatherman's mother probably asked him why? At least the name Frost fits both of them since they're both concerned with precipitation.

(5) Robert Frost is, to some people, one of the greatest American poets. He was chosen to speak at the 1960 presidential inauguration. He was very old at this time and had some difficulty in reciting his own poetry. He died a short while after his television appearance in 1960. This was the last time I saw or heard Robert Frost.

I am not very familiar with the works of Robert Frost though I am sure I must have read some of his poetry in high school.

(6) Above all else Robert Frost was a man—in no way related to the beloved Jack Frost who stains windows. Perhaps the poet Frost had something over other men because he could always express himself in verse. But no matter— he was still a man. He lived, he aged, and he died. He had the same emotions as any man but he was able to do something with them. We all have hate, love, fear, and the ability for satire within us. But how many can express these feelings as Robert Frost was able to do? Because of this he was perhaps a little more of a man than the average. Still a man of course but with just a little something added for good measure.

(7) An American poet. His poems are loved by the American people. He died not too long ago. Snow white hair and a face that was wrinkled like a dried prune. I can't recall the names of any of his poems although I have read some of them. Ice. I think he read a poem at Kennedy's inauguration. His name reminds me of Jack Frost. Feel very guilty that I can't recollect more about such a noted poet.

(8) Robert Frost—snowy headed, senile poet. Wander through the forest across the snow-laden, glistening paths that converge. The old man of song and verse rides through the winter days on his dottering nag, touching the branches and smiling in his vague, peculiar way. The snow falls softly about him, and he feels the velvet softness about him. A simpering old man, simple, but sensitive.

(9) To me, he is cool, crisp, stopping by a woods on a snowy evening.

He is silent, thoughtful, pensive, possessing an understanding of the relationship between man and nature akin to God.

He is everything his name suggests—white-haired, biting, refreshing, rude awakening, ice on the grass.

He is old in my mental picture of him before his death, but this age only contributes to his superior understanding of mankind.

(10) Robert Frost is perhaps America's most well known poet, although the merit of much of his work is rather dubious. Frost's poetry supposedly brings to light the intrinsic beauty of the New England countryside, but I believe much of what literary critics see in Frost's poetry is a product of their imagination.

The great American bard's popularity became most evident at President Kennedy's inauguration. Frost was chosen by Kennedy to read a poem commemorating the occasion, since he was considered the poet truly representative of our country. Unfortunately Frost did not have much to say and even had trouble remembering what he had planned to say. Kennedy, the supposed new breed of politician-intellect, should have chosen a poet more in keeping with the changing scene. Perhaps Allen Ginsberg would have been more appropriate.

(11) Robert Frost—poet. The first feeling or thought I have about Robert Frost is that he was a great poet. Why? I don't know why really because I've never read that much of his works.

I remember when I saw him on television. Here was the very old gray-haired man reading poetry and all I could think of was "gosh, he'd make someone a nice grandfather."

I have positive good feelings toward Frost. I mean he must be great because he's famous. Now there's a cockeyed analogy. Of course what I've read I've liked. But of course that makes little sense either.

Frost must have been a wonderful man. I mean any man with the last name of Frost who wrote about winter and snow must have some good in him or at least a sense of humor.

(12) Robert Frost was an American poet who was known as a "people's poet." His poetry was written in a style which can be easily understood by most of the people who read it. He wrote about things and places which are familiar to the masses of people.

Frequently during his lifetime, Robert Frost read his own poetry before an audience. One of these times was at a Presidential inauguration.

I don't believe him to have been a very great poet, but he is a poet whom I and many other people enjoy reading.

(13) Robert Frost was a 20th century American poet. His poems were mostly about New England, where he lived all his life. One of his poems was "Stopping by a Woods" and described his feelings when he came upon a woods one lonely, snowy night. He died in the early 1960's and is the best known American poet of this century. His poems often depicted folksy scenes and his style was simple and colloquial.

(14) If the United States had ever had such a thing as a "Poet Laureate," Robert Frost would surely have been chosen to fill that position. In a way, in

fact, perhaps he was our unofficial Poet Laureate since he was chosen to speak at John Kennedy's inauguration, and this was sure an honor.

When I think of Robert Frost I think, of course, of New England, for this is the section in which he lived and which he wrote about. I remember his "mending wall" and "a swinger of birches." I remember his attitude toward nature and toward his fellow man. I remember all these things, but, most of all, I remember a small elderly man with "frost" white hair.

(15) Robert Frost, New England poet. He loved to create international images through his descriptions of local scenery and happenings. His poems seem to represent thoughtful solitude which brings the reader to a point of active thinking.

He dealt mainly with objects of nature and their relationship to the human experience. He sees the birches as being swung by young boys rather than by an inanimate ice storm. He sees two roads diverging in a wood and sees them as choices people must make. He stops by a woods and says the owner lives far away and is missing the beauty of it.

(16) I don't know that much about Robert Frost as a person. I've read quite a bit of his poetry and like it. One of my favorite poems of his is "Fire and Ice." I don't really know why. I memorized it once for something and it's always stuck with me.

I like what Frost has to say in his poems—in a lot of cases I don't like to tear his poetry apart and analyze it. I like to read them and enjoy them at face value. Too many times, for me, a value loses its beauty and meaning by being picked apart.

(17) Robert Frost's poetry is very appealing to me. I like it because of its seeming simplicity. His poetry is regional in the sense that so much of it deals with New England, but I think that beyond the New England setting it is quite universal. Having studied some of Frost's poetry last semester, I think that because of the things I mentioned above I am more sensitive to his poetry than the blurt poetry of Carl Sandburg.

(18) First, Robert Frost is All-American. Nice, comfortable, likable American. *Everybody* has read some Frost or at least can chant "miles to go before I sleep." You really can't go wrong saying you like him—almost no one will argue with you. I mean, it would be like saying Lincoln was an early Soviet spy or something. Frost is simple. That is why he is found in all school literature books after Mother Goose has been mastered. Of course lots of teachers read lovely obscure meanings into his poems. He doesn't really read his poems period; he sort of mumbles and stumbles them out in a very gruff down-to-earth way. Comfortable. Frost is simply a comfortable poet. No controversy, no Freudian meaning, full sentences, comfortable.

(19) The first time I came into contact with Robert Frost was in high school and like most tenth graders I really had no feelings for the man. Actually I disliked poetry at that time so I probably didn't even read "Stopping by the Woods" more than once. It wasn't until last year that I was confronted by Frost again. That time our meeting was more cordial. Since I was in a poetry class I wanted to read poetry. And since I read Frost at the same time I read Wallace Stevens and Marianne Moore I naturally became attached to Frost more readily than some other 20th century American poets. No doubt because I at

least thought I could understand him.

My first feelings toward Frost are now that I enjoy his style. I know that he writes about fairly simple ideas and uses very homely physical objects and relationships in his poetry. This simpleness is no doubt what I like about him.

(20) Robert Frost is an American poet from New England and much of his poetry reflects New England's customs and geography. I especially like "The Mending" wall [*sic*] and "Home Burial." I think I like "Home Burial" because it is hard to tell who is right, the husband or the wife. Is the wife too sensitive and unwilling to go on living because of the child's death or is the husband too cold and insensitive to it.

"Stopping in a Woods" is another Frost poem I like. I enjoy reading his poetry because unlike many other poets of our century, especially those of the 1940's, he is not so ambiguous as to be impossible to comprehend.

(21) Robert Frost was America's white-haired, New England poet who had this beautiful image of a grandfatherly, kindly, cryptic manner. He wrote beautiful poems, most of which I like. Right now Mr. Frost is something of a puzzle to me because according to *Time*'s review of his biography which recently came out (I haven't read the book), he really wasn't a grandfatherly, kindly, cryptic man. According to *Time*, according to the biography, he had many problems and really had to polish and polish his poetry to get that rough-hewn edge on his work. They also said he wasn't kindly either, but that he tended to be nasty and to begrudge the fact that he didn't have any money when he was young. All this completely ruins my image of him as a kindly, crusty man, but I don't mind. It makes him more of a person to me, and I like that.

These statements are arranged more or less according to the ascending order of familiarity with Frost and his work claimed by each respondent. The writers of the first statements say they are hardly acquainted with Frost, while the last few are able to compare him with other poets; respondent 21 understood the significance of Thompson's biography for Frost's popular reputation. Yet, regardless of this understandably wide range of acquaintance with Frost, elements of knowledge common to all or most of the respondents make it possible to observe certain features of a collectively held *public* image of him.

Over half of the respondents identify Frost as American. Although some of the identifications are just labels—e.g., "American male poet of the twentieth century" (3)—most add a cultural connotation to the name ("all-American," in paragraph 18) or the regional specification ("American poet from New England and much of his poetry reflects New England's customs and geography," in paragraph 20). Two respondents, 15 and 17, understand Frost to have transformed his local concerns into ones of "international" or "universal" relevance. The frequent association of Frost with New England, while not wholly false, suggests the dimension of mythology that Frost's reputation has gained from it. Very little of his poetry can be positively identified as referring to "New England customs and geography," and he did not, as respondent 13 says, live there "all his life." Respondent 10, who says that Frost's poetry "supposedly brings to light the intrinsic beauty of the New England countryside," senses that he is dealing with a myth, but he does not actually name the mythological elements. Such hazy knowledge of Frost must have grown from an awareness that Frost lived in New England at least much of his life and from primary and secondary school acquaintance with New England's role in American history and the group of well-known, frequently anthologized nineteenth-century New England poets. These extremely common school experiences facilitate the subsequent conception of Frost as "the great American bard" (10), the "people's poet" (12), the "best-known American poet of the century" (13), or "poet laureate" (14). From the "cradle of the Revolution" came the poet of the inauguration.

It is difficult to determine whether the image of Frost as a popular national leader of American culture grew out of the respondents' viewing of his appearance at John Kennedy's inauguration in 1961; six do cite the event as contributing to their conception of Frost. The invitation by Kennedy (who was born in New England but also cannot be identified with Revolutionary New England) could not have been only a matter of aesthetic taste; Frost's then-existing personal mythology must have seemed an appropriate contribution to the new president's own attempts to build an atmosphere of enlightened, cultivated leadership. It is highly unlikely, however, that T. S. Eliot's appearance in the same capacity would have rendered him the "great American bard" or the "all-American" poet. Respondents 10 and 14 each ascribe Frost's appearance at the inaugural to his having been "chosen" (as opposed to "invited"), with the former's reason being that "he was considered the poet truly representative of our country." Although this reader is skeptical of the value of Frost's work ("the merit of much of his work his rather dubious"), he sees his appearance at the inauguration as the president's conscious invocation of Americana, as if in the best national interest: this is the sense in which I think the word *chosen* is used by both respondents. For most of those who cited the inauguration reading, it was an image-using as much as an image-making event.

A major aspect of this image is literally visual, the elements of which contribute to the readers' frequent personal sense of Frost as a "grandfather" (11, 21). He is not simply old, but is the "old man of song and verse" (8), a "little more of a man than the average" (6); and his age "only contributes to his superior understanding of mankind" (9), an understanding earlier characterized by this respondent as "akin to God." The striking visual feature of this wise old man is—in addition to his wrinkled face (7)—his white hair, which is mentioned prominently by eight of the respondents. Respondent 4's invidious comparison of the lab instructor with the white-haired poet of the same name suggests how the sheer image projects an elevated personal and perhaps spiritual value for her. The same image makes respondent 3 aware of her own sense of inadequate knowledge of Frost: "He is the one person an English major should know about." Similarly, respondent 7, in comparing the poet of "snow white hair" with Jack Frost, feels "very guilty" that she cannot advance beyond this mythical knowledge. Although only respondent 21 claims to have documented the mythical dimension of the awe-inspiring, white-haired grandfather poet, the others are also aware of the tenuous grounds of the image, yet subscribe to it nevertheless. The image represents a collectively held subjective value.

This value is related to what many perceive as a real feature of his poetry—its simplicity, cited by respondents 12, 13, 17, 18, 19, and 20. Most of those who are not widely read or otherwise familiar with literature, like respondents 1 and 2, find poetry in general a distant and difficult subject. If their attitude is receptive, Frost becomes an exception to their belief that poetry is inaccessible to them. Respondent 19 describes how, once he took the initiative to read poetry, he preferred Frost over the others: "This simpleness is no doubt what I like about him." Respondent 18, who seems the most aware of Frost as a mythic figure, presents this situation most directly: "Frost is simple." To him, more than the language is simple; the poet himself is "comfortable" because he and his work involve "no controversy, no Freudian meaning, full sentences." Simplicity in this sense is an American value so incontrovertible and widely accepted as to be in the class of objective goods that include Abraham Lincoln and Mother Goose; at least, this is how Frost appears to the reader. Put another way, the value is "the universal *accessibility*, to me the unsophisticated reader, of a wise and important leader."

I do not know how much Frost's name and the color of his hair contributed to the broad familiarity of some of his winter poems and imagery. The statements above suggest that the poetic images are very often identified with the name, age, or personality of the poet. Although respondent 11's thought may be partly ironic, it is similar to what several other readers observed: "Any man with the last name of Frost who wrote about winter and snow must have some good in him or at least a sense of humor." Respondent 9 is more direct: "He is everything his name suggests—white-haired, biting, refreshing, rude awakening, ice on the grass." The ease with which relatively uninformed readers make the association of the name, the hair, and the subject matter is a major factor in the common feeling of his accessibility.

Even though Frost's poetry is perceived as easily comprehended, very few poems, with the exception of "Stopping by Woods on a Snowy Evening," enter into the respondents' images of Frost. Only one respondent (20) presented a substantive interpretation of a poem as part of her knowledge of the poet. One or two others commented on specific images in poems, such as respondent 15's observation on "Birches" and "The Road Not Taken." "Fire and Ice" and "Mending Wall" are each mentioned by two respondents, but in no instance— except for "Stopping by Woods"—does familiarity with a particular poem contribute to the respondents' images and sense of the poet. While many of the respondents claimed they did read the poetry on more than just a casual basis, they did not seem to consider the actual reading experiences important enough to include in their presentation of their "knowledge of Frost." In valuing accessibility over experiential complexity, these readers reflect the concerns of their pedagogical training—but more in a mode of discomfort with these concerns than acceptance. The poet whose work permits personal contact with himself is more valuable than the one who demands "close reading" of "the text." At the same time, those readers who feel embarrassed or guilty at not being familiar with Frost, his work, or poetry in general— respondents 1 and 2—are aware of a coercive pedagogical demand for knowledge: "It was asked of me this morning. . . ." The popularity of Frost and his work is due in large part to the motives of younger readers (in our culture, at this time) to find authorities and heroes who express traditional American values, to engage the sentiments attached to these values, but to bypass moralistic pressures for objective knowledge. For most of these respondents, the "real" Robert Frost is less important than the imagined poet who ameliorates pedagogical difficulties while encouraging a sense of personal integration into the culture.

"Stopping by Woods" answers these motives as well as other, related ones, as I will discuss shortly in the context of a longer response statement. Because of its brevity and simple vocabulary, it is usually taught earlier in school than other poems; and as many students report, it is a work they are asked to memorize. Although many students come to dislike the poem because they associate it with coercive pedagogy, their familiarity with it spans a longer period of growth than for other poems, and they feel their opinion about the poem has more authority than their views on other, less familiar works.

It is easy to point to "errors" these readers made in citing or alluding to even this well-known poem. But it is more important to understand which values the conceptions of the poem represent, and to view these idiosyncratic readings as instances of negotiable subjective knowledge and collective interests. Respondent 8, for example, imagines the speaker riding a "dottering, nag, touching the branches and smiling in his vague peculiar way." Obviously, none of this is in the poem, but it is a metaphor for the reader's affective response. Respondent 9 uses the title as a metaphor for the poet. Respondent 13 identifies the poet with the speaker of the poem. Respondent 15 says the owner of the woods "lives far away and is missing the beauty of it." (The speaker says only that the "owner" lives in the village and "will not see me stopping here.") Each of these observations come as part of a personal idea of the poet and as participation in a collective interest in him. The motive for a shared cultural interest cannot be "close reading" or technical accuracy: a perfectly accurate reading would mean only the repetition of the poem. The mythological aspect of this author derives from a variety of commonly held motives, values, perceptual habits, and pedagogical trainings. The benign and peaceful way in which the poem is associated with the image of the author intimates what some of the commonly held motives are—simplicity and accessibility of venerable leadership; reverence for and enjoyment of nature; rootedness in the most wholesome traditions of American life. Because values such as these appear regularly among Americans regardless of whether they read poetry, it is no surprise that at least one American poet mobilizes them, as Frost did in these respondents. (It is probably surprising to many, as it was to respondent 21, that Frost deliberately aimed for such responses.)

The strong association of "Stopping by Woods" with the mythic personality of its author has produced an almost equally strong prevailing interpretation of the poem. It is taught in high schools, in the universities, and in the published criticism, and it was repeated in the dozens of response statements I have collected after readings of the poem. The speaker, in a peaceful moment, is watching the lonely, snowy woods unobserved; it is very dark; he is tempted to lie down in the woods and die; but he renounces the temptation in order to go on living and keep his promises (obligations to family and society); he redoubles his resolve by repeating the last line. The meaning of this reading is its affirmation of social responsibility; often the "owner" of the woods is interpreted as God, who is giving "man" a chance to decide his own destiny in a responsible way; "man" does, after being tempted, make the "right" decision. If Frost is identified with the speaker, he becomes the temptable, frail mortal, articulate yet simple in his longing. Finally, in his simple way, he is heroic: he chooses to keep his promises rather than go to sleep. Among student respondents, this interpretation takes on several common forms. The speaker is Santa Claus, pausing on his busy schedule, but then continuing on to give gifts to little children; or, the speaker is an obstetrician called out on this dark night, weary, but nevertheless trudging on to deliver happy children; or, the speaker is a father on his way home, tempted by the mysteries of the universe, but called back to his normal role by ongoing obligations; and so on. From these homely scenarios comes the interest in wise old men with white hair living peacefully in New England and maintaining a stable family and community in spite of hardship and temptation. The poem is understood as an allegory of a plain, decent man's victory over idle temptations and even death. In its religious dimension, it is also an especially American value; God, to the readers, is intimated, if not actually present, and lies behind the traditional Puritan value of austere hard work and self-denial. Frost is perceived as mellowing this tradition, humanizing it, secularizing it through nature, while retaining its seriousness and dedication. These are the values brought out in pedagogical and sometimes homiletic interpretation which elaborate and fill out the topical values suggested by the respondents' various images of Frost.

An extended response statement turns up different aspects of these values. It suggests a commonly held emotional substrate which forms a motive for affirming the values. Relative to the present pedagogical motives, the response statement outlines possibilities for the collective rearticulation of the myth into more locally adaptive knowledge.

The Response Statement of Ms. J to Frost's
"Stopping by Woods on a Snowy Evening"

(1) Frost's "Stopping by Woods on a Snowy Evening" has always been one of my favorite poems. It helped me get through the difficulty of growing up. As I re-read it I see how it served functionally as a scapegoat to justify the extreme loneliness I always used to feel and sometimes feel now.

(2) I think my problem was that I took life too seriously when I was about 15. When I began junior high school I knew how to have fun goofing around with the gang and I certainly was reliable for getting into all kinds of trouble, but when I reached high school I spent most of the time resenting the responsibilities I had at home and it seemed right that I should feel sorry for myself as often as I did. It's strange though, when I did feel sorry for myself I didn't actually realize that that was what I was doing. Instead I felt proud that I was more mature than my infantile friends and had responsibilities which I knew none of them had because they all had 2 parents. Since my father died when I was 11 and my mother went to work, I had to clean the entire house, wash the clothes, cook some of the meals, and I felt it was *my* house more than anyone else's. I didn't like to spend time lurking around the local suburban shopping center with my girlfriends waiting for beautiful boys to flirt with. My flirting days passed with the carefreeness of junior high; I had more important things to attend to. Besides, I didn't have the confidence any more in my beauty and charm, and when I tried to be with my friends and talk to the boys, I always felt rejected.

(3) "Whose woods these are I think I know. His house is in the village though; He will not see me stopping here . . ." However, there were the good

old days when I was usually happy and felt confident with all kinds of people, kids my age as well as adults. Whenever I had the opportunity to get away with some mischievous prank, or lie to get out of trouble when I had been caught, I seized it with delight! However, I rarely got caught since I always made up necessary stories beforehand to defend my fantastic deviltry. And lying was always great fun and games since I was capable of the most beautiful and believable stories. When there was no one around to prove my very naughty conduct, man, I took full advantage. In seventh grade it just happened that all of my best friends were in most of my classes. We had a really flipped-out and senile, white-haired old man for a science teacher, Mr. German. Just to illustrate what a weird guy he was, we were doing experiments on the content of starches, sugars, acids, etc., in different foods and solutions. Mr. German took a glass beaker and stood out in the hall in between classes asking kids to "spit in the jar." He wanted to put it to the iodine test to see if it would turn purple like potato starch. This guy wasn't satisfied with his own sample or one other person's saliva, he had to go collecting everybody's enzymes in jars and storing them in his closet! That was really weird. Anyway, my best friend, Suzie, and I used to get into trouble for passing notes to each other. Mr. German had us seated on opposite sides of the room but this didn't stop us. As soon as he'd turn his back to us to draw some elaborate amoeba on the blackboard with his favorite colored chalk, we'd stand up and with full pitching power, hurl crazy notes at each other. When this happened simultaneously we'd inevitably break out in such hysterical laughter that the entire class would crack up, contagiously. Suzie had one of those hilarious laughs! Then Mr. German would turn around and scream, "Who is causing this ruckus?" Without waiting for an answer he'd throw one or both of us out of the room and Cathy, Karen, Steve, and Paul would follow in succession. I think we spent more time in the hall than in class, and he defeated his own purpose because we all ended up together. Then there were the lies we made up for getting out of detention after school. Now I feel sorry for Mr. German, though, because clearly, we didn't respect him, and as a teacher he was competent. But I guess at the age of 13 it's more important for a kid to have the status as a *wise guy* than to learn science.

(4) As I got older, I stopped going around with the gang after school hours. I spent time alone at home writing romantic poetry, doing homework or some chore for my mother, or crying to my dog, Peewee, who was the only person that understood me. I think the person in Frost's poem must have had this kind of relationship with his horse. The horse seems to have the responsibility of keeping his master from freezing in the cold and wind on the darkest night of the year with no one else near by. He doesn't understand why his master acts irrationally by stopping in the woods when it is getting late and he has "promises to keep." Peewee didn't know why I cried so much and so hard but she would crawl into my lap looking very hurt and sorry that I felt so badly. She would lick my hand and face wherever the tears fell and it made me happier to know the most important person in my life was alleviating some of the burden of my sorrow. But sometimes when I felt really angry and hurt for reasons beyond my comprehension, I'd accuse her of not really feeling compassion and merely enjoying the salt in my tears.

(5) The person in the poem really appreciates the quiet, lovely solitude of the woods. He must have been a busy person with many responsibilities. My high school English teachers never failed to inform the class that he was a middle-aged, hard working family man with a wife and a tribe of kids to feed, and that everyone needs to get away from it all every so often. Gee, what insight these guys had! It's too bad that everything can't be defined as stereotypically and simplistically as that. Whenever I would receive that shallow interpretation year after year from every Tom, Dick, and Harry English teacher, and I would begin each course by trusting them to give me some great insights into literature, they'd certainly leave me by the wayside when we got to this poem. I never really trusted them after that. Life just wasn't structured like that for me.

(6) My mother had some widowed friends who were also fairly young like she was, and they'd always go somewhere together every Saturday night, like to a dance or something. I always felt relieved when I got her ready with her hair set and looking pretty, and her clothes fitting beautifully and she got the hell out of the house. It wasn't as though I didn't like my mother; in fact I loved her. But she was really spaced-out after my father died and it was a good thing I was such a self-sufficient kid. I was sincerely happy for her to go out because I wanted her to try to have some fun. I never resented the fact that she wanted to remarry. She was certainly young and beautiful and I didn't want her life to end. Even selfishly, I wished she would get married, and I say "selfishly" because I wasn't sure if what I wanted more was a husband for her or a father for me. Anyway, when she'd leave I appreciated the solitude. She was a comfort to me and yet a threat. I was pretty lonely. I lived in a middle class section of town and although it wasn't a particularly dangerous neighborhood my mother always warned me to be careful at night that I didn't get beat up or raped or killed or something. In fact, she didn't want me to walk around at night, which my friends commonly did. "I'll drive you any place you want to go, but please don't walk." She always gave me a hassle about that and if I did walk I'd have to call her when I reached my destination. When I went next door to my friend's house for a few minutes, she'd leave the light on outside and watch from the window sometimes to see if I was O.K. I guess she really cared and was worried about me but I still felt hassled. So when she went out on Saturday nights I went out too, walking alone. I knew there were some punky kids in town who probably would act violent if given the opportunity but I wasn't really scared. One night I went out and walked about three miles feeling very brave and sorry for myself and not giving too much of a damn if I got jumped or raped or killed. I walked past a group of boys on the other side of the street at about one a.m. I frequently crossed the street whenever there were boys or other people I felt like avoiding. These boys were involved in some sort of argument and I didn't want to seem obvious by staring, yet I caught a glimpse of what seemed like a rifle. This made me a little nervous. But although there was no traffic on the road and this lone, feminine, rapable figure was approaching them, they didn't seem to notice. I guess what they were doing was more intriguing for them. I walked on feeling invisible, relieved yet a little shook up, and turned the next corner towards home. I was frightened back to reality by something, and sped up my pace. I remember

going past the clock in the window of an office. It was one-thirty. I went home pretty quickly. I knew Peewee would be waiting, my mother would be home soon and I didn't want to be hassled about where I had been. I didn't feel much like lying to her and I also had things to think out. And not to sound corny or melodramatic, but "miles to go before I sleep."

(7) Frost's poem "Stopping by Woods on a Snowy Evening" had a terrific impact on me as an adolescent. I was so lonely, even when I was with other people; I felt self-conscious all the time. Lacking confidence, I enjoyed wallowing in my sorrow within the safe and sheltering confines of my own room. I must have read that poem hundreds of times since it always made me feel so much better and seemed to tell me that somewhere out there in the lovely, dark deepness of the woods was someone who was experiencing a feeling of loneliness, and yet loving every breathtaking second of the peaceful solitude. He would know how I felt and be my friend. The woods and horse and snow and lake would all be my friends; they would cheer me up. In fact, the poem seemed to cry out, "I know you're lonely but it's O.K. to be lonely; it's a beautiful experience we can share. Trust me."

The value of "thoughtful solitude," which respondent 15 believes Frost's poems represent is part of the "crusty grandfather" image of the poet. Ms. J's response statement presents the private, and usually unmentioned, component of this value—anxious loneliness. The feelings she reports as having come in response to a long acquaintance with this poem grew from her repeated perception of the poem as a statement that loneliness, not solitude, was "O.K." (7). From the perspective of Ms. J's response alone, however, it is not possible to claim that loneliness is usually associated with solitude in the syndrome of values mobilized by Frost. On the other hand, conflictual or painful feelings are rarely included in any conception of a society's collective "interests." Rather, such interests represent a collectivity's best image of itself and express which of its strong features are retained and enhanced in any new enterprises. Moreover, few will deny that the idealism of Frost's image and the apparent moral responsiveness of the speaker in "Stopping by Woods" (as well as in other poems) actually represent the complex balance of feelings in real reading experiences of the poetry. A series of response statements from the group I have surveyed could suggest collectively held private values that normally accompany the popular image of Frost. Nevertheless, Ms. J's statement presents, in briefer (if less authoritative) form, a motivational explanation of the collective image from her own standpoint. The quality and value of the feelings which comprise the explanation give some indication of the collective motivational premium in maintaining the benign image.

In paragraph 5, Ms. J elaborates her perception of the speaker's appreciation of the "lovely solitude" of the woods. The trustable quality of the imagined scene—which is also cited in the opening and concluding paragraphs—is stereotyped and simplified for her by the reiterated "shallow" thinking of her English teachers. Through her derisive remarks, Ms. J shows the distance between her own responsive language and that of her teachers. She, of course, is not a middle-class father with a "tribe of kids to feed," and more importantly, she *does not have* such a father. Her own version of the common adolescent feelings of loneliness and rejection is related to her other more unique situation of loss. Her teachers only seem to aggravate the already painful feelings. She reports that she "trusts" the teachers for "insights," which means to her, as to any other reader, "insight into one's own feelings and reading experiences." The teachers, she felt, left her "by the wayside," so that she feels alone with the poem as well as alone in response to the poem. For Ms. J in this response the origin of the feelings of "peaceful solitude" is their appearance as a compensation for strong feelings of anxious adolescent loneliness.

The detailed association in paragraph 6 is Ms. J's subjective definition of adolescent loneliness. It emerges partially in response to the concluding observation of paragraph 5 and partially in response to the last stanza of the poem.[2] In the earlier parts of the paragraph, Ms. J describes how her life was "structured" during her adolescence, when her mother went out on weekends, presumably in her efforts to remarry. The different degrees of admiration, cooperation, envy, and need are not unusual for a girl in this situation. Furthermore, the ordinary expressions of maternal concern—about not walking alone at night—had become so oppressive that Ms. J appreciated the solitude. All of these expectable circumstances contributed to a distinct affective condition: "I was pretty lonely." The subsequent parts of the paragraph describe Ms. J's handling of the feeling at the time and also suggest specific psychological ramifications which adolescent loneliness entails.

In her self-asserting walks through dangerous neighborhoods, Ms. J, in a daring born of loneliness, challenges the "punky kids" (mostly in her imagination) to notice this "lone, feminine, rapable figure." The walk is a test of sexual potential and personal courage; although there is a real risk, there is also the challenge to avoid the danger. The whole report in this paragraph is a subjective perception of the last stanza of the poem—the temptation and the challenge to avoid it. In the concluding parts of the paragraph, Ms. J describes how she did avoid it:

2. This double origin of several of the associations in this response statement may not be apparent to those who do not know the person who wrote it. Ms. J was aware of doing two things—re-responding to a new reading and reporting the history of her response to this poem. In discussing her statement, however, it is hardly necessary to separate out the feelings according to unrecoverable intentions. It is simpler and emotionally truer to the response to understand it simply as the result of a present reading; obviously memories of other readings will enter the statement as a contribution to the present sense of it.

she crossed the street, quickened her pace, and was "frightened back to reality," which meant her dog, her home, her mother. Reality, however, also meant her reflective, rather than her active, self—she defines the last line of the poem as "things to think about." The assertion of responsibility referred to herself as much as to her mother. At the level of specific psychological experience the "temptation to die" usually associated with the speakers' pause at the lovely woods can be understood as a temptation toward sex or violence or interpersonal transgression. These are as much a part of the list of Puritan prohibitions as the vague wish to be distracted or swallowed by transcendental mysteries. Furthermore, Frost's biography shows how he was often distracted in his youth—and repeatedly later—by the aesthetic pull of poetry, whose claims on his energies conflicted with his responsibilities as the head of a family—first as protector of his mother and subsequently, of his wife and children. In the real experiences of Ms. J's response, and of Frost's life, the determination to "keep promises" came out of difficult struggles, and was anything but the quiet choice usually attributed to the poem's speaker.

Ms. J's associations in paragraph 3 define the sense in which the poem's nominal situation, watching woods, introduces psychological complexity from the outset. Readers whose attention is caught by the third line of the first stanza, "He will not see me stopping here," begin to change their existing understanding of the poem toward a meaning which gives more prominence to the thought that the speaker's experience is stolen to begin with. Ms. J's remarks give the particular sense in which she is among this group of readers. The classroom behavior she describes is, like the speaker's, ultimately harmless. Yet, her considerable exuberance in describing the release of energy in defiance of the authority figure whose back is turned communicates psychological importance. In the response, the teacher's obsessive behavior is an object of derision, and this feeling indirectly justifies the pleasurable triumph over him and the successful reunion of the group of classmates he had earlier split up. Such forceful feelings may seem alien to the familiar mood of this poem, but inconsequential feelings could not be the occasion for its wide popularity. It is one form of experience to enjoy solitude; it is something else to consciously note that a specific individual—an owner or other authoritative figure— "will not see me" relate to something that belongs to him. Ms. J's association makes this awareness of experience stolen from a specific person explicit and suggests the kind of pleasure it entails.

Ms. J's response to the horse in paragraph 4 is a preamble to the more aggressive feelings (described in her next paragraph) accruing from loneliness: pain and sadness precede the initiatives to ameliorate the loneliness. Her dog is a dependent figure, and even though he seems to offer consolation and love, these attentions are, after all, insufficient, insofar as they are coming from "someone" whose own needs are actually taking precedence over hers: Peewee is "merely enjoying the salt in my tears." The aggressive feelings Ms. J then presents are a response as much to her dependency as to the last stanza of the poem.

As Ms. J makes clear in paragraphs 1 and 7, the material of this response, though recorded in the present, also represents important feelings that occurred in the past, over a long period of time during which the poem was read repeatedly. In lonely circumstances, reading this poem was an ameliorating activity because she understood the speaker as someone who, in a situation like her own, was able to love "every breathtaking second of the peaceful solitude." The reading experience brings out, in addition to memories of actual events, the awareness of a psychological habit in which loneliness was translated into aggressive and defiant feelings and then into a cultivation of solitude. The tradition of objective interpretation conceives this psychological journey as having arrived back to the poem and its values. Subjectively conceived, however, the response is a redefinition of the way Ms. J participates in a collective value whose idealistic character is reduced in proportion to the degree of experiential specificity it acquired.

Understanding the value as defined by the response is similar to viewing it in the context of Frost's biography; both sets of subjective material show the partial nature of a common image. Frost did have white hair, but only when he was old; he did write about winter, but only a small part of the time; and he did have many moments of thoughtful solitude, but usually as a consequence of the severe stresses of loneliness, bitterness, anger, frustration, and impatience with the needs and demands of others. As different as Ms. J's reports are from Frost's personal experiences, her response and Frost's biography each suggest ways in which a trying sense of loneliness is part of the collectively held reassuring value this poem is believed to express.

Adolescent loneliness is an important part of American culture, and the various aspects of this feeling relate to the collective image developed by the twenty-one respondents above and to the psychology in Ms. J's response statement. For example, Frost is perceived as a "nature" poet. In America, *nature* means many things, but one of its most common senses is the "frontier," where the task, for generations, was to subdue, control, and appropriate natural resources with few thoughts for the destruction this might entail. Those most responsible for the taming of the American frontier were the nation's young men, who went out alone to take command of "the territory." Many of Frost's poems show a lone figure in a natural setting, contemplating it or himself or both. The original history is, in such poems, itself "subdued" from action to meditation. The value of "nature," however, has never been such a purely meditative one; but the collectively held motive for stressing the peaceful side was created by a history that was anything but peaceful. Frost's own childhood in San Francisco in the 1880s was deeply immersed in the atmosphere of violence and lawlessness of this history, and his father was victimized by his own participation in it.

Frost is perceived as a purveyor of grandfatherly wisdom, "akin to God," as respondent 9 observes. The traditional hero in American life has never been the old man; it has always been the young athletic type whose authority derived from a historical rejection of the European "fathers" as well as from the success in cultivating the frontier. Thoughtful wisdom was not the virtue of such heroes, who were bold, aggressive, and oriented toward survival and "freedom." But they share in common with the grandfather an impulse of generosity to strangers (though mainly those who appear in the same lonely position as themselves) and, more importantly, asexuality. The image of the grandfather legitimizes these two aspects of the historical hero, regardless of Frost's actual lack of personal generosity and his actual difficulties in coping with sexuality. Ms. J's response suggests both the violent thoughts which grow from loneliness and the sexuality that is inhibited by it; her "wisdom" is her discovery that she needed to accommodate these realities through the conscious effort to appreciate solitude.

One of the grounds on which respondent 15 reached the generalization of "thoughtful solitude" for Frost's poems was her understanding of "Stopping by Woods" as presenting the owner "far away" from his woods and "missing the beauty of it." Neither of these perceptions can have been derived from the verbal meaning of the poem, since we are not told if the village is far, and we are told only that the owner "will not see" the speaker. These "errors," however, are consistent with the myth of the poem and with the psychology of the myth. Perceiving the owner as distant emphasizes the speaker's isolation; perhaps, to this respondent, the owner *feels* distant. Perceiving the owner as missing the beauty transforms the poem's third line from one having ambiguous implication for the speaker to one which holds him in a more cultivated light; the speaker's observation of the beauty is a more definite contrast with the owner who is missing it. This reading greatly reduces, and perhaps eliminates, the implication that the speaker may be "stealing" a pleasurable experience. This initial innocence helps to promote the subsequent perception of his moral strength in renouncing even an innocent pleasure for "promises."

For some years, Americans have begun to reunderstand their history in light of the fact that much of the territory (if not all of it) was actually taken from another people. But for a long time, "manifest destiny" was considered a normal explanation of how the territory was acquired. Nevertheless, even today, few Americans other than the descendents of the Indian nations take seriously the implication that all of the bounty of our civilization grows from conquests and thefts, which are psychologically "unseen"—that is, in general, unfelt—even if they are factually present in most people's minds. Frost's biography shows that he was aware of the psychological ramifications of knowing who is *not* observing him. Similarly, Ms. J's response presents a common portrayal of the aggressive opportunities created by the turned back of the "owner." The public image of Frost also does not "see" either the historical realities or the psychological complexity which are important sources of its set of values.

In the ten-year period since the preceding responses were collected, it is probable that the popular acquaintance with Frost and his work has changed, especially in the light of Thompson's biography; more teachers, like respondent 21, have the documentation at their disposal for making this "simple" poet more interesting and less stereotyped. Yet regardless of what new information comes to light about Frost, his work is going to represent a collective interest for some time to come. Other, less accessible poets remain the concern of one sort of collectivity or another even though they have not articulated national mythic values to the same degree Frost did. In each instance, biographical information is a major contributor to the dialectic that creates and reduces collective interests. Nevertheless, just what a collective interest is remains an abstraction until a particular group surveys what its constituents have in common and investigates how individual response habits manifest shared values and perceptions. The idea of collectivity is always vague until a particular group defines its own "groupness." For example, the meaning of "freedom" to Democrats depends on one collective psychological syndrome, and to Republicans, on another; the interests of each group set forth what the "same" value "actually is."

The pedagogical situation is a natural context for initiating inquiries into collective interests. Most such situations are already defined by certain obvious commonalities, such as "young people of age 20." The psychological functions of these commonalities, however, are not usually obvious, and few believe in the importance of appropriating them to the purpose of synthesizing new knowledge. Just because no single individual can alone define a collective interest, a group's responsibility to its own existence is to *consciously* establish what it shares. The establishment of shared interests is fundamental to authorizing any new knowledge, since knowledge of personal taste, of meaning, and of authors—as discussed in the previous chapter as well as in this one—is strongly influenced by unspoken, collectively held psychological paradigms.

Literary regularities perceived as outside of or independent of one's own collectivity are nevertheless defined by this group's collective interests. The regularity which holds the greatest sway in the contemporary study of literature is historical; the most widely accepted means of perceiving different aspects of Western civilization's literary heritage has been through conceptualization of a definitive character for each historical epoch. Although it seems that the chronological presentation of literature is itself value-free, most teachers know that this is not the case: the old is always presented, through the use of the word "classic," as superior to the contemporary; from this presentation comes the belief that, in general, older is better. In addition to such implicit values, each age is usually given a qualitative characterization whose actual function is to form a basis for comparing the mores of past societies with our own. For example, if Victorian mores were not compared to our own, it would be very difficult to associate sexual repression with mid-nineteenth-century life; only because our society has paid more *public* attention to sexuality does the retrospective characterization of Victorians become meaningful—that is, true relative to our collective self-image. The use of historical chronology derives from the assumed value of quantitative description which renders works having more years generally better than those having less; quantitative description is one of the main consequences of the objective paradigm. Qualitative characterization invokes, implicitly, the idea of progress, which also derives from the objective paradigm: the mores of the present are necessarily an improvement over those of the past. Therefore, both of the defining features in the contemporary use of historical periodization follow from the assumptions of the objective paradigm, which is one of the interests of the collectivity to which my discussion is presented.

In some quarters, thinking has shifted away from these traditional habits into a more subjective framework. Rachel Trickett writes, for example, that "the real difficulty of defining and categorizing in the Augustan or any other age, is to avoid over-simplification and the feeling that in some way we have succeeded in fixing the period and its characteristics for good."[3] From a different viewpoint, George Boas observes that "we may as well say, however, dogmatically, that when one is in search of an age, one ends with human beings."[4] Trickett's

3. Rachel Trickett, "The Difficulties of Defining and Categorizing in the Augustan Period," *New Literary History*, 1 (1969), 178.

4. George Boas, "In Search of the Age of Reason," in *Aspects of the Eighteenth Century*, ed. Earl Wasserman (Baltimore, 1965), p. 18.

remark tries to increase awareness of the great effect of our own perspective on our thinking; Boas says that what seems a group of people from our perspective were in their own society several individuals with no necessary connection with one another. These remarks were offered in contexts whose explicit purpose was to reopen inquiry into the prevailing conceptualizations of eighteenth-century literature, and to discover if this historical phase still remains susceptible to the generalizations that have been widely accepted for a long time: the "age of order," or the "age of reason." The result of these inquiries was less that the habitual epithets were cast into disfavor than that the whole process of searching for such titles seemed a more questionable enterprise.

The study of response statements aims to disclose collective motives for defining literary regularities. In the discussion to follow, I will suggest what I think are some consequences of conceiving Jonathan Swift as a characteristic mind of the eighteenth century—that is, a writer thought to confirm the title "age of order"—and then I will propose how a response statement to his poem "A Beautiful Young Nymph Going to Bed" confirms instead Trickett's and Boas's doubts about such generalization. The knowledge derivable from the response will then concern our own collective interest in Swift and in the eighteenth century; and it will also suggest a collective basis for admitting alternative definitions of literary regularity in that period.

The traditional concept of eighteenth-century culture emphasizes the rise of the middle class, a concern with everyday life, the ideal of reason (meaning common sense), and increasing faith in common sense as the essence of human rationality. The harmony in nature, especially in the motion of celestial bodies as described by Newton, was understood as a divine manifestation of common sense. There was a social and natural order that was regular in all its details; there was an increased concern with landscaping, architecture, and furniture; music was balanced, contrapuntal, and regular in its rhythms. Historically in England, order meant social stabilization after the Restoration, a new emphasis on the ancient "classical" authors, and political propriety and regularity. Order seemed to describe the literary habits of the heroic couplet; the serialized, epistolary, and episodic novel; and comedies of the well-mannered. The growth of the middle class seemed to "order" the historical conflict between aristocracy and peasantry. This modern picture of eighteenth-century life carries truth value in ways similar to the image of Frost developed by the twenty-one respondents: the picture is not mendacious—it just stresses certain features over others.

Bonamy Dobrée's discussion of Swift in the *Oxford History of English Literature* shows the critical effects of the traditional view of that age:

The scatological had been an element in Swift's work ever since "The Problem" of 1699. . . . The decay, the collapse of the body, how appalling! his own vertigo, how humiliating! how nauseating the whole business of physical being! Yet if this is the human body, the condition of existence, very well, then, he will accept it (it is one of the hells beneath), he will face it, defeat it by outfacing it. What is abnormal about this attitude is not its rarity, but its intensity; the intensity itself is the abnormality, as it is in much that Swift wrote.
. . .

The subject can be dropped in discussing Swift's contribution to literature (though not in discussing Swift himself); but there is just one comment to be made with respect to one of the malodorous poems of the period—"A Beautiful Young Nymph Going to Bed." . . . Swift was not the only person at this time to write that sort of poem: we get it in Prior, Parnell, and others. . . . Like a good deal of verse and prose printed during this period, it is what we might term schoolboy rather than anything else. The age, of course, was less squeamish than ours—it had to be or die of aromatic pain, not of a rose. . . . Having said that, we can return to a consideration of Swift's more central contributions to literature.[5]

In the first paragraph, Dobree treats Swift's scatological concerns as having an "abnormal" intensity. Were they abnormal relative to Swift, to his time, or to our time? If Swift's intensity "itself is the abnormality," is his other work also atypical in that regard? Dr. Johnson was also intense; is he typical or atypical? If the age was "less squeamish than ours," as Dobree allows in his second paragraph, wouldn't normality and abnormality then have features different from those now? If other important figures of the age also wrote "malodorous" poetry, why should the subject be "dropped"? Did schoolboys actually write such verse, and should we ignore the fact that Swift wrote "A Beautiful Young Nymph" when he was over sixty? Each of my questions implies contradictory thinking in Dobree's comments. But there are no contradictions if those comments are understood as a manifestation of a distinct set of values, and his judgments as serving the society which holds those values. Dobree and those who share his perspective reject the scatological material to the extent of diminishing its importance to almost nothing. The extremely "disorderly" nature of this material does not seem to be consistent with the picture of the age of order. If Dobree's remarks are taken as representative of a collective exercise of taste, they are more pedagogically negotiable than if they are understood as judgments of historical fact, as the title of the volume in which they appear suggests.

Norman O. Brown's opinion of the excremental theme in Swift is considerably different from Dobree's: "Whereas for Rabelais and Aristophanes the anal function is a part of the total human being which

5. Bonamy Dobree, *English Literature in the Early Eighteenth Century* (Oxford, 1959), pp. 462-63.

they make us love because it is part of life, for Swift it becomes the decisive weapon in his assault on the pretensions, the pride, even the self-respect of mankind. . . . The understanding of Swift . . . begins with the recognition that Swift's anatomy of human nature, in its entirety and at the most profound and profoundly disturbing level, can be called 'The Excremental Vision.' "[6] Brown understands Swift's scatological concerns as a definitive feature of his work. Furthermore, Brown interprets the "excremental vision" as part of a complex of Western values and not necessarily a hallmark of the eighteenth century. This complex is the "universal neurosis" of mankind which pervades history.[7] Therefore, both in his local view of Swift and his general view of history, Brown's system of intellectual categories derives from values which contradict Dobree's. Even so, the system is no less local or peculiar to the contemporary perspective. The differences with Dobree only emphasize their analogous anchorage in widely held intellectual formulas and their attempts to have their own values define an objective reality. Even though Brown's remarks seem more fully governed by an attitude of argumentation, he assumes, like Dobree, that there is an ultimate essence of Swift's thought and work that the best form of reasoning will reveal.

Viewing Swift through the language of response statements permits the self-conscious use of contemporary perspectives to disclose the extent to which collective interests *define* the past and its collectivities. Samuel Novey's reasoning (discussed in Chapter Three) obtains in this context also: we shall always be dealing with our own motives for reconceiving the past, so it is advantageous to take these motives into account from the outset. Mr. G's response to "A Beautiful Young Nymph" and my discussion of it should be understood analogously to Ms. J's response to "Stopping by Woods" and its discussion: it is a suggestion of the motives that may be at work in contemporary attempts to generalize Swift and his "age." It is not an attempt to prove such motives exist in all cases. Most concretely, the response presents specific grounds for accepting Boas's observation that the search for an age leads mainly to knowledge of human beings.

The Response Statement of Mr. G to Swift's
"A Beautiful Young Nymph Going to Bed"

(1) The title is promising; it sounds as if it may possibly be erotic (i.e., the poem), so I am prepared to be "turned on." Nymphs are associated (for me) with delightful naked women (small ones, like my wife) who, proverbially, sport in the open fields, etc. Also associated are literary works, like Ovid's (classical nymphs), and Nabakov's (contemporary ones)—the former type of

6. Norman O. Brown, "The Excremental Vision," in *Life Against Death* (New York, 1959), p. 179.
7. Ibid., p. 185.

nymph being less aggressive than the latter, both delightful in their own way. "Bed" is to me the best of all places in that sexual love most often takes place there. But I have on further thoughts, more humorous ideas of associations with bed—the scene in *Tristram Shandy* with Mr. and Mrs. Shandy having their discussions. So the title promises much to me in the way of enjoyment, possibly erotic.

(2) Moving into the poem, I find I am almost immediately deceived about the nature of it; more clearly, it is a letdown from the title. The first two lines give me to understand that we are in for a "pastoral" type of nymph—possibly not erotic. I'm a little frustrated, but not mad—after all, she has yet to go to bed and that could be exciting. I then find out it is not pastoral, but urban (Covent Garden) and that she's not a nymph, but a prostitute ("strolling toast . . ." I think) who has had no luck (I feel like I missed my chance, I wish I had been there to get her). I begin to feel sorry for her (lines 7-9): I think of coming home (in the summer, when I worked) after a hard day's work, coming home late, trudging up the stairs, feeling as if I haven't really done anything, unless it was pay day. My 'pity' for her begins to diminish (beginning line 10) as she pulls her 'self' apart, and I'm on the verge of becoming scornful of her; I remember girls I had gone out with who were not quite as deceitful, but more false than I knew or understood—in fact, I liked artificiality at one point. Anyway I smirk as I read lines 10-20, thinking of all the jokes I had heard years ago: your eyes are like stars (or your teeth are like stars)—they come out every night, etc. Coming to lines 20-21 which follow in the same line, I get disgusted—"flabby dugs" repulses me. I once went out with a girl (in high school) when I first had a car and could go "parking" on the beach; this was the first girl I ever "tried" anything with, and she was receptive; for months I had planned or dreamed or fantasized how to go about it all, what to do first and all that, so I read books on the matter and found out that the breasts of a woman were a good place to begin after preliminary kisses and all that—so finally the day came when I was going to put my plans into action; she always presented to me what appeared to be nice breasts, a good size for me, and I quite naturally thought they would be firm—how else could they stay up and look so pointed (I never understood, at that point in my life, the function of bras; I thought they were like underpants, something you wore to cover up something that was to be covered up). Well, I was enraged to find that her breasts were unbelievably unfirm, and to me they were anti-breasts. So at that point I went no farther, not wanting to be any more disillusioned than I was. To come back to the poem, I can see how it functions: Swift is presenting things that could be disillusioning situations, hoping to hit the reader somewhere in a soft spot—as he did me. From lines 23-28 I get a little bored; my emotional peak came at the disgust of the breasts; from there it's a letdown and his listing of one appearance-reality situation after another doesn't keep me going—my disgust is kept up (realizing one disillusionment, I can "sympathize" with others), but it is less personal.

(3) Lines 38-9 bring back some sympathy, but alternating with a kind of gothic vision of this naked anti-woman who becomes almost like a Graham Wilson cartoon—grotesque but funny as hell; I think the diction—"Pains of Love" doesn't fit the picture of the woman. A strange thing now happens: she

is tormented by thoughts of prison, so she has my sympathy—but in line 42 I feel a sadistic delight and lose sympathy; what seems to happen is that the object of my emotions is transferred from her to whoever is whipping her; ever since I read DeSade (and lots of him) I have had the desire to be sadistic; at the same time I really don't want to hurt anybody—so here in the poem, I can be sadistic (by not being sympathetic, by forgetting the victim and identifying with the sadist) without participating; I can be a voyeur . . . something I also enjoy. Again I now become somewhat bored to line 56; the remainder of the series (which often is not understandable to me) of items which she dreams about are nothing compared with the first. Now the heroine reenters (Corinna wakes), I immediately remember her and feel a sympathetic disgust; "A dreadful sight" reminds me of her, reinforces my sympathetic disgust; then "Behold the Ruins of the Night" keeps up my orientation which is back with Corinna—but now I see that the last two exclamations also move forward to the situation of the apartment and of Corinna's make-up . . . This is delightful play on Swift's part. This is the first linguistic play which I got caught up in and enjoyed. Lines 59-64 I roar at: "And Puss had on her Plumpers pissed" sends me into a good hearty belly laugh. It is partly the phrasing (the "alas" in the preceding line) which is mock-tragic; so I'm laughing, while I'm saying the poor bitch—it's a W. C. Fields bit. Somehow it's O.K. to laugh even without being sympathetic. Here the list of "disasters" is short enough so I don't get bored. Swift doesn't push the situation into boredom; I laugh and then can move on. Urine is perhaps funny to me because of a mix-up of urinating and ejaculating which confused me in my immediate post-pubic state when I didn't know how to masturbate—realizing soon after the difference, I may still chuckle at my youthful stupidity. I move to the last verse paragraph. I wish the poem ended with line 70; I would be happily deceived somehow (even line 72 would be O.K.) . . . I guess I have forgotten the woman and the disgust surrounding her and I am amused at the situation she is in without really thinking of her . . . the last lines, however, bring her and her disgusting qualities back into the poem and force me to be disgusted when I'd much rather be amused.

(4) I sense that Swift has performed a verbal rape which is enjoyable, but sometimes not swift moving enough to keep boredom off; the rape of an anti-woman is sometimes disgusting to me, sometimes pleasing; but ending on a sour note, Swift has frustrated a conceivable situation of humor.

Although Dobree's and Brown's views of Swift are opposite, each emphasizes parts of the same descriptive paradigm for the eighteenth century: the issue of order and disorder. Mr. G raises altogether different matters: disillusionment with women and sexuality and the problems of presenting these thoughts in poetry. Also, the origin of Mr. G's thoughts is different; he *reports* his reading experience while Dobree and Brown abstracted theirs before reporting. Abstraction and report may be equally credible by themselves, but the report of the actual experience is a more authoritative starting point for the pedagogical development of knowledge sought in Mr. G's community.

His response statement discloses ways in which the excremental theme is a function of psychological concerns that do not appear in either of the two critics' comments. Furthermore, these concerns have been biographically documented as prominent (so far as such things are ascertainable) in Swift's life. The resulting view of Swift as an individual and as a representative of an epoch is less assimilable to the traditional abstraction but more comprehensible in the contexts usually used today to discuss living people whom we know and deal with.

The excremental theme is part of Mr. G's response, but only as a consolation for the frustrated expectation of an erotic scene. The first and second paragraphs describe a long subjective dialectic between what he feels various lines augur and what he actually finds in the reading. He observes the "deceitfulness" of women (or girls in the association), but as the response continues in the third and fourth paragraphs, Mr. G gradually localizes the source of his frustration in Swift, the speaker-author. By the time he observes that "Swift has frustrated a conceivable situation of humor" (4), a frustration in his responding fantasies has been converted into a more conscious sense of frustration in the overall reading experience. Regardless of whether the frustration is sexual or artistic, however, it is not possible to understand this feeling as Mr. G's rejection of the disgusting material (and the poem with it), or even as a compensatory celebration of the excremental thoughts. His orientation is interpersonal—toward the heroine and toward the author.

Two parts of the response relate Mr. G's feelings about the experiences that first enlightened him about sex: paragraph 2 describes his ignorance about bras and the results of this ignorance; paragraph 3 reports how his "mix-up" of urinating and ejaculating is now amusing to him, and therefore, "urine is perhaps funny to me." In the last paragraph, he sees Swift's role in this poem as having "performed a verbal rape," though he is critical that there was perhaps not enough action; too much was either boring or disgusting. Mr. G's feelings introduce a set of issues not usually brought into the understanding of Swift—sexuality, voyeurism, and sadism. Swift's manifest rejection of such feelings and of their appearance in society helps to inhibit discussion of their role in Swift's life except as something he rejected. The poem must also reflect an authentic part of its author's mind; if it is "schoolboy" verse, it is to some extent conventional. Mr. G's schoolboy feelings of sexuality (his innocence and voyeurism) in response help to validate Dobree's judgment. The response introduces the possibility that a conception of Swift can include a better-defined sexual dimension as well as features of a schoolboy mentality.

Mr. G's conception of Swift played a definite role in his response. In entering into the response inquiry, he consciously sought more knowledge about the author. His reading was done in a seminar he helped to organize as a consequence of his long-standing interest in Swift, his familiarity with other works, and his rudimentary biographical knowledge.[8] Mr. G's favorable disposition toward Swift was responsible for his anticipation that he would feel the author "working on" him in some way. On several occasions in the response, he perceives Swift's action on him. In paragraph 2, he observes that Swift was "hoping to hit the reader in a soft spot—as he did me." He understands his own disillusionment as having been perpetrated by Swift, and Mr. G's language—"soft spot" and "letdown"—places him in the same position relative to the imagined author as Corinna and his own first sexual partner. In the last paragraph, Mr. G feels more removed from the scene of the poem; here, he finds Swift's "verbal rape" of interest but not quite satisfactory. Mr. G conceives Swift as a sexual figure whose wit does not compensate for the high degree of sexual disillusionment of the reading experience.

Irvin Ehrenpreis's biographical discussions of Swift suggest that disillusionment and frustration are probably more explanatory of Swift's personal history than is the presumed scatological obsession. In *The Personality of Jonathan Swift* (1958), he outlines how the important women in Swift's life were usually inaccessible to him. When he was a child, his prenatally widowed mother "lost" him to a nurse yet kept his older sister, Jane. In adulthood, Swift had at least three major relationships similar to one another; he married none of the women, received maternal ministrations and affections often, and always gave paternal guidance and tutelage. Ehrenpreis believes these relationships were always in a fundamental way, and in either direction, those between a parent and a child:

A pattern of fatherless girls much younger than himself, and all in bad health, can be linked to his own posthumous birth, his early lack of an immediate family, and his constant wrestling with illness. The role of the parent gave him a double pleasure: first, he could provide his beloved with that guidance and warmth which he himself had missed and therefore valued intensely; secondly, he could make up to himself for the inadequacy of his childhood, since the women he chose had needs much like his own, so that (without realizing it) he might imagine that he was reaching back into the 1670's and in an odd but vivid way treat the other person as deputy for his younger self. This was one reason—though far from the only reason—that he praised in women

8. The context in which Mr. G's response was recorded is especially noteworthy for its independent motivation. Several students and faculty gathered regularly to study Swift. One of the techniques agreed upon in advance was to solicit responses to three "scatological" poems, the other two being "Strephon and Chloe" and "Cassinus and Peter."

traits often classified as masculine: these facilitated his identification with them. . . . Sexuality and marriage were not elements in such a scheme as Swift's.[9]

This analysis emphasizes that the constructive motives in Swift's life have more to do with attempts to reconstitute parent-child relationships than with a perverse hatred of sex and dirt. As a parent, he was paternal, but Ehrenpreis suggests that he was also maternal— mothering women who were effigies of his own dependent childhood; in some ways in his adult relationships, he was extremely independent, yet he needed the distant women deeply. The emotional priority of these needs rendered sex only a secondary consideration, even though it was just as strong an impulse in him as in anyone else. One likely result of this configuration of motives is that sexuality became "sour grapes."[10] So on several prominent literary occasions, Swift stressed its connection with the excremental functions. Being an author by profession, he was especially articulate and imaginative in the service of whatever thought he recorded; his characteristic satiric talents came into play; his awareness of contemporary conventions on the subject was mobilized; and poems like "A Beautiful Young Nymph" were written in consequence.

It is probably not coincidental that Ehrenpreis's biographical views of Swift and Mr. G's response to the poem speak similar languages: the subjective motives for biographical inquiry and for investigation of one's own responses are similar. Both aim to understand literary experience in terms of preliterary language habits that are governed by

9. Irvin Ehrenpreis, *The Personality of Jonathan Swift* (New York, 1958), pp. 22-23.

10. Two psychoanalysts draw similar conclusions in more technical terms. Ferenczi says: "From the psychoanalytical standpoint one would describe his neurotic behavior as an inhibition of normal potency, with a lack of courage in relation to women of good character and perhaps with a lasting aggressive tendency toward women of a lower type" (Sandor Ferenczi, *Final Contributions to the Problems and Methods of Psycho-Analysis*, London, 1955, p. 59). Greenacre writes: "One gets the impression that the anal fixation was intense and binding and the genital demands so impaired or limited at best that there was a total retreat from genital sexuality in his early adult life, probably beginning with his unhappy relationship with Jane Waring, the first of the goddessess" (Phyllis Greenacre. "The Mutual Adventures of Jonathan Swift and Lemuel Gulliver," *Psychoanalytic Quarterly*, 24, 1955, 60). The two psychoanalysts are explaining the alleged "anal fixation" in Swift as the result of regression: the substitution of attention to an infantile mode of behavior when there are emotional difficulties with a later developmental stage. Because genital sexuality did not seem to fit in with the direction in which Swift was developing, he "retreated" from it—which means he may have renounced it, rejected it, avoided it, forgot about it, found substitutions for it, or all of these things. Although the psychoanalysts' descriptions seem somewhat clinical, there is no ambivalence in their view of Swift as struggling with heterosexual inhibitions and interpersonal struggles accruing from those inhibitions; this is extremely different from viewing the scatalogical interest as an originating and characteristic feature of his personality. The excremental emphasis is a secondary result of the main difficulty he had in coping with women at almost all levels, except at a distance. This is the sense in which sexuality is "sour (or excremental) grapes."

each person's history of interpersonal development. This aim, in turn, is part of a growing orientation in contemporary thought around subjectivity and the nature of intellection. The interest in subjectivity is itself the expression of the collective interests of present-day interpretive communities.

These interests propose new literary regularities with which to conceptualize Swift's poem, Swift, or his "age." The question of whether Swift was an instance of or an exception to his culture becomes idle; if he lived in a specific culture, he was necessarily a part of it. The various emphases in his literature are explainable as a synthesis of personal experiences each of which is common to only a part of his culture and some of which are completely idiosyncratic. Any regularity in Swift's work is inevitably seen relative to our own collective interests. For example, while Dobree says that "schoolboy" verse was conventional, Ehrenpreis documents how literary dissection of women's cosmetic artifices is common to many ages. Is Swift's poem therefore to be related to a local convention, a convention of Western civilization, a literary convention, a feminine convention, a masculine view of women through history, or to all or some of these? Which convention applies depends on what questions *we* ask, which knowledge is sought *now*, and for what purpose. The definition of literary regularities cannot proceed without a prior inquiry into contemporary collective interests. The multiplicity of directions in current literary scholarship suggests that these interests are by no means self-evident and that a systematic way of disclosing them in communities of all sizes would be advantageous. Awareness of the motivated conceptual categories in our own community creates the options and the motives for defining regularities in other communities, past or present.

The inquiry of a pedagogical community into its motives for thought is not an "exercise for the student"; it is the first step in formulating mental procedures that any thinker and any group uses in proposing new knowledge. Regardless of how similar the thousands of classrooms seem to one another, each is different from the others in just the ways that bear on the development of knowledge. It is a pragmatic necessity, and not a democratic sentimentality, that urges each group to understand its uniqueness. This necessity arises from abiding human motives that have never been doubted—motives of self-regulation, self-interest, social stability, and the natural common interest of prolonging, protecting, and preserving life. The classroom is the child's first collectivity, where first-person groups and other-person groups are first formed. Interests in knowledge grow from these actions, and it would seem only natural to cultivate awareness of group interests from the outset.

# Conclusion

# KNOWLEDGE, RESPONSIBILITY, AND COMMUNITY

Subjective criticism is a way of reaching knowledge of language and literature, of bearing responsibility for it, and of assembling collective interests in the pursuit of such knowledge. In practice (as opposed to in imagination) none of these purposes are separable from one another. Once you and I enter either a conversation or a classroom, we are proposing knowledge, bearing responsibility, and defining a community of common interests. There is no way to reduce the scope of these simple activities; when taken seriously, they become difficult and complex. The only recourse is to increase awareness of them and to establish a vocabulary of subjective initiatives that can command our thoughts and regulate our relationships. Beyond these thoughts and relationships there is no way to authorize knowledge.

Those who are uncomfortable with this attitude toward knowledge justify their opposition on the grounds that subjectivity is the same as solipsism.[1] Solipsism, however, is much more a description of the attitudes of objectivity. If a subjective perception—such as, for

1. Norman N. Holland writes, for example, that "merely calling reality 'subjective' leads to the familiar dead-end solipsism or extreme idealism" ("The New Paradigm: Subjective or Transactive?" *New Literary History*, 7, No. 2, Winter 1976, 339; see also Chapter Four, n. 29, above). A statement such as this can only come from a paradigmatic difference between my mind and Holland's. From the beginning of this study, I have contested the use of the term *reality* as an absolute denotative. So I cannot be calling "reality" subjective. When Holland uses the term *reality*, he means "objective reality," which remains as absolute for him as God is for the fundamentalist. Yes, to call objective reality subjective does not change anything. The subjective paradigm, however, proposes a mental outlook which casts a diminished value on those experiences considered by Holland as "objective reality" and places a great deal of authority in those experiences traditionally understood as subjective. The *shift of values* is the change in paradigm. Holland's "new paradigm" is a denial of the mental capability that makes thought possible at all: "One cannot separate subjective and objective perspectives" (ibid.). This can be the case only for a solipsistic mind.

example, "The earth is flat"—is directly objectified without an intervening intersubjective negotiation—such as "Does it seem flat to you?"—one arrives at what most people believe is a falsehood. It is solipsistic to believe that all of my own perceptions will be all of everyone else's perceptions. As a philosophical principle, solipsism cannot mean that only I exist, because this is a psychotic state of mind; rather, it can only mean that all people perceive things in the same way, and this is the assumption of the objective paradigm. Once it is admitted that intersubjective negotiation is the source of knowledge and that such negotiation regulates whether any experience is considered the same or different among different people, the subjective paradigm is the operating assumption.

If I stub my toe and then claim to you that stone must exist for you, and then we enter into a dispute over whether the stone exists, the discussion is solipsistic insofar as the existence of the stone is inconsequential. If you and I are discussing our eyesight, about which we care a great deal, the existence of the stone matters, but only in its function as a test of our eyesight. The stone thus exists subjectively and not objectively; belief in its objective existence is idle and represents solipsism as indulgence in reiterating one's perceptions to no end. In the case of Dr. Johnson's example, the objectification of the stone has no function except as an explanation of the pain. To understand the existence of an object as subjective is not the same as to understand it as imaginary. The subjective mode of understanding supposes a *conscious shift* of perceptual and ratiocinative priority to the undisputable experiences of the mind and a devaluation of essences presumed to exist outside of mental functioning.

Objectivity is additionally solipsistic in that it is considered independent of human ethics.[2] The convenient separation may then be made between the discovery of knowledge and its function among people. To commit oneself to objective knowledge is not a commitment at all, because the "true" knowledge bears all the responsibility of its consequences; that is, the individual bears no responsibility since he is only affirming true things. If a piece of "true" knowledge has different values to two groups of people, however, it is no longer the same knowledge; each group has actually created, and not discovered, its knowledge. The separation of discovery from function (of knowledge) is a pretense whose purpose is for each group to bluff the other into accepting its point of view. When the subjective authorization of knowledge is allowed, the pretense of truth is replaced by

2. The ethical argument against objectivity and for "deep subjectivity" is presented by Roger Poole, whose treatise I discussed in Chapter One.

intersubjective negotiation. The responsibility of each knower for his knowledge and to the other party is necessarily an item in the discussion. The consistent influence of mutual responsibility is the opposite of solipsism.

If two individuals are obligated to one another, they are in the same community. The pedagogical relationship in pursuit of common knowledge incurs a mutual obligation to either synthesize the knowledge or to form a new community defined by other common knowledge. To know anything at all is to have assigned a part of one's self to a group of others who claim to know the same thing. In Chapter Ten, several of those who reported they knew nothing of Robert Frost also said that their lack of knowledge reduced the viability of their membership in the "group" of English majors or prospective teachers. It is not possible to "have" an interpretation of a work of literature in isolation from a community. Even though one can read a poem, decide what it means, and then keep it a secret, such an interpretation has the same epistemological status as an unremembered dream. Its lack of negotiative presence renders it functionally nonexistent. If it is forgotten, it might as well not have taken place; if it subsequently emerges in unexpected contexts, it has acquired a negotiative value. For example, when a person who reads voluminously in private then reports his reading in a casual context, that context is the community which defines the knowledge. There are many individuals who do read in just this way and who, in principle, may recursively resymbolize their experience, but who for one reason or another never do it, or otherwise make their reading public. The degree to which knowledge is not part of a community is the degree to which it is not knowledge at all.[3]

The interconnection of knowledge, responsibility for it, and its necessary action in human pluralities is founded on the conception of language as symbolization and motivated resymbolization. In each child, language originates and grows in a community of two or more people where the identification of experience and its explanation are the same set of behaviors. To an adult or to a child over two, an explanation usually appears different from a simple identification because of the asker's awareness of having requested an explanation. He is aware of wanting to know—that is, aware of his motivation. As a consequence of this awareness, linguistic resymbolization becomes explanatory interpretation. The most general means of distinguishing linguistic acts from one another is on the basis of motivation for their appearance. Formulating a motivational explanation for a language experience involves assigning a responsibility for it and defining its community of address.

3. This point was previously discussed, in a somewhat different context, at the beginning of Chapter Five.

Except for speaking, reading is the most typical language experience and (as discussed in Chapter Five) is an outgrowth of childhood conversational activity. Commenting on reading experiences is likewise derived from infantile talking habits and motives. Each reader's language system, therefore, must be a determining factor in the knowledge he develops. When the reader takes account of his own language in his proposal of knowledge, the proposal is subjectively authorized and collectively negotiable. In this process, the response statement makes room for the reader to objectify himself and his experience—relative to himself. He sets his reading experience apart as the object of study and establishes the extent of his responsibility for his thoughts. The responsibility becomes functional within a prearticulated collective purpose. In this way, critical knowledge is inseparable from the reader's responsibility for it and from the collective interests of the reader's community. Subjective criticism is the disciplined study of language and literature under the assumption of the subjective paradigm.

In my experience as a student and teacher of "English," I consider two features of my community to have led to the proposals of subjective criticism. The first is the division of language and literature into two separate disciplines; the second is the tacit, but overwhelming, assumption on the part of English teachers at all levels that knowledge of language and literature, while often interesting or "enriching," is ultimately less important and less authoritative than most other knowledge that is more consciously "scientific." The first feature is the consequence of the long-standing existence of the second. That is, those interested in language perceived that it might be isolated and studied with quantitative and logical precision. As a result, language and psychology were considered subjects separate from literature and criticism. My intuitions, my pleasures in speaking the language of certain authors and of articulating my own language, as well as the multifarious factors of my upbringing and school career, led me to think that knowledge of all four of these traditional academic subjects were indispensable to one another. The problem was to show why this was the case and how a single, differently conceived discipline could lead to changes in existing pedagogical institutions that will reflect the forms of thought more commensurate with today's most authoritative knowledge. Subjective criticism is my proposal of what that discipline is, how it can create a new community of interest, how it supersedes the traditional authority of quantitative science, and how it may involve every interested individual, of any age, in the formulation of consequential knowledge.

Subjective criticism assumes that each person's most urgent motivations are to understand himself, and that the simplest path to this understanding is awareness of one's own language system as the agency of consciousness and self-direction. The distinction, first broached in Chapter Three and subsequently invoked on many occasions in this study, between real objects, symbolic objects, and people, suggests that in English, the "real" objects are words and texts; the symbolic objects are language and literature. The subject is people, who speak, read, and write.

# INDEX

*Acquisition of Language, The* (McNeill), 49n
*Acquisition of Syntax in Children of Five to Ten, The* (C. Chomsky), 47n
Action language (Schafer), as problem of objectification, 73-74n
Adler, Richard, on responding to readers' responses, 106n
*Alice's Adventures in Wonderland* (Carroll), 201; Ms. H's present response to, 205-8; Ms. H's remembered response to, 202-4
*Approaches to Poetics* (Chatman), 129n
Aristotle, on audience response, 98
*Art and Illusion* (Gombrich), on relativity of visual perception, 32-33
*Aspern Papers, The* (James), Mr. P's partial interpretation of, 145
Author: David Bleich's response to and biographical treatment of, 260-62; as imagined by Mr. G, 291; judgments of real and symbolized, 159-62; parent as child's first, 135; rationale for biographical documentation of, 259-60; reader's conception and documentation of, 238-63; role of, in reading (Harding), 108. *See also* Author's intention; Biographical criticism
Authority: child's first awareness of, in others, 135; collective interests as highest, 264; communal, of interpretation, 69; Freud's increase of, in therapist and patient, 77n; as issue in Ms. M's response statement, 199; Mr. P's attitude toward David Bleich's, 143; of Mr. P's work in class, 144; of Ms. M in consequence of her response, 199; need for, in reading, 159; possible objectivity of, in pedagogy, 151; Rosenblatt on moral, 110; stipulation of therapist's, 78

Author's intention: communally defined, 124; difficulty of defining, 238; inaccessibility of, in regard to generic choice, 164; lacking in Freud's interpretation of Michelangelo's "Moses," 89, 92, 93; as new predication, 160; role of biographical research in understanding, 160-61; as sought by Freud, 89; in "subjective" literature, 36. *See also* Author; Biographical criticism

Barrett, Cyril, 70n
Beach, Richard, 106n
"Beautiful Young Nymph Going to Bed, A" (Swift), 286; response statement of Mr. G to, 287-89
Becker, Carl L., 86
*Behind Appearance* (Waddington), 12n
Belief, 4-7; as determinant of interpretive authority, 69; "erroneous," and superstition, 39; and knowledge, 7
Benstock, Bernard, 259
Bernays, Martha, 92
Bible: Freud on Moses, 91; interpretation in response to, 68; as received today, 6
Biographical criticism: affected by biographer's subjectivity, 263; connections of, with reading and pedagogy, 161; in consequence of reader's conception of author, 239-58; effects of, seen in Mr. D's response statement, 254-58; as means of authorizing interpretations, 161-62; Mr. D's efforts at, between response statements, 245; as part of subjective criticism, 160; as practiced by David Bleich, 260-62; psychological origins of, 159-60
*Biology and Knowledge* (Piaget), 29n

*299*